MICROSOFT OFFICE 2010 CERTIFICATION PREP: MICROSOFT OFFICE SPECIALIST 2010

LAURA STORY
DAWNA WALLS

COURSE TECHNOLOGY
CENGAGE Learning™

Australia • Brazil • Japan • Korea • Mexico • Singapore • Spain • United Kingdom • United States

COURSE TECHNOLOGY
CENGAGE Learning™

Microsoft Office 2010 Certification Prep:
Microsoft Office Specialist 2010
Laura Story, Dawna Walls

Executive Editor: Donna Gridley

Product Manager: Allison O'Meara McDonald

Development Editor: Fran Marino

Associate Product Manager: Chad Kirchner

Editorial Assistant: Brandelynn Perry

Content Project Manager: Lisa Weidenfeld

Associate Marketing Manager: Julie Schuster

Manufacturing Coordinator: Julio Esperas

Manuscript Quality Assurance Lead: Jeff Schwartz

Manuscript Quality Assurance Reviewers: John
    Freitas, Susan Pedicini

Proofreader: Kathy Orrino

Indexer: Rich Carlson

Art Director: Faith Brosnan

Cover Designer: © Wing-ip Ngan, Ink design, inc.

Cover Image: magewerks/ Getty Images

Compositor: GEX Publishing Services

For product information and technology assistance, contact us at
Cengage Learning Customer & Sales Support, 1-800-354-9706

For permission to use material from this text or product, submit all requests online at **www.cengage.com/permissions**
Further permissions questions can be emailed to
permissionrequest@cengage.com

ISBN-13: 978-1-133-19107-0

ISBN-10: 1-133-19107-X

Course Technology
20 Channel Center Street
Boston, Massachusetts 02210
USA

Cengage Learning is a leading provider of customized learning solutions with office locations around the globe, including Singapore, the United Kingdom, Australia, Mexico, Brazil, and Japan. Locate your local office at:
www.cengage.com/global

Cengage Learning products are represented in Canada by Nelson Education, Ltd.

To learn more about Course Technology, visit **www.cengage.com/coursetechnology**

To learn more about Cengage Learning, visit **www.cengage.com**

Any fictional data related to persons or companies or URLs used throughout this book is intended for instructional purposes only. At the time this book was printed, any such data was fictional and not belonging to any real persons or companies.

Please visit **login.cengage.com** and log in to access instructor-specific resources.

Printed in the United States of America
1 2 3 4 5 6 7 15 14 13 12 11

ABOUT THIS BOOK

The Microsoft Office Specialist program is the only performance-based certification program approved by Microsoft to validate desktop computer skills using Office 2010 and Windows 7. The new credential is a globally recognized standard that meets the demand for the most up-to-date skills using the latest technologies from Microsoft.

HOW TO USE THIS BOOK

Microsoft® Office 2010 Certification Prep: Microsoft® Office Specialist 2010 Exam Practice is a study tool designed to prepare you for the Microsoft Office Specialist exams. This book assumes that you already understand the concepts that are the basis for the skills covered in this book, and, therefore, the book can be used as a companion to review and practice skills before taking the exam, or as a desk reference when using Microsoft Office programs.

The Structure of this Book

There are eight sections in this book, plus an appendix covering basic features of the Windows 7 operating system to help extend students' learning. The first section, Exam Tips, provides some background information on the Microsoft Office Specialist program, the general process for taking an exam, and some helpful hints for preparing for and successfully passing the exams.

The remaining seven sections each cover a different Microsoft program or exam: Word Core, Word Expert, Excel Core, Excel Expert, Access, PowerPoint, and Outlook. Each program-specific section begins with a brief Getting Started section that reviews the basic skills that are not specifically covered in the Microsoft Office Specialist exams, but that are essential to being able to work in the program.

Each skill is presented in bulleted steps containing clear instructions. Because there are often different ways to complete a task, the book provides multiple methods where appropriate, including Ribbon, Shortcut, Menu, Mouse, and Task Pane methods. The Microsoft Office Specialist exams allow you to use any one of these methods, so you can choose the one with which you are most comfortable to complete the task. In addition, full-color screen shots and icons provide visual reinforcement of topics. A "Note" feature is inserted throughout the book, providing helpful tips to further students' understanding of the material.

Review Questions, Projects, and Critical Thinking activities are provided at the end of each Objective. Review Questions include a mix of True/False, Fill-in-the-Blank, Multiple Choice, and Matching questions to test students on their knowledge of the skills and concepts for the Objective. Projects provide step-by-step instructions that help students put into practice the skills they have learned while creating a real-world document. Critical Thinking activities provide less instruction, and give the students the opportunity to observe training demonstrations, explore advanced skills, and solve problems on their own or in a group.

Technical Concerns

This book assumes the following regarding your computer's setup:

☐ You have installed Office 2010 using the Typical installation.

☐ You have installed Windows 7.

☐ You have a document open and ready to use when required to work within a specific application. Also, if the steps instruct you to format an Excel worksheet or a Word document, you can format the open document or worksheet in any way you want, choosing options that are appropriate for your needs.

☐ You have access to the data files provided on the CD that accompanies this book so that you may complete the Projects and Critical Thinking Activities at the end of each objective, and you have the ability to save and access files on your hard drive or a network drive.

☐ You have an Internet connection to complete certain steps, and you are familiar with how to connect to the Internet.

☐ Your screen may look different from some of the figures in the book depending on your computer's screen resolution and any additional programs you have installed. These differences will not affect your ability to use the book and complete the steps.

To complete all lessons and End-of-Lesson material, this book will require approximately 40 hours.

START-UP CHECKLIST

Hardware

☐ Computer and processor: 500-megahertz (MHz) processor or higher

☐ Memory: 256 megabytes (MB) of RAM or higher

☐ Hard disk: 3.5 gigabyte (GB) available disk space

☐ Display: 1024×768 or higher-resolution monitor

Software:

☐ Operating system: Windows XP with Service Pack 3, Windows Vista with SP1, or Windows 7

INSTRUCTOR RESOURCES DISK

ISBN-10: 1133191061; ISBN-13: 9781133191063

Instructor Resources CD or *DVD* contains the following teaching resources:

☐ The Data and Solution files for this course.

☐ ExamView® tests for each lesson. ExamView is a powerful testing software package that allows instructors to create and administer printed, computer (LAN-based), and Internet exams.

☐ Instructor's Manual that includes lecture notes for each lesson and references to the end-of-lesson activities and Unit Review projects.

☐ Answer Keys that include solutions to the lesson and unit review questions.

☐ Copies of the figures that appear in the student text.

☐ Grids that show skills required for the Microsoft Certification Application Specialist (MCAS) exam, SCANS workplace competencies and skills, and activities that apply to cross-curricular topics.

☐ Suggested Syllabus with block, two quarter, and 18-week schedule

☐ Annotated Solutions and Grading Rubrics

☐ PowerPoint presentations for each lesson.

ABOUT THIS BOOK

The Microsoft Office Specialist program is the only performance-based certification program approved by Microsoft to validate desktop computer skills using Office 2010 and Windows 7. The new credential is a globally recognized standard that meets the demand for the most up-to-date skills using the latest technologies from Microsoft.

HOW TO USE THIS BOOK

Microsoft® Office 2010 Certification Prep: Microsoft® Office Specialist 2010 Exam Practice is a study tool designed to prepare you for the Microsoft Office Specialist exams. This book assumes that you already understand the concepts that are the basis for the skills covered in this book, and, therefore, the book can be used as a companion to review and practice skills before taking the exam, or as a desk reference when using Microsoft Office programs.

The Structure of this Book

There are eight sections in this book, plus an appendix covering basic features of the Windows 7 operating system to help extend students' learning. The first section, Exam Tips, provides some background information on the Microsoft Office Specialist program, the general process for taking an exam, and some helpful hints for preparing for and successfully passing the exams.

The remaining seven sections each cover a different Microsoft program or exam: Word Core, Word Expert, Excel Core, Excel Expert, Access, PowerPoint, and Outlook. Each program-specific section begins with a brief Getting Started section that reviews the basic skills that are not specifically covered in the Microsoft Office Specialist exams, but that are essential to being able to work in the program.

Each skill is presented in bulleted steps containing clear instructions. Because there are often different ways to complete a task, the book provides multiple methods where appropriate, including Ribbon, Shortcut, Menu, Mouse, and Task Pane methods. The Microsoft Office Specialist exams allow you to use any one of these methods, so you can choose the one with which you are most comfortable to complete the task. In addition, full-color screen shots and icons provide visual reinforcement of topics. A "Note" feature is inserted throughout the book, providing helpful tips to further students' understanding of the material.

Review Questions, Projects, and Critical Thinking activities are provided at the end of each Objective. Review Questions include a mix of True/False, Fill-in-the-Blank, Multiple Choice, and Matching questions to test students on their knowledge of the skills and concepts for the Objective. Projects provide step-by-step instructions that help students put into practice the skills they have learned while creating a real-world document. Critical Thinking activities provide less instruction, and give the students the opportunity to observe training demonstrations, explore advanced skills, and solve problems on their own or in a group.

Technical Concerns

This book assumes the following regarding your computer's setup:

- ☐ You have installed Office 2010 using the Typical installation.
- ☐ You have installed Windows 7.
- ☐ You have a document open and ready to use when required to work within a specific application. Also, if the steps instruct you to format an Excel worksheet or a Word document, you can format the open document or worksheet in any way you want, choosing options that are appropriate for your needs.
- ☐ You have access to the data files provided on the CD that accompanies this book so that you may complete the Projects and Critical Thinking Activities at the end of each objective, and you have the ability to save and access files on your hard drive or a network drive.
- ☐ You have an Internet connection to complete certain steps, and you are familiar with how to connect to the Internet.
- ☐ Your screen may look different from some of the figures in the book depending on your computer's screen resolution and any additional programs you have installed. These differences will not affect your ability to use the book and complete the steps.

To complete all lessons and End-of-Lesson material, this book will require approximately 40 hours.

START-UP CHECKLIST

Hardware

- ☐ Computer and processor: 500-megahertz (MHz) processor or higher
- ☐ Memory: 256 megabytes (MB) of RAM or higher
- ☐ Hard disk: 3.5 gigabyte (GB) available disk space
- ☐ Display: 1024 × 768 or higher-resolution monitor

Software:

- ☐ Operating system: Windows XP with Service Pack 3, Windows Vista with SP1, or Windows 7

INSTRUCTOR RESOURCES DISK

ISBN-10: 1133191061; ISBN-13: 9781133191063

Instructor Resources CD or *DVD* contains the following teaching resources:

- ☐ The Data and Solution files for this course.
- ☐ ExamView® tests for each lesson. ExamView is a powerful testing software package that allows instructors to create and administer printed, computer (LAN-based), and Internet exams.
- ☐ Instructor's Manual that includes lecture notes for each lesson and references to the end-of-lesson activities and Unit Review projects.
- ☐ Answer Keys that include solutions to the lesson and unit review questions.
- ☐ Copies of the figures that appear in the student text.
- ☐ Grids that show skills required for the Microsoft Certification Application Specialist (MCAS) exam, SCANS workplace competencies and skills, and activities that apply to cross-curricular topics.
- ☐ Suggested Syllabus with block, two quarter, and 18-week schedule
- ☐ Annotated Solutions and Grading Rubrics
- ☐ PowerPoint presentations for each lesson.

ExamView®

This textbook is accompanied by ExamView, a powerful testing software package that allows instructors to create and administer printed, computer (LAN-based), and Internet exams. ExamView includes hundreds of questions that correspond to the topics covered in this text, enabling students to generate detailed study guides that include page references for further review. The computer-based and Internet testing components allow students to take exams at their computers, and save the instructor time by grading each exam automatically.

To access additional course materials, please visit www.cengagebrain.com. At the CengageBrain.com home page, search for the ISBN of your title (from the back cover of your book) using the search box at the top of the page. This will take you to the product page where these resources can be found.

SAM 2010 *SAM*

SAM 2010 helps bridge the gap between the classroom and the real world by allowing students to train and test on important computer skills in an active, hands-on environment.

SAM 2010's easy-to-use system includes powerful interactive exams, training or projects on critical applications such as Word, Excel, Access, PowerPoint, Outlook, Windows, the Internet, and much more. SAM simulates the application environment, allowing students to demonstrate their knowledge and think through the skills by performing real-world tasks.

SAM 2010 includes built-in page references so students can print helpful study guides that match the textbooks used in class. Powerful administrative options allow instructors to schedule exams and assignments, secure tests, and run reports with almost limitless flexibility.

What is the Microsoft® Office Specialist Program?

The Microsoft Office Specialist Program enables candidates to show that they have something exceptional to offer – proven expertise in certain Microsoft programs. Recognized by businesses and schools around the world, over 4 million certifications have been obtained in over 100 different countries. The Microsoft Office Specialist Program is the only Microsoft-approved certification program of its kind.

What is the Microsoft Office Specialist Certification?

The Microsoft Office Specialist certification validates through the use of exams that you have obtained specific skill sets within the applicable Microsoft Office programs and other Microsoft programs included in the Microsoft Office Specialist Program. The candidate can choose which exam(s) they want to take according to which skills they want to validate.

The available Microsoft Office Specialist Program 2007 exams include*:

Using Windows Vista®
Using Microsoft® Office Word 2007
Using Microsoft® Office Word 2007 - Expert
Using Microsoft® Office Excel® 2007
Using Microsoft® Office Excel® 2007 - Expert
Using Microsoft® Office PowerPoint® 2007
Using Microsoft® Office Access® 2007
Using Microsoft® Office Outlook® 2007
Using Microsoft SharePoint® 2007

The Microsoft Office Specialist Program 2010 exams will include*:

Microsoft Word 2010
Microsoft Word 2010 Expert
Microsoft Excel® 2010
Microsoft Excel® 2010 Expert
Microsoft PowerPoint® 2010
Microsoft Access® 2010
Microsoft Outlook® 2010
Microsoft SharePoint® 2010

What does the Microsoft Office Specialist Approved Courseware logo represent?

The logo indicates that this courseware has been approved by Microsoft to cover the course objectives that will be included in the relevant exam. It also means that after utilizing this courseware, you may be better prepared to pass the exams required to become a certified Microsoft Office Specialist.

For more information:

To learn more about Microsoft Office Specialist exams, visit www.microsoft.com/learning/msbc

To learn about other Microsoft approved courseware from Course Technology, visit www.cengage.com/ct/certification

* The availability of Microsoft Office Specialist certification exams varies by Microsoft program, program version and language. Visit www.microsoft.com/learning for exam availability.

Microsoft, Access, Excel, the Office Logo, Outlook, PowerPoint, SharePoint, and Windows Vista are either registered trademarks or trademarks of Microsoft Corporation in the United States and/or other countries. The Microsoft Office Specialist logo and the Microsoft Office Specialist Approved Courseware logo are used under license from Microsoft Corporation.

AUTHOR ACKNOWLEDGEMENTS

We would like to thank Donna Gridley for yet another awesome opportunity, to Fran Marino for her important role in shaping this book, to Allison O'Meara McDonald for her expert management of this project, to Jeffrey Schwartz and the MQA team for helping us fine-tune this baby, and to Lisa Weidenfeld, Louise Capulli, and the GEX team for their excellent production work.

Dawna Walls: Many thanks to Laura for agreeing to work with me on this project, even though she has a 'real' job. I don't know how you did it. I would also like to thank my family for continuing to put up with my demanding work schedule and occasional grumpiness. John, Luke, and Leah, you rock!

Laura Story: Much gratitude to Dawna for taking on more than her share of this book so I could remain in my Fusionary cube and for always being willing to go the extra mile to produce quality products. Thanks also to Debbie McClure for so enthusiastically supporting my work, both within the office and without.

BRIEF TABLE OF CONTENTS

TABLE OF CONTENTS

WHAT IS MICROSOFT OFFICE SPECIALIST CERTIFICATION?

Certification is a growing trend in the Information Technology industry. A software or hardware company devises and administers exams for users that enable them to demonstrate their ability to use the software or hardware effectively. By passing a certification exam, users prove their competence and knowledge of the software or hardware to current or prospective employers and colleagues.

The Microsoft Office Specialist program is the only comprehensive, performance-based certification program approved by Microsoft to validate desktop computer skills using the Microsoft Office 2010 programs:

- ☐ Microsoft Word
- ☐ Microsoft Excel®
- ☐ Microsoft Access™
- ☐ Microsoft PowerPoint®
- ☐ Microsoft Outlook®
- ☐ Microsoft SharePoint

The Microsoft Office Specialist program provides computer program literacy, measures proficiency, and identifies opportunities for enhancing skills. Successful candidates receive a certificate that sets them apart from their peers in the competitive job market. The certificate is a valuable credential, recognized worldwide as proof that an individual has the desktop computing skills needed to work productively and efficiently. Certification is a valuable asset to individuals who want to begin or advance their computer careers.

NOTE

If you have earned a Microsoft Certified Application Specialist (MCAS) certification in Microsoft Office 2007, it is still valid. The name has just been changed to Microsoft Office Specialist (MOS). You can request an updated certificate from Microsoft that contains the new name.

The Microsoft Office Specialist exams are developed, marketed, and administered by Certiport, Inc., a company that has an exclusive license from Microsoft. The exams are available in a variety of languages. Exams must be taken at an authorized Certiport Center, which administers exams in a quiet room with the proper hardware and software and has trained personnel to manage and proctor the exams.

WHAT ARE THE BENEFITS OF ACHIEVING CERTIFICATION?

Achieving Microsoft Office Specialist certification in one or several of the Microsoft Office 2010 programs can be beneficial to you and your current or prospective employer. Earning certification acknowledges that you have the expertise to work with Microsoft Office programs. Individuals who are Microsoft Office Specialist certified report increased competence and productivity with Microsoft Office programs, as well as increased credibility with their employers, co-workers, and clients. Certification sets you apart in today's competitive job market, bringing employment opportunities, greater earning potential and career advancement, and increased job satisfaction.

For example, if you have passed the Microsoft Word 2010 certification exam and you are interviewing for a job that requires knowledge and use of Word to complete business-related tasks, certification will indicate to your prospective employer that you not only have the necessary skills to perform that aspect of the job, but that you also have the initiative to prepare for, sign up for, pay for, and take the exam. Certification can help you increase your productivity within your current job and is a great way to enhance your skills without taking courses to obtain a new degree. Another benefit of Microsoft certification is that you gain access to a member Web site, career-building tools, and training.

More information about the benefits of getting certified can be found on the Certiport Web site, shown in Figure ET-1.

Figure ET-1   Certiport Web site

Courtesy of Certiport, Inc. www.certiport.com

THE MICROSOFT OFFICE SPECIALIST CERTIFICATION PROCESS

The steps to successfully completing Microsoft Office Specialist certification are outlined in Table ET-1 and discussed in the remainder of this section.

NOTE

The Web addresses may change. If you cannot find what you are looking for, go to the main site (*www.microsoft.com* or *www.certiport.com*) and do a search for the topic you are looking for.

Table ET-1

Steps to Achieving Certification	
1. Choose an exam	Choose from one of the following exams, based on your skills and interests: • Microsoft Office Word 2010 • Microsoft Office Word 2010 Expert • Microsoft Office Excel 2010 • Microsoft Office Excel 2010 Expert • Microsoft Office PowerPoint 2010 • Microsoft Office Outlook 2010 • Microsoft Office Access 2010 • Microsoft Office SharePoint 2010
2. Find a testing center	Find an authorized testing center near you using the Certiport Center locator at *www.certiport.com/Portal/Pages/LocatorView.aspx.*
3. Prepare for the exam	Select the method that is appropriate for you, including taking a class or purchasing self-study materials.
4. Take a practice test	It is recommended that candidates take a Practice Test before taking an exam. • To view the practice tests available, go to *www.certiport.com/portal.* • Follow the online instructions for purchasing a voucher and taking the practice test.
5. Take the exam	• Contact the Certiport Center and make an appointment for the exam you want to take. Check the organization's payment and exam policies.
	• Purchase an exam voucher at *www.certiport.com/portal.*
	• Go to the Certiport Center to take the test, and bring a printout of the exam voucher, your Certiport username and password, and a valid picture ID.
6. Receive exam results	You will find out your results immediately. If you pass, you will receive your certificate two to three weeks after the date of the exam.

1. CHOOSE AN EXAM

The Microsoft Office Specialist certification program offers exams for the main applications of Microsoft Office 2010, including Word, Excel, Access, PowerPoint, and Outlook. You can also take a Microsoft Office Specialist exam for expert levels of Word and Excel that cover more advanced skills. You can earn the highest level of certification, Microsoft Office Specialist Master, by passing three required exams—Word 2010 Expert, Excel 2010 Expert, and PowerPoint 2010—and one elective exam—Access 2010 or Outlook 2010. Choose one or more applications that will help you in your current position or job search, or one that tests skills that match your abilities and interests. You can find the list of skills covered in each exam on the exam Web site. Go to *www.microsoft.com/learning/en/us/certification/mos.aspx#certifications* to access the Microsoft Office Specialist Certification page, as shown in Figure ET-2.

Exam Tips

Figure ET-2   Microsoft Office Specialist Certification page

To display more detailed information, click the exam number link for the exam you want to take, as shown in Figure ET-3.

Figure ET-3 **Microsoft Office Specialist exam info**

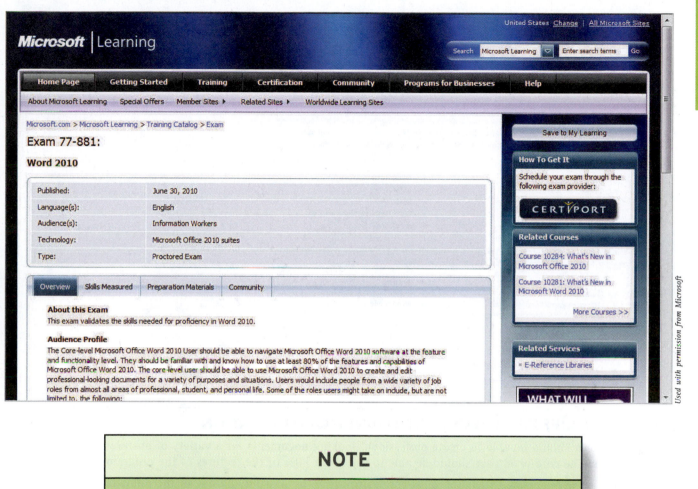

Used with permission from Microsoft

NOTE

You can also find the list of Objective Domains under exams at *http://www.certiport.com/Portal/desktopdefault. aspx?page=common/pagelibrary/MOS2010-objectives.html.*

Click on the objective domain that you want to prepare for to view a list of software features and capabilities that you should know, as shown in Figure ET-4.

Figure ET-4   **Software features and capabilities**

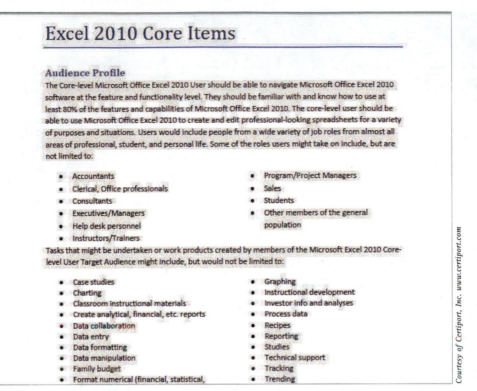

Courtesy of Certiport, Inc. www.certiport.com

MICROSOFT OFFICE SPECIALIST (CORE) CERTIFICATION

The core-level user should be able to create professional-looking documents for a variety of business, school, and personal situations. The core-level user should be able to use about 80% of the features of the program.

You can achieve the Microsoft Office Specialist core certification by passing any one of the following exams:

- ☐ Word 2010
- ☐ Excel 2010
- ☐ PowerPoint 2010
- ☐ Access 2010
- ☐ Outlook 2010
- ☐ Sharepoint 2010

MICROSOFT OFFICE SPECIALIST EXPERT CERTIFICATION

The expert user should be able to perform many of the advanced skills in the program.

You can earn the Microsoft Office Expert certification by passing one of the following exams:

- ☐ Word 2010 Expert
- ☐ Excel 2010 Expert

MICROSOFT OFFICE SPECIALIST MASTER CERTIFICATION

To achieve the Microsoft Office Master certification, you need to pass three required exams and one elective exam.

REQUIRED

□ Word 2010 Expert

□ Excel 2010 Expert

□ PowerPoint 2010

ELECTIVE

□ Access 2010

OR

□ Outlook 2010

More information about the Microsoft Office Specialist 2010 certification series can be located on the Certiport Web site at *www.certiport.com/portal*, as shown in Figure ET-5.

Figure ET-5   Certiport certification information

Courtesy of Certiport, Inc. www.certiport.com

2. FIND A TESTING CENTER

You must take Microsoft Office Specialist certification exams at an authorized testing center, called a Certiport Center. Certiport Centers are located in educational institutions, corporate training centers, and other such locations. You can find a testing center near you using the Certiport Center locator at *www.certiport.com/portal/Pages/LocatorView.aspx*, as shown in Figure ET-6.

Figure ET-6   Certiport Center locator

Courtesy of Certiport, Inc. www.certiport.com

---

3. PREPARE FOR THE EXAM

Completing the exercises in this book will help you prepare for the exam. Reading through the exam objectives and taking a practice test can help you determine where you may need extra practice. If you are new to an Office program, you might want to take an introductory class and learn the program in its entirety. If you are already familiar with the program, you may only need to purchase study materials and learn unfamiliar skills on your own.

Take a Class

Taking a class—such as one that uses this book—is a good way to help you prepare for a certification exam, especially if you are a beginner. If you are an experienced user and know the basics, consider taking an advanced class. The benefits of taking a class include having an instructor as a resource, having the support of your classmates, and receiving study materials such as a lab book. Your local community college, career education center, or continuing education programs will most likely offer such courses. You can also check the Certiport Center in your area.

Purchase Materials for Self-Study

You can prepare on your own to take an exam by purchasing materials at your local bookstore or from an online retailer. To ensure that the study materials you are purchasing are well-suited to your goal of passing the Microsoft Office Specialist certification exam, you should consider the following: favorable reviews (reviews are often available when purchasing online); a table of contents that covers the skills you want to master; and the Microsoft Office Specialist Approved Courseware logo, as shown in Figure ET-7.

Figure ET-7   Microsoft Office Specialist Approved Courseware logo

This logo indicates that Microsoft has reviewed the book and recognizes it as being an adequate tool for certification preparation.

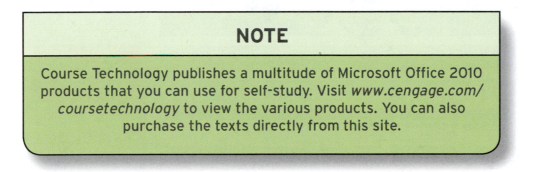

NOTE

Course Technology publishes a multitude of Microsoft Office 2010 products that you can use for self-study. Visit *www.cengage.com/ coursetechnology* to view the various products. You can also purchase the texts directly from this site.

4. TAKE A PRACTICE TEST

Consider taking an online practice test if one is available for the certification exam that you want to take. A practice test lets you determine the areas you should brush up on before taking the certification exam and helps you become familiar with the structure and format of the exam so you'll know what to expect. It is a self-assessment tool that tests you on the exam objectives and indicates your level of proficiency. You can view the available practice tests from Certiport and register and pay for a practice test voucher at *www.certiport.com/portal*.

5. TAKE THE EXAM

Make an Appointment

Contact a Certiport Center near you and make an appointment for the exam you want to take. The Certiport Center staff can answer any questions you may have about scheduling, vouchers, and exam administration. Verify the materials that you should bring with you when you take the exam.

Purchase an Exam Voucher

If your Certiport Center verifies that you need a voucher to take the test, go online and purchase a voucher from Certiport. The voucher is your proof that you registered and paid for the exam in advance. To pay for the exam and obtain a voucher, go to *www.certiport.com/portal*. Click the Login link and create a user account with a username and password of your choice. At the MyCertiport screen, click the Purchase Exam Voucher button and follow the onscreen instructions to purchase a voucher, as shown in Figure ET-8.

Figure ET-8 **Purchase an exam voucher**

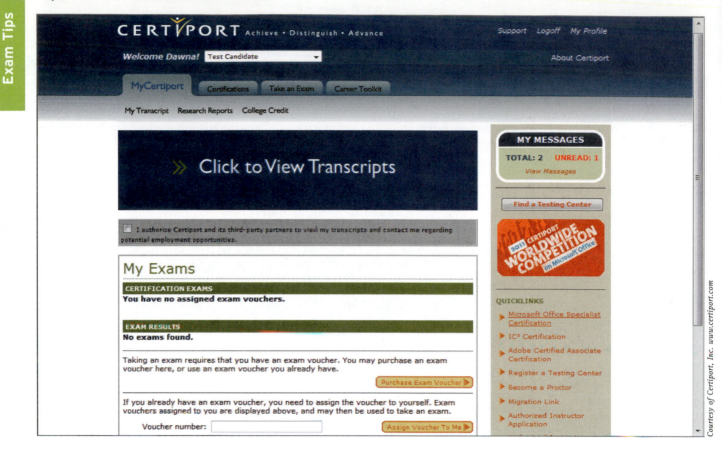

Take the Exam

You must bring the following to the Certiport Center on the day of the test:

☐ Your **voucher**, which is a printout of the electronic document you received when you paid for the test online. You will need to enter the voucher number when you log in to the test. If necessary, check with the Certiport Center to see if bringing just the voucher number, rather than a printout, is acceptable.

☐ Your **Certiport username and password**, which you will also have to enter at test login. You will have created a username and password when you paid for the voucher online.

☐ A valid **picture ID** (driver's license or valid passport).

If you are late or forget any of these required items, you may not be permitted to take the exam, and may need to reschedule your test for another time.

You may not bring any study or reference materials into the exam. You may not bring writing implements, calculators, or other materials into the test room.

Each exam is administered within a functional copy of the Microsoft program corresponding to the exam that you are taking. The exam tests your knowledge of the program by requiring you to complete specific tasks in the program. The exam is "live in the program," which means that you will work with an actual document, spreadsheet, presentation, etc., and must perform tasks on that document. You cannot use Office Online Help during the exam; the Help feature is disabled during the exam. The overall exam is timed, although there is no time limit for each question. Most exams take up to 90 minutes, but the allotted time depends on the subject and level.

> ## NOTE
>
> For more information about the exam, view the FAQ documents at *www.microsoft.com/certification* or *www.certiport.com/portal.*

6. RECEIVE EXAM RESULTS

☐ Exam results appear on the screen as soon as you complete the exam, so you'll know your score right away.

☐ You will receive a printout of your score to take with you. If you need additional copies, go to *www.certiport.com/portal*, and then log in and go to MyCertiport, where you can always access your exam results. If you pass the exam, you will receive an official certificate in the mail in approximately two to three weeks.

☐ The exam results are confidential.

If you do not pass the exam, refunds will not be given. Keep in mind that the exams are challenging; do not become discouraged if you do not pass the first time around. If you purchased a voucher with a retake, you will be given a second chance to take the exam. Be sure to study the results of your first exam and note the areas you need to work on. Check your Certiport Center's exam retake policies for more information.

MICROSOFT WORD 2010 CERTIFICATION PREP

Getting Started with Word 2010

The Word Microsoft Office Specialist (MOS) exam assumes a basic level of proficiency in Word. This section is intended to help you reference these basic skills while you are preparing to take the Word exam.

☐ Starting and exiting Word
☐ Viewing the Word window
☐ Using the Ribbon
☐ Opening, saving, and closing documents
☐ Navigating in the document window
☐ Using views
☐ Using keyboard KeyTips
☐ Getting Help

START AND EXIT WORD

Start Word

Shortcut Method

☐ Click the **Start button** on the Windows taskbar, then point to **All Programs**
☐ Click **Microsoft Office**, then click **Microsoft Word 2010**

OR

☐ Double-click the **Microsoft Word program icon** on the desktop

OR

☐ Click the **Microsoft Word 2010 program icon** listed on the Start menu

Exit Word

Ribbon Method

☐ Click the **File tab**, then click **Exit**

OR

☐ Click the **Close button** on the Word program window title bar

Shortcut Method

☐ Press **[Alt][F4]**

VIEW THE WORD WINDOW

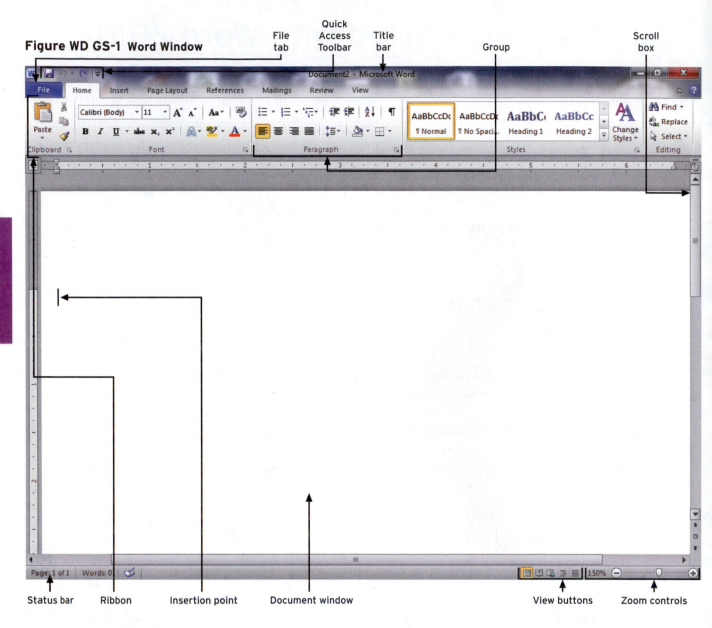

Figure WD GS-1 Word Window

Labels: File tab · Quick Access Toolbar · Title bar · Group · Scroll box · Status bar · Ribbon · Insertion point · Document window · View buttons · Zoom controls

USE THE RIBBON

Display Tabs on the Ribbon

Ribbon Method

☐ Open a document, then click any tab

Hide the Ribbon
Ribbon Method
☐ Double-click the active tab to show only the tabs
Shortcut Method
☐ Right-click any tab, then click **Minimize the Ribbon** to select it

Work with the Ribbon
Ribbon Method
☐ Click a **button**, a **button list arrow**, or the **More button** ⊡ (when available) in any group, then click a command or gallery option, if necessary
  OR
☐ Click a **dialog box launcher** ⊡ to open a dialog box or a pane offering more options

Customize the Quick Access Toolbar
Ribbon Method
☐ Right-click any button on the Quick Access toolbar
☐ To hide that button, click **Remove from Quick Access Toolbar**
☐ To add or remove a button, click **Customize Quick Access Toolbar**, click a command in the left or right column of the Word Options dialog box, then click **Add** or **Remove** in the Word Options dialog box

Reposition the Quick Access Toolbar
Ribbon Method
☐ Right-click any button on the Quick Access toolbar
☐ Click **Show Quick Access Toolbar Below the Ribbon**

OPEN, SAVE, AND CLOSE DOCUMENTS

Open a New Document
Ribbon Method
☐ Click the **File tab**, then click **New**
☐ Click **Blank document** under Available Templates, then click **Create**
Shortcut Method
☐ Press **[Ctrl][N]**

Open an Existing Document
Ribbon Method
☐ Click the **File tab**, then click **Open**
☐ In the Open dialog box, shown in Figure WD GS-2, navigate to the drive and folder where you stored your file
☐ Click the file, then click **Open**

Word

Figure WD GS-2 Open dialog box

Navigate to the drive and folder where the file is stored

Shortcut Method
☐ Press **[Ctrl][O]**

☐ In the Open dialog box, navigate to the drive and folder where you stored your file

☐ Click the file, then click **Open**

Use Save As

Ribbon Method
☐ Click the **File tab**, then click **Save As**

☐ In the Save As dialog box, shown in Figure WD GS-3, navigate to the appropriate drive and folder, if necessary

☐ Type an appropriate filename in the File name text box, then click **Save**

Figure WD GS-3 Save As dialog box

Navigate to the drive and folder where you want to save the file

Type a file name

Shortcut Method
□ Press **[F12]**
□ Follow the steps in bullets 2–3 of the Use Save As Ribbon Method above

Save an Existing Document
Ribbon Method
□ Click the **File tab**, then click **Save**
Shortcut Method
□ Press **[Ctrl][S]**
   OR
□ Click the **Save button** 🖫, on the Quick Access toolbar

Close a Document
Ribbon Method
□ Click the **File tab**, then click **Close**
□ If prompted to save the file, click **Save**, **Don't Save**, or **Cancel**, as appropriate
Shortcut Method
□ Click the **Close button** ❌ on the title bar
□ If prompted to save the file, click **Save**, **Don't Save**, or **Cancel**, as appropriate
   OR
□ Press **[Ctrl][W]** or **[Alt][F4]**
□ If prompted to save the file, click **Save**, **Don't Save**, or **Cancel**, as appropriate

NAVIGATE IN THE DOCUMENT WINDOW

Ribbon Method

☐ Click the **Home tab**, click the **Find list arrow** in the Editing group, then click **Go To**

☐ In the Find and Replace dialog box, shown in Figure WD GS-4, select an option in the Go to what list; in the related text box, type the go to identifier, then click **Go To**

Figure WD GS-4 **Find and Replace dialog box**

Shortcut Method

☐ Press **[Ctrl][G]**

☐ Follow the step in bullet 2 of the Navigate in the Document Window Ribbon Method above
  OR

☐ Use Table WD GS-1 as a reference to navigate through the document using keyboard shortcuts

Table WD GS-1 **Navigation Keyboard Shortcuts**

Key	Moves the insertion point
[Ctrl][Home]	To the beginning of the document
[Ctrl][End]	To the end of the document
[Home]	To the beginning of the current line
[End]	To the end of the current line
[Page Up]	One screen up
[Page Down]	One screen down
[→], [←]	To the right or left one character at a time
[Ctrl][→], [Ctrl][←]	To the right or left one word at a time
[↓],[↑]	Down or up one line at a time

Mouse Method

To change the view without moving the insertion point, do one of the following:

☐ Drag the **scroll box** in a scroll bar to move within the document

☐ Click above the scroll box in the vertical scroll bar to move up a screen without moving the insertion point

☐ Click below the scroll box in the vertical scroll bar to move down a screen without moving the insertion point

☐ Click the up scroll arrow in the vertical scroll bar to move up one line

☐ Click the down scroll arrow in the vertical scroll bar to move down one line

☐ Repeat bullets 2–5 above using the horizontal scroll bar and replacing up and down with left and right

☐ Click the **Next Page button** ⬇ or the **Previous Page button** ⬆ on the vertical scroll bar to move to the next or previous page

USE VIEWS

Refer to Table WD GS-2 to change document views.

Table WD GS-2 Document Views

View	What you see	Ribbon Method-View tab	Shortcut Method-status bar
Print Layout view	Displays a document as it will look on a printed page	Click the **Print Layout button**	Click the **Print Layout button** 🖳
Full Screen Reading view	Displays document text so it is easy to read and annotate	Click the **Full Screen Reading button**	Click the **Full Screen Reading button** 📖
Web Layout view	Displays a document as it will appear when viewed in a Web browser	Click the **Web Layout button**	Click the **Web Layout button** 🖥
Outline view	Displays the headings and their related subtext in hierarchical order	Click the **Outline View button**	Click the **Outline button** 📄
Draft view	Displays a simplified layout of a document, without margins, etc.	Click the **Draft View button**	Click the **Draft button** 🖹

USE KEYBOARD KEYTIPS

Display KeyTips

Shortcut Method

☐ Press **[Alt]** to display the KeyTips for any active tab on the Ribbon and on the Quick Access toolbar as shown in Figure WD GS-5

☐ Press the letter or number for the specific command for the active tab on the Ribbon

☐ Press additional letters or numbers as needed to complete the command sequence

☐ If two letters appear, press each one in order; for some commands you will find that you have to click an option from a gallery or menu to complete the command sequence

☐ The KeyTips turn off automatically at the end of the command sequence

Figure WD GS-5 KeyTips   KeyTip

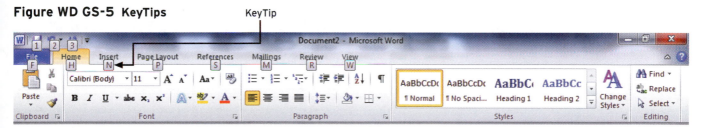

Hide KeyTips

Shortcut Method

☐ Press **[Alt]** to hide the KeyTips for each Ribbon command

GET HELP

Ribbon Method

☐ Click the **Microsoft Word Help button** [?] to display the Word Help window shown in Figure WD GS-6

☐ Use Table WD GS-3 as a reference to select the most appropriate way to search for help using the Microsoft Word Help window

OR

☐ Point to any button on the Ribbon, then read the ScreenTip text

☐ If you see "Press F1 for more help." at the bottom of the ScreenTip, continue pointing to the button, then press **[F1]** to see targeted help on that button from Word Help

Figure WD GS-6 Word Help window

Shortcut Method

☐ Press **[F1]**

☐ Use Table WD GS-3 as a reference to select the most appropriate way to search for help using the Microsoft Word Help window

Table WD GS-3 Microsoft Word Help Window Options

Option	To use
Getting started with Word 2010	Click a link representing a topic you want to read about; click subtopics that appear until you see help text for the topic
Browse Word 2010 support	Click a link representing a topic you want to read about; click subtopics that appear until you see help text for the topic
Back button	Click to return to the previously displayed information
Forward button	Click to go forward in the sequence of previously displayed information
Stop button	Click to stop searching on a topic
Refresh button	Click to refresh the Help window content
Home button	Click to return to the Word Help window
Print button	Click to print the current page
Change Font Size button	Click to enlarge or shrink the help text
Show Table of Contents	Click to show the Table of Contents pane, showing topic links you can click
Keep on Top	Click to keep the Help window on top as you work; button becomes the Not On Top button, which you click to let the Help window go behind the current window as you work
Type words to search for box	Type a word, then click the Search button
Search button list arrow	Click the list arrow, then click the area, such as Content from Office.com, All Word, or Word Help
Microsoft Office Search help using Bing	Type a word, then click the Search button or Type a word, then click the link downloads, images, or templates to search for those items on Office.com

REVIEW QUESTIONS

FILL IN THE BLANK

Complete the following sentences by writing the correct word or words in the blanks provided.

1. Double-click the active tab to _____ the Ribbon.

2. To open a new document, click the File tab, then click _____.

3. The Microsoft Word Help button is usually located in the top _____ corner of the window.

4. Press _____ to display the KeyTips for any active tab.

5. _____ view displays the headings and their related subtext in hierarchical order.

MATCHING

Match the correct term in Column 2 to its description in Column 1.

Column 1	Column 2
_____ 1. Save an existing document	A. [Ctrl][Home]
_____ 2. Exit Word	B. [Ctrl][S]
_____ 3. Open the Go To tab of the Find and Replace dialog box	C. [Alt][F4]
_____ 4. Navigate to the end of the document	D. [Ctrl][End]
_____ 5. Navigate to the beginning of the document	E. [Ctrl][G]

Word

PROJECTS

Project WD GS-1

1. Open Word.

2. Open a new document.

3. Reposition the Quick Access Toolbar below the Ribbon.

4. Customize the Quick Access Toolbar by adding a button for a commonly used command.

5. Display the KeyTips.

6. Use the KeyTips to display the Page Layout tab.

7. Display the Home tab.

8. Hide the Ribbon.

9. Reposition the Quick Access Toolbar above the Ribbon.

10. Remove the button you added to the Quick Access Toolbar in step 4.

11. Close the document without saving it.

Project WD GS-2

1. Open Word.

2. Open the **Project GS-2.docx** file.

3. Use keyboard shortcuts to move to the end of the document.

4. Use keyboard shortcuts to move to the beginning of the line.

5. Drag the vertical scroll box to the top of the scroll bar.

6. Use the Ribbon to display the document in Outline view.

7. Use the status bar to display the document in Print Layout view.

8. Display the Word Help window and show the Table of Contents.

9. Hide the Table of Contents and close the Word Help window.

10. Save the document as **Realtors.docx** and close the document.

11. Exit Word.

CRITICAL THINKING

Activity WD GS-1

Open the Word Help window. Click the Getting started with Word 2010 link. Scroll down and click the play button to view the Getting Started with Microsoft Word 2010 video. What other videos are available? Browse through Help to see all the material available for you to learn more about using Word. Refer to Table WD GS-3 as a reference if you need help using the Word Help window.

Activity WD GS-2

With the Word Help window open, search to find out what's new in Word 2010. Open a new blank document and explore each tab on the Ribbon to familiarize yourself with where the commands are located. What is Microsoft Office Backstage view? Use Word Help to find out more about this new feature for managing your files and the data about them.

Word Objective 1: Sharing and Maintaining Documents

Apply Different Views to a Document

Select Zoom options

Ribbon Method
☐ Click the **View tab**, then click the **Zoom button** in the Zoom group
☐ In the Zoom dialog box, select appropriate options, then click **OK**

Shortcut Method
☐ Click the **Zoom level button** `100%` on the status bar
☐ In the Zoom dialog box, shown in Figure WD 1-1, select appropriate options, then click **OK**

Figure WD 1-1   Zoom dialog box

Split Windows

Ribbon Method
☐ Click the **View tab**, then click the **Split button** in the Window group
☐ Drag the horizontal split bar to the location where you want to split the window then click
☐ To adjust the split, drag the horizontal split bar to a new location
☐ To remove the split, click the **Remove Split button** in the Window group

Arrange Windows

Ribbon Method
☐ Click the **View tab**, then click the **Arrange All button** in the Window group
☐ To view only one document, click the **Maximize button** on the title bar of that document

View Windows Side by Side

Ribbon Method
☐ Click the **View tab**, then click the **View Side by Side button** in the Window group

Use Synchronous Scrolling

Ribbon Method
☐ Click the **View tab**, click the **View Side by Side button** in the Window group, then click the **Synchronous Scrolling button** if necessary

Reorganize a Document Outline

Ribbon Method

- ☐ Click the **View tab**, then click the **Outline button** in the Document Views group
- ☐ Use the options in the Outline Tools group to rearrange items in the document
- ☐ Click the **Close Outline View button** in the Close group

Shortcut Method

- ☐ Click the **Outline button** 🔲 on the status bar
- ☐ Follow the steps in bullets 2–3 in Reorganize a Document Outline Ribbon Method above

View Master Documents

Ribbon Method

- ☐ Open a master document
- ☐ Click the **View tab**, then click the **Outline button** in the Document Views group
- ☐ Click the **Show Document button** in the Master Document group
- ☐ Use the commands in the Master Document group to work with the master document and subdocuments

Shortcut Method

- ☐ Open a master document
- ☐ Click the **Outline button** 🔲 on the status bar
- ☐ Follow the steps in bullets 2-3 of the View Master Documents Ribbon Method above

View Subdocuments

Ribbon Method

- ☐ Open a master document
- ☐ Click the **View tab**, then click the **Outline button** in the Document Views group
- ☐ Click the **Collapse Subdocuments button** in the Master Document group to show the links containing the full paths to the subdocuments

  OR

- ☐ Click the **Expand Subdocuments button** in the Master Document group to show the content of the subdocuments

Shortcut Method

- ☐ Open a master document
- ☐ Click the **Outline button** 🔲 on the status bar
- ☐ Follow the steps in bullets 3-4 in the View Subdocuments Ribbon Method

View a Document in Web Layout view

Ribbon Method

- ☐ Click the **View tab**, then click the **Web Layout button** in the Document Views group

Shortcut Method

- ☐ Click the **Web Layout button** 🔲 on the status bar

View a Document in Draft view

Ribbon Method

- ☐ Click the **View tab**, then click the **Draft button** in the Document Views group

Shortcut Method

- ☐ Click the **Draft button** 🔲 on the status bar

Switch Between Windows

Ribbon Method

☐ Click the **View tab**, click the **Switch Windows button** in the Window group, then click the document you want to view in the window from the available documents listed in the menu

Open a Document in a New Window

Ribbon Method

☐ Click the **View tab**, then click the **New Window button** in the Window group

APPLY PROTECTION TO A DOCUMENT

Apply Formatting Restrictions

Ribbon Method

☐ Click the **File tab**, click the **Protect Document button**, then click **Restrict Editing**

☐ In the Restrict Formatting and Editing task pane, shown in Figure WD 1-2, select the Limit formatting to a selection of styles check box in the Formatting restrictions section, click **Settings**, select the appropriate options in the Formatting Restrictions dialog box, click **OK**, then click **Yes**, **Start Enforcing Protection**

☐ In the Start Enforcing Protection dialog box, click **OK** to start enforcement without protecting the document with a password or type a password, press **[Tab]**, then type the password again to password protect the document, or click the **User authentication** option to encrypt the document and use Information Rights Management Service to authenticate the owners of the document and click **OK** or click **Cancel** if you do not want to start enforcing protection

Figure WD 1-2   Restrict Formatting and Editing task pane

OR

☐ Click the **Review tab**, click the **Restrict Editing button** in the Protect group, then follow the steps in bullets 2–3 of the Apply Formatting Restrictions Ribbon Method

Apply Editing Restrictions and Limit Access to a Document

Ribbon Method

☐ Click the **File tab**, click the **Protect Document button**, then click **Restrict Editing**

☐ In the Restrict Formatting and Editing task pane, select the **Allow only this type of editing in the document check box** in the Editing restrictions section, click the list arrow to select the type of editing to allow, then select the users in the Exceptions section that this editing restriction will not apply to, then click **Yes, Start Enforcing Protection**

☐ In the Start Enforcing Protection dialog box, click **OK** to start enforcement without protecting the document with a password or type a password, press **[Tab]**, then type the password again to password protect the document, or click the **User authentication** option to encrypt the document and use Information Rights Management Service to authenticate the owners of the document and click **OK** or click **Cancel** if you do not want to start enforcing protection

OR

☐ Click the **Review tab**, click the **Restrict Editing button** in the Protect group, then follow the steps in bullets 2–3 of the Apply Editing Restrictions and Limit Access to a Document Ribbon Method above

Password-protect a Document

Ribbon Method

☐ Open a Word document, click the **File tab**, click the **Protect Document button**, then click **Encrypt with Password**

☐ Type a password in the Encrypt Document dialog box, shown in Figure WD 1-3, then click **OK**

☐ Reenter the password in the Confirm Password dialog box, then click **OK**

Figure WD 1-3   **Encrypt Document dialog box**

OR

☐ Follow the steps in bullets 1–3 of the Apply Formatting Restrictions or Apply Editing Restrictions and Limit Access to a Document Ribbon Methods above

Mark a Document as Final

Ribbon Method

☐ Click the **File tab**, click the **Protect Document button**, click **Mark as Final**, then click **OK**

OR

☐ Click the **File tab**, click the **Protect Document button**, then click **Restrict Editing**

☐ In the Restrict Formatting and Editing task pane, select the **Allow only this type of editing in the document check box** in the Editing restrictions section, click the list arrow and select **No changes (Read only)**, then click **Yes, Start Enforcing Protection**

☐ In the Start Enforcing Protection dialog box, type a password, press **[Tab]**, then type the password again to password protect the document, or click the **User authentication** option and click **OK** or click **Cancel** if you do not want to password protect the document
OR

☐ Click the **Review tab**, then click the **Restrict Editing button** in the Protect group

☐ Follow the steps in bullets 2-3 in the Mark Document as Final Ribbon Method on the previous page

MANAGE DOCUMENT VERSIONS

Modify AutoRecover Options

☐ Click the **File tab**, click **Options**, then click **Save**

☐ In the Word Options dialog box, under the Save documents section, click the **Save AutoRecover information checkbox** to turn on the feature or remove the checkbox to turn off the feature, use the up and down arrows to change the number of minutes to have AutoRecover save information, choose whether or not to keep the last auto-save version of a file if you close without saving, or change the location where your AutoRecover files are saved

> ### NOTE
>
> Word's AutoRecover feature automatically saves your document at regular intervals so that you can recover at least some of your work in case of a power outage or other unexpected shutdown.

Recover Draft Versions

Ribbon Method

☐ Click the **File tab**, click the **Manage Versions button**, then click **Recover Unsaved Documents**

☐ In the Open dialog box, click an unsaved document from the list and click **Open** to open the document

☐ In the Recovered Unsaved File bar at the top of the document, click **Save As**

☐ In the Save As dialog box, type a filename, and click **Save**

Delete All Draft Versions

Ribbon Method

☐ Click the **File tab**, click the **Manage Versions button**, then click **Delete All Unsaved Documents**

☐ In the Microsoft message box, click **Yes** to delete all unsaved files

SHARE DOCUMENTS

Send Documents via E-mail

Ribbon Method

☐ Click the **File tab**, click **Save & Send**, make sure **Send Using E-mail** is selected in the Save & Send pane, then click the **Send as Attachment button** in the Send Using E-mail pane to open a new e-mail message with the file attached and the filename in the subject line of the e-mail message

☐ Enter an e-mail address in the To: box, type a message in the box if necessary, then click the **Send button** to send the e-mail with the file attachment

Send Documents via SkyDrive

Ribbon Method

□ Click the **File tab**, click **Save & Send**, then click the **Save to Web button** in the Save & Send pane

□ Click the **Sign In button** in the Save to Windows Live SkyDrive pane, shown in Figure WD 1-4, to sign in with your Windows Live ID and to gain access to Windows SkyDrive or click the **Sign up for Windows Live SkyDrive link** to open the Welcome to Windows Live web page where you can sign up for a Windows Live ID then use it to sign in

□ Click the folder where you want to save the file from the Personal Folders or Shared Folders list in the Save to Windows Live SkyDrive pane, then click the **Save As button**

□ In the Save As dialog box, type an appropriate filename in the File name text box, click the **Save as type list arrow**, select the file format you want to save as, then click **Save**

Figure WD 1-4   **Save to Windows Live SkyDrive pane**

Send Documents via Internet Fax

Ribbon Method

□ Click the **File tab**, click **Save & Send**, make sure **Send Using E-mail** is selected in the Save & Send pane, then click the **Send as Internet Fax button** in the Send Using E-mail pane

□ A Microsoft Office message is displayed explaining that you need to choose an Internet Fax service in order to send a fax. Click **OK** to open a web page that lists Internet Fax service providers

□ Follow the instructions for choosing a provider then repeat the steps in the first bullet

> ### NOTE
>
> Windows Live SkyDrive is a free online storage service from Microsoft which makes documents accessible from any computer with Internet access.

Change File Types

Ribbon Method

□ Click the **File tab**, click **Save & Send**, click **Change File Type** in the File Types section of the center pane

□ Click the appropriate file type in the Change File Type pane, then click the **Save As button**

□ In the Save As dialog box, type an appropriate filename in the File name text box, then click **Save**

OR

□ Click the **File tab**, then click **Save As**

□ In the Save As dialog box, type an appropriate filename in the File name text box, click the **Save as type list arrow**, select the file format you want to save as, then click **Save**

Shortcut Method

□ Press **F12**

□ In the Save As dialog box, type an appropriate filename in the File name text box, click the **Save as type list arrow**, select the file format you want to save it as, then click **Save**

Create PDF documents

Ribbon Method

□ Click the **File tab**, click **Save & Send**, click **Create PDF/XPS document** in the File Types section of the center pane, then click the **Create PDF/XPS button** in the Create a PDF/XPS Document pane

□ In the Publish As PDF or XPS dialog box, type an appropriate filename in the File name text box, click the appropriate **Optimize for button**, change any other options as necessary, then click **Publish**

OR

□ Click the **File tab**, then click **Save As**

□ In the Save As dialog box, type an appropriate filename in the File name text box, click the **Save as type list arrow** and click the PDF (*.pdf) file type, click the appropriate **Optimize for button**, change any other options as necessary, then click **Save**

Shortcut Method

□ Press **F12**

□ In the Save As dialog box, type an appropriate filename in the File name text box, click the **Save as type list arrow** and click the PDF (*.pdf) file type, click the appropriate **Optimize for button**, change any other options as necessary, then click **Save**

Create a Shared Document

Ribbon Method

□ Create or open a document you want to share

☐ Click the **File tab**, click **Save & Send**, click **Save to SharePoint** in the Save & Send section of the center pane, then click **Browse for a location** in the Save to SharePoint pane to locate the SharePoint server on your network

☐ Click the **Save As button** in the Save to SharePoint pane

☐ In the Save As dialog box, type an appropriate filename in the File name text box, click the **Save as type list arrow**, select the file format you want to save it as, then click **Save**

NOTE

Saving to an organization's SharePoint site provides opportunities for collaboration, such as editing documents with multiple people at the same time.

Register a Blog Account

Ribbon Method

☐ Visit Office.com to view a list of blog providers compatible with Microsoft Word. Choose one of the blog providers and set up a blog account at their website.

☐ Click the **File tab**, click **New**, click **Blog post** in the Available Templates section of the center pane, then click the **Create button** in the right pane

☐ Click **Register Now** in the Register a Blog Account dialog box

☐ In the New Blog Account dialog box, click the down arrow to choose your blog provider, then click the **Next button**

☐ Follow the directions to register the account with Word, usually by entering the username and password you use to login to the blog account, click **OK**, specify your picture provider in the Picture Options dialog box, then click **OK**

☐ In the Microsoft Word message box that states that other people may be able to see your information when it is sent, click **Yes**

☐ Click **OK** in the Microsoft Word message box that states that your account registration was successful

---

NOTE

You must create an account with an Internet blog provider that is compatible with Microsoft Word, then register that account with Word, to be able to publish blog posts using Microsoft Word.

Create and Publish a Blog Post

Ribbon Method

☐ Click the **File tab**, click **New**, click **Blog post** in the Available Templates section of the center pane, then click the **Create button** in the right pane

☐ In the new blog post, click **Enter Post Title Here** and type a title for the blog post, type the text of the blog post below the line, and then save document

□ Click the **Publish button** in the Blog group, enter the username and password for access to your blogging space, and click **OK**

□ In the **Microsoft Office message box** that states that other people may be able to see your information when it is sent, click **Yes** to publish the blog anyway (or click **No** to cancel publishing). A date and time stamp will appear at the top of the blog post stating the time, date, and location of the blog post

OR

□ Open the document you would like to post as a blog

Click the **File tab**, click **Save & Send**, click **Publish as Blog Post** in the Save & Send section of the center pane, then click the **Publish as Blog Post button** in the right pane

□ Follow the steps in bullets 2-4 under Create and Publish a Blog Post Ribbon Method above

> ### NOTE
>
> Word cannot publish blog posts saved with the .doc extension, so be sure to save blog posts in the .docx format. Also, be sure to include a title on your blog posts, because some Internet blog providers require it.

SAVE A DOCUMENT

Use Compatibility Mode

Ribbon Method

□ Open a document saved with a .docx extension, click the **File tab**, click **Save As**, click **Word 97-2003 Document** in the Save as type list, type a name for the document in the File name box, then click **Save** to save the document as a .doc file that can be used in an earlier version of Word

OR

□ Open a .doc file, click the **File tab**, click the **Convert button**, then click **OK** to convert the .doc file to a .docx file that enables the new features in Word 2010

Use Protected Mode

Ribbon Method

□ Click the **File tab**, then click **Options** to open the Word Options dialog box

□ Click **Trust Center** in the left pane, then click the **Trust Center Settings button** in the right pane to open the Trust Center dialog box

□ Click **Protected View** in the right pane, select appropriate options to disable or enable protected view options in the right pane, then click **OK**

> ### NOTE
>
> When a file from the internet or other potentially unsafe location is opened on your computer, it is opened in protected view. Click the Enable Editing button on the protected view message bar to exit protected view.

Use Save As Options

Ribbon Method

☐ Click the **File tab**, then click **Save As**

☐ In the Save As dialog box, shown in Figure WD 1-5, type an appropriate filename in the File name text box, click the **Save as type list arrow**, select the file format you want to save as such as .dotx for a Word Template or .pdf for a PDF file format, then click **Save**

Figure WD 1-5   Save As dialog box

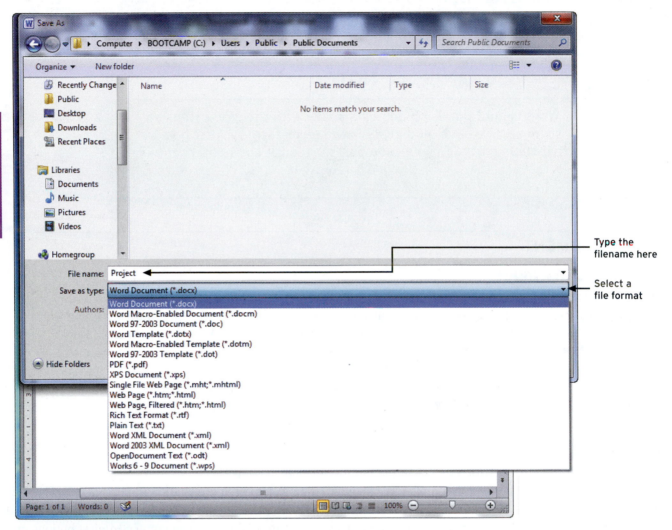

Shortcut Method

☐ Press **[F12]**

☐ Follow the steps in bullet 2 of the Use Save As Options Ribbon Method above

OR

☐ To select the Save As file format for a file that has not been saved previously, click the **Save button** on the Quick Access toolbar, then follow the steps in bullet 2, Use Save As Options Ribbon Method above

OR

☐ To select the Save As file format for a file that has not been saved previously, press **[Ctrl][S]**, then follow the steps in bullet 2 of the Use Save As Options Ribbon Method above

APPLY A TEMPLATE TO A DOCUMENT

Locate a Template on your Disk

Ribbon Method

☐ Click the **File tab**, click **New**, in the Available Templates pane (shown in Figure WD 1-6), click **Sample templates**, click an appropriate template in the center pane, click the **Document** or **Template button** in the right pane to select whether to open as a document or a template, then click the **Create button**

OR

☐ Click the **File tab**, click **New**, in the Available Templates pane (shown in Figure WD 1-6), click **My templates**, click an appropriate template from the Personal Templates tab in the New dialog box, click the Document or Template button to select whether to open as a document or a template, then click **OK**

Figure WD 1-6   Available Templates pane

Find Templates on the Web

Ribbon Method

☐ Click the **File tab**, click **New**, and click a category from the Office.com Templates section of the center pane (shown in Figure WD 1-6), click an appropriate template, then click the **Download button** to download a template from Office.com

OR

☐ Click the **File tab**, click **New**, type a keyword in the Search Office.com for templates box (shown in Figure WD 1-6), click the **Start searching button** ➡, click an appropriate template from the center pane, then click the **Download button** to download the template from Office.com

Replace Placeholder Text in a Template

Mouse Method

☐ Locate and open a template following the steps under Locate a Template on your Disk Ribbon Method or Find Templates on the Web Ribbon Method on the previous page

☐ Click the placeholder text in brackets, such as [Type the document title] and type your own text (Some placeholders, such as those for the date, may have an arrow you can click to choose the date from a calendar)

REVIEW QUESTIONS

TRUE/FALSE

Circle T if the statement is true or F if the statement is false.

T   F   1. To save a document in a different file format, use the Save command.

T   F   2. When you split the screen, you can drag the horizontal split bar to the location where you want the screen to be split.

T   F   3. You can manage master documents in Draft view.

T   F   4. It is possible to restrict editing without protecting a document with a password.

T   F   5. The Sample Templates button displays templates available on Office.com.

T   F   6. Templates include one or more subdocuments.

T   F   7. You usually need to confirm a new password by typing it twice.

T   F   8. The Full Screen Reading button is located on the Page Layout tab.

T   F   9. The Word 97-2003 file format saves a document with the .docx extension.

T   F   10. You must register a blog account before you can publish it with Word.

MATCHING

Match the correct term in Column 2 to its description in Column 1.

Column 1	Column 2
_____ 1. A command that lets you recover or delete unsaved files	A. Restrict Editing
_____ 2. A way to save a file that disables some new features so that the file can be used with earlier versions of Word	B. Mark as Final
_____ 3. Used to control access to a document	C. Manage Versions
_____ 4. A way in which a file from the Internet or other potentially unsafe locations is opened to prevent damage to your computer	D. Compatibility Mode
_____ 5. Saves a document as read-only	E. Protected Mode

PROJECTS

Project WD 1-1

1. Create a new document using the Equity Report in the Sample templates category of Backstage view.
2. Save the document as **First Quarter Report.docx**.
3. Click the document title placeholder, and then type **First Quarter Report**.
4. Click the document subtitle placeholder tab, then type **2015**.
5. Click the down arrow on the date placeholder and choose April 1, 2015.
6. If necessary, type your name as the author.
7. View the document in Outline view.
8. Close Outline view.
9. View the document in Web Layout view.
10. View the document in Draft view.
11. View the document in Print Layout view.
12. Save and close the document.

Project WD 1-2

1. Open the data file **Project WD 1-2.doc**.
2. The document is currently saved in the Word 97-2003 .doc file format. Save the document as **Draft Letter** in the Word Document .docx format.
3. Apply editing restrictions to only allow comments in the document.
4. Start enforcing the restrictions and type **watkinsL2c*** as the password.
5. Save and close the document.
6. Open the document. Attempt to change the salary to $42,000.
7. In the Restrict Formatting and Editing task pane, click **Stop Protection**.
8. Type **watkinsL2c*** as the password.
9. Change the salary to $42,000.
10. Save the document.
11. Send the document to yourself via E-mail.
12. Close the document.

Project WD 1-3

1. Open the data file **Project WD 1-3.docx**.
2. Change the Zoom setting to 200% and scroll through the document.
3. Change the Zoom setting to 100%.
4. Click the **Two Pages** button on the View tab to see both pages.
5. Click the **One Page** button.
6. Click the **100%** button.
7. Split the window, dragging the horizontal split bar just above the **Employment History** heading.
8. Scroll down through the bottom half of the window.

Word

9. Click in the top half of the window. Position the insertion point after the period after the word *machinery*, at the end of the fourth line of the **Skills Profile** list.

10. Press **Enter** and type **Eager to learn new skills.**

11. Click the **Remove Split** button.

12. Save the document as **Watkins Resume.docx** and close it.

CRITICAL THINKING

Activity WD 1-1

Open a new blank document. Type your name and e-mail address and then use the Encrypt with Password command to protect the document with a password. (Remember to use a password you can remember or write it down and keep it in a safe place.) Save the document with a meaningful name and close it. Reopen it using the password you created. Close the document.

Activity WD 1-2

Use Word Help to find out what makes a strong password. Write a short paragraph explaining what makes a strong password. What kind of characters should the password contain? Should they be uppercase or lowercase? What does case-sensitive mean? How many characters should you use? How would you rate the password you created in Activity WD 1-1? How would you rate the password used in Project WD 1-2?

Word

WORD OBJECTIVE 2: FORMATTING CONTENT

APPLY FONT AND PARAGRAPH ATTRIBUTES

Apply Character Attributes

☐ Select the text to which you want to apply a character format, then use Table WD 2-1 as a reference to apply the character formatting you want

Table WD 2-1   Applying Character Attributes

Attribute to apply	Ribbon Method: Home tab/Font group	Shortcut Method: Mini toolbar	Shortcut Method: Keyboard	Launcher in the Font group: Font dialog box
Apply a new font	Click the **Font list arrow**, then click a font	Click the **Font list arrow**, then click a font	Press **[Ctrl] [Shift] [F]**, click the **Font list arrow**, then click a font	Click the **Font scroll bar**, then click a font
Apply a new font size	Click the **Font Size list arrow**, then click a font size, or type a value in the Font Size text box	Click the **Font Size list arrow**, then click a font size, or type a value in the Font Size text box	Press **[Ctrl] [Shift] [F]**, then click the Font Size list arrow and click a font size; or type the value in the Font Size text box	Click the **Font size scroll bar**, then click a font size; or type the value in the Font Size text box
Increase the font size one increment	Click the **Grow Font button** A	Click the **Grow Font button** A	Press **[Ctrl] [>]**	
Decrease the font size one increment	Click the **Shrink Font button** A	Click the **Shrink Font button** A	Press **[Ctrl] [<]**	
Clear formatting	Click the **Clear Formatting button**		Right-click, the click the **Styles command** on the Shortcut menu, then click **Clear Formatting**	
Apply bold	Click the **Bold button** B	Click the **Bold button** B	Press **[Ctrl] [B]**	Click **Bold** in the Font style list
Apply italics	Click the **Italic button** I	Click the **Italic button** I	Press **[Ctrl] [I]**	Click **Italic** in the Font style list
Apply underlining	Click the **Underline button** U, or click the **Underline list arrow** U, select a pre-formatted underline or click More Underlines to open the Font dialog box, then refer to the directions in the last column	Click the **Underline button** U	Press **[Ctrl] [U]**	Click the **Underline style list arrow** and select a style, click the **Underline color list arrow**, select a color, then click OK
Apply strikethrough	Click the **Strikethrough button**			Click the **Strikethrough check box** in the Effects section
Apply subscript	Click the **Subscript button** x_2		Press **[Ctrl] [=]**	Click the **Subscript check box** in the Effects section
Apply superscript	Click the **Superscript button** x^2		Press **[Ctrl] [Shift] [+]**	Click the **Superscript check box** in the Effects section

Word

(continued)

Table WD 2-1 Applying Character Attributes (continued)

Attribute to apply	Ribbon Method: Home tab/Font group	Shortcut Method: Mini toolbar	Shortcut Method: Keyboard	Launcher in the Font group: Font dialog box
Apply highlighting to text	Click the **Text Highlight Color button** to apply the active highlight color or click the **Text Highlight Color list arrow**, then select a new color	Click the **Text Highlight Color button** to apply the active highlight color or click the **Text Highlight Color list arrow**, then select a new color		
Apply a new font color	Click the **Font Color button** to apply the active font color or click the **Font Color list arrow**, then select a color from a palette of available colors; or click **More Colors**, then create a custom color	Click the **Font Color button** to apply the active font color or click the **Font Color list arrow**, then select a color from a palette of available colors; or click **More Colors**, then create a custom color		Click the **Font Color list arrow** to select a color from a palette of available colors; or click **More Colors** to create a custom color
Change Case	Click the **Change Case button**			Click an option in the Effects section then click **OK**
Text Effects	Click the **Text Effects button**			Click the **Text Effects** button and choose options in the Format Text Effects dialog box, click **Close**, then click **OK**

Apply Styles

Ribbon Method
☐ Select the text, click the **Home tab**, click the **More button** in the Styles group, then click an appropriate Quick Style from the gallery, as shown in Figure WD 2-1
  OR
☐ Click the **Home tab**, click the **Change Styles button** in the Styles group, click **Style Set**, then click an appropriate style set
  OR
☐ Select the text, click the **Home tab**, then click the **launcher** in the Styles group to open the Styles task pane
☐ Scroll the list of available styles, then click an appropriate style

Shortcut Method
☐ Select the text, right-click, then click the **Styles command** on the shortcut menu
☐ Click a **Quick Style** in the gallery that opens or click **Apply Styles** at the bottom of the gallery to open the Apply Styles dialog box, click the **Style Name list arrow**, select a style, then close the dialog box

Figure WD 2-1   Quick Style gallery

Use the Format Painter to Copy Formatting

Ribbon Method

- □ Select the text that has the formatting you want to copy, then click the **Home tab**
- □ Click the **Format Painter button** 🖌 in the Clipboard group one time, then select the text you want to format
  OR
- □ Click the **Format Painter button** 🖌 in the Clipboard group two times, select the text you want to format and apply the same formatting to multiple places in the document, then click 🖌 to turn off the Format Painter

Shortcut Method

- □ Select the text that has the formatting you want to copy, then press **[Ctrl] [Shift] [C]** to copy the formatting
- □ Select the text you want to format, then press **[Ctrl] [Shift] [V]** to apply the formatting
- □ Repeat for each instance

Cut and Paste Text

Ribbon Method

- □ Select the text you want to cut, click the **Home tab**, then click the **Cut button** ✂
- □ Position the insertion point where you want to paste the text, then click the **Paste button**

Shortcut Method

- □ Select the text you want to cut, right-click, then click **Cut** on the shortcut menu
- □ Position the insertion point where you want to paste the text, right-click, click **Paste Options** on the shortcut menu, then click Keep Source Formatting, Merge Formatting, or Keep Text Only depending on how you want the pasted text to be formatted
  OR
- □ Select the text you want to cut, then press **[Ctrl] [X]**
- □ Position the insertion point where you want to paste the text, then press **[Ctrl] [V]**

Copy and Paste Text

Ribbon Method

- □ Select the text you want to copy, click the **Home tab**, then click the **Copy button** 📋
- □ Position the insertion point where you want to paste the text, then click the **Paste button**

Shortcut Method

- □ Select the text you want to copy, right-click, then click **Copy** on the shortcut menu
- □ Position the insertion point where you want to paste the text, right-click, then click **Paste** on the shortcut menu
  OR
- □ Select the text you want to copy, then press **[Ctrl] [C]**
- □ Position the insertion point where you want to paste the text, then press **[Ctrl] [V]**

Word

NAVIGATE AND SEARCH THROUGH A DOCUMENT

Display the Navigation Pane

Ribbon Method

☐ Click the **View tab**, then click the **Navigation Pane check box** in the Show group
  OR
☐ Click the **Home tab**, then click the **Find button** in the Editing group

Shortcut Method

☐ Press **[CTRL][F]**

Use the Navigation Pane to Browse Document Headings

Ribbon Method

☐ Make sure your document's headings are formatted with heading styles
☐ Display the Navigation pane using the steps in the Display the Navigation Pane Ribbon or Shortcut Method above
☐ Click the **Browse the headings in your document tab** 🗐
☐ Click a heading listed in the Navigation pane to display that section of the document on the right side of the screen

Use the Navigation Pane to Browse Document Pages

Ribbon Method

☐ Display the Navigation pane using the steps in the Display the Navigation Pane Ribbon or Shortcut Method above
☐ Click the **Browse the pages in your document tab** 🔡
☐ Click a page thumbnail in the Navigation pane to display that page on the right side of the screen

> ## NOTE
>
> A thumbnail is a small picture of a page.

Use the Navigation Pane to Browse the Results of a Search

Ribbon Method

☐ Click the **Home tab**, then click the **Find button** in the Editing group
☐ Type a keyword in the **Search Document text box**
☐ If necessary, click the **Browse the results from your current search tab** 🗐 to display the results of the search in the navigation pane. Notice that all instances of the keyword are highlighted in the document, as shown in Figure WD 2-2.
☐ Click a result in the Navigation pane to display that page on the right side of the screen

Shortcut Method

☐ Press **[CTRL][F]**
☐ Follow the steps in the bullets 2-4 under Use the Navigation Pane to Browse the Results of a Search Ribbon Method above

Figure WD 2-2   Navigation Pane

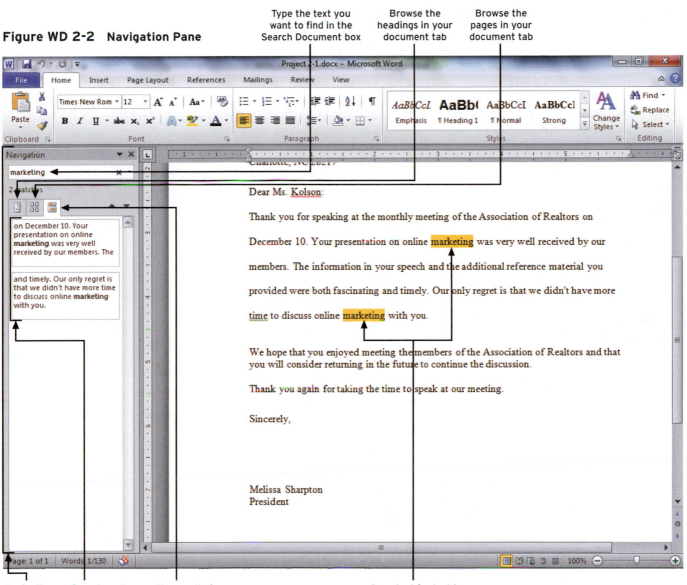

| Type the text you want to find in the Search Document box | Browse the headings in your document tab | Browse the pages in your document tab |

| Navigation pane | Search results | Browse the results from your current search tab | Searched-for text is highlighted in the document |

Use Go To

Ribbon Method

☐ Click the **Home tab**, click the **Find list arrow** in the Editing group, then click **Go To**

☐ Select an option in the Go to what list; in the related text box, type the go to identifier, then click **Go To**

Shortcut Method

☐ Press **[Ctrl][G]** to open the Find and Replace dialog box with the Go To tab active

☐ Follow the step in bullet 2 of the Use Go To Ribbon Method above

Use the Select Browse Object button

Ribbon Method

☐ Click the **Select Browse Object button** 🔘 at the bottom of the vertical scroll bar

☐ Click a button on the menu, shown in Figure WD 2-3, to move quickly to the next occurrence of that object or to display the Find and Replace dialog box in the case of Find and Go To

Figure WD 2-3   Select Browse Object pop-up menu

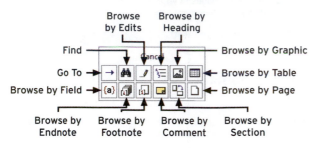

Find Text

Ribbon Method

□ Click the **Home tab**, click the **Find list arrow** in the Editing group, then click **Advanced Find** to open the Find and Replace dialog box with the Find tab active

□ Type the text you want to find in the Find what text box

□ Click the **More button** to view and select additional search options

□ Click the **Find Next button** to view each instance of the text in the Find what text box

□ Click **Cancel** to close the Find and Replace dialog box

Shortcut Method

□ Press **[Ctrl] [F]** to open the Find and Replace dialog box with the Find tab active

□ Follow the steps in bullets 2–5 of the Find Text Ribbon Method above

Find and Replace Text

Ribbon Method

□ Click the **Home tab**, then click the **Replace button** in the Editing group to open the Find and Replace dialog box with the Replace tab active

□ Type the text you want to find and replace in the **Find what text box**

□ Type the replacement text in the **Replace with text box**

□ Click the **More** button to view additional search options, then select the appropriate search options

□ Click the **Find Next button** to view the next instance of the text in the Find what text box, review the selected text, then click **Replace** to replace the selected text or click **Find Next** to leave the selected text as is and move to the next instance

□ Click **Cancel** to close the Find and Replace dialog box

Shortcut Method

□ Press **[Ctrl] [H]** to open the Find and Replace dialog box with the Replace tab active

□ Follow the steps in bullets 2–6 of the Find and Replace Text Ribbon Method above

Use Replace All

Ribbon Method

□ Follow the steps in bullets 1–4 of the Find and Replace Text Ribbon Method above

□ Click **Replace All** to replace all instances without preview

□ Click **Cancel** to close the Find and Replace dialog box

Search for and Highlight Text

Ribbon Method

□ Click the **Home tab**, click the **Find list arrow** in the Editing group, then click **Advanced Find**

□ In the Find and Replace dialog box, type a keyword in the **Find what box**, then click the **Reading Highlight button** and click **Highlight All** to highlight all occurrences of the keyword in the document

☐ Click the **Find Next button** to move to the next occurrence of the highlighted word

OR

☐ Follow the steps in bullets 1-4 under Use the Navigation Pane to Browse the Results of a Search Ribbon Method on the previous page

Find and Replace Formatting

Ribbon Method

☐ Click the **Home tab**, then click the **Replace button** in the Editing group to open the Find and Replace dialog box with the Replace tab active

☐ Click the **More button** to view additional search options

☐ Click in the **Find what box** to change the bottom portion of the dialog box to Find commands, then leave it blank since you are searching for a format only

☐ Click the **Format button** under Find, then click a format from the list, as shown in Figure WD 2-4

☐ Click in the **Replace with box** to change the bottom portion of the dialog box to Replace commands, then leave it blank since you are replacing a format only

☐ Click the **Format button** under Replace, then click a format from the list

☐ Click the **Find Next button** to view the next instance of the format you are searching for, review the selection, then click **Replace** to replace the selected format or click **Find Next** to leave the selected format as is and move to the next instance

☐ Click **Cancel** to close the Find and Replace dialog box

Shortcut Method

☐ Press **[Ctrl] [H]** to open the Find and Replace dialog box with the Replace tab active

☐ Follow the steps in bullets 2–8 of the Find and Replace Formatting Ribbon Method above

Figure WD 2-4   Find and Replace dialog box

Find and Replace Text with Specific Formatting
Ribbon Method
- ☐ Click the **Home tab**, then click the **Replace button** in the Editing group to open the Find and Replace dialog box with the Replace tab active
- ☐ Click the **More button** to view additional search options
- ☐ Type the text that you want to find in the Find what box
- ☐ Click the **Format button** under Find, then click a format from the list
- ☐ Type the replacement text in the Replace with box
- ☐ Click the **Format button** under Replace, then click a format from the list
- ☐ Click the **Find Next button** to view the next instance of the text with the format you are searching for, review the selection, then click **Replace** to replace the selected text with the new text and the new format or click **Find Next** to leave the selection as is and move to the next instance
- ☐ Click **Cancel** to close the Find and Replace dialog box

Shortcut Method
- ☐ Press **[Ctrl] [H]** to open the Find and Replace dialog box with the Replace tab active
- ☐ Follow the steps in bullets 2–8 of the Find and Replace Text with Specific Formatting Ribbon Method above

Find and Replace Special Characters, Formatting, or Fields
Ribbon Method
- ☐ Click the **Home tab**, then click the **Replace button** in the Editing group to open the Find and Replace dialog box with the Replace tab active
- ☐ Click the **More button** to view additional search options
- ☐ Click in the **Find what text box** to change the bottom portion of the dialog box to Find commands, then leave the box blank
- ☐ Click the **Special button** under Find, then click a format or special character from the list
- ☐ Click in the **Replace with text box** to change the bottom portion of the dialog box to Replace commands, then leave the box blank
- ☐ Click the **Special button** under Replace, then click a format or character from the list
- ☐ Click the **Find Next button** to view the next instance of the format or special character, review the selection, then click **Replace** to replace the selection or click **Find Next** to leave the selection as is and move to the next instance
- ☐ Click **Cancel** to close the Find and Replace dialog box

Shortcut Method
- ☐ Press **[Ctrl] [H]** to open the Find and Replace dialog box with the Replace tab active
- ☐ Follow the steps in bullets 2–8 of the Find and Replace Special Characters, Formatting, or Fields Ribbon Method above

APPLY INDENTATION AND TAB SETTINGS TO PARAGRAPHS

Apply Indentation
- ☐ Click anywhere in the paragraph you want to indent, then use Table WD 2-2 as a reference to apply the indent formatting you want

Table WD 2-2   Applying Indentation Formatting

Indent formatting to apply	Ribbon Method	Shortcut Method: Mini toolbar	Shortcut Method: ruler	Paragraph dialog box/ Indents and Spacing tab*
Increase indent by preset .5"	Click the **Home tab**, click the **Increase indent button** in the Paragraph group	Click the **Increase indent button**		
Decrease indent by preset .5"	Click the **Home tab**, click the **Decrease indent button** in the Paragraph group	Click the **Decrease indent button**		
Left indent	Click the **Page Layout tab**, then use the arrows or enter a value in the Indent Left text box in the Paragraph group		Drag the **Left Indent marker** to the desired position	Use the arrows or enter a value in the Left text box in the Indentation section
Right indent	Click the **Page Layout tab**, then use the arrows or enter a value in the Indent Right text box in the Paragraph group		Drag the **Right Indent marker** to the desired position	Use the arrows or enter a value in the Right text box in the Indentation section
First Line Indent			Drag the **First Line Indent marker** to the desired position OR Scroll to the **First Line Indent marker** in the tab indicator, click the **First Line Indent marker** to select it, then click the ruler at the desired position	Click the list arrow under Special, click **First Line**, then if necessary, use the arrows or enter a value in the By text box in the Indentation section
Hanging Indent			Drag the **Hanging Indent marker** to the desired position OR Scroll to the **Hanging Indent marker** in the tab indicator, click the **Hanging Indent marker** to select it, then click the ruler at the desired position	Click the list arrow under Special, click **Hanging**, then if necessary, use the arrows or enter a value in the By text box in the Indentation section
Negative Indent (Outdent)	Click the **Page Layout tab**, then use the arrows OR enter a negative value in the Indent Left text box in the Paragraph group		Drag the **Left Indent marker** to the desired position on the ruler (the position is to the left of the current paragraph)	Use the arrows or enter a negative value in the Left text box in the Indentation section

* Click the launcher in the Paragraph group on the Home tab or on the Page Layout tab to open the Paragraph dialog box.

Word

Set Tabs

Use Table WD 2-3 as a reference on how to set tabs

Table WD 2-3   Setting Tabs

Tab setting to apply	Ribbon Method	Shortcut Method: Ruler
	To open the Tabs dialog box: Click the **launcher** in the Paragraph group on the Home tab or the Page Layout tab to open the Paragraph dialog box, then click the **Tabs button**. Click the appropriate Alignment option button in the Tabs dialog box	To use the tab indicators: Click the **View Ruler button** at the top of the vertical scroll bar to display the rulers if necessary, then click the tab indicator at the left end of the horizontal ruler until the desired tab indicator is active
Left tab	Type the value in the Tab stop position text box, then click **OK**	With the Left tab indicator active, click the horizontal ruler
Center tab	Type the value in the Tab stop position text box, then click **OK**	With the Center tab indicator active, click the horizontal ruler
Right tab	Type the value in the Tab stop position text box, then click **OK**	With the Right tab indicator active, click the horizontal ruler
Decimal tab	Type the value in the Tab stop position text box, then click **OK**	With the Decimal tab indicator active, click the horizontal ruler
Bar tab	Type the value in the Tab stop position text box, then click **OK**	With the Bar tab indicator active, click the horizontal ruler

Set Tabs with Leaders

Ribbon Method

☐ Open the **Tabs dialog box** (refer to Table WD 2-3 as needed), shown in Figure WD 2-5, select the tab stop in the Tab stop position list box that you want to modify, click the **leader style option button** for an appropriate leader style, then click **OK**

Figure WD 2-5   Tabs dialog box

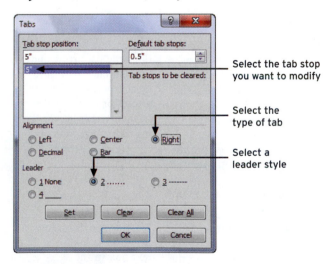

Clear a Tab

Ribbon Method

☐ Open the **Tabs dialog box** (refer to Table WD 2-3 as needed), select the tab stop in the Tab stop position list box that you want to modify, click the **Clear button**, then click **OK**

Mouse Method

☐ Position the pointer over the tab stop you want to remove
☐ Use the pointer ⬚ to drag the tab stop off the horizontal ruler

Clear All Tabs

Ribbon Method

☐ Open the **Tabs dialog box** (refer to Table WD 2-3 as needed), click the **Clear All button**, then click **OK**

Move a Tab Stop

Mouse Method

☐ Position the pointer ⬚ over the tab stop you want to move
☐ Drag the tab stop to its new location on the horizontal ruler and release the mouse button

---

APPLY SPACING SETTINGS TO TEXT AND PARAGRAPHS

Set Line Spacing

Ribbon Method

☐ Click anywhere in the paragraph you want to format
☐ Click the **Line and Paragraph Spacing list arrow** ⬚, then click a preset line spacing option or click **Line Spacing Options**
☐ On the Indents and Spacing tab in the Paragraph dialog box, click the appropriate line spacing option, then click **OK**

OR

☐ Click the **launcher** ⬚ in the Paragraph group, click the **Indents and Spacing tab** if necessary, select the appropriate line spacing option, then click **OK**

Set Paragraph Spacing

Ribbon Method

☐ Click the **Page Layout tab**
☐ Click the **Spacing Before arrows** in the Paragraph group to increase or decrease the amount of space before a paragraph or type the value in the Before text box
☐ Click the **Spacing After arrows** in the Paragraph group to increase or decrease the amount of space after a paragraph or type the value in the After text box

OR

☐ Click the **launcher** ⬚ in the Paragraph group on the Page Layout tab or the Home tab to open the Paragraph dialog box
☐ Click the **Indents and Spacing tab** if necessary, select the appropriate Before and After options in the Spacing section of the dialog box, then click **OK**

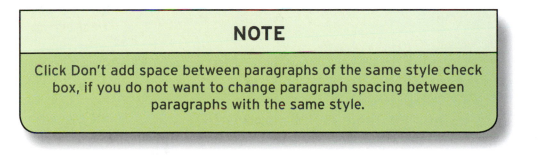

NOTE

Click Don't add space between paragraphs of the same style check box, if you do not want to change paragraph spacing between paragraphs with the same style.

Apply Alignment

☐ Click anywhere in the paragraph you want to align, then use Table WD 2-4 as a reference to apply the alignment formatting you want

Table WD 2-4   Applying Alignment

Alignment to apply or modify	Ribbon Method: Home tab/ Paragraph group	Shortcut Method: Mini toolbar	Shortcut Method: Keyboard	Paragraph dialog box/ Indents and Spacing tab*
Left	Click the **Align Text Left button** ▤		Press **[Ctrl] [L]**	In the General section, click the **Alignment list arrow**, then click **Left**
Center	Click the **Center button** ▤	Click the **Center button** ▤	Press **[Ctrl] [E]**	In the General section, click the **Alignment list arrow**, then click **Centered**
Right	Click the **Align Text Right button** ▤		Press **[Ctrl] [R]**	In the General section, click the **Alignment list arrow**, then click **Right**
Justify	Click the **Justify button** ▤		Press **[Ctrl] [J]**	In the General section, click the **Alignment list arrow**, then click **Justified**

* Click the launcher ▣ in the Paragraph group on the Home tab or on the Page Layout tab to open the Paragraph dialog box.

CREATE TABLES

Create a Table Using the Insert Table Dialog Box

Ribbon Method

☐ Click the **Insert tab**, click the **Table button** in the Tables group, then click **Insert Table** to display the Insert Table dialog box, shown in Figure WD 2-6

☐ Type a number in the Number of columns text box, then type a number in the Number of rows text box

☐ Set other options as appropriate, then click **OK**

Figure WD 2-6   Insert Table dialog box

Create a Table Using the Table Button and Grid

Ribbon Method

☐ Click the **Insert tab**, click the **Table button** in the Tables group, drag over the grid to select the number of columns and rows, then click the mouse

Draw a Table
Ribbon Method
- ☐ Click the **Insert tab**, click the **Table button** in the Tables group, then click **Draw Table**
- ☐ Use the **Draw Table pencil** ✐ to draw a rectangular boundary, then draw vertical and horizontal lines to create columns and rows

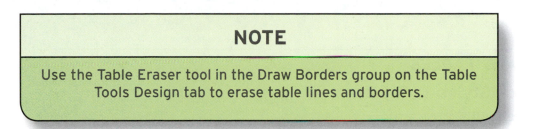

NOTE
Use the Table Eraser tool in the Draw Borders group on the Table Tools Design tab to erase table lines and borders.

Insert a Quick Table
Ribbon Method
- ☐ Click the **Insert tab**, click the **Table button** in the Tables group, point to **Quick Tables**, then click a table option from the Built-in gallery

Convert Text to a Table
Ribbon Method
- ☐ Select the desired text, then click the **Insert tab**
- ☐ Click the **Table button** in the Tables group, then click **Convert Text to Table**
- ☐ Enter the appropriate options in the Convert Text to Table dialog box shown in Figure WD 2-7 then click **OK**

Figure WD 2-7   Convert Text to Table dialog box

Use a Table to Control Page Layout
- ☐ Click the **Insert tab**, click the **Table button** in the Tables group, then click **Insert Table**
- ☐ In the Insert Table dialog box, specify the number of rows and columns appropriate for the content and orientation of the page
- ☐ Insert text, graphics, and other contents in separate table cells instead of using tabs for alignment
- ☐ Select the table, click the **Bottom Border List Arrow** ▦▾, then click **No Border** to remove table borders from view, if desired

> **NOTE**
>
> Tables are often used to control page layout in Web pages, such as adding text in a table cell and a graphic in the cell beside it to keep them aligned on the page.

MANIPULATE TABLES

Apply Quick Styles To Tables

Ribbon Method

☐ Click anywhere in a table, click the **Table Tools Design tab**, then click the **More button** in the Table Styles group

☐ In the Table Styles gallery, click the Quick Style you want to apply or click **Modify Table Style**

☐ In the Modify Style dialog box, select appropriate options, then click **OK**

Sort Content

Ribbon Method

☐ Click anywhere in the table you want to sort, click the **Table Tools Layout tab**, then click the **Sort button** in the Data group

☐ In the Sort dialog box shown in Figure WD 2-8, choose appropriate options to identify primary, secondary, and tertiary criteria, then click **OK**

Figure WD 2-8   Sort dialog box

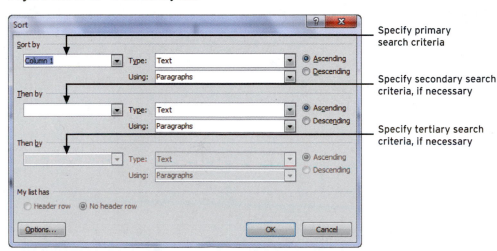

Add a Row to a Table

Ribbon Method

☐ Click in a table row

☐ Click the **Table Tools Layout tab**, then click the **Insert Above button** or **Insert Below button** in the Rows & Columns group

OR

☐ To insert multiple rows, select two or more rows

☐ Click the **Table Tools Layout tab**, then click the **Insert Above button** or **Insert Below button** in the Rows & Columns group to add the number of rows above or below the selected rows

Shortcut Method

☐ Right-click in a table row
☐ Point to **Insert** on the shortcut menu, then click **Insert Rows Above** or **Insert Rows Below** from the submenu

Add a Column to a Table

Ribbon Method

☐ Click in a table column
☐ Click the **Table Tools Layout tab**, then click the **Insert Left button** or **Insert Right button** in the Rows & Columns group
  OR
☐ To add multiple columns at a time, select the number of columns you want to add
☐ Click the **Table Tools Layout tab**, then click the **Insert Left button** or **Insert Right button** in the Rows & Columns group to add the number of columns to the right or left of the selected columns

Shortcut Method

☐ Right-click in a table column
☐ Point to **Insert** on the shortcut menu, then click **Insert Columns to the Left** or **Insert Columns to the Right** from the submenu

Merge Table Cells

Ribbon Method

☐ Select the cells you want to merge into one cell, click the **Table Tools Layout tab**, then click the **Merge Cells button** in the Merge group

Shortcut Method

☐ Select the cells you want to merge into one cell, right-click, then click **Merge Cells** on the shortcut menu

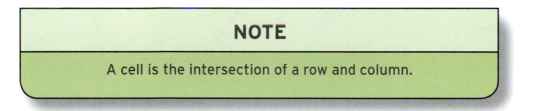

NOTE

A cell is the intersection of a row and column.

Split Table Cells

Ribbon Method

☐ Click the cell you want to split, click the **Table Tools Layout tab**, then click the **Split Cells button** in the Merge group
☐ In the Split Cells dialog box, enter the appropriate options, then click **OK**

Shortcut Method

☐ Select the cell you want to split, right-click, then click **Split Cells** on the shortcut menu
☐ In the Split Cells dialog box, enter the appropriate options, then click **OK**

Move Columns and Rows

Ribbon Method

☐ Select the row(s) or column(s) that you want to move, click the **Home tab**, then click the **Cut button** ✄ in the Clipboard group

☐ Select a row or a column in the table, then click the **Paste button** to insert the row(s) above the selected row or to insert the column(s) to the left of the selected column

Mouse Method

☐ Select the row(s) or column(s) that you want to move, click the **Drag and drop pointer** and drag the dotted insertion point to the new location, then release the mouse button to insert the row(s) above the row with the dotted insertion point or to insert the column(s) to the left of the column with the dotted insertion point

Resize Columns and Rows

Ribbon Method

☐ Click in the column or row, click the **Table Tools Layout tab**, then click the up and down arrows in the Table Row Height text box or the Table Column Width text box in the Cell Size group to increase or decrease the width of a column or height of a row

OR

☐ Click in the column or row, click the **Table Tools Layout tab**, then click the **AutoFit list arrow** and click an option for automatically resizing the column width to the size of the contents, window, or a fixed width

Mouse Method

☐ Position the mouse pointer on a vertical or horizontal cell border, drag the **Resize pointer** vertically or horizontally to increase or decrease the size of the column or row

Delete Columns and Rows

Ribbon Method

☐ Select the column(s) or row(s), click the **Table Tools Layout tab**, click the **Delete button** in the Rows & Columns group, then click **Delete Columns** or **Delete Rows**

Shortcut Method

☐ Select the column(s) or row(s), right-click, then click **Delete Rows** or **Delete Columns** from the shortcut menu

OR

☐ Select the column(s) or row(s), then press **[Shift][Delete]**

Define the Header Row

Ribbon Method

☐ Click in the table, click the **Table Tools Design tab**, click the **Header Row check box** in the Table Style Options dialog box

Convert Tables to Text

Ribbon Method

☐ Click anywhere in the table you want to convert to text, then click the **Table Tools Layout tab**

☐ Click the **Convert to Text button** in the Data group, enter the appropriate options in the Convert Table to Text dialog box, then click **OK**

View Gridlines

Ribbon Method

☐ Click anywhere in the table, click the **Table Tools Layout tab**, then click **View Table Gridlines** in the Table group

> ## NOTE
>
> It is most helpful to view gridlines on tables without borders.

FORMAT LISTS

Apply Bullets to Existing Text

Ribbon Method

□ Select the text you want to convert to a list
□ Click the **Home tab**, then click the **Bullets button** ☷ in the Paragraph group to apply the current bullet style
OR
□ Click the **Home tab**, then click the **Numbering button** ☷ in the Paragraph group to apply the current numbering

Shortcut Method

□ Select the text you want to convert to a bulleted list, right-click, point to **Bullets** on the shortcut menu, then click a bullet format from the Bullets gallery
OR
□ Select the text you want to convert to a numbered list, right-click, point to **Numbering** on the shortcut menu, then click a number format from the Numbering Library

Select a New Symbol Format for Bullets

Ribbon Method

□ Click anywhere in the list, click the **Home tab**, then click the **Bullets list arrow** ☷ ▾ in the Paragraph group
□ Click a new bullet style from the Bullets gallery, shown in Figure WD 2-9, or click **Define New Bullet**
□ In the Define New Bullet dialog box, shown in Figure WD 2-10, click **Symbol** to open the Symbol dialog box, click a new bullet style, then click **OK**

Figure WD 2-10   Define New Bullet dialog box

Figure WD 2-9   Bullets gallery

Define a Picture to be used as a Bullet

Ribbon Method

□ Click anywhere in the list, click the **Home tab**, then click the **Bullets list arrow** ☷ ▾ in the Paragraph group
□ Click a new bullet style from the Bullets gallery or click **Define New Bullet**
□ In the Define New Bullet dialog box, click **Picture** to open the Picture Bullet dialog box of options, click a new bullet style or click **Import** to select a picture to import as a bullet, then click **OK**

Shortcut Method

□ Select the bulleted list, right-click, point to **Bullets** on the menu, then click **Define New Bullet**
□ In the Define New Bullet dialog box, click **Picture** to open the Picture Bullet dialog box of options, click a new bullet style or click **Import** to select a picture to import as a bullet, then click **OK**

Use AutoFormat to Create a Bulleted, Numbered, or Multilevel List

Ribbon Method

- ☐ Position the insertion point where you want a list to begin
- ☐ Click the **Home tab**, then click the **Bullets button** ▤ in the Paragraph group to apply the current bullet style

  OR
- ☐ Click the **Home tab**, then click the **Numbering button** ▤ in the Paragraph group to apply the current numbering style

  OR
- ☐ Click the **Home tab**, click the **Multilevel List arrow** ▤ in the Paragraph group, then click a style from the gallery
- ☐ Type a list item, press **[Enter]** at the end of each item
- ☐ Follow the steps in the Demote and Promote List Items section below to change the level of an item in a list

Shortcut Method

- ☐ Right-click where you want to create a bulleted list, point to **Bullets** on the shortcut menu, then click a bullet format from the Bullets gallery

  OR
- ☐ Right-click where you want to create a numbered list, point to **Numbering** on the shortcut menu, then click a numbering format from the Numbering gallery
- ☐ Type a list item, press **[Enter]** at the end of each item

Demote and Promote List Items

Ribbon Method

- ☐ To demote a list item, click anywhere in the item you want to demote, click the **Home tab**, then click the **Increase Indent button** ▤ in the Paragraph group
- ☐ To promote a list item, click anywhere in the item you want to promote, click the **Home tab**, then click the **Decrease Indent button** ▤ in the Paragraph group

Shortcut Method

- ☐ Select the item you want to demote or promote, then click the **Increase Indent button** ▤ or the **Decrease Indent button** ▤ on the Mini toolbar

  OR
- ☐ Position the insertion point in front of the item you want to demote or promote, then press **[Tab]** to demote the item or press **[Shift][Tab]** to promote the item

Sort List Items

Ribbon Method

- ☐ Select the appropriate items to sort, click the **Home tab**, then click the **Sort button** ▤ in the Paragraph group
- ☐ In the Sort dialog box, choose appropriate options to identify primary, secondary, and tertiary criteria, then click **OK**

REVIEW QUESTIONS

TRUE/FALSE

Circle T if the statement is true or F if the statement is false.

T   F   1. You can search for words in a document using the Navigation pane.

T   F   2. Leaders can be dots, dashes, or lines.

T   F   3. You can increase spacing before a paragraph, but not after a paragraph.

T   F   4. The Text Highlight Color button makes text look like it has been marked with a highlighter pen.

T   F   5. To demote a list item, click the Increase Indent button.

MATCHING

Match the correct term in Column 2 to its description in Column 1.

Column 1	Column 2
_____ 1. Highlights all instances of the text in the Find What text box	A. Merge Cells
_____ 2. A negative indent	B. Clear Formatting button
_____ 3. Changes a table to text	C. Browse the pages in your document tab
_____ 4. Increases the font size one increment	D. AutoFormat
_____ 5. Lets you move table columns or rows to a new location	E. Convert to Text
_____ 6. Combines multiple cells into one	F. Outdent
_____ 7. Replaces all instances of text without a preview	G. Drag and drop pointer
_____ 8. Removes all formatting, leaving only plain text	H. Highlight All button
_____ 9. Displays pages as thumbnails	I. Grow Font button
_____ 10. Helps you create a formatted bulleted list	J. Replace All

PROJECTS

Project WD 2-1

1. Open the data file **Project WD 2-1.docx**.

2. Select all the text and change the font to Calibri.

3. Change the font size to 11.

4. Click in the first paragraph, which begins ("Thank you...") and change the line spacing to 1.0.

5. Add 6 pt line spacing before the first paragraph.

6. Add a first line indent of .5 inches.

7. Use the Format Painter to apply the format from the first paragraph to the next two paragraphs in the body of the letter.

8. Insert a blank line before the date.

9. Center the three lines of the return address, which begins with Melissa Sharpton.

10. Select Melissa Sharpton and apply the following formatting:
    - Apply Bold.
    - Change the font size to 14.
    - Change the case to uppercase.
    - Change the color to Blue.

11. Save the document as **Thank You Letter.docx** and close it.

Project WD 2-2

1. Open the **Project WD 2-2.docx** document from the data files for this objective.

2. Select the title and apply the **Title** style.

3. Select Daily Specials and apply the **Heading 1** style.

4. Select the quotation after the title and cut it from that location. Position the insertion point three blank lines after the last paragraph and paste it.

5. Apply the **Intense Quote** style to the quotation.

6. Change the font size of the quotation to 11.

7. Select the line that begins with *Monday*. Clear the tab that is set at 4 inches and set a new right tab with dot leaders at 6 inches.

8. Use the Format Painter to copy the formatting from the Monday line to the Tuesday, Wednesday, Thursday, and Friday lines.

9. Use the Navigation pane to find and highlight all occurrences of the word *tomato* in the document.

10. Find the words *garlic pizza* and replace all three occurrences with the words *homemade pizza*.

11. Save the document as **Pizzeria Menu.docx** and close it.

Project WD 2-3

1. Open a new blank document.

2. Create a table that has 5 columns and 5 rows.

3. Enter the following data in the table:

2015 Sales by Quarter				
	First Quarter	**Second Quarter**	**Third Quarter**	**Fourth Quarter**
Region 1	942,987	789,490	835,987	787,678
Region 2	987,456	698,320	900,234	896,783
Totals				

4. Select the first row and merge the cells.

5. Insert a new row below the Region 2 row and enter the following data:

Region 3	787,698	894,439	649,421	904,685

6. Delete the Totals row.

7. Apply the Light Grid - Accent 5 table style.

8. Save the document as **2015 Sales.docx** and close it.

Project WD 2-4

1. Open the data file **Project WD 2-4.docx**.

2. Select the text under the heading *What do you want to do?* and sort the list in ascending order.

3. Format the list as a bulleted list.

4. Select the text under the heading *Top Ten Places to Go* and format it as a numbered list.

5. Select the bulleted list and change the bullet style to the black square bullets.

6. Select the numbered list and change the numbering style to the style with the closed parenthesis.

7. Save the document as **Flyer.docx** and close it.

CRITICAL THINKING

Activity WD 2-1

Open the **Activity WD 2-1.docx**. Convert the table to text, separated by tabs. Then, convert the text to a table with 5 rows and 5 columns, separating text by tabs. Save the document as **2015 Sales Converted.docx**.

Activity WD 2-2

Create your own resume. Use what you have learned to apply styles and format the document to give it a professional appearance. Save and close the document.

WORD OBJECTIVE 3: APPLYING PAGE LAYOUT AND REUSABLE CONTENT

FORMAT PAGES

Set Margins

Ribbon Method

☐ Click the **Page Layout tab**, then click the **Margins button** in the Page Setup group

☐ Click a **preset margin option** or click **Custom Margins**, enter values in the Top, Bottom, Left, and Right text boxes of the Page Setup dialog box (shown in Figure WD 3-1), then click **OK**

Figure WD 3-1 **Page Setup dialog box**

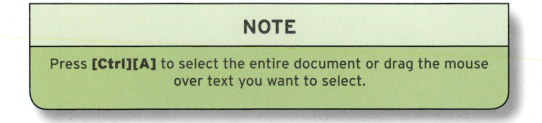

Enter values to create Custom margins

OR

☐ Click the **Page Layout tab**, click the **dialog box launcher** 🖻 in the Page Setup group, then click the **Margins tab** in the Page Setup dialog box, if necessary

☐ Enter values in the Top, Bottom, Left, and Right text boxes, then click **OK**

Mouse Method

☐ Click the **View Ruler button** 🖾 at the top of the vertical scroll bar to display the rulers if necessary, then select appropriate text to apply new margins

---

NOTE

Press **[Ctrl][A]** to select the entire document or drag the mouse over text you want to select.

☐ Drag the **Left Indent marker** ▣ to an appropriate location on the horizontal ruler
☐ Drag the **Right Indent marker** △ to an appropriate location on the horizontal ruler

Insert Nonbreaking Spaces

Ribbon Method

☐ Position the insertion point in the location where you want to insert a nonbreaking space
☐ Click the **Insert tab**, click the **Symbol button** in the Symbols group, then click **More Symbols**
☐ In the Symbol dialog box, click the **Special Characters tab**, click **Nonbreaking Space**, as shown in Figure WD 3-2, then click **Insert**

Figure WD 3-2   **Symbol dialog box**

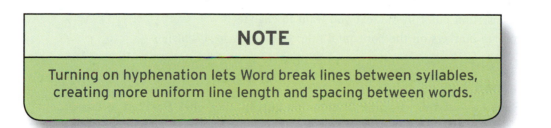

Shortcut Method

☐ Position the insertion point in the location where you want to insert a nonbreaking space
☐ Press **[CTRL][SHIFT][SPACE]**

Add Hyphenation

Ribbon Method

☐ Click the **Page Layout tab**, click the **Hyphenation button** in the Page Setup group, then click **Automatic** to turn on hyphenation or click **Hyphenation Options** to open the Hyphenation dialog box, specify hyphenation settings, then click **OK**

> ## NOTE
>
> Turning on hyphenation lets Word break lines between syllables, creating more uniform line length and spacing between words.

Add Columns

Ribbon Method

☐ Select the text you want to format as columns

☐ Click the **Page Layout tab**, then click the **Columns button** in the Page Setup group
☐ Select one of the **predefined options** in the menu that opens or click **More Columns** to open the Columns dialog box, select the desired settings, then click **OK**

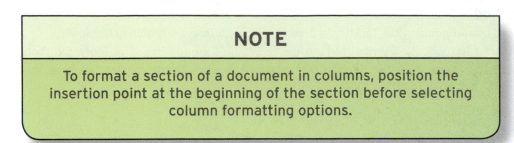

> ## NOTE
>
> To format a section of a document in columns, position the insertion point at the beginning of the section before selecting column formatting options.

Change Column Width and Spacing

Ribbon Method

☐ Position the insertion point in the text you want to change
☐ Click the **Page Layout tab**, click the **Columns button** in the Page Setup group, then click **More Columns** to open the Columns dialog box shown in Figure WD 3-3
☐ Enter the desired settings in the width and spacing text boxes, then click **OK**

Figure WD 3-3 **Columns dialog box**

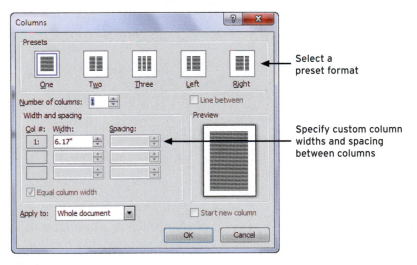

Mouse Method

☐ Position the insertion point in the text you want to change
☐ Drag the column markers on the horizontal ruler to the new location(s)

Set Page Orientation

Ribbon Method

☐ Click the **Page Layout tab**, click the **Orientation button**, then click **Portrait** or **Landscape**
  OR
☐ Click the **Page Layout tab**, click the **dialog box launcher** in the Page Setup group to open the Page Setup dialog box, click the **Margins tab** if necessary, then click **Portrait** or **Landscape**

Set Paper Size

Ribbon Method

☐ Click the **Page Layout tab**, click the **Size button** in the Page Setup group, then select a paper size from the menu
   OR

☐ Click the **Page Layout tab**, click the **dialog box launcher** 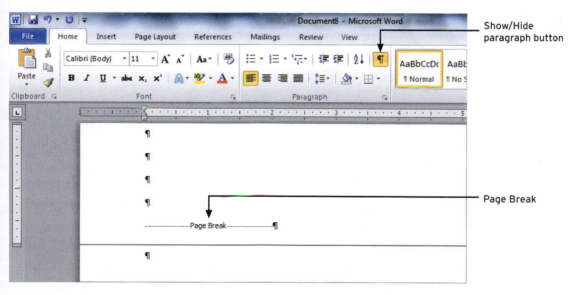 in the Page Setup group to open the Page Setup dialog box, click the **Paper tab** if necessary, click the **Paper Size list arrow**, then select a paper size or enter values in the Width and Height text boxes

Force a Page Break

Ribbon Method

☐ Position the insertion point where you want the page break to occur

☐ Click the **Page Layout tab**, click the **Breaks button** in the Page Setup group, then click **Page** in the Page Breaks section

Shortcut Method

☐ Position the insertion point where you want the page break to occur, then press **[Ctrl] [Enter]**

Remove a Page Break

Shortcut Method

☐ Click the **Home tab**, click the **Show/Hide button** ¶ in the Paragraph group to display formatting marks

☐ Click to the left of the page break, shown in Figure WD 3-4, to select it, then press **[Delete]**
   OR

☐ Double-click a **page break** to select it, then press **[Delete]**

Figure WD 3-4   Page Break

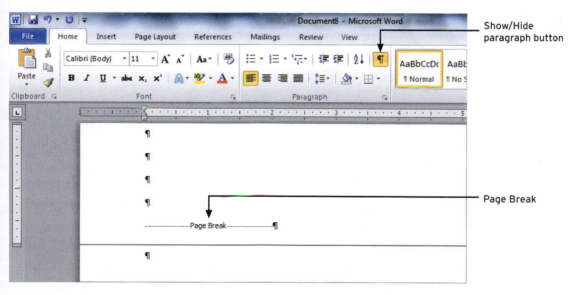

Insert a Section Break

Ribbon Method

☐ Position the insertion point where you want the section break to occur

☐ Click the **Page Layout tab**, click the **Breaks button**, then click the type of break you want to insert—Continuous, Next page, Odd Page, or Even Page—from the Section Breaks area of the menu shown in Figure WD 3-5

Figure WD 3-5   Breaks button and menu

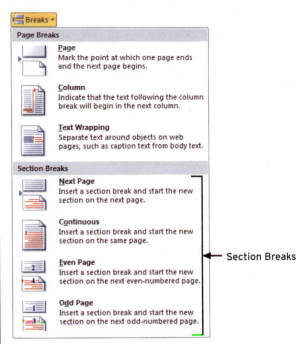

Section Breaks

Remove a Section Break

Ribbon Method

☐ Click the **Home tab**, then click the **Show/Hide button** ¶ in the Paragraph group to display formatting marks

☐ Position the insertion point to the left of the section break, then press **[Delete]**

Insert a Blank Page

Ribbon Method

☐ Click the **Insert tab**, then click **Blank Page** in the Pages group to add a blank page at the location of the Insertion point

APPLY THEMES

Use a Theme to Apply Formatting

Ribbon Method

☐ Click the **Page Layout tab**, click the **Themes button** in the Themes group to display a gallery of options, as shown in Figure WD 3-6, then move the pointer over each theme in the gallery to preview the theme

☐ Click an appropriate theme

Figure WD 3-6   Themes button and menu

Customize Theme Effects

Ribbon Method

☐ Click the **Page Layout tab**, then click the **Theme Effects button** 🔘▾ in the Themes group

☐ Click an appropriate option

Customize Theme Fonts

Ribbon Method

☐ Click the **Page Layout tab**, then click the **Theme Fonts button** 🅰▾ in the Themes group

☐ Click an appropriate option

   OR

☐ Click **Create New Theme Fonts**, select a Heading font and a Body font, type a name in the **Name text box**, then click **Save**

Customize Theme Colors

Ribbon Method

☐ Click the **Page Layout tab**, then click the **Theme Colors button** ▦▾, in the Themes group

☐ Click an appropriate option

   OR

☐ Click **Create New Theme Colors**, select appropriate options, type a name in the **Name text box**, then click **Save**

CONSTRUCT CONTENT USING QUICK PARTS

Insert Pull Quotes

Ribbon Method

☐ Position the insertion point in the location where you want the pull quote to appear, click the **Insert tab**, then click the **Text Box button** in the Text group

☐ Click a preformatted quote style from the gallery shown in Figure WD 3-7

☐ Replace the placeholder text with appropriate text

Figure WD 3-7   Text Box button and gallery

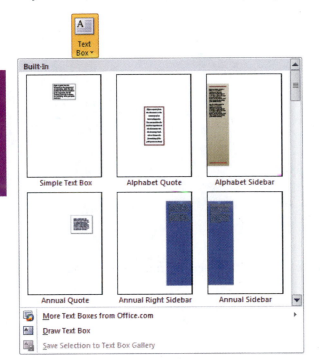

Insert a Text Box

Ribbon Method

☐ Position the insertion point where you want the text box to appear, click the **Insert tab**, then click the **Text Box button** in the Text group

☐ Select a preformatted text box from the gallery

☐ Replace the placeholder text with appropriate text

Insert a Header

Ribbon Method

☐ Click the **Insert tab**, then click the **Header button** in the Header & Footer group

☐ Scroll the Header gallery, click the **built-in Header Quick Part** you want to insert

☐ Replace the placeholder text with your content

☐ Click the **Close Header and Footer button**

Insert a Footer

Ribbon Method

- ☐ Click the **Insert tab**, then click the **Footer button** in the Header & Footer group
- ☐ Scroll the Footer gallery, click the **built-in Footer Quick Part** you want to insert
- ☐ Replace the placeholder text with your content
- ☐ Click the **Close Header and Footer button**

Insert a Cover Page

Ribbon Method

- ☐ Click the **Insert tab**, click **Cover Page**, scroll through the gallery of choices, then click an appropriate cover page to be inserted at the beginning of the document
- ☐ Replace the placeholder text with your content

Insert a Watermark

Ribbon Method

- ☐ Click the **Page Layout tab**, then click **Watermark** in the Page Background group
- ☐ Scroll to see the preset watermarks available, then click an appropriate watermark from the gallery

---

NOTE

A watermark is shaded text or a graphic that appears behind text in a document.

Insert Equations

Ribbon Method

- ☐ Click the **Insert tab**, click the **Equation list arrow** in the Symbols group, then click an appropriate equation from the gallery

---

CREATE AND MANIPULATE PAGE BACKGROUNDS

Format a Document's Background

Ribbon Method

- ☐ Click the **Page Layout tab**, click the **Page Color button** in the Page Background group, then click **Fill Effects**
- ☐ In the Fill Effects dialog box, shown in Figure WD 3-8, click the Gradient, Texture, Pattern, or Picture tab, select appropriate options, then click **OK**

Figure WD 3-8   **Fill Effects dialog box**

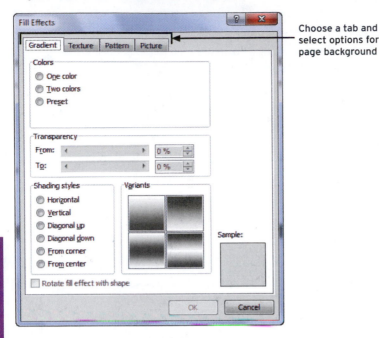

Choose a tab and select options for page background

Set a Colored Background

Ribbon Method

☐ Click the **Page Layout tab**, click **Page Color** in the Page Background group, then click an appropriate color

Add a Custom Watermark

Ribbon Method

☐ Click the **Page Layout tab**, click **Watermark** in the Page Background group, click **Custom Watermark** to display the Printed Watermark dialog box, shown in Fig WD 3-9

☐ Click the **Picture watermark option button**, click **Select Picture**, navigate to an appropriate drive and folder, double-click the picture, click **Apply**, then click **Close**

OR

☐ Click the **Text watermark option button**, use the list arrows to select appropriate options, click **Apply**, then click **Close**

Figure WD 3-9   **Printed Watermark dialog box**

Set Page Borders

Ribbon Method

☐ Click the **Page Layout tab**, click **Page Borders** in the Page Background group, click appropriate options from the Borders and Shading dialog box, shown in Figure WD 3-10, then click **OK**

Figure WD 3-10   Borders and Shading dialog box

CREATE AND MODIFY HEADERS AND FOOTERS

Insert Page Numbers

Ribbon Method

☐ Click the **Insert tab**, click the **Page Number button** in the Header & Footer group, point to the **location** (Top of Page, Bottom of Page, Page Margins, or Current Position) where you want the page number to appear, view the options in the gallery that opens, then click the option you want

OR

☐ Double-click in the header or footer area, click the **Page Number button** in the Header & Footer group, point to the **location** (Top of Page, Bottom of Page, Page Margins, or Current Position) where you want the page number to appear, view the options in the gallery that opens, then click the option you want

OR

☐ Click the **Insert tab**, click the **Header or Footer button**, then select a header or footer option from the gallery that contains a page number

Format Page Numbers

Ribbon Method

☐ Click the **Insert tab**, click the **Page Number button** in the Header & Footer group, then click **Format Page Numbers** to open the Page Number Format dialog box, shown in Figure WD 3-11

☐ Choose appropriate options then click **OK**

Shortcut Method

☐ Select a **page number** in a header or footer area, right-click, then click **Format Page Numbers** from the shortcut menu

☐ In the Page Number Format dialog box, select appropriate options, then click **OK**

Figure WD 3-11   Page Number Format dialog box

Insert the Current Date and Time

Ribbon Method

☐ Click the **Insert tab**, then click the **Date & Time button** in the Text group

☐ In the Date and Time dialog box, select an appropriate format in the Available formats list

☐ Check the **Update automatically** check box to automatically update the date and time stamp each time the document is opened

☐ Click **OK**

OR

☐ Double-click in a header or footer area, click the **Date & Time button** in the Insert group

☐ Follow the steps in bullets 2-4 of the Insert the Current Date and Time Ribbon Method above

Insert a Built-in Header or Footer

Ribbon Method

☐ Click the **Insert tab**, then click the **Header** or **Footer button** in the Header & Footer group

☐ Click a **built-in Quick Part** from the Header or Footer gallery, shown in Figure WD 3-12

☐ Replace the placeholder text with your content

☐ Click the **Close Header and Footer button**

Figure WD 3-12   Header button and gallery

Add Content to a Header or Footer

Ribbon Method

☐ Insert a built-in header or footer using the steps in bullets 1-4 under Insert a Built-in Header or Footer Ribbon Method on the previous page

☐ Click the placeholder text in brackets, such as [Type the document title] and type your own text (Some place-holders, such as those for the date, may have an arrow you can click to choose the date from a calendar)

Delete a Header or Footer

Ribbon Method

☐ Click the **Insert tab**, then click the **Header** or **Footer button** in the Header & Footer group

☐ Click **Remove Header** or **Remove Footer**

Change the Margins of a Header or Footer

Mouse Method

☐ Double-click in a header or footer area

☐ Move the **left indent marker** ▦ or **right indent marker** ⌂ to change the header margins

☐ Click the **Close Header and Footer button**

Apply a Different First Page Attribute

Ribbon Method

☐ Press **[Ctrl][Home]** to move to the beginning of the document, click the **Insert tab**, click the **Header button**, then click one of the built-in headers or click **Edit Header** to open the Header area or click the **Footer button**, then click one of the built-in footers or click **Edit Footer** to open the Footer area

☐ Click the **Different First Page check box** in the Options group to select it

☐ Type the text or insert the content you want to appear in the first page header, if any

☐ Click the **Show Next button**, then type the text or insert the content you want to appear in the header for the remaining pages in the section

REVIEW QUESTIONS

FILL IN THE BLANK

Complete the following sentences by writing the correct word or words in the blanks provided.

1. Use the _____ button on the Insert tab to insert a nonbreaking space.

2. You can customize a _____ by changing the effects, colors, or fonts.

3. To add a color to the background of a page, use the _____ button.

4. To create custom _____, enter values in the Top, Bottom, Left, and Right text boxes of the Page Setup dialog box.

5. Page numbers are inserted in _____ or footers.

MULTIPLE CHOICE

Select the best response for the following statements.

1. The shortcut method for inserting a page break is _____.
   - A. [CTRL][A]
   - B. [CTRL][Enter]
   - C. [CTRL][SHIFT][SPACE]
   - D. [CTRL][Home]

2. Continuous is a type of _____.
   - A. watermark
   - B. column
   - C. section break
   - D. header

3. The _____ button turns off the page number or other header and footer elements on the first page of a document.
   - A. Page Number
   - B. Quick Parts
   - C. Breaks
   - D. Different First Page

4. The _____ button allows you to create a pull quote.
   - A. Pull Quote
   - B. Text Box
   - C. Cover Page
   - D. Equations

5. The _____ button contains a gallery of pages that can be added to the beginning of the document.
   - A. Cover Page
   - B. Blank Page
   - C. Page Break
   - D. Page Color

PROJECTS

Project WD 3-1

1. Open **Project WD 3-1.docx**.
2. Change the paper size to 4 × 6 in.
3. Set the orientation to landscape.
4. Change the margins to **Moderate**.
5. Set the layout to a two-column **Right** format with a line between the columns.
6. Change the theme to **Equity**.
7. Add a **1 1/2 pt** solid line **Box** style page border.
8. Change the page color to **black**.
9. Change the width of column #1 to **2.8"** and the spacing to **0.2"**. Change the width of column #2 to **1.5"**. Notice that the zip code now fits on the same line as the city and state.
10. Change the page color to **No Color**.
11. Save the document as **Meeting Postcard.docx** and close the document.

Project WD 3-2

1. Open **Project WD 3-2.docx**.
2. Change the Theme of the document to **Urban**.
3. Change the Theme Font to **Horizon**.
4. Change the Theme Colors to **Essential**.
5. Apply the **Confidential 1** Watermark to the second page of the document (the page after the cover page).
6. Save the document as **First Quarter Report 2.docx**.

Project WD 3-3

1. Open **Project WD 3-3.docx**.
2. Insert the **Perspective** header.
3. Use the Different First Page option to remove the header from the first page.
4. Remove the header.
5. Insert the **Alphabet** footer.
6. Replace the [Type text] placeholder with **Perry Watkins**.
7. Change the Page Format to the -1-, -2-, -3- number format.
8. Change the theme to Elemental.
9. Change the margins to normal.
10. Add a blank page to the end of the document.
11. Show/hide paragraph marks and delete the page break on the second page.
12. Turn off the show/hide paragraph marks.
13. Save the document as **Watkins Resume 2.docx** and close it.

CRITICAL THINKING

Activity WD 3-1

Create a positive, inspirational poster for the classroom using a standard 8.5" × 11" page. Search the Internet for an appropriate quote for your poster. Use the Text Box button to insert the quotation on your page. Adjust the size and position if necessary. Customize the theme and add a page border, color, or background.

WORD OBJECTIVE 4: INCLUDING ILLUSTRATIONS AND GRAPHICS IN A DOCUMENT

INSERT AND FORMAT PICTURES IN A DOCUMENT

Insert Pictures from Files

Ribbon Method

☐ Position the insertion point in the desired location

☐ Click the **Insert tab**, then click the **Insert Picture from File button** in the Illustrations group

☐ In the Insert Picture dialog box, navigate to the appropriate drive and folder, then select an appropriate picture

☐ Click **Insert**

Shortcut Method

☐ Follow the steps in bullets 1–3 of the Insert Pictures from Files Ribbon Method above

☐ Double-click an appropriate picture

Add Captions

Ribbon Method

☐ Select a picture in the document

☐ Click the **References tab**, then click **Insert Caption** from the Captions group

☐ In the Caption dialog box, shown in Figure WD 4-1, click the **Label list arrow** to choose a label or click **New Label** to type the name of a new label and click **OK**

OR

☐ Click the **Exclude label from caption check box** to remove the label

☐ Click the **Position list arrow** to choose a position for the label, type a caption in the Caption text box, choose any other options as necessary, then click **OK**

Shortcut Method

☐ Right-click a picture in your document, then click **Insert Caption** from the shortcut menu

☐ In the Caption dialog box, click the **Label list arrow** to choose a label or click **New Label** to type the name of a new label and click **OK**

OR

☐ Click the **Exclude label from caption check box** to remove the label

☐ Click the **Location list arrow** to choose a position for the label, type a caption in the Caption text box, choose any other options as necessary, then click **OK**

Figure WD 4-1 **Caption dialog box**

Apply Artistic Effects

Ribbon Method

□ Click the picture to select it, then click the **Picture Tools Format tab**

□ Click the **Artistic Effects button** in the Adjust group, then click the effect you want to apply from the gallery

OR

□ Click the **launcher** ⬚ in the Picture Styles group to open the Format Picture dialog box

□ Click **Artistic Effects** in the left pane, then click the **Artistic Effect list arrow**, click the effect you want to apply, then click **Close**

Shortcut Method

□ Right-click the picture, then click **Format Picture** on the shortcut menu to open the Format Picture dialog box

□ Click **Artistic Effects** in the left pane, then click the **Artistic Effect list arrow** in the right pane, click the effect you want to apply, then click **Close**

Apply Corrections and Color to a Picture

Ribbon Method

□ Click the picture to select it, then click the **Picture Tools Format tab**

□ Click the **Corrections list arrow** in the Adjust group on the Picture Tools Format tab, then click a Soften and Sharpen option or a Brightness and Contrast option from the gallery

OR

□ Click the **Color list arrow** in the Adjust group, then click an option from the gallery

OR

□ Click the **launcher** ⬚ in the Picture Styles group to open the Format Picture dialog box

□ Click **Picture Corrections** or **Picture Color** in the left pane if necessary, then select the appropriate options in the right pane

Apply Picture Styles

Ribbon Method

□ Click the picture to select it, then click the **Picture Tools Format tab**

□ Click the **More button** ⬚ in the Picture Styles group to display the gallery shown in Figure WD 4-2, then select a **Quick Style**

Figure WD 4-2   Picture Styles gallery

OR

□ Select a picture

- ☐ Click the **Picture Tools Format tab**, click the **launcher** 🔲 in the Picture Styles group to open the Format Picture dialog box
- ☐ Click a category in the left pane, then select specific options in the right pane

  OR

- ☐ Select a picture
- ☐ Click the **Picture Tools Format tab**
- ☐ Click the **Picture Border button list arrow** in the Picture Styles group and click an option from the palette to change the picture's border color or click the **Picture Effects button** and click an option from the effects menu

Shortcut Method

- ☐ Right-click a picture, then click **Format Picture** on the shortcut menu to open the Format Picture dialog box
- ☐ Click a category in the left pane, then select specific options in the right pane

Compress Pictures

Ribbon Method

- ☐ Select the picture to compress, then click the **Picture Tools Format tab**
- ☐ Click the **Compress Pictures button** 🔳 in the Adjust group to open the Compress Pictures dialog box
- ☐ Click the **Apply only to this picture check box** if necessary to select it
- ☐ Select a Target output option, then click **OK**

Modify the Shape of a Picture Using the Crop Tool

Ribbon Method

- ☐ Click the picture to select it, then click the **Picture Tools Format tab**
- ☐ Click the **Crop button** in the Size group to display cropping handles on the sides and corners of the picture
- ☐ Position the **Crop Tool pointer** ┳ over a cropping handle (solid black line), then drag the cropping handle inward and repeat with the other cropping handles as necessary to specify unwanted parts of the picture
- ☐ Click the **Crop button** in the Size group to remove the unwanted parts of the picture

  OR

- ☐ Click the picture to select it, then click the **Picture Tools Format tab**
- ☐ Click the **Crop button list arrow** in the Size group, click **Crop to Shape**, then click a shape from the gallery

Shortcut Method

- ☐ Right-click the picture, then click the **Crop button** 🔲 on the mini toolbar to display the cropping handles on the sides and corners of the picture
- ☐ Position the **Crop Tool pointer** ┳ over a cropping handle (solid black line), then drag the cropping handle inward and repeat with the other cropping handles as necessary to specify unwanted parts of the picture
- ☐ Click the **Crop button** in the Size group on the Picture Tools Format tab to remove the unwanted parts of the picture

Adjust Position

Ribbon Method

- ☐ Click the graphic, then click the **Picture Tools Format tab**
- ☐ Click the **Position button** in the Arrange group, then click an appropriate option from the menu shown in Figure WD 4-3 or click **More Layout Options** to open the Layout dialog box and apply advanced options

  OR

Shortcut Method

- ☐ Right-click the graphic, then click **Size and Position** from the shortcut menu
- ☐ In the Layout dialog box, click the **Position tab** to specify horizontal, vertical, and additional position options and click **OK**

Figure WD 4-3   Position button and menu

Adjust Size

Ribbon Method

☐ Click the graphic to select it, then click the **Picture Tools Format tab**

☐ Type values in the Shape Height and Shape Width text boxes in the Size group
OR

☐ On the Picture Tools Format tab, click the **launcher** ⬚ in the Size group to open the Layout dialog box, shown in Figure WD 4-4

☐ On the Size tab, enter appropriate values in the Height, Width, Rotate, and Scale sections, then click **OK** to resize the graphic precisely

Figure WD 4-4   Layout dialog box

Shortcut Method

□ Right-click the graphic, then click **Size and Position** from the shortcut menu

□ In the Layout dialog box, click the **Size tab**, enter appropriate values in the Height, Width, Rotate, and Scale sections and click **OK**

Mouse Method

□ Click a picture to select it, move the mouse over a corner sizing handle, then drag the Diagonal Resize pointer ⬉ or the Diagonal Resize pointer ⬈ to resize the graphic proportionally

OR

□ Move the mouse over a side, top, or bottom sizing handle, then press **[Ctrl]** and drag the Horizontal Resize pointer ↔ or the Vertical Resize pointer ↕ to resize the graphic vertically or horizontally while keeping the center position fixed

OR

□ Move the mouse over a corner sizing handle, then press **[Ctrl]** and drag the Diagonal Resize pointer ⬉ or the Diagonal Resize pointer ⬈ to resize the graphic diagonally while keeping the center position fixed

OR

□ Move the mouse over a corner sizing handle, then press **[Shift][Ctrl]** and drag the Diagonal Resize pointer ⬉ or the Diagonal Resize pointer ⬈ to resize the graphic proportionally while keeping the center position fixed

Insert Screenshots

□ Open the document or window that you would like to use in a screenshot; make sure it is not minimized

□ Position the insertion point in the document where you want to insert the screenshot

□ Click the **Insert tab**, click the **Screenshot button** in the Illustrations group, then click a thumbnail from the Available Windows gallery, shown in Figure WD 4-5, to insert it

Figure WD 4-5   Screenshot button and Available Windows gallery

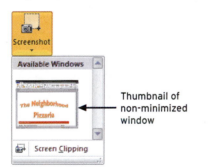

Thumbnail of non-minimized window

> # NOTE
>
> A screenshot is a picture of a computer screen or part of a screen, such as a window or button.

Insert Screen Clippings

Ribbon Method

□ Open the document or window that you would like to use in a screenshot; make sure it is not minimized

□ Position the insertion point in the document where you want to insert the screenshot clipping

□ Click the **Insert tab**, click the **Screenshot button** in the Illustrations group, then click **Screen Clipping**
□ Use the **Crosshair pointer** ╋ to draw a rectangle around the area of the window that you want to cut out and insert into your document
□ Release the mouse button to insert the screen clipping into your document

INSERT AND FORMAT SHAPES, WORDART, AND SMARTART

Insert Shapes

Ribbon Method

□ Position the insertion point in the desired location
□ Click the **Insert tab**, then click the **Shapes button** in the Illustrations group
□ In the gallery of shapes, shown in Figure WD 4-6, click an appropriate shape, then click and drag the **Crosshair pointer** ╋ to draw the shape

Figure WD 4-6   Shapes button and gallery

Insert WordArt

Ribbon Method

□ Click the **Insert tab**, then click the **WordArt button** in the Text group
□ Select a **WordArt style** from the gallery shown in Figure WD 4-7, type the text in the text box that appears, and drag the WordArt into position in your document
□ Use the Drawing Tools Format tab as needed to format and customize the WordArt graphic

Word

Figure WD 4-7 **WordArt button and gallery**

Word

Modify WordArt

Ribbon Method

☐ Click the **WordArt object**, then click the **Drawing Tools Format tab**, if necessary

☐ Use the buttons in the Text group to change the text direction, align the text vertically, or create a link to another text box

☐ Use the buttons in the WordArt Styles group to change the style, the text fill color, the text outline color, or the text effects

☐ Use the buttons in the Shape Styles group to change the style, shape fill, shape outline, or shape effects

☐ Use the buttons in the Arrange group to position and add text wrapping

☐ Use the buttons in the Size group to resize the WordArt object

Insert SmartArt Graphics

Ribbon Method

☐ Position the insertion point where you want the SmartArt graphic to be inserted in the document

☐ Click the **Insert tab**, then click the **SmartArt button** in the Illustrations group

☐ In the Choose a SmartArt Graphic dialog box, shown in Figure WD 4-8, click the category of diagram in the left pane, select a specific diagram layout and design in the middle pane, then preview your selection in the right pane

☐ Click **OK**

☐ Replace the placeholder text and use the SmartArt Tools Design and Format tabs as needed to format and customize the SmartArt graphic

Figure WD 4-8   Choose a SmartArt Graphic dialog box

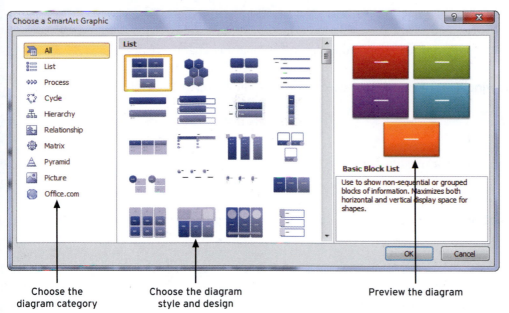

Choose the
diagram category   Choose the diagram   Preview the diagram
                                style and design

Modify SmartArt Graphics
Ribbon Method
☐ Click the **SmartArt graphic**, then click the **SmartArt Tools Design tab**, if necessary
☐ Use the buttons in the Create Graphic group to move and arrange SmartArt shapes
☐ Use the buttons in the Layouts group to change the SmartArt graphic layout
☐ Use the buttons in the SmartArt Styles group to change colors and styles
☐ Click the **SmartArt Tools Format tab** to modify shapes, shape styles, WordArt styles, arrangement, and size

Insert Text in SmartArt Graphics
Ribbon Method
☐ Select the SmartArt graphic
☐ Click the **SmartArt Tools Design tab**, then click the **Text Pane button** in the Create Graphic group to display the text pane, then type appropriate text
Shortcut Method
☐ Click the placeholder box, then type appropriate text
☐ Press **[Shift][Enter]** to move to a new line in a placeholder box
    OR
☐ Click the **Text pane control** to expand the text pane, then type appropriate text
☐ Press **[↓]** or **[↑]** to move between placeholder boxes or click the placeholder box
☐ Press **[Shift][Enter]** to move to a new line in a placeholder box

Add Text to a Shape
Mouse Method
☐ Select a shape, then type the text
Shortcut Method
☐ Right-click the shape, then click **Add Text** on the shortcut menu
☐ Type the text

Word

Modify Text on a Shape

Ribbon Method

☐ Select the text

☐ Click the **Home tab**, then click buttons in the Font group to apply formatting characteristics

OR

☐ Select the text, click the **Drawing Tools Format tab**, select options in the WordArt Styles group to apply formatting characteristics

Shortcut Method

☐ Select the text in a shape

☐ Point to a button on the mini toolbar to modify the text

OR

☐ Select text in a WordArt or SmartArt shape

☐ Right-click the text, click **Font** on the Shortcut menu to open the Font dialog box, then specify formatting options

Add Captions

Ribbon Method

☐ Select a shape, WordArt graphic, or SmartArt graphic

☐ Click the **References tab**, then click **Insert Caption** from the Captions group

☐ In the Caption dialog box, click the **Label list arrow** to choose a label or click **New Label** to type the name of a new label and click **OK**

OR

☐ Click the **Exclude label from caption check box** to remove the label

☐ Click the **Position list arrow** to choose a position for the label, type a caption in the Caption text box, choose any other options as necessary, then click **OK**

Shortcut Method

☐ Right-click a shape, WordArt graphic, or SmartArt graphic in your document, then click **Insert Caption** from the shortcut menu

☐ In the Caption dialog box, click the **Label list arrow** to choose a label or click **New Label** to type the name of a new label and click **OK**

OR

☐ Click the **Exclude label from caption check box** to remove the label

☐ Click the **Position list arrow** to choose a position for the label, type a caption in the Caption text box, choose any other options as necessary, then click **OK**

Set Shape Styles

Ribbon Method

☐ Select a shape

☐ Click the **Drawing Tools Format tab,** click the **More button** in the Shape Styles group, then click a style from the gallery

OR

☐ Select a shape

☐ Click the **Drawing Tools Format tab**, click the **launcher** in the Shape Styles group to open the Format Shape dialog box, shown in Figure WD 4-9

☐ Click a category in the left pane, then select specific options in the right pane

OR

☐ Select a shape

☐ Click the **Drawing Tools Format tab**

☐ Click the **Shape Fill list arrow** in the Shape Styles group and click an option from the palette to change the shape fill, click the **Shape Outline list arrow** and click an option from the palette to change the shape's border, or click the **Shape Effects list arrow** to choose an effect from the menu

Figure WD 4-9   **Format Shape dialog box**

Shortcut Method

☐ Right-click a shape, then click **Format Shape** on the shortcut menu to open the Format Shape dialog box

☐ Click a category in the left pane, then select specific options in the right pane

OR

☐ Right-click a shape, then click the **Shape Fill list arrow** 🎨▾ on the mini toolbar and click an option from the palette to change the shape fill or click the **Shape Outline list arrow** 🖊▾ on the mini toolbar and click an option from the palette to change the shape's border

Adjust Position

Ribbon Method

☐ Select the shape or WordArt graphic, then click the **Drawing Tools Format tab** or select a SmartArt graphic and click the **SmartArt Tools Format tab**

☐ Click the **Position button** in the Arrange group, then click an appropriate option from the menu or click **More Layout Options** to open the Layout dialog box and apply advanced options

OR

☐ On the Drawing Tools Format tab or the SmartArt Tools Format tab, click the **launcher** ⸬ in the Size group to open the Layout dialog box

☐ Click the **Position tab** to specify horizontal, vertical, and additional position options, then click **OK**

Shortcut Method

☐ Right-click the shape, WordArt, or SmartArt graphic, then click **More Layout Options** from the shortcut menu

☐ In the Layout dialog box, click the **Position tab** to specify horizontal, vertical, and additional position options and click **OK**

> ## NOTE
>
> Use the Text Wrapping options to specify the way text flows around an object.

Adjust Size

Ribbon Method

□ Select the WordArt graphic or shape, then click the **Drawing Tools Format tab** or select a SmartArt graphic and click the **SmartArt Tools Format tab**

□ Type values in the Shape Height and Shape Width text boxes in the Size group
  OR

□ On the Drawing Tools Format tab or the SmartArt Tools Format tab, click the **launcher** 🔲 in the Size group to open the Layout dialog box

□ On the Size tab, enter appropriate values in the Height, Width, Rotate, and Scale sections, then click **OK** to resize the graphic precisely

Shortcut Method

□ Right-click the shape, WordArt, or SmartArt graphic, then click **More Layout Options** from the shortcut menu

□ In the Layout dialog box, click the **Size tab**, enter appropriate values in the Height, Width, Rotate, and Scale sections and click **OK**

Mouse Method

□ Select the shape, WordArt, or SmartArt graphic, move the mouse over a corner sizing handle, then drag the Diagonal Resize pointer ⬃ or the Diagonal Resize pointer ⬀ to resize the graphic proportionally
  OR

□ Move the mouse over a side, top, or bottom sizing handle, then press **[Ctrl]** and drag the Horizontal Resize pointer ⟷ or the Vertical Resize pointer ↕ to resize the graphic vertically or horizontally while keeping the center position fixed
  OR

□ Move the mouse over a corner sizing handle, then press **[Ctrl]** and drag the Diagonal Resize pointer ⬃ or the Diagonal Resize pointer ⬀ to resize the graphic diagonally while keeping the center position fixed
  OR

□ Move the mouse over a corner sizing handle, then press **[Shift][Ctrl]** and drag the Diagonal Resize pointer ⬃ or the Diagonal Resize pointer ⬀ to resize the graphic proportionally while keeping the center position fixed

INSERT AND FORMAT CLIP ART

Insert Clip Art

Ribbon Method

□ Position the insertion point in the desired location

□ Click the **Insert tab**, then click the **Clip Art button** in the Illustrations group

□ In the Clip Art task pane, type the search criteria in the Search for text box, use the **Results should be list arrow** to identify the format to find, click the Include Office.com content check box if you want to search for clip art on Office.com, then click **Go**

□ Position the ▸ pointer over the image you want to insert

□ Click the list arrow that appears, then click **Insert**, as shown in Figure WD 4-10, or click an image to insert it

Figure WD 4-10   Clip Art task pane

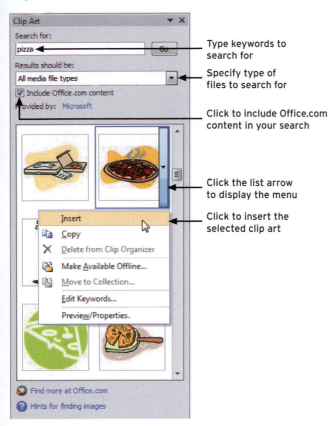

Type keywords to
search for

Specify type of
files to search for

Click to include Office.com
content in your search

Click the list arrow
to display the menu

Click to insert the
selected clip art

Add Clip Art to the Clip Organizer

Menu Method

☐ In the Clip Art task pane, position the Normal Word pointer ⬚ over the online image that you want to add to the
Clip Organizer

☐ Click the list arrow that appears, then click **Make Available Offline**

☐ In the Copy to Collection dialog box, click a collection folder in which to store the clip art, then click **OK** or click
New to create and name a new folder, then click **OK**

Add Clip Art to a Collection in the Clip Organizer

Menu Method

☐ In the Clip Art task pane, position the Normal Word pointer ⬚ over the image that you want to add to a collection in the Clip Organizer

☐ Click the list arrow that appears, then click **Copy to Collection**

☐ In the Copy to Collection dialog box, click a collection folder in which to store the clip art, then click **OK** or click
New to create and name a new folder, then click **OK**

Remove Clip Art from the Clip Organizer

Menu Method

☐ In the Clip Art task pane, position the pointer Normal Word pointer ⬚ over the image you want to remove from
the Clip Organizer

☐ Click the list arrow that appears, then click **Delete from Clip Organizer**

☐ Click **OK** in the Microsoft Clip Organizer message box that appears stating that, "This will delete the selected
clip(s) from all collections in Clip Organizer"

Add Captions

Ribbon Method

☐ Select a graphic

☐ Click the **References tab**, then click **Insert Caption** from the Captions group

☐ In the Caption dialog box, click the **Label list arrow** to choose a label or click **New Label** to type the name of a new label and click **OK**

OR

☐ Click the **Exclude label from caption check box** to remove the label

☐ Click the **Position list arrow** to choose a position for the label, type a caption in the Caption text box, choose any other options as necessary, then click **OK**

Shortcut Method

☐ Right-click a graphic in your document, then click **Insert Caption** on the shortcut menu

☐ In the Caption dialog box, click the **Label list arrow** to choose a label or click **New Label** to type the name of a new label and click **OK**

OR

☐ Click the **Exclude label from caption check box** to remove the label

☐ Click the **Position list arrow** to choose a position for the label, type a caption in the Caption text box, choose any other options as necessary, then click **OK**

Compress Pictures

Ribbon Method

☐ Select the clip art graphic to compress, then click the **Picture Tools Format tab**

☐ Click the **Compress Pictures button** ▨ in the Adjust group to open the Compress Pictures dialog box

☐ Click the **Apply only to this picture check box** if necessary to select it

☐ Select a Target output option, then click **OK** to reduce the file size of the graphic

Adjust Position

Ribbon Method

☐ Follow the steps in the bullets under Adjust Position Ribbon Method under Insert and Format Pictures in a Document on page 62

Shortcut Method

☐ Follow the steps in the bullets under Adjust Position Shortcut Method under Insert and Format Pictures in a Document

Adjust Size

Ribbon Method

☐ Follow the steps in the bullets under Adjust Size Ribbon Method under Insert and Format Pictures in a Document on page 63

Shortcut Method

☐ Follow the steps in bullets 1-2 under Adjust Size Shortcut Method under Insert and Format Pictures in a Document on page 63

Mouse Method

☐ Follow the steps in the bullets under Adjust Size Mouse Method under Insert and Format Pictures on page 63

Rotate a Graphic

Ribbon Method

☐ Click the graphic to select it, then click the **Picture Tools Format tab** or **Drawing Tools Format tab** depending on the graphic type selected

□ Click the **launcher** ▣ in the Size group to open the Layout dialog box, enter appropriate values in the Rotate section on the Size tab, then click **OK** to rotate the graphic precisely

OR

□ Click the **Rotate button** ▤▾ in the Arrange group, click the appropriate option or click **More Rotation Options** to open the Layout dialog box, then enter the rotation value

Mouse Method

□ Click the graphic, position the pointer over the green rotation handle, then click the **Rotation pointer** ⟲ and drag the green rotation handle

OR

□ Click the graphic, position the pointer over the green rotation handle, press **[Shift]**, then click the **Rotation pointer** ⟲ to drag the green rotation handle in 15-degree increments

---

APPLY AND MANIPULATE TEXT BOXES

Insert a Text Box

Ribbon Method

□ Position the insertion point where you want the text box to appear, click the **Insert tab**, then click the **Text Box button** in the Text group

□ Select a preformatted text box from the gallery shown in Figure WD 4-11

OR

□ Position the insertion point where you want the text box to appear, click the **Insert tab**, click the **Text Box button** in the Text group, then click **Draw Text Box** or click the **Shapes button** in the Illustrations group, then click the **Text Box icon** ▣

□ Click and drag the **Crosshair pointer** ╋ to draw a text box, then type text

Figure WD 4-11   Text box button and gallery

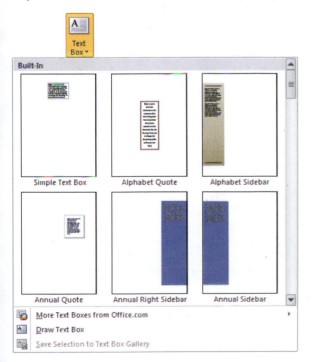

Format a Text Box

Ribbon Method

☐ Select a text box

☐ Click the **Drawing Tools Format tab**, click the **launcher** [⬚] in the Shape Styles group to open the Format Shape dialog box

☐ Click **Text Box** in the left pane, then select Text layout, Autofit, and Internal margin options in the right pane

Shortcut Method

☐ Right-click a text box, then click **Format Shape** on the shortcut menu to open the Format Shape dialog box

☐ Click **Text Box** in the left pane, then select Text layout, Autofit, and Internal margin options in the right pane

Save a Selection to the Text Box Gallery

Ribbon Method

☐ Select a text box you'd like to save to the Text Box gallery

☐ Click the **Insert tab**, click the **Text Box button**, then click **Save Selection to Text Box Gallery**

☐ In the Create New Building Block dialog box, shown in Figure WD 4-12, type a name for the text box in the Name box, select other options as desired, then click **OK**

OR

☐ Select a text box you'd like to save to the Text Box gallery

☐ Click the **Insert tab**, click the **Quick Parts button**, then click **Save Selection to Quick Part Gallery**

In the Create New Building Block dialog box, type a name for the text box in the Name box, click the **Gallery list arrow** and click **Text Boxes**, select other options as desired, then click **OK**

Figure WD 4-12   Create New Building Block dialog box

> # NOTE
>
> Building blocks are reusable parts accessible in galleries and stored in the Building Blocks Organizer.

Apply Text Box Styles

Ribbon Method

☐ Select a text box

☐ Click the **Drawing Tools Format tab**, click the **More button** in the Shape Styles group, then click a style from the gallery

OR

☐ Select a text box

☐ Click the **Drawing Tools Format tab**, click the **launcher** ⬚ in the Shape Styles group to open the Format Shape dialog box

☐ Click a category in the left pane, such as Fill or Line Color, then select specific options in the right pane

OR

☐ Select a text box

☐ Click the **Drawing Tools Format tab**

☐ Click the **Shape Fill button list arrow** in the Shape Styles group and click an option from the palette to change the shape fill, click the **Shape Outline button list arrow** and click an option from the palette to change the shape's border, or click the **Shape Effects button** to choose an effect from the menu

Shortcut Method

☐ Right-click a text box, then click the **Shape Fill list arrow** 🎨 ⁻ on the mini toolbar and choose an option from the palette to change the fill of the text box or click the **Shape Outline list arrow** ✏ ⁻ on the mini toolbar and choose an option from the palette to change the text box outline

OR

☐ Right-click a text box, then click **Format Shape** on the shortcut menu to open the Format Shape dialog box

☐ Click a category in the left pane, then select specific options in the right pane

Change Text Direction
Ribbon Method

☐ Select a text box

☐ Click the **Drawing Tools Format tab**, click the **Text Direction button** in the Text group, click an option from the menu, or click **Text Direction Options** to open the Text Direction - Text Box dialog box and select additional options

Apply Shadow Effects
Ribbon Method

☐ Select a text box

☐ Click the **Drawing Tools Format tab**, click the **Shape Effects button** in the Shape Styles group, click **Shadow** from the menu, then click an option from the submenu or click **Shadow Options** to open the Format Shape dialog box where you can specify advanced options

OR

☐ Select a text box

☐ Click the **Drawing Tools Format tab**, click the **launcher** ⬚ in the Shape Styles group to open the Format Shape dialog box

☐ Click **Shadow** in the left pane, then select advanced options in the right pane

Shortcut Method

☐ Right-click a text box, click **Format Shape** on the shortcut menu to open the Format Shape dialog box

☐ Click **Shadow** in the left pane, then select advanced options in the right pane

Apply 3-D Effects
Ribbon Method

☐ Select a text box

☐ Click the **Drawing Tools Format tab**, click the **Shape Effects button** in the Shape Styles group, click **Bevel** from the menu, then click an option from the menu or click **3-D Options** to open the Format Shape dialog box In the left pane, click **3-D Format** or **3-D Rotation**, then select advanced options in the right pane

OR

☐ Select a text box

☐ Click the **Drawing Tools Format tab**, click the **launcher** ⬚ in the Shape Styles group to open the Format Shape dialog box

☐ Click **3-D Format** or **3-D Rotation** in the left pane, then select advanced options in the right pane

Shortcut Method

☐ Right-click a text box, click **Format Shape** on the shortcut menu to open the Format Shape dialog box

☐ Click **3-D Format** or **3-D Rotation** in the left pane, then select advanced options in the right pane

REVIEW QUESTIONS

FILL IN THE BLANK

Complete the following sentences by writing the correct word or words in the blanks provided.

1. Press _____ and drag a side, top, or bottom sizing handle to resize a graphic vertically and horizontally while keeping the center position fixed.

2. The _____ command cuts out a portion of a window and inserts it into your document.

3. The _____ button is used to remove unwanted parts of a picture.

4. You can create diagrams using _____ graphics.

5. _____ is enhanced text that can be treated as a graphic.

MULTIPLE CHOICE

Select the best response for the following statements.

1. To resize a graphic proportionally, drag a _____ sizing handle.

   A. Middle

   B. Top

   C. Bottom

   D. Corner

2. The _____ button reduces a document's file size.

   A. Save

   B. Compress Pictures

   C. Position

   D. Text box

3. By default, a(n) _____ includes a label and a number.

   A. caption

   B. artistic effect

   C. picture style

   D. screenshot

4. When you save a selection to the Text Box gallery, you are creating a new _____.

   A. caption

   B. WordArt graphic

   C. building block

   D. SmartArt graphic

5. Rotate all text 270° is an option for _____.

   A. changing text direction

   B. adding clip art to the Clip Organizer

   C. adding shadow effects to a Text box

   D. inserting SmartArt graphics

PROJECTS

Project WD 4-1

1. Open the data file **Project WD 4-1.docx**.

2. In the second column, leave one blank line below the heading *Your world tour planning experts* and insert a picture from clip art. Search for the keywords *sand dunes*. Results should be all media file types and include Office.com content. Insert the picture of the sand dunes shown in Figure WD 4-13.

3. Apply the Glass artistic effect, the fifth option in the third row.

4. Apply the **Simple Frame, Black** quick style.

5. Leave a blank line after the second paragraph in column three and insert the **Lighthouse.jpg** picture from the Sample Pictures folder on your computer and apply the **Simple Frame, Black** quick style.

6. Insert the Puzzle Quote text box and type the following text:

   Our mission is to provide you with the most comprehensive and complete planning and travel services so that you can have the adventure of a lifetime that is exciting, comfortable, and worry-free. We look forward to showing you the world!

7. Drag the text box up into position below the *Adventure Works TOURS* heading.

8. Center the text in the quote.

9. Change the style of the text box to the Moderate Effect—Dark Red, Accent 2 shape style, the third option in the fifth row.

10. Adjust spacing, if necessary, so that your document looks similar to Figure WD 4-13.

11. Save the document as **Adventure Brochure.docx**.

Figure WD 4-13 **Adventure Brochure.docx**

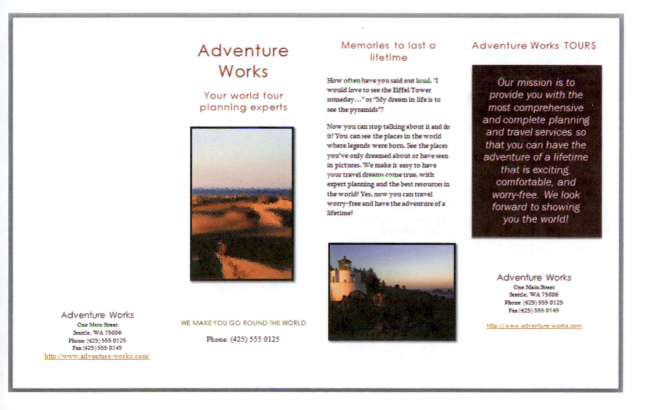

Project WD 4-2

1. Open the data file **Project WD 4-2.docx**.

2. Select the title, *The Neighborhood Pizzeria* and insert WordArt using the Fill-Orange, Accent 6, Warm Matte Bevel, the second option on the sixth row.

3. Add the Transform, Warp, Stop text effect.

4. Position the insertion point after the Friday paragraph and search for clip art using the keywords pizza pies.

5. Find the picture of a hot pizza pie with an orange background and add it to the first Favorites folder in the Clip Organizer.

6. Insert the picture of a hot pizza pie with an orange background.

7. Resize the clip art to 1.37" high and 2" wide.

8. Use the Position command to position the clip art in bottom center with square text wrapping.

9. Save the document as **Pizza Pies.docx** and close it.

Project WD 4-3

1. Open a new blank document.

2. Create the document shown in Figure WD 4-14.

3. Save the document as **Org Chart.docx** and close it.

Figure WD 4-14   Org Chart.docx

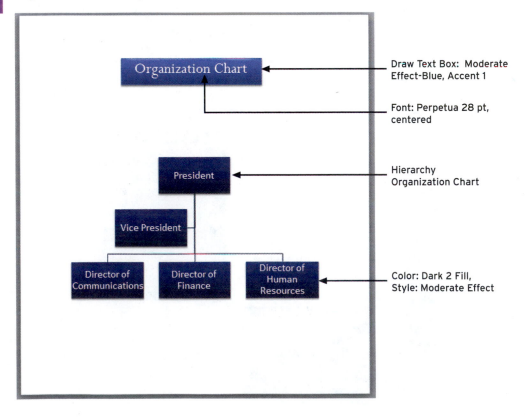

CRITICAL THINKING

Activity WD 4-1

Create your own letterhead. Insert a shape, picture, clip art, WordArt, or SmartArt graphic as your logo. Make at least two modifications to the graphic. Use what you have learned to format your letterhead with a professional appearance.

Word

WORD OBJECTIVE 5: PROOFREADING DOCUMENTS

VALIDATE CONTENT BY USING SPELLING AND GRAMMAR CHECKING OPTIONS

Check the Spelling and Grammar in a Document

Ribbon Method

☐ Click the **Review tab**, then click the **Spelling & Grammar button** in the Proofing group

☐ In the Spelling and Grammar dialog box, shown in Figure WD 5-1, make appropriate selections and use the buttons to ignore or change possible spelling or grammar errors

Shortcut Method

☐ Press **[F7]** to open the Spelling and Grammar dialog box, then follow the steps in bullet 2 of the Check the Spelling and Grammar in a Document Ribbon Method

Figure WD 5-1   Spelling and Grammar dialog box

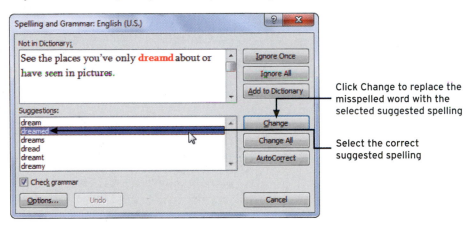

NOTE

Word automatically checks spelling and grammar as you type.
Word flags words that might be misspelled with a wavy red
underline, questionable grammatical construction with a green
wavy line, and words that might be used incorrectly with a blue
wavy line. You can right-click a word that has a red, green,
or blue wavy line and see a shortcut menu with suggestions
for corrections.

Turn Grammar Checking On or Off

Ribbon Method

☐ Click the **File tab**, then click the **Options button** to display the Word Options dialog box

☐ Click **Proofing** in the left pane

☐ In the When correcting spelling and grammar section of the right pane, click the **Check grammar with spelling check box**, if necessary, to insert a checkmark to turn on grammar checking or to remove the checkmark to turn off grammar checking

☐ Click **OK**

OR

☐ Click the **Review tab**, click the **Spelling & Grammar button** in the Proofing group

☐ In the Spelling and Grammar dialog box, click the **Check grammar check box** to insert a checkmark to turn on grammar checking or remove the checkmark to turn off grammar checking

Change Grammar Settings

Ribbon Method

☐ Click the **Review tab**, click the **Spelling & Grammar button** in the Proofing group

☐ In the Spelling and Grammar dialog box, click the **Options button** to open the Word Options dialog box, shown in Figure WD 5-2

☐ In the right pane, in the When correcting spelling and grammar section, click the **Writing Style list arrow** and choose **Grammar Only**, if necessary, then click the **Settings button**

☐ In the Grammar Settings dialog box, shown in Figure WD 5-3, select appropriate options and click **OK**

☐ Click **OK** in the Word Options dialog box to return to the Spelling and Grammar dialog box

OR

☐ Click the **File tab**, then click the **Options button** to display the Word Options dialog box

☐ Click **Proofing** in the left pane

☐ In the When correcting spelling and grammar section of the right pane, click the **Writing Style list arrow** and choose **Grammar & Style**, then click the **Settings button**

☐ In the Grammar Settings dialog box, select appropriate options and click **OK**

☐ Click **OK** to close the Word Options dialog box

Figure WD 5-2   Word Options dialog box

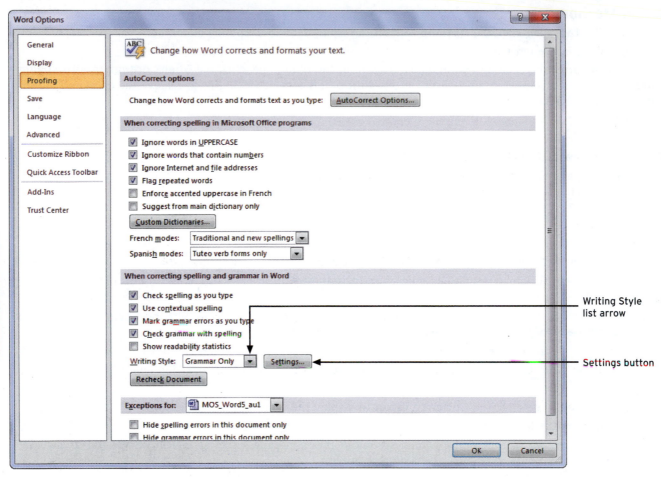

Figure WD 5-3   Grammar Settings dialog box

Set Style Options
Ribbon Method
□ Click the **Review tab**, click the **Spelling & Grammar button** in the Proofing group

□ In the Spelling and Grammar dialog box, click the **Options button**

□ In the When Correcting Spelling and Grammar section of the Word Options dialog box, click the **Writing Style list arrow** and choose **Grammar & Style**, then click the **Settings button**

□ In the Grammar Settings dialog box, select appropriate options and click **OK**

□ Click **OK** in the Word Options dialog box to return to the Spelling and Grammar dialog box

OR

□ Click the **File tab**, then click the **Options button** to open the Word Options dialog box

□ Click **Proofing** in the left pane

□ In the When Correcting Spelling and Grammar section of the right pane, click the **Writing Style list arrow** and choose **Grammar & Style**, then click the **Settings button**

□ In the Grammar Settings dialog box, select appropriate options and click **OK**

□ Click **OK** to close the Word Options dialog box

CONFIGURE AUTOCORRECT SETTINGS

Add or Remove Exceptions
Ribbon Method
□ Click the **File tab**, then click **Options** to open the Word Options dialog box

□ Click **Proofing** in the left pane

□ In the right pane, click the **AutoCorrect Options button**

□ Click the **AutoCorrect tab** in the AutoCorrect dialog box, if necessary

□ Click the **Exceptions button** to open the AutoCorrect Exceptions dialog box shown in Figure WD 5-4

□ Make appropriate selections within each tab, click **Delete** or type an exception in the text box and click **Add** then click **OK**

□ Click **OK** in the AutoCorrect dialog box, then click **OK** in the Word Options dialog box

Figure WD 5-4   AutoCorrect Exceptions dialog box

Turn On and Off AutoCorrect
Ribbon Method
□ Click the **File tab**, then click **Options** to display the Word Options dialog box

□ Click **Proofing** in the left pane

☐ In the right pane, click the **AutoCorrect Options button** to open the AutoCorrect dialog box, shown in Figure WD 5-5

☐ To turn off AutoCorrect, click the **Replace text as you type check box** to remove the check mark

☐ To turn AutoCorrect on, click the **Replace text as you type check box** to insert a checkmark

☐ In the AutoCorrect dialog box, click **OK**, then click **OK** in the Word Options dialog box

Figure WD 5-5   AutoCorrect dialog box

Click to remove checkmark and turn off AutoCorrect

INSERT AND MODIFY COMMENTS IN A DOCUMENT

Insert a Comment

Ribbon Method

☐ Select the text (or existing comment) that you want to comment on, click the **Review tab**, then click the **New Comment button** in the Comments group

☐ Type the text for your comment in the balloon

Edit a Comment

Ribbon Method

☐ Click the **Review tab**, click the **Track Changes list arrow** in the Tracking group, then click **Change Tracking Options**

☐ In the Markup section in the Track Changes Options dialog box, click the **Comments list arrow**, then select a color

OR

☐ In the Balloons section in the Track Changes Options dialog box, select appropriate options, then click **OK**

Mouse Method

☐ Click in a comment, then make text changes

Delete a Comment
Ribbon Method
☐ Click a comment to select it
☐ Click the **Review tab**, click the **Delete list arrow** in the Comments group, then click **Delete** or another appropriate option as shown in Figure WD 5-6

Shortcut Method
☐ Right-click a comment
☐ Click **Delete Comment** on the shortcut menu

Figure WD 5-6   Delete button and menu

View a Comment from Another User
Ribbon Method
☐ Open a document that contains comments from another user
☐ If the comments are not displayed, click the **Review tab**, click **Show Markup list arrow** in the Tracking group, then click **Comments** to insert a checkmark beside it to indicate that comments should be displayed in the document

OR

☐ Click the **Review tab**, click **Show Markup list arrow** in the Tracking group, point to **Reviewers**, then click **All Reviewers** to show all comments in the document or click the **name** of the reviewer whose comments you want to show

View Comments Inline
Ribbon Method
☐ Click the **Review tab**, click the **Show Markup list arrow** in the Tracking group, point to **Balloons**, then click **Show All Revisions Inline**

View Comments as Balloons
Ribbon Method
☐ Click the **Review tab**, click the **Show Markup list arrow** in the Tracking group, point to **Balloons**, then click **Show Only Comments and Formatting in Balloons**

REVIEW QUESTIONS

TRUE/FALSE
Circle T if the statement is true or F if the statement is false.

T   F   1. F7 opens the Spelling and Grammar dialog box.

T   F   2. You cannot turn off grammar checking.

T   F   3. You can delete all comments in a document at once.

T   F   4. The Spelling & Grammar button is located in the References tab.

T   F   5. AutoCorrect can be turned off on the Review tab.

MATCHING

Match the correct term in Column 2 to its description in Column 1.

Column 1

_____ 1. Lets you choose whether or not to show comments in a document.

_____ 2. A comment window.

_____ 3. Replaces text as you type.

_____ 4. Display comments, revisions, and formatting within the text of a document.

_____ 5. Contains Spelling and Grammar option settings.

Column 2

A. AutoCorrect

B. Word Options dialog box

C. Show Markup list arrow

D. Show All Revisions Inline

E. Balloon

PROJECTS

Project WD 5-1

1. Open the data file **Project WD 5-1.docx**.

2. Check the spelling and grammar, and correct any errors.

3. Click on the second comment and insert a new comment. Type the following in the comment:

   No. I double-checked and it is still $8,000.

4. Delete Comment 1.

5. Click on the comment you inserted. Position the insertion point at the end of the sentence and type the following:

   It will change to $10,000 next year.

6. View the comments inline.

7. View the comments as balloons.

8. Turn off AutoCorrect.

9. In the first paragraph under Memories to last a lifetime, position the insertion point before the p in pyramids.

10. Type the misspelled word **hte**. Notice that AutoCorrect did not change it for you. Delete the misspelled word.

11. Turn on AutoCorrect. With the insertion point in the same position, type the misspelled word **hte**. Notice that AutoCorrect automatically corrects the spelling for you to *the*.

12. Save the document as **Brochure.docx** and close it.

CRITICAL THINKING

Activity WD 5-1

Add or delete an AutoCorrect exception, and create an AutoCorrect option that will replace a misspelled form of your name with the correct spelling.

Activity WD 5-2

Create teams of three classmates. Each classmate should write a paragraph about their favorite sport, book, movie, or hobby. The documents should be checked for spelling and grammar errors and then electronically traded among the team members. Team members should make at least two positive comments on each document, and change the color of their comments. After the documents are returned to their owners, each team member should practice hiding and showing reviewer comments, and then delete all the comments in the document.

Word Objective 6: Applying References and Hyperlinks

Apply a Hyperlink

Apply a Hyperlink to Text or Graphic

Ribbon Method

□ Select the text or picture you want to create as a hyperlink, click the **Insert tab**, then click the **Hyperlink button** in the Links group

□ In the Insert Hyperlink dialog box, shown in Figure WD 6-1, click the option you want to link to in the Link to list, complete the rest of the Insert Hyperlink dialog box based on the Link to option you selected, then click **OK**

Shortcut Method

□ Right-click the text or picture you want to create as a hyperlink, then click **Hyperlink** on the shortcut menu that opens

□ Follow the steps in bullet 2 of the Apply a Hyperlink to Text or Graphic Ribbon Method above

  OR

□ Select the text or picture you want to create as a hyperlink, then press **[CTRL][K]**

□ Follow the steps in bullet 2 of the Apply a Hyperlink to Text or Graphic Ribbon Method above

Figure WD 6-1   Insert Hyperlink dialog box

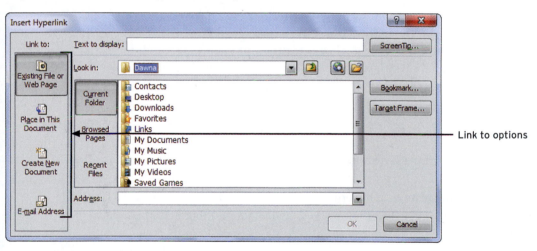

Link to options

Use a Hyperlink as a Bookmark

Ribbon Method

□ Select the text you want to create as a hyperlink, click the **Insert tab**, then click the **Hyperlink button** in the Links group

□ In the Insert Hyperlink dialog box, click the **Bookmark button** to open the Select Place in Document dialog box, shown in Figure WD 6-2

□ Click an option under Select an existing place in the document, click **OK**, then click **OK** in the Insert Hyperlink dialog box

Shortcut Method

□ Right-click the text or picture you want to create as a hyperlink, then click **Hyperlink** on the shortcut menu that opens

□ Follow the steps in bullets 2-3 of the Use a Hyperlink as a Bookmark Ribbon Method above

  OR

□ Select the text or picture you want to create as a hyperlink, then press **[CTRL][K]**

□ Follow the steps in bullets 2-3 of the Use a Hyperlink as a Bookmark Ribbon Method above

Word

Figure WD 6-2 Select Place in Document dialog box

Link a Hyperlink to an E-Mail Address

Ribbon Method

☐ Select the text that you want to create as a hyperlink to an e-mail address, click the **Insert tab**, then click the **Hyperlink button** in the Links group

☐ In the Insert Hyperlink dialog box, click the **E-mail Address option** in the Link to list

☐ In the Insert Hyperlink dialog box, shown in Figure WD 6-3, type the text to display, if necessary, type the e-mail address that you want to link to in the E-mail address text box or choose one from the list of recently used e-mail addresses at the bottom of the text box, type a subject for the e-mail message, if necessary, then click **OK**

Shortcut Method

☐ Right-click the text or picture you want to create as a hyperlink to an e-mail address, then click **Hyperlink** on the shortcut menu that opens

☐ Follow the steps in bullets 2–3 of the Link a Hyperlink to an E-mail Address Ribbon Method above

OR

☐ Select the text or picture you want to create as a hyperlink to an e-mail address, then press **[CTRL][K]**

☐ Follow the steps in bullets 2–3 of the Link a Hyperlink to an E-mail Address Ribbon Method above

Figure WD 6-3 Insert Hyperlink dialog box

CREATE ENDNOTES AND FOOTNOTES IN A DOCUMENT

Insert Endnotes and Footnotes

Ribbon Method

☐ Position the insertion point where you want to insert the note reference mark, click the **References tab**, then click the **Insert Footnote button** or **Insert Endnote button** in the Footnotes group

☐ Type the text for the endnote or footnote

> ## NOTE
>
> Footnotes are used to provide details about the text and are located below the text or at the bottom of the page. Endnotes are used to provide references for text and are located at the end of the section or end of the document.

Shortcut Method

☐ Position the insertion point where you want to insert the note reference mark

☐ To insert a footnote, press **[CTRL][ALT][F]**

☐ To insert an endnote, press **[CTRL][ALT][D]**

☐ Type the text for the endnote or footnote

Manage Footnote and Endnote Locations

Ribbon Method

☐ Click the **References tab**, then click the dialog box launcher 🔲 in the Footnotes group to open the Footnote and Endnote dialog box, shown in Figure WD 6-4

☐ To change the location, click the list arrow beside Footnotes or Endnotes and choose a new location

☐ Click **Apply**

Figure WD 6-4   Footnote and Endnote dialog box

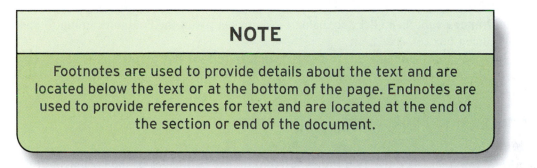

Convert Footnotes to Endnotes or Endnotes to Footnotes

Ribbon Method

- ☐ Click the **References tab**, then click the dialog box launcher ⬚ in the Footnotes group to open the Footnote and Endnote dialog box
- ☐ In the Location section of the dialog box, click the **Convert button** to open the Convert Notes dialog box
- ☐ Choose an appropriate option, then click **OK**

Configure Footnote and Endnote Format

Ribbon Method

- ☐ Click the **References tab**, then click the dialog box launcher ⬚ in the Footnotes group to open the Footnote and Endnote dialog box
- ☐ In the Format section of the dialog box, click the **Number format list arrow** and choose a new format or click the **Symbol button** to open the Symbol dialog box where you can select a symbol and click **OK**
- ☐ Click **Insert**

View Endnotes and Footnotes for Presentation

Ribbon Method

- ☐ Click the **View tab**, then click the **Two Pages button** to view two pages of the document at once in Page Layout view

  OR
- ☐ Click the **View tab**, then click the **Full Screen Reading button** to view the document on the full screen and scroll through the document

Change Footnote and Endnote Numbering

Ribbon Method

- ☐ Click the **References tab**, then click the dialog box launcher ⬚ in the Footnotes group to open the Footnote and Endnote dialog box
- ☐ In the Format section of the dialog box, click the **Start at up and down arrows** and choose a new starting value or click the **Numbering list arrow** to choose a different numbering method
- ☐ Click **Insert**

CREATE A TABLE OF CONTENTS IN A DOCUMENT

Create a Table of Contents

Ribbon Method

- ☐ Assign headings and subheadings using the buttons in the Styles group
- ☐ Position the insertion point where you want the Table of Contents to appear
- ☐ Click the **References tab**, then click the **Table of Contents list arrow** in the Table of Contents group
- ☐ Select an option from the Table of Contents menu, shown in Figure WD 6-5

  OR
- ☐ On the Table of Contents menu, click **Insert Table of Contents**
- ☐ In the Table of Contents dialog box, select the desired settings, then click **OK**

Figure WD 6-5   **Table of Contents button and menu**

Set Levels

Ribbon Method

☐ Click the **References tab**, then click the **Table of Contents button** in the Table of Contents group, and click **Insert Table of Contents** to open the Table of Contents dialog box

☐ In the General area, use the Show levels up and down arrows to change the number of levels to show in the table of contents, then click **OK**

☐ Click **Yes** if a Microsoft Word box opens asking to replace the current table of contents
   OR

☐ Click the **References tab**, then click the **Table of Contents button** in the Table of Contents group, and click **Insert Table of Contents** to open the Table of Contents dialog box

☐ Click the **Options button** to open the Table of Contents Options dialog box

☐ Set the Table of Contents level in the right column that matches the style you want to use in the left column, then click **OK**

☐ Click **OK** in the Table of Contents dialog box, then click **Yes** in the Microsoft Word box that opens asking to replace the current table of contents

Set Alignment

Ribbon Method

☐ Click the **References tab**, then click the **Table of Contents button** in the Table of Contents group, and click **Insert Table of Contents** to open the Table of Contents dialog box

☐ In the General area, click the **Right align page numbers check box** to remove the checkmark and align the page number after the heading in the table of contents or click the **Right align page numbers check box** to insert a checkmark and right align the page numbers, then click **OK**

☐ Click **Yes** if a Microsoft Word dialog box opens asking to replace the current table of contents

Set Tab Leaders

Ribbon Method

☐ Click the **References tab**, click the **Table of Contents button** in the Table of Contents group, then click **Insert Table of Contents** to open the Table of Contents dialog box shown in Figure WD 6-6

☐ In the Print Preview area, make sure the **Right align page numbers check box** contains a checkmark, click the **Tab Leader list arrow** and choose an appropriate option, then click **OK**

☐ Click **Yes** in the Microsoft Word dialog box to replace the selected table of contents

Figure WD 6-6 Table of Contents dialog box

Modify Styles

Ribbon Method

☐ Use styles to assign headings and subheadings to your document

☐ Click the **References tab**, then click the **Table of Contents button** in the Table of Contents group, and click **Insert Table of Contents** to open the Table of Contents dialog box

☐ Click the **Modify button** to open the Style dialog box, shown in Figure WD 6-7

☐ Select the style you want to modify from the Styles list and click the **Modify button** to open the Modify Style dialog box shown in Figure WD 6-8

☐ Select appropriate options and click **OK**

☐ Click **OK** in the Style dialog box, click **OK** in the Table of Contents dialog box

☐ Click **OK** in the Microsoft Word box asking to replace the current table of contents

Figure WD 6-7   **Style dialog box**

Figure WD 6-8   **Modify Style dialog box**

Apply a Different Format to the Table of Contents

Ribbon Method

☐ Use styles to assign headings and subheadings to your document
☐ Click the **References tab**, then click the **Table of Contents button** in the Table of Contents group, and click **Insert Table of Contents** to open the Table of Contents dialog box
☐ Click the **Formats list arrow** in the General section, scroll as needed to select a new format, click the format you want to apply, then click **OK**
☐ Click **OK** if a Microsoft Word dialog box opens asking to replace the current table of contents

Update a Table of Contents

Ribbon Method

☐ Make changes to the document (such as changing page numbers or deleting heads and their subtext)

☐ Click an entry in the table of contents to select the table of contents, click the **References tab**, then click the **Update Table button** in the Table of Contents group

☐ In the Update Table of Contents dialog box, shown in Figure WD 6-9, click **Update page numbers only** or **Update entire table**, then click **OK**

☐ Click the **Table of Contents head** (or anywhere in the document) to deselect the table of contents

Shortcut Method

☐ Make changes to the document (such as changing page numbers, deleting heads and their subtext)

☐ Right-click the **table of contents**, then click **Update Field** on the shortcut menu that opens

☐ Follow the steps in bullets 3–4 of the Update a Table of Contents Ribbon Method above
    OR

☐ Make changes to the document (such as changing page numbers, deleting heads and their subtext)

☐ Click the **table of contents** to select it, then click the **Update Table tab**

☐ Follow the steps in bullets 3–4 of the Update a Table of Contents Ribbon Method above

Figure WD 6-9   **Update Table of Contents dialog box**

REVIEW QUESTIONS

FILL IN THE BLANK

Complete the following sentences by writing the correct word or words in the blanks provided.

1. _____ provide details about the text and are usually located at the bottom of the page.

2. The Insert Endnote button is located on the _____ tab.

3. To create a table of contents, the headings in the document must be formatted with _____.

4. _____ can be text or pictures.

5. Footnotes can be _____ to endnotes and vice versa.

MULTIPLE CHOICE

Select the best response for the following statements.

1. A table of contents that contains headings using three different styles would have three _____.

    A. Endnotes

    B. Leaders

    C. Tables

    D. Levels

2. _____ are dots, dashes, or lines that fill the empty space before a tab stop.

    A. Bookmarks

    B. Styles

    C. Tab Leaders

    D. Hyperlinks

3. After you make changes to a document that affect headings or page numbers, you should _____.

    A. Update page numbers only in the table of contents

    B. Update the entire table of contents

    C. Create a new table of contents

    D. Create a hyperlink to the table of contents

4. The Hyperlink button is located on the _____ tab.

    A. Insert

    B. References

    C. Page Layout

    D. View

5. Note reference marks for footnotes and endnotes can be _____.

    A. symbols

    B. numbers

    C. letters

    D. all of the above

PROJECTS

Project WD 6-1

1. Open the **Project WD 6-1.docx**.

2. Position the insertion point on the first page of the document after the cover page and insert a blank page.

3. Click the **Show/Hide ¶ button**, and position the insertion point at the beginning of the Page Break on the new page.

4. Insert the Table of Contents format named Automatic Table 2.

5. Scroll down to the third page. Select First Quarter Sales and apply the **Heading 2** quick style.

6. Apply the **Heading 3** quick style to Regional Sales, National Sales, and International Sales.

7. On the second page, update the entire table of contents.

8. Change the tab leaders in the table of contents to solid lines.

9. Modify the style of the first level heading. Change the font of the style to Arial Black.

10. On the third page, type **Conclusion** under the text for International Sales and format it with the **Heading 1** quick style.

11. Update the entire table of contents.

12. Click the **Show/Hide ¶ button**.

13. On the third page, position the insertion point after the International Sales heading and insert a footnote with the following text:

    These figures are not final at time of publication.

Word

14. Change the number format of the footnotes to the format that begins with an asterisk (*) and apply it to the document.

15. Select **Your Name** on the first page, and insert a hyperlink to your own e-mail address or one provided by your instructor.

16. Save the document as **Report.docx**.

CRITICAL THINKING

Activity WD 6-1

Create a new document and insert the four different kinds of hyperlinks in the Link to section of the Insert Hyperlink dialog box:

- Existing File or Web Page
- Place in This Document
- Create New Document
- E-mail Address

WORD OBJECTIVE 7: PERFORMING MAIL MERGE OPERATIONS

SET UP MAIL MERGE

Perform a Mail Merge using the Mail Merge Wizard

Task Pane Method

- ☐ Click the **Mailings tab**, click the **Start Mail Merge button** in the Start Mail Merge group, then click **Step by Step Mail Merge Wizard**, as shown in Figure WD 7-1
- ☐ In the Mail Merge task pane, shown in Figure WD 7-2, click the **Letters option button** (or another type of document you are working on), then click **Next: Starting document**
- ☐ In Step 2 of 6, click the **option button** next to the description of your starting document; if you select Start from a template or Start from an existing document, follow the onscreen directions to navigate to the file you want to use, click it, then click **OK** or **Open**; then click **Next: Select recipients**
- ☐ In Step 3 of 6, click the **option button** next to the recipient list you want to use, then follow the onscreen directions to create the list or navigate to and open an existing list, then click **Next: Write your letter**
- ☐ In Step 4 of 6, write your letter inserting merge fields where appropriate, click **More items** to select individual merge fields to insert, then click **Next: Preview your letters**
- ☐ In Step 5 of 6, use the arrow buttons in the task pane to preview your letters, make changes if necessary, then click **Next: Complete the merge**
- ☐ In Step 6 of 6, click **Print** to send the merged document directly to a printer or click **Edit individual letters** to create a merge file that you can edit if you'd like to personalize one or more of the letters before printing
- ☐ Click the **Close box** ☒ to close the task pane

Figure WD 7-1   Start Mail Merge button and menu

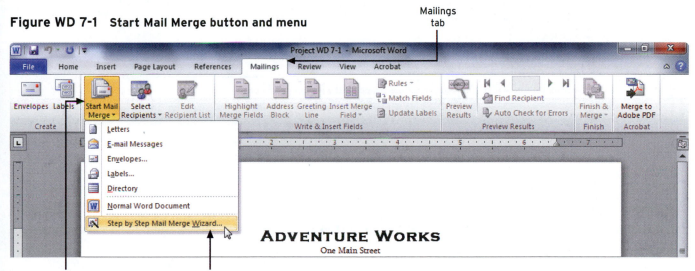

Mailings
tab

Start Mail Merge button   Step by Step Mail Merge Wizard

Figure WD 7-2   Mail Merge task pane

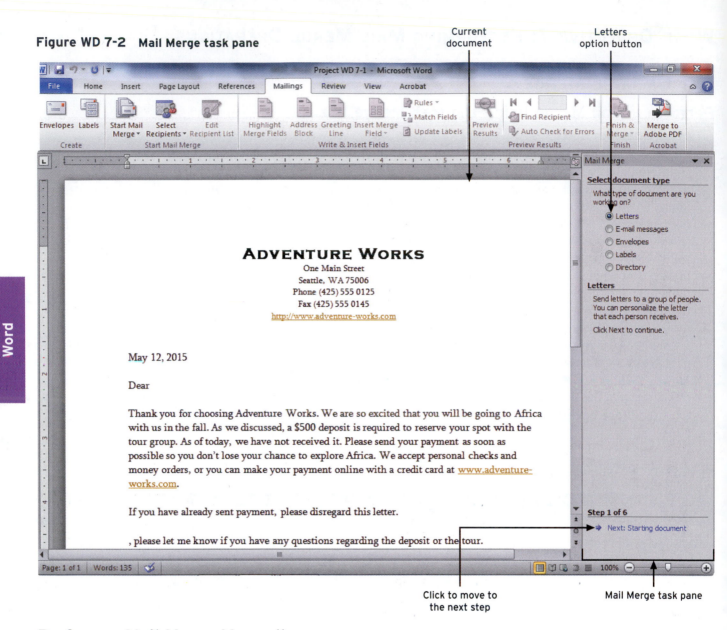

Current document

Letters option button

Click to move to the next step

Mail Merge task pane

Perform a Mail Merge Manually

Ribbon Method

☐ Click the **Mailings tab**, click the **Start Mail Merge button** in the Start Mail Merge group, then click **Letters** as shown in Figure WD 7-3

Figure WD 7-3   Start Mail Merge button and menu

□ Click the **Select Recipients button** in the Start Mail Merge group, click **Type New List** and, if necessary, type a new list in the New Addresses list dialog box shown in Figure WD 7-4, click **Use Existing List** to use a list that was created previously, or click **Select from Outlook Contacts**, then create the list or navigate to the file, select the file, then click **OK**

Figure WD 7-4   New Address List dialog box

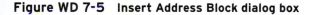

□ Position the insertion point where you want to insert a field in the document, then use the buttons in the Write & Insert Fields group to insert an Address Block (see Figure WD 7-5), a Greeting Line, or select a field from the menu that opens when you click the **Insert Merge Field button list arrow**

Figure WD 7-5   Insert Address Block dialog box

□ Repeat the step in bullet 3 until you have inserted all merge fields in your document

□ Click the **Preview Results button** in the Preview Results group

□ Click the **Finish & Merge button** in the Finish group, then click **Edit Individual Documents** to create a merge file that you can edit, click **Print Documents** to send the merged document directly to the printer, or click **Send E-mail Messages** to create e-mail messages

□ Select appropriate options in the dialog box that opens, then click **OK**

Use Auto Check for Errors

Ribbon Method
☐ Click the **Mailings tab**, then click **Auto Check for Errors** in the Preview Results group
☐ In the Checking and Reporting Errors dialog box, shown in Figure WD 7-6, select an appropriate option, then click **OK**

Shortcut Method
☐ Press **[Alt][Shift][K]**
☐ In the Checking and Reporting Errors dialog box, select an appropriate option, then click **OK**

Figure WD 7-6 · Checking and Reporting Errors dialog box

REVIEW QUESTIONS

TRUE/FALSE

Circle T if the statement is true or F if the statement is false.

T   F   1. The address block contains the greeting line.

T   F   2. The Step by Step Mail Merge Wizard is located on the Start Mail Merge button.

T   F   3. First Name is an example of a merge field.

T   F   4. The Mail Merge task pane opens when you start the Step by Step Mail Merge Wizard.

T   F   5. To create a mail merge from a list, use the Use Existing List command on the Insert Merge Field button.

MATCHING

Match the correct term in Column 2 to its description in Column 1.

Column 1	Column 2
_____ 1. Replaces fields with merged data so you can see what the document looks like.	A. Auto Check for Errors button
_____ 2. A placeholder for recipient information.	B. Type New List dialog box
_____ 3. Where you can create a new list.	C. Preview Results button
_____ 4. Creates a new document that contains all the merged documents.	D. Edit Individual Documents command
_____ 5. Allows you to specify how to handle errors if they occur during a merge.	E. Field

PROJECTS

Project WD 7-1

1. Open the data file **Project WD 7-1.docx**.

2. Save the document as **Africa Letters.docx**.

3. Use the Step by Step Mail Merge Wizard to start a mail merge for the letter and choose **africatourlist.accdb** from the data files for this objective as the data source.

4. Using the default formats, insert an **Address Block**, a **Greeting Line**, and a **First Name** field in the letter as shown in Figure WD 7-7.

Figure WD 7-7   **Letter with mail merge fields**

5. Preview the letters. Notice that there is an extra *Dear* in the greeting line. Delete the first occurrence of the word *Dear.*

6. Save the file.

7. Complete the merge. Choose to edit individual letters, and merge all records.

8. Scroll through the document to view the letters.

9. Save the document as **Africa Merged Letters.docx** and close it. Close **Project WD 7-1.docx** without saving.

Project WD 7-2

1. Create a new blank document.

2. Start a mail merge for size 10 envelopes to go with the letters created in the previous project. Use the default formatting settings and choose **africatourlist.accdb** as the data source.

3. Open **Project WD 7-1.docx** and copy the first three lines of the company name and address and paste it onto the envelope, then left-align the address block. Close the **Project WD 7-1.docx** without saving.

4. Insert the default Address Block format for the delivery address, as shown in Figure WD 7-8.

Figure WD 7-8 Mail merge envelope document

> **ADVENTURE WORKS**
> One Main Street
> Seattle, WA 75006
>
>
>
>   «AddressBlock»

5. Preview an envelope.

6. Simulate the merge and report errors in a new document using Auto Check for Errors. If there are no errors, click OK.

7. Finish and merge the envelopes and choose to edit individual documents. Merge all records.

8. Scroll through the envelopes.

9. Save the document as **Africa Envelopes** and close it.

10. Close the envelope design document without saving.

CRITICAL THINKING

Activity WD 7-1

Use your school's name and address to create a single label. Create an entire sheet of the same label using your choice of label format. Save or print the label.

Activity WD 7-2

Create an invitation to a party using a Word document. Type a new list of 3–5 people who you want to invite and use it to merge the documents. Insert a first name and last name field and any other fields of your choice to personalize each invitation. Merge the documents and save the merged file using a meaningful name of your choice.

Word

Word Expert Objective 1: Sharing and Maintaining Documents

Customize Word Options

Change the Default Save Location

Ribbon Method

☐ Click the **File tab**, click **Options**, click **Save** in the left pane, then write down the contents of the Default file location text box

☐ Click **Browse** next to the Default file location text box, shown in Figure WDX 1-1, to navigate to the folder where you want to save your files, select the folder, click **OK** to select the location, then click **OK** as needed to exit the Word Options dialog box

☐ Start a new blank document, click the **Save button** 🖫 on the Quick Access toolbar, then verify that the default file location you specified appears as the location where the document should be saved

Figure WDX 1-1   Word Options dialog box

Change Username and Initials

Ribbon Method

☐ Click the **File tab**, click **Options** to open the Word Options dialog box shown in Figure WDX 1-2, then click **General** in the left pane, if necessary

☐ Select the **contents** of User name text box, type a new user name, press **[Tab]**, type new initials in the Initials text box, then click **OK**

OR

☐ Click the **Review tab**, click the **Track Changes list arrow**, then click **Change User Name**

☐ Select the **contents** of User name text box, type a new user name, press **[Tab]**, type new initials in the Initials text box, then click **OK**

Figure WDX 1-2   Word Options dialog box

Change Advanced Options

Ribbon Method

☐ Click the **File tab**, click **Options**, then click **Advanced** in the left pane

☐ Select appropriate options, then click **OK**

Change Spelling Options

Ribbon Method

☐ Click the **File tab**, click **Options**, then click **Proofing** in the left pane

☐ Select appropriate options in the When correcting spelling and grammar in Word section, then click **OK**

Change Grammar Checking Options

Ribbon Method

☐ In a document that contains grammar or spelling errors, click the **Review tab**, then click the **Spelling & Grammar button** in the Proofing group

☐ In the Spelling and Grammar dialog box, click the **Options button** to open the Word Options dialog box

☐ Select appropriate options in the When correcting spelling and grammar in Word section of the right pane, then click **OK** or click the **Writing Style list arrow** and choose **Grammar Only**, if necessary, then click the **Settings button**

☐ In the Grammar Settings dialog box, shown in Figure WDX 1-3, select appropriate options and click **OK**

☐ Click **OK** in the Word Options dialog box to return to the Spelling and Grammar dialog box

   OR

☐ Click the **File tab**, then click **Options** to display the Word Options dialog box

☐ Click **Proofing** in the left pane

☐ Select appropriate options in the When correcting spelling and grammar in Word section of the right pane, then click **OK** or click the **Writing Style list arrow** and choose **Grammar & Style**, then click the **Settings button**

☐ In the Grammar Settings dialog box, select appropriate options and click **OK**

☐ Click **OK** to close the Word Options dialog box

Figure WDX 1-3   Grammar Settings dialog box

APPLY PROTECTION TO A DOCUMENT

Apply Formatting Restrictions

Ribbon Method

☐ Click the **File tab**, click the **Protect Document button**, then click **Restrict Editing**

☐ In the Restrict Formatting and Editing task pane, select the **Limit formatting to a selection of styles check box** in the Formatting restrictions section, click **Settings**, select the appropriate options in the Formatting Restrictions dialog box, click **OK**, then click **Yes, Start Enforcing Protection**

☐ In the Start Enforcing Protection dialog box, click **OK** to start enforcement without protecting the document with a password

   OR

☐ Type a password, press **[Tab]**, then type the password again to password protect the document

   OR

☐ Click the User authentication option to encrypt the document and use Information Rights Management Service to authenticate the owners of the document

☐ Click **OK** or click **Cancel** if you do not want to start enforcing protection

   OR

☐ Click the **Review tab**, click the **Restrict Editing button** in the Protect group, then follow the steps in bullets 2–4 of the Apply Formatting Restrictions Ribbon Method above

Apply Editing Restrictions and Limit Access to a Document

Ribbon Method

☐ Click the **File tab**, click the **Protect Document button**, then click **Restrict Editing**

☐ In the Restrict Formatting and Editing task pane, shown in Figure WDX 1-4, click the **Allow only this type of editing in the document check box** in the Editing restrictions section. Click the list arrow to select the type of editing to allow, select the users in the Exceptions section that this editing restriction will not apply to, then click **Yes, Start Enforcing Protection**

☐ In the Start Enforcing Protection dialog box, click **OK** to start enforcement without protecting the document with a password

OR

☐ Type a password, press **[Tab]**, then type the password again to password protect the document

OR

☐ Click the User authentication option to encrypt the document and use Information Rights Management Services to authenticate the owners of the document

☐ Click **OK** or click **Cancel** if you do not want to start enforcing protection

OR

☐ Click the **Review tab**, click the **Restrict Editing button** in the Protect group, then follow the steps in bullets 2–3 of the Apply Editing Restrictions and Limit Access to a Document Ribbon Method above

Figure WDX 1-4   **Restrict Formatting and Editing task pane**

Restrict Access to a Document Using Information Rights Management

Ribbon Method

☐ Click the **File tab**, click the **Protect Document button**, click **Restrict Permission by People**, then click **Restricted Access**

☐ In the Service Sign-Up dialog box, click **Yes, I want to sign up for this free service from Microsoft** and click **Next**

☐ Follow the instructions to sign in with your Windows Live ID and follow instructions to sign up for the service

Encrypt a Document with a Password

Ribbon Method

☐ Open a Word document, click the **File tab**, click the **Protect Document button**, then click **Encrypt with Password**

☐ Type a password in the Encrypt Document dialog box, shown in Figure WDX 1-5, then click **OK**

☐ Reenter the password in the Confirm Password dialog box, then click **OK**

Figure WDX 1-5   Encrypt Document dialog box

NOTE

A digital signature confirms that a document is authentic and has not been altered.

Insert a Line for a Digital Signature

Ribbon Method

☐ Position the insertion point where you want the digital signature line to appear, click the **Insert tab**, click the **Signature Line button** in the Text group, then click **OK** if a Microsoft Word dialog box appears as shown in Figure WDX 1-6

☐ In the Signature Setup dialog box, shown in Figure WDX 1-7, fill in the appropriate information, then click **OK**

Figure WDX 1-6   Microsoft Word dialog box

Figure WDX 1-7   Signature Setup dialog box

> **NOTE**
>
> To add a digital signature to the signature line, you must obtain a digital ID from a Microsoft partner or create your own ID.

APPLY A TEMPLATE TO A DOCUMENT

Modify an Existing Template

Ribbon Method

☐ Click the **File tab**, click **New**, click the **Sample templates button**, click a template, click the **Template option button** in the right pane, then click **Create**

☐ Make any formatting or layout changes, click the **Save button** 🖫 on the Quick Access Toolbar to open the Save As dialog box, type a meaningful name in the File name text box, navigate to an appropriate location, then click **Save**

OR

☐ Click the **File tab**, click **New**, click the **My templates button**

☐ In the New dialog box, click a template from the Personal Templates tab, click the **Template option button**, then click **OK**

☐ Make any formatting or layout changes, click the **Save button** 🖫 on the Quick Access Toolbar to open the Save As dialog box, type a meaningful name in the File name text box, navigate to an appropriate location, then click **Save**

Create a New Template

Ribbon Method

☐ Open or create a document, click the **File tab**, click **Save As**, click the **Save as type list arrow**, click **Word Template**, type a meaningful name in the File name text box, navigate to an appropriate location, then click **Save**

OR

☐ Click the **File tab**, click **New**, click the **Sample templates button**, click a template, click the **Template option button** in the right pane, then click **Create**

☐ Make any formatting or layout changes, click the **Save button** 🖫 on the Quick Access Toolbar to open the Save As dialog box

☐ Type a meaningful name in the File name text box, navigate to an appropriate location, then click **Save**

  OR

☐ Click the **File tab**, click **New**, click the **My templates button**

☐ In the New dialog box, click a template from the Personal Templates tab, click the **Template option button**, then click **OK**

☐ Make any formatting or layout changes, click the **Save button** 🔲 on the Quick Access Toolbar to open the Save As dialog box

☐ Type a meaningful name in the File name text box, navigate to an appropriate location, then click **Save**

Apply a Template to an Existing Document

Ribbon Method

☐ Click the **File tab**, click **New**, click the **New from existing button**, navigate to an existing template or document, then click **Create New**

☐ Make any formatting or layout changes, click the **Save button** 🔲 on the Quick Access Toolbar to open the Save As dialog box

☐ Type a meaningful name in the File name text box, navigate to an appropriate location, then click **Save**

Manage Templates by Using the Organizer

Ribbon Method

☐ Open a template

☐ Click the **File tab**, click **Options** to open the Word Options dialog box

☐ Click **Add-Ins** in the left pane, click the **Manage list arrow** in the right pane, click **Templates**, then click the **Go button**

☐ In the Templates and Add-Ins dialog box, click the **Organizer button**

☐ In the Organizer dialog box, shown in Figure WDX 1-8, select styles in the left column from the open template to delete, rename, or copy to the normal template in the right column and vice versa, then click **Close**

Figure WDX 1-8   **Organizer dialog box**

Review Questions

True/False

Circle T if the statement is true or F if the statement is false.

T   F   1. You cannot change the default save location.

T   F   2. You can change spelling and grammar checking options in the Proofing section of the Word Options dialog box.

T   F   3. You can save any Word document as a template using the Save As dialog box.

T   F   4. The Signature Line button is located on the Review tab.

T   F   5. A Word template is saved with a .docx extension.

Matching

Match the correct term in Column 2 to its description in Column 1.

Column 1	**Column 2**
_____ 1. Contains commands for restricting editing and encrypting documents with a password.	A. Restrict Editing
_____ 2. A choice in the New section of backstage view that lets you open a template as a template.	B. Protect Document button
_____ 3. A command used to control who can make changes to a document and what kind of changes they can make.	C. Organizer dialog box
_____ 4. Used with a digital ID to authenticate a document.	D. Template option button
_____ 5. Lets you rename and delete styles in a template or copy styles between templates.	E. Signature Line

Projects

Project WDX 1-1

1. Open the data file **Project WDX 1-1.docx**.

2. Save the document as **Signature Letter.docx**.

3. Position the insertion point at the bottom of the letter below the *Mark Hanson* line.

4. Insert a line for a digital signature with the following information:

   Perry Watkins

   Courier

   perrywatkins@mail.net

5. Apply editing restrictions to the document, allowing no changes (Read only).

6. Start enforcing protection and use the password **Sig#1***

7. Change the date to August 10. Notice that you cannot make changes to the document.

8. Stop the protection, enter the password, and change the *7* to **10** in the date.

9. Save and close the document.

Project WDX 1-2

1. Locate the Equity Fax template in the Sample Templates category in backstage view.

2. Create a new template based on the Equity Fax template.

3. Select the word *Fax* and change the font to Wide Latin.

4. Select the remaining text and change the font size to 14.

5. Save the template as **NewFax.dotx** in the location where you save your data files and close the document.

6. In the New section of backstage view, click the New from existing button and navigate to the NewFax template and then click **Create New**.

7. Replace the placeholder data in the fax with the following:

   To: **James Smith**

   Fax: **214-555-0123**

   Phone: **214-555-0019**

   Re: **Receipts**

   From: **Mary Washington**

   Pages: **2**

   Date: **3.2.2015**

   Comments: **Here is a copy of the receipt for my purchases related to our project. Thank you for reimbursing these expenses in a timely manner.**

8. Save the file as a document named **SmithFax.docx** and close the document.

CRITICAL THINKING

Activity WDX 1-1

Open a template that you think would be of use to you, such as a letter that you could use again and again. Modify the template to your specifications with your name and information. Save it as a new template with a meaningful name.

Activity WDX 1-2

Personalize your copy of Word by completing the following tasks. If you are working on a shared computer or in a lab, reverse all of the steps after you finish.

- Change the default save location to the folder where you save your solution files.
- In the Word Options dialog box, change the username and initials to yours. If yours are already there, add a third name, such as your middle name, and a third initial.

WORD EXPERT OBJECTIVE 2: FORMATTING CONTENT

APPLY ADVANCED FONT AND PARAGRAPH ATTRIBUTES

Use Character Attributes

☐ Select the text to which you want to apply a character format, then use Table WDX 2-1 as a reference to apply the character formatting you want

Table WDX 2-1   Applying Character Attributes

Attribute to apply	Ribbon Method: Home tab/Font group	Shortcut Method: Mini toolbar	Shortcut Method: Keyboard	Launcher in the Font group: Font dialog box
Apply a new font	Click the **Font list arrow**, then click a font	Click the **Font list arrow**, then click a font	Press **[Ctrl] [Shift] [F]**, click the **Font scroll bar**, then click a font	Click the **Font scroll bar**, then click a font
Apply a new font size	Click the **Font Size list arrow**, then click a font size, or type a value in the Font Size text box	Click the **Font Size scroll bar**, then click a font size, or type a value in the Font Size text box	Press **[Ctrl] [Shift] [P]**, then click the **Font Size scroll bar** and click a font size; or type the value in the Font Size text box	Click the **Font size scroll bar**, then click a font size; or type the value in the Font Size text box
Increase the font size one increment	Click the **Grow Font button** A˙	Click the **Grow Font button** A˙	Press **[Ctrl] [>]**	
Decrease the font size one increment	Click the **Shrink Font button** A˅	Click the **Shrink Font button** A˅	Press **[Ctrl] [<]**	
Clear formatting	Click the **Clear Formatting button**		Right-click, click the **Styles command** on the Shortcut menu, then click **Clear Formatting**	
Apply bold	Click the **Bold button** B	Click the **Bold button** B	Press **[Ctrl] [B]**	Click **Bold** in the Font style list
Apply italics	Click the **Italic button** I	Click the **Italic button** I	Press **[Ctrl] [I]**	Click **Italic** in the Font style list
Apply underlining	Click the **Underline button** U, or click the **Underline list arrow** U ˅, select a preformatted underline or click More Underlines to open the Font dialog box, then refer to the directions in the last column	Click the **Underline button** U	Press **[Ctrl] [U]**	Click the **Underline style list arrow** and select a style, click the **Underline color list arrow**, select a color, then click **OK**
Apply strikethrough	Click the **Strikethrough button** abc			Click the **Strikethrough check box** in the Effects section
Apply subscript	Click the **Subscript button** x₂		Press **[Ctrl] [=]**	Click the **Subscript check box** in the Effects section

(continued)

Table WDX 2-1 Applying Character Attributes (continued)

Attribute to apply	Ribbon Method: Home tab/Font group	Shortcut Method: Mini toolbar	Shortcut Method: Keyboard	Launcher in the Font group: Font dialog box
Apply superscript	Click the **Superscript button** x^2		Press **[Ctrl] [Shift] [+]**	Click the **Superscript check box** in the Effects section
Apply highlighting to text	Click the **Text Highlight Color button** 🖍 to apply the active highlight color or click the **Text Highlight Color list arrow** 🖍, then select a new color	Click the **Text Highlight Color button** 🖍 to apply the active highlight color or click the **Text Highlight Color list arrow** 🖍, then select a new color		
Apply a new font color	Click the **Font Color button** **A** to apply the active font color or click the **Font Color list arrow** **A**, then select a color from a palette of available colors; or click **More Colors**, then create a custom color	Click the **Font Color button** **A** to apply the active font color or click the **Font Color list arrow** **A**, then select a color from a palette of available colors; or click **More Colors**, then create a custom color		Click the **Font Color list arrow** to select a color from a palette of available colors; or click **More Colors** to create a custom color
Change Case	Click the **Change Case button** **Aa**			Click an option in the Effects section then click **OK**
Apply Text Effects	Click the **Text Effects button** **A**			Click the **Text Effects button** and choose options in the Format Text Effects dialog box, click **Close**, then click **OK**
Scale Fonts				Click the **Advanced tab**, click the **Scale list arrow**, choose an appropriate option, then click **OK**
Expand or Condense Character Spacing				Click the **Advanced tab**, click the **Spacing list arrow**, click **Expanded** or **Condensed**, click an appropriate option in the By box, then click **OK**
Raise or Lower Font Position				Click the **Advanced tab**, click the **Position list arrow**, choose Raised or Lowered, click an appropriate option in the By box, then click **OK**
Adjust Kerning				Click the **Advanced tab**, click the **Kerning for fonts check box**, click an appropriate option in the Points and above box, then click **OK**

Word

Use Character-Specific Styles
Ribbon Method
☐ Select the text, click the **Home tab**, click the **More button** ⬇ in the Styles group, then click an appropriate character Quick Style from the gallery, as shown in Figure WDX 2-1

Figure WDX 2-1   Quick Styles gallery

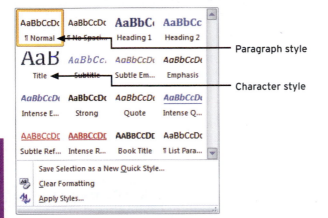

OR
☐ Select the text, click the **Home tab**, then click the **launcher** ▧ in the Styles group to open the Styles task pane
☐ Scroll the list of available styles, then click an appropriate character style

Shortcut Method
☐ Select the text, right-click, then click the **Styles command** on the shortcut menu
☐ Click a character Quick Style in the gallery that opens or click **Apply Styles** at the bottom of the gallery to open the Apply Styles dialog box, click the **Style Name list arrow**, select a style, then close the dialog box

> ## NOTE
>
> A character style contains attributes that only apply to text, such as font, font size, and font color. A paragraph style contains attributes that include paragraph formatting, such as alignment and spacing. A paragraph style contains a ¶ symbol next to it in the Quick Styles gallery.

CREATE TABLES AND CHARTS

Insert a Table
Ribbon Method
☐ Click the **Insert tab**, click the **Table button** in the Tables group, then click **Insert Table** to display the Insert Table dialog box
☐ Type a number in the Number of columns text box, then type a number in the Number of rows text box
☐ Set other options as appropriate, then click **OK**
☐ Use the Table Tools Design and Layout tabs to modify the table to your specifications

Insert Tables by Using Microsoft Excel Data in Tables

Ribbon Method

☐ Click the **Insert tab**, click the **Table button** in the Tables group, then click **Excel Spreadsheet** to open a blank spreadsheet, as shown in Figure WDX 2-2

☐ Type data in the spreadsheet and use the commands on the Ribbon as needed to format data

☐ Click outside the spreadsheet

> ### NOTE
>
> You can double-click a spreadsheet to edit the data.

Figure WDX 2-2   **Excel Spreadsheet**

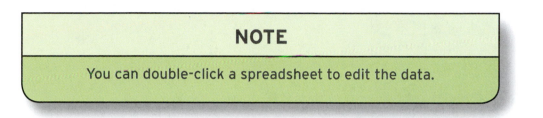

Excel Spreadsheet
in a Word document

Apply Formulas or Calculations on a Table
Ribbon Method
- ☐ Create the table, click the cell, click the **Table Tools Layout tab**, then click the **Formula button** in the Data group
- ☐ In the Formula dialog box, shown in Figure WDX 2-3, enter the appropriate options, then click **OK**

Figure WDX 2-3 **Formula dialog box**

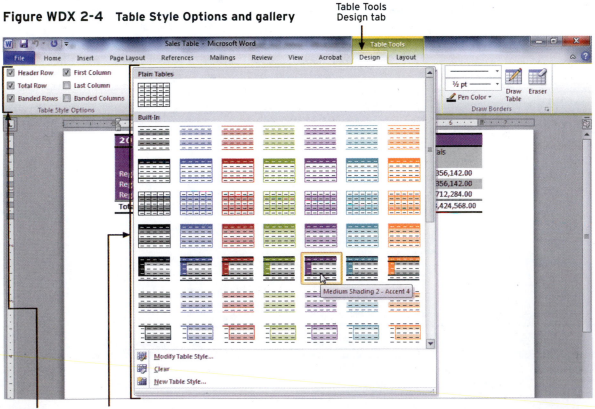

Apply Table Styles and Options
Ribbon Method
- ☐ With a table selected, click the **Table Tools Design tab**
- ☐ In the Table Style Options group, as shown in Figure WDX 2-4, click the check boxes next to the special formatting options that you want to apply to the table
- ☐ Click the **More button** ⬇ in the Table Styles group to display the Table Styles gallery
- ☐ Click a **table style** in the gallery

Figure WDX 2-4 **Table Style Options and gallery**

Insert a Chart
Ribbon Method
☐ Click the **Insert tab**, then click the **Chart button** in the Illustrations group
☐ In the left pane of the Insert Chart dialog box, shown in Figure WDX 2-5, click the **chart type**, click the **thumbnail** for the desired chart in the center pane, then click **OK**
☐ The screen splits into two windows: A Word window on the left with the sample chart on the document, and an Excel window on the right with sample data in the worksheet
☐ Replace the sample data in the Excel worksheet with the labels and values for your chart
☐ Close the Microsoft Excel window
☐ Use the Chart Tools Design, Layout, and Format tabs to modify the chart to your specifications

Figure WDX 2-5   Insert Chart dialog box

Modify Chart Data
Ribbon Method
☐ Select the chart, click the **Chart Tools Design tab**, then click the **Edit Data button** in the Data group
☐ Modify the data in the Excel spreadsheet and close it

Save a Chart as a Template
☐ Select the chart, click the **Chart Tools Design tab**, then click the **Save As Template button** in the Type group
☐ Navigate to the location where you want to save the template, type a name in the file name box, then click **Save**

Modify Chart Layout

Ribbon Method

☐ With a chart selected, click the **Chart Tools Design tab**, then click the **More button** ▾ in the Chart Layouts group to open the Chart Layouts gallery, shown in Figure WDX 2-6

☐ Click a **chart layout** in the gallery

Figure WDX 2-6 **Chart Layouts gallery**

Modify Chart Styles

Ribbon Method

☐ With a chart selected, click the **Chart Tools Design tab**, then click the **More button** ▾ in the Chart Styles group

☐ Click a **chart style** in the gallery

Change Chart Type

Ribbon Method

☐ With a chart selected, click the **Chart Tools Design tab**, then click the **Change Chart Type button** in the Type group

☐ In the Change Chart Type dialog box, click a **chart type**, then click **OK**

Add or Modify a Chart Title

Ribbon Method

☐ With a chart selected, click the **Chart Tools Layout tab**, then click the **Chart Title button** in the Labels group

☐ Click an option from the menu

☐ Click the chart title to edit it

Add or Change the Location of the Legend

Ribbon Method

☐ With a chart selected, click the **Chart Tools Layout tab**, then click the **Legend button** in the Labels group

☐ Click an option from the menu

Add or Change the Location of Data Labels

Ribbon Method

☐ With a chart selected, click the **Chart Tools Layout tab**, then click the **Data Labels button** in the Labels group

☐ Click an option from the menu

CONSTRUCT REUSABLE CONTENT IN A DOCUMENT

Create Customized Building Blocks

Ribbon Method

- ☐ Position the insertion point in the desired location of a header, footer, or other building block
- ☐ Click the **Insert tab**, click the **Quick Parts button** in the Text group, click **Document Property**, then click an option from the menu
- ☐ Type the text for the document property
- ☐ Position the insertion point at another location and follow the steps in bullets 2-3 to insert additional document properties, if desired

  OR

- ☐ Position the insertion point in the desired location, click the **Insert tab**, click the **Quick Parts button** in the Text group, then click **Field**
- ☐ In the Field dialog box, shown in Figure WDX 2-7, scroll the Field names list box as needed, click the name of the appropriate field, select additional properties associated with the field in the Field properties list box as needed, then click **OK**

Figure WDX 2-7   Field dialog box

Save a Selection as a Quick Part

Ribbon Method

□ Create the frequently used data, including text and/or images, then select it

□ Click the **Insert tab**, click the **Quick Parts button** in the Text group, then click **Save Selection to Quick Part Gallery**

□ In the Create New Building Block dialog box, shown in Figure WDX 2-8, type a unique name, make any other appropriate changes or selections in the dialog box, then click **OK**

Figure WDX 2-8 **Create New Building Block dialog box**

Save Quick Parts After a Document is Saved

Ribbon Method

□ Create and save the quick part using the steps in bullets 1-3 of Save a Selection as a Quick Part Ribbon Method

□ Save and close all open documents and exit Word

□ In the Microsoft Word dialog box that opens, shown in Figure WDX 2-9, click **Save** to save the quick part to the Building Blocks Gallery

Figure WDX 2-9 **Microsoft Word dialog box**

Insert Text as a Quick Part

Ribbon Method

☐ Position the insertion point in the desired location

☐ Click the **Insert tab**, click the **Quick Parts button** in the Text group, click **AutoText**, then click an option from the gallery to insert it

Add Content to a Header or Footer

Ribbon Method

☐ Create a quick part using the steps in bullets 1-3 of the Save Selection as a Quick Part Ribbon Method

☐ Insert a blank header or footer and position the insertion point in the desired location

☐ Click the **Header & Footer Tools Design tab**, click the **Quick Parts button** in the Insert group, then click a quick part displayed in the gallery to insert it

☐ Click the **Close Header and Footer button** in the Close group

LINK SECTIONS

Link a Text Box to Another Text Box

Ribbon Method

☐ Create a text box and fill it with text, then create a second empty text box

☐ Select the first text box, be sure the Drawing Tools Format tab is the active tab, then click the **Create Link button** in the Text group to activate the Pitcher pointer

☐ Click the second text box with the Pitcher pointer to link it to the first text box

Break Links Between Text Boxes

Ribbon Method

☐ Select the first text box that is linked

☐ On the Drawing Tools Format tab, click the **Break Link button** in the Text group

Link Different Sections

Ribbon Method

☐ Position the insertion point where you want to insert a section break

☐ Click the **Page Layout tab**, click the **Breaks button**, then click the appropriate section break

☐ Click in the header or footer in the new section

☐ On the Header & Footer Tools Design tab, in the Navigation group, the **Link to Previous button** will be turned on automatically and will be displayed with an orange background. If you want to break the link and use a different header or footer in the new section, click the **Link to Previous button** to turn it off

REVIEW QUESTIONS

FILL IN THE BLANK

Complete the following sentences by writing the correct word or words in the blanks provided.

1. A _____ is used to calculate data in a table.

2. Pie, line, and bar are all types of _____.

3. The Link to Previous button is used to link headers or footers in different _____.

4. The options for adjusting Kerning are located in the _____ tab of the Font dialog box.

5. A _____ identifies the patterns or colors of the data series or categories in a chart.

MULTIPLE CHOICE

Select the best response for the following statements.

1. A _____ style contains attributes that only apply to text.
   - A. paragraph
   - B. character
   - C. quick
   - D. gallery

2. The command for inserting an Excel spreadsheet is located on the _____ button.
   - A. Excel
   - B. Quick Parts
   - C. Table
   - D. Chart

3. _____ are saved in the Building Blocks Organizer.
   - A. Tables
   - B. Charts
   - C. Fields
   - D. Quick Parts

4. Use the _____ button to link two text boxes.
   - A. Create Link
   - B. Link to Previous
   - C. Break Link
   - D. Text Box

5. AutoText is a type of _____.
   - A. table
   - B. text box
   - C. chart
   - D. quick part

PROJECTS

Note: If you are working in a lab or on a shared computer, use the Building Blocks Organizer to delete any Quick Parts you create or modify after completing all projects and activities.

Project WDX 2-1

1. Open the data file **Project WDX 2-1.docx**.
2. Insert a new row below the Region 3 row and type **Totals** in the first cell of the new row.
3. Insert a new column to the right of the Fourth Quarter column and type **Totals** in the row to the right of Fourth Quarter.
4. Merge the cells in the title row.
5. Enter a formula in the last row of each column that sums all the numbers in the columns. Use the number format with the dollar sign ($) at the beginning.
6. Position the insertion point in the last column.
7. Enter a formula in the last column of each row that sums all the numbers in the rows. Use the number format with the dollar sign ($) at the beginning.
8. Change the title of the table to **2015 Sales by Quarter and by Region**.
9. Scale the title to 150% and use expanded spacing of 1 pt.
10. Apply the Medium Shading 2 – Accent 4 table style, the fifth option on the fifth row.
11. Turn on the Total Row Table Style Option.
12. Save the document as **Sales Table.docx** and close it.

Project WDX 2-2

1. Create a new blank document.
2. Create a Line with Markers chart using the following data:

	Product 1	Product 2	Product 3
North	10,003	13,980	5,456
South	8,098	14,098	7,376
East	11,345	15,584	10,986
West	23,004	9,345	20,098

3. Change the chart to a Clustered Column chart.
4. Add data labels using the Outside End option.
5. Format the chart using Style 23 from the Chart Styles gallery.
6. Change the chart to a Stacked Cylinder chart.
7. Change the chart layout to Layout 1.
8. Type **Sales by Region** as the chart title.
9. Save the document as **Profits.docx** and close it.

Project WDX 2-3

1. Open the data file **Project WDX 2-3.docx**.
2. Select the Consolidated Messenger clip art and text at the top of the document and save it as a quick part to the Building Blocks Organizer using Consolidated Messenger as the title.
3. Close the document without saving.
4. Create a new blank document.

5. Insert the Consolidated Messenger quick part.

6. Save the document as **Letterhead.docx** and close it.

7. Don't save changes to the Building Blocks gallery.

CRITICAL THINKING

Activity WDX 2-1

Create a new blank document and insert the Consolidated Messenger building block that you saved in Project WDX 2-3. Change the Consolidated Messenger title to a different color, style, and font, and resave it as a quick part using the same name. If you work on a shared computer, you may need to delete this Quick Part using the Building Blocks Organizer.

Activity WDX 2-2

Create a pie chart that shows how you use your time on a typical day. Be sure to account for all 24 hours in a day. Replace the sample data with your own data. Experiment with the format and change chart attributes until your chart is complete. Be prepared to present your chart to the class. Do you think you spend your time wisely? Why or why not? Save it with a meaningful name.

Word

WORD EXPERT OBJECTIVE 3: TRACKING AND REFERENCING DOCUMENTS

REVIEW, COMPARE, AND COMBINE DOCUMENTS

Apply Tracking
Ribbon Method
- ☐ To turn on the Track Changes feature, click the **Review tab**, then click the **Track Changes button** in the Tracking group
- ☐ To turn off the Track Changes feature, click the **Review tab**, then click the **Track Changes button** in the Tracking group

Shortcut Method
- ☐ To turn on the Track Changes feature, press **[CTRL][SHIFT][E]**
- ☐ To turn off the Track Changes feature, press **[CTRL][SHIFT][E]**

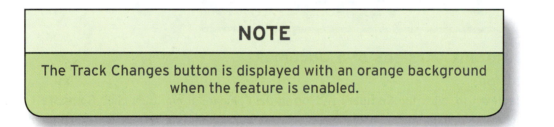

NOTE

The Track Changes button is displayed with an orange background when the feature is enabled.

Accept and Reject Changes
Ribbon Method
- ☐ Click the **Review tab**, click the **Next button** in the Changes group, then review the tracked change
- ☐ Click the **Reject list arrow** in the Changes group, then select the appropriate option
  - OR
- ☐ Click the **Accept list arrow** in the Changes group, then select the appropriate option
- ☐ Click the **Next button** to move to the next tracked change or click the **Previous button** to move to the previous tracked change

Merge Different Versions of a Document
Ribbon Method
- ☐ Click the **Review tab**, click the **Compare button** in the Compare group, then click **Combine**
- ☐ In the Combine Documents dialog box, navigate to and select the original document, then navigate to and select the revised document
- ☐ Click the **More button**, if necessary, to display additional options
- ☐ Click the **New document option button** in the Show changes in section, as shown in Figure WDX 3-1, select other options as appropriate, then click **OK**
- ☐ To change which document versions are displayed, click the **Compare button** in the Compare group, click **Show Source Documents**, then click to hide, show the original, show the revised, or show both documents
- ☐ If you wish to save the new combined document, click the **Save button** 🖫 on the Quick Access Toolbar, type a name in the file name box, then click **Save**. If you do not want to save the combined document, click the **Close button** ✖, then click **Don't Save**

Figure WDX 3-1   Combine Documents dialog box

Combine Documents	? ✕

Original document:
Project WDX 3-3a

Label unmarked changes with: Your Name

Revised document:
Project WDX 3-3b

Label unmarked changes with: Your Name

⇄

<< Less   OK   Cancel

Comparison settings

☑ Insertions and deletions   ☑ Tables
☑ Moves   ☑ Headers and footers
☑ Comments   ☑ Footnotes and endnotes
☑ Formatting   ☑ Textboxes
☑ Case changes   ☑ Fields
☑ White space

Show changes

Show changes at: Show changes in:
○ Character level   ○ Original document
◉ Word level   ○ Revised document
                                  ◉ New document

Compare Different Versions of a Document

Ribbon Method

☐ Click the **Review tab**, click the **Compare button** in the Compare group, then click **Compare**

☐ In the Compare Documents dialog box, navigate to and select the original document, then navigate to and select the revised document

☐ Click the **More button**, if necessary, to display additional options

☐ Click the **New document option button** in the Show changes in section, select other options as appropriate, then click **OK**

☐ To change which document versions are displayed, click the **Compare button** in the Compare group, click **Show Source Documents**, then click to hide, show the original, show the revised, or show both documents

Track Changes and Review Comments in a Combined Document

Ribbon Method

☐ Click the **Review tab**, click the **Compare button** in the Compare group, then click **Combine**

☐ In the Combine documents dialog box, navigate to and select the original document, then navigate to and select the revised document

☐ Click the **More button**, if necessary, to display additional options

☐ In the Comparison Settings section, make sure check marks appear beside all desired options

☐ In the Show changes section, click the Character level or Word level option button as desired

☐ Click the **New document option button** in the Show changes in section, then click **OK**

☐ View a summary of tracked changes and comments in the Reviewing pane, shown in Figure WDX 3-2

☐ View tracked changes in the Combined Document pane

☐ To change which document versions are displayed, click the **Compare button** in the Compare group, click **Show Source Documents**, then hide, show the original, show the revised, or show both documents

☐ Click the **Track Changes button** in the Tracking group to turn on tracking changes for future revisions

☐ Click the **Save button** 💾 on the Quick Access Toolbar, type a name in the file name box, then click **Save**

Figure WDX 3-2 Combine Result

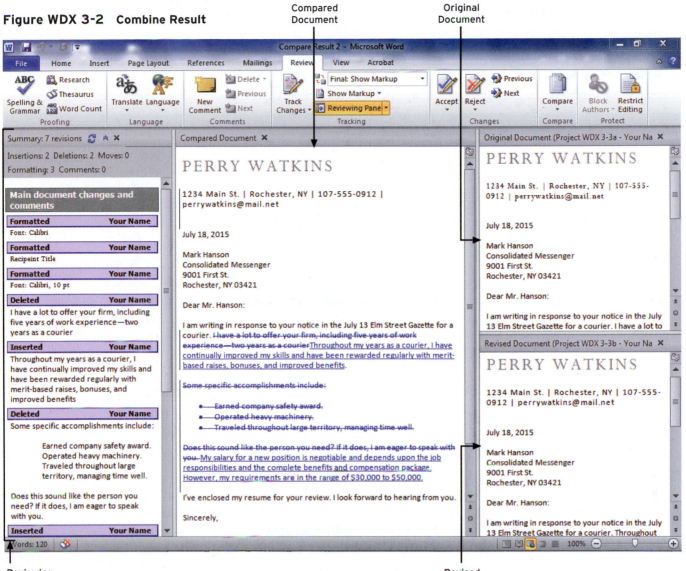

Compared Document

Original Document

Reviewing Pane

Revised Document

Show Tracked Changes and Comments by Reviewer

Ribbon Method

☐ Click the **Review tab**, click the **Display for Review list arrow** in the Tracking group, then click **Final: Show Markup** to show all tracked changes

OR

☐ Click the **Show Markup list arrow** in the Tracking group, point to **Reviewers**, then **All Reviewers** or select the reviewer(s) you want to view

CREATE A REFERENCE PAGE

Add Citations

Ribbon Method

☐ Click the **References tab**, click the **Insert Citation list arrow** in the Citations & Bibliography group, then click **Add New Source**

☐ In the Create Source dialog box, shown in Figure WDX 3-3, enter the appropriate information, then click **OK**

Figure WDX 3-3   Create Source dialog box

Manage Sources

Ribbon Method

☐ Click the **References tab**, then click the **Manage Sources button** in the Citations & Bibliography group

☐ In the Source Manager dialog box, select the **source** you want to edit, then click the **Edit button**

☐ Enter the appropriate information in the Edit Source dialog box, click **OK**, answer **Yes/No** if prompted, then click **Close**

   OR

☐ Click a citation, click the **content control list arrow**, click **Edit Source**, then follow bullet 3 in the Manage Sources Ribbon Method above

Compile a Bibliography

Ribbon Method

☐ Press **[Ctrl][End]** to move to the end of the document, then press **[Ctrl][Enter]** to create a new blank page

☐ Click the **References tab**, then click the **Bibliography button** in the Citations & Bibliography group to display the gallery shown in Figure WDX 3-4

☐ To insert a built-in Bibliography content control, click **Bibliography** in the Built-In section

☐ To insert a built-in Works cited content control, click **Works Cited** in the Built-In section

☐ To insert a bibliography, click **Insert Bibliography**

Figure WDX 3-4   Bibliography button and gallery

Modify Bibliographies

Shortcut Method

☐ Add sources and citations as needed, then select the **Bibliography**

☐ Right-click, then click **Update Field** or click **Update Citations and Bibliography** in the title bar of a content control

Apply Cross References

Ribbon Method

☐ Position the insertion point where you want to insert the cross reference

☐ Click the **Insert tab**, then click the **Cross-reference button** in the Links group

☐ In the Cross-reference dialog box, click the **Reference type list arrow** and click an appropriate option from the list

☐ Click the **Insert reference to list arrow** and click an appropriate option from the list

☐ In the For which section, click the appropriate option from the list

　OR

☐ Position the insertion point where you want to insert the cross reference

☐ Click the **References tab**, then click the **Cross-reference button** in the Captions group

☐ Follow the steps in bullets 3-5 in the Apply Cross References Ribbon Method above

Select Reference Styles such as APA or MLA

Ribbon Method

☐ Open a document with references, click the **References tab**, click the **Style list arrow** in the Citations & Bibliography group, then click an appropriate style

CREATE A TABLE OF AUTHORITIES IN A DOCUMENT

Mark Citations and Create a Table of Authorities

Ribbon Method

- ☐ Select all or part of the text you want to include as a reference in the Table of Authorities, click the **References tab**, then click the **Mark Citation button** in the Table of Authorities group
- ☐ In the Mark Citation dialog box, enter the appropriate information, then click **Mark**
- ☐ Continue to follow the steps in bullets 1–2 above to mark references to include in the Table of Authorities
- ☐ Position the insertion point where you want the Table of Authorities to be placed, click the **Insert Table of Authorities button** 🖼 in the Table of Authorities group, enter appropriate information on the Table of Authorities tab in the Table of Authorities dialog box, then click **OK**

Apply Default Formats to a Table of Authorities

Ribbon Method

- ☐ Click the **Insert Table of Authorities button** 🖼 in the Table of Authorities group to open the Table of Authorities dialog box, shown in Figure WDX 3-5
- ☐ Click the **Formats list arrow**, choose a format from the list, then click **OK**
- ☐ Click **OK** in the Microsoft Word dialog box that opens asking if you want to replace the selected category of the Table of Authorities

Figure WDX 3-5 **Table of Authorities dialog box**

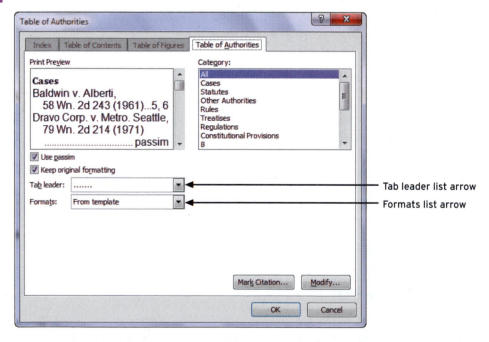

Adjust Alignment

Ribbon Method

- ☐ Select the Table of Authorities title, click **Home tab**, then click an alignment option in the Paragraph group
  OR
- ☐ Click the **Insert Table of Authorities button** 🖼 in the Table of Authorities group, then click the **Modify button** on the Table of Authorities tab in the Table of Authorities dialog box
- ☐ In the Style dialog box, enter appropriate information or click the **Modify button** to open the Modify Style dialog box and select alignment options, then click **OK** as needed to close all open dialog boxes

Apply a Tab Leader
Ribbon Method
☐ Click the **Insert Table of Authorities button** 🗃 in the Table of Authorities group to open the Table of Authorities dialog box
☐ Click the **Tab leader list arrow**, choose a format from the list, then click **OK**
☐ Click **OK** in the Microsoft Word dialog box that opens asking if you want to replace the selected category of the Table of Authorities

Modify Styles
Ribbon Method
☐ Click the **Insert Table of Authorities button** 🗃 in the Table of Authorities group, then click the **Modify button** on the Table of Authorities tab in the Table of Authorities dialog box
☐ In the Style dialog box, enter appropriate information or click the **Modify button** to open the Modify Style dialog box and select options, then click **OK** as needed to close all open dialog boxes

Use Passim (Short Form)
Ribbon Method
☐ Click the **Insert Table of Authorities button** 🗃 in the Table of Authorities group to open the Table of Authorities dialog box
☐ Click the **Use passim check box**, then click **OK**
☐ Click **OK** in the Microsoft Word dialog box that opens asking if you want to replace the selected category of the Table of Authorities

Update a Table of Authorities
Ribbon Method
☐ Click the **Update Table of Authorities button** 🗃 in the Table of Authorities group
Shortcut Method
☐ Right-click a section (such as cases, rules, and so on) of the Table of Authorities, then click **Update Field**

CREATE AN INDEX IN A DOCUMENT

Mark Index Entries
Ribbon Method
☐ Select the text you want to mark as an index entry, click the **References tab**, then click the **Mark Entry button** in the Index group to open the Mark Index Entry dialog box
☐ Verify that the text you selected appears in the Main entry text box in the Index section, or adjust the Mark Index Entry dialog box as needed to create an appropriate type of index entry (such as subentry, cross-reference)
☐ Click **Mark** to mark only the selected text as the index entry or click **Mark All** to include all instances of the selected text in the index, then click **Close**

Create an Index and Specify Type, Columns, and Language
Ribbon Method
☐ Position the insertion point where you want the index to appear
☐ Click the **References tab**, then click the **Insert Index button** in the Index group to open the Index dialog box shown in Figure WDX 3-6
☐ In the Type section, click the Indented or Run-in option button
☐ In the Columns box, click the up and down arrows to specify the number of columns
☐ Click the Language list arrow to specify the language
☐ Select a predefined Format, select other desired settings, then click **OK**

Figure WDX 3-6   Index dialog box

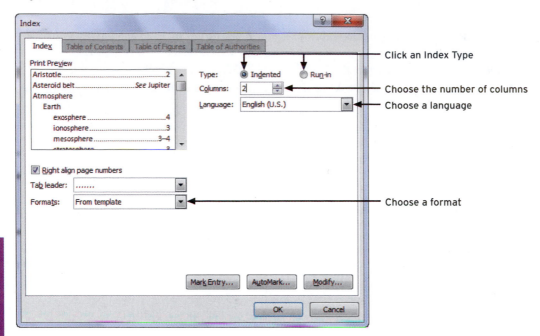

Modify an Index

Ribbon Method

☐ Scroll to the index, click the **References tab**, then click the **Insert Index button** in the Index group

☐ In the Index dialog box, select a new format and make other changes as appropriate, then click **OK**

☐ Click **Yes** to replace the selected index

Update an Index

Ribbon Method

☐ Mark more entries or change marked entries

☐ Click an entry in the Index to select the index, click the **References tab**, then click the **Update Index button** in the Index group

☐ Click the Index head (or anywhere in the document) to deselect the index

Shortcut Method

☐ Mark more entries or change marked entries

☐ Right-click the index, then click **Update Field** on the shortcut menu that opens

☐ Click the Index head (or anywhere in the document) to deselect the index

REVIEW QUESTIONS

TRUE/FALSE

Circle T if the statement is true or F if the statement is false.

T   F   1. A cross-reference refers the reader to another place in the document.

T   F   2. A citation refers to a source in the bibliography.

T   F   3. You cannot combine two documents into an existing document.

T   F   4. The Track Changes button toggles off and on to enable and disable track changes.

T   F   5. You do not have to mark entries to create and Index.

MATCHING

Match the correct term in Column 2 to its description in Column 1.

Column 1	Column 2
_____ 1. Used to agree with a change and move to the next one.	A. Compare button
_____ 2. Allows you to identify words or phrases for the index.	B. Bibliography
_____ 3. Used to combine revisions from multiple authors.	C. Accept button
_____ 4. Allows you to modify the sources in a document.	D. Mark Entry button
_____ 5. Lists all the sources cited in a document.	E. Manage Sources button

PROJECTS

Project WDX 3-1

1. Open the data file **Project WDX 3-1.docx**.

2. On page 3, select the First Quarter Sales heading and mark it as an entry for indexing.

3. Mark the Regional Sales, National Sales, and International Sales headings as entries for indexing.

4. Insert a blank page at the end of the document and insert an index. Use the Modern format with 2 columns.

5. On page 3, select Introduction and mark it as an entry for indexing.

6. Select the index and update it.

7. Select the index and change the format to Bulleted with 1 column. *Note:* replace the index if necessary.

8. Position the insertion point before the F at the top of the last page, type **Index**, and press **Enter**.

9. Save the document as **Indexed Report.docx** and close the document.

Project WDX 3-2

1. Open the data file **Project WDX 3-2.docx**.

2. Save the document as **Newsletter Article.docx**.

3. Change the reference style to the MLA Sixth Edition style.

4. Position the insertion point after the first sentence of the second paragraph and insert a new citation. Add a new source as shown in Figure WDX 3-7.

Figure WDX 3-7   Create Source dialog box

5. Position the insertion point after the last sentence of the first paragraph under the Purpose heading.

6. Insert a new citation. Add a new source as shown in Figure WDX 3-8.

Figure WDX 3-8   Create Source dialog box

7. Position the insertion point after the last sentence of the third paragraph under the Purpose heading.

8. Insert a new citation. Choose the Cook source from the menu.

9. Position the insertion point after the last sentence of the fifth paragraph under the Content heading.

10. Insert a new citation. Add a new source as shown in Figure WDX 3-9.

Figure WDX 3-9   Create Source dialog box

11. Position the insertion point at the end of the document and insert the Built-in Bibliography.

12. Edit the Cook source. Change the month of publication from January to February.

13. Update the Bibliography.

14. Save the document and close it.

Project WDX 3-3

1. Open the following data files: **Project WDX 3-3a** and **Project WDX 3-3b**.

2. Compare and combine both documents into a new document, using Project WDX 3-3a as the original document and Project WDX 3-3b as the revised document.

3. Show both of the source documents.

4. Choose **Final** on the Display for Review button.

5. Choose **Final: Show Markup** on the Display for Review button.

6. Accept all the insertions and reject all the deletions.

7. Adjust spacing as necessary.

8. Hide both source documents.

9. Save the document as **Watkins Letter** and close it.

CRITICAL THINKING

Activity WDX 3-1

Search the Internet or the local classified ads for a job you are interested in. Write a letter to the potential employer, introducing yourself and describing your qualifications for the job. Name and save the file. Swap files with a classmate and review each other's work. Provide professional, helpful comments using the Reviewing tools in Word. Do not mark your formatting changes, but make sure that any text that you move is marked. Switch files again and use the Reviewing tools to accept or reject all the suggested changes. Compare the original version and the edited version and combine the changes to the original.

Word Objective 4: Performing Mail Merge Operations

Execute Mail Merge

Perform a Mail Merge

Ribbon Method

☐ Click the **Mailings tab**, click the **Start Mail Merge button** in the Start Mail Merge group, then click **Letters**

☐ Click the **Select Recipients button** in the Start Mail Merge group, click **Type New List** to display the New Address List dialog box, click **Use Existing List** to use a list that was created previously, or click **Select from Outlook Contacts**, then create the list or navigate to the file, select the file, then click **OK**

☐ Position the insertion point where you want to insert a field in the document, then use the buttons in the Write & Insert Fields group to insert an Address Block, a Greeting Line, or select a field from the menu that opens when you click the Insert Merge Field button arrow

☐ Repeat the step in bullet 3 until you have inserted all merge fields in your document

☐ Click the **Preview Results button** in the Preview Results group

☐ Click the **Finish & Merge button** in the Finish group, then click **Edit Individual Documents** to create a merge file that you can edit, click **Print Documents** to send the merged document directly to the printer, or click **Send E-mail Messages** to create e-mail messages

☐ Select appropriate options in the dialog box that opens, then click **OK**

Task Pane Method

☐ Click the **Mailings tab**, click the **Start Mail Merge button** in the Start Mail Merge group, then click **Step by Step Mail Merge Wizard**

☐ In the Mail Merge task pane, click the **Letters option button** (or another type of document you are working on), then click **Next: Starting document**

☐ In Step 2 of 6, click the **option button** next to the description of your starting document; if you select Start from a template or Start from an existing document, follow the onscreen directions to navigate to the file you want to use, click it, then click **OK** or **Open**; then click **Next: Select recipients**

☐ In Step 3 of 6, click the **option button** next to the recipient list you want to use, then follow the onscreen directions to create the list or navigate to and open an existing list, then click **Next: Write your letter**

☐ In Step 4 of 6, write your letter inserting merge fields where appropriate, click **More items** to select individual merge fields to insert, then click **Next: Preview your letters**

☐ In Step 5 of 6, use the **arrow buttons** in the task pane to preview your letters, make changes if necessary, then click **Next: Complete the merge**

☐ In Step 6 of 6, click **Print** to send the merged document directly to a printer or click **Edit individual letters** to create a merge file that you can edit if you'd like to personalize one or more of the letters before printing

Set Merge Rules

Ribbon Method

☐ Start the mail merge and select recipients using the steps in bullets 1-2 of Perform a Mail Merge Ribbon Method or bullets 1–4 of the Task Pane method above

☐ Click the **Rules button** in the Write & Insert Fields group, then click a rule to insert. Use Table WDX 4-1 as a reference

☐ If a dialog box opens, choose appropriate options and click **OK**

Table WDX 4-1   Merge Fields and Rules

Rule	Description
Ask	Repeats the same information in more than one place in a document
Fill-in	Allows you to insert information only once
If...Then...Else	Displays information based on a condition
Merge Record #	Displays the ordinal position of the current data record, reflecting any sorting or filtering applied to the data source
Merge Sequence #	Numbers each merged record sequentially
Next Record	Merges the next data record into the current merged document
Next Record If	Compares two expressions. Merges the next data record into the current merged document if the comparison is true, or it merges the next data record into a new merged document if the comparison is false
Set Bookmark	Allows you to assign text, a number, or other information to a bookmark
Skip Record If	Compares two expressions. Cancels the current merge document and moves to the next data record if the comparison is true, or it continues the current merge document if the comparison is false

Send Personalized E-Mail Messages to Multiple Recipients

Ribbon Method

☐ Click the **Mailings tab**, click the **Start Mail Merge button** in the Start Mail Merge group, then click **E-mail Messages**

☐ Click the **Select Recipients button** in the Start Mail Merge group, click **Type New List** to display the New Address List dialog box, click **Use Existing List** to use a list that was created previously and includes an e-mail address field, or click **Select from Outlook Contacts**, choose the contacts you want to include in the merge, then click **OK**

☐ Write the e-mail message, and position the insertion point where you want to insert a field, then use the buttons in the Write & Insert Fields group to insert fields in the e-mail message

☐ Click the **Preview Results button** in the Preview Results group

☐ Click the **Finish & Merge button** in the Finish group, then click **Send E-mail Messages** to open the Merge to E-mail dialog box, shown in Figure WDX 4-1

☐ Click the **To list arrow** and click the field that contains the e-mail addresses, choose other appropriate options, then click **OK** to send the merged e-mail messages

Figure WDX 4-1   Merge to E-mail dialog box

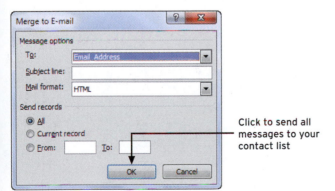

Click to send all messages to your contact list

Task Pane Method

☐ Click the **Mailings tab**, click the **Start Mail Merge button** in the Start Mail Merge group, then click **Step by Step Mail Merge Wizard**

☐ In the Mail Merge task pane, click the **E-mail messages button**, then click **Next: Starting document**

□ In Step 2 of 6, click the **option button** next to the description of your starting document; if you select Start from a template or Start from an existing document, follow the onscreen directions to navigate to the file you want to use, click it, then click **OK** or **Open**; then click **Next: Select recipients**

□ In Step 3 of 6, click the **option button** next to the recipient list you want to use, then follow the onscreen directions to create the list or navigate to and open an existing list, then click **Next: Write your e-mail message**

□ In Step 4 of 6, write your e-mail message, inserting merge fields where appropriate, click **More items** to select individual merge fields to insert, then click **Next: Preview your e-mail messages**

□ In Step 5 of 6, use the **arrow buttons** in the task pane to preview your letters, make changes if necessary, then click **Next: Complete the merge**

□ In Step 6 of 6, click **Electronic Mail** to open the Merge to E-mail dialog box

□ Click the **To list arrow**, click the field that contains the e-mail addresses, choose other appropriate options, then click **OK** to send the merged e-mail messages

CREATE A MAIL MERGE BY USING OTHER DATA SOURCES

Use Microsoft Outlook Tables as Data Sources for a Mail Merge Operation

Ribbon Method

□ Click the **Mailings tab**, click the **Start Mail Merge button** in the Start Mail Merge group, then click the **Letters** (or another option)

□ Click the **Select Recipients button** in the Start Mail Merge group, click **Select from Outlook Contacts**

□ In the Select Contacts dialog box, shown in Figure WDX 4-2, click a contact folder, then click **OK**

□ In the Mail Merge Recipients dialog box, select recipients for the merge, then click **OK**

□ Follow the steps in bullets 3-7 of Perform a Mail Merge Ribbon Method on page WDX-136

Figure WDX 4-2 **Select Contacts dialog box**

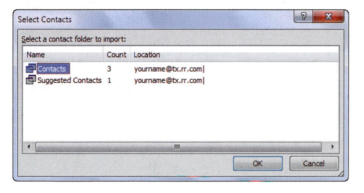

NOTE

Be thorough and cautious when selecting the contacts you want to send merged e-mail messages to. Once you click OK in the Merge to E-mail dialog box, the messages are sent.

Task Pane Method

☐ Click the **Mailings tab**, click the **Start Mail Merge button** in the Start Mail Merge group, then click **Step by Step Mail Merge Wizard**

☐ In the Mail Merge task pane, click the **Letters option button** (or another type of document you are working on), then click **Next: Starting document**

☐ In Step 2 of 6, click the **option button** next to the description of your starting document; if you select Start from a template or Start from an existing document, follow the onscreen directions to navigate to the file you want to use, click it, then click **OK** or **Open**; then click **Next: Select recipients**

☐ In Step 3 of 6, click the **Select from Outlook contacts option button**, click **Choose Contacts Folder** to open the Select Contacts dialog box, choose a contacts folder to use in the merge, then click **OK**

☐ In the Mail Merge Recipients dialog box, select contacts to include in the merge, click **OK**, then click **Next: Write your letter**

☐ Follow the steps in bullets 5-7 of Perform A Mail Merge Task Pane Method on page WDX-136

Use an Access Table as a Data Source for a Mail Merge Operation

Ribbon Method

☐ Click the **Mailings tab**, click the **Start Mail Merge button** in the Start Mail Merge group, then click the **Letters** (or another option)

☐ Click the **Select Recipients button** in the Start Mail Merge group, click **Use Existing List** as shown in Figure WDX 4-3

☐ In the Select Data Source dialog box, shown in Figure WDX 4-4, navigate to the location of the Access table, click it, then click **Open**

☐ Follow the steps in bullets 3-7 of Perform a Mail Merge Ribbon Method on page WDX-136

Figure WDX 4-3   **Select Recipients button and menu**

Figure WDX 4-4   Select Data Source dialog box

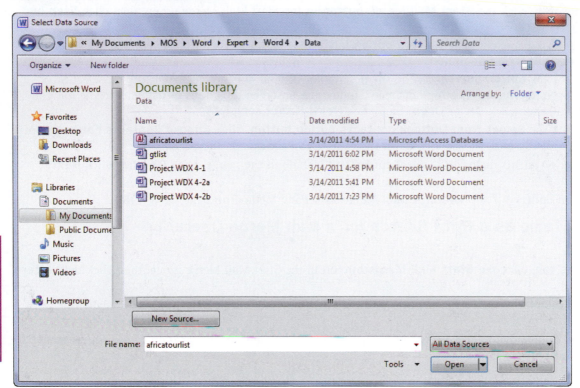

Task Pane Method

☐ Click the **Mailings tab**, click the **Start Mail Merge button** in the Start Mail Merge group, then click **Step by Step Mail Merge Wizard**

☐ In the Mail Merge task pane, click the **Letters option button** (or another type of document you are working on), then click **Next: Starting document**

☐ In Step 2 of 6, click the **option button** next to the description of your starting document; if you select Start from a template or Start from an existing document, follow the onscreen directions to navigate to the file you want to use, click it, then click **OK** or **Open**; then click **Next: Select recipients**

☐ In Step 3 of 6, click the **Use an existing list option button**, click **Browse** to open the Select Data Source dialog box, navigate to the location of the Access table, click it, then click **Open**

☐ Follow the steps in bullets 5-7 of Perform A Mail Merge Task Pane Method on page WDX-136

Use an Excel Table as a Data Source for a Mail Merge Operation

Ribbon Method

☐ Click the **Mailings tab**, click the **Start Mail Merge button** in the Start Mail Merge group, then click the **Letters** (or another option)

☐ Click the **Select Recipients button** in the Start Mail Merge group, click **Use Existing List**

☐ In the Select Data Source dialog box, navigate to the location of the Excel table, click it, then click **Open**

☐ Follow the steps in bullets 3-7 of Perform a Mail Merge Ribbon Method on page WDX-136

Task Pane Method

☐ Click the **Mailings tab**, click the **Start Mail Merge button** in the Start Mail Merge group, then click **Step by Step Mail Merge Wizard**

☐ In the Mail Merge task pane, click the **Letters option button** (or another type of document you are working on), then click **Next: Starting document**

☐ In Step 2 of 6, click the **option button** next to the description of your starting document; if you select Start from a template or Start from an existing document, follow the onscreen directions to navigate to the file you want to use, click it, then click **OK** or **Open**; then click **Next: Select recipients**

☐ In Step 3 of 6, click the **Use an existing list option button**, click **Browse** to open the Select Data Source dialog box, navigate to the location of the Excel table, click it, then click **Open**

☐ Follow the steps in bullets 5-7 of Perform A Mail Merge Task Pane Method on page WDX-136

Create a Word Table to Use as a Data Source for a Mail Merge Operation

Ribbon Method

☐ Open a blank word document, click the **Insert tab**, click the **Table button**, then click **Insert Table** to open the Insert Table dialog box, select appropriate options, then click **OK**

☐ Enter data in the table, reserving the top row for data fields (such as First, Last, Address, City, or E-mail Address)

☐ Save the table with a meaningful name in a location where you can find it easily, such as the My Data Sources folder in your Documents Library

Use a Word Table as a Data Source for a Mail Merge Operation

Ribbon Method

☐ Click the **Mailings tab**, click the **Start Mail Merge button** in the Start Mail Merge group, then click the **Letters** (or another option)

☐ Click the **Select Recipients button** in the Start Mail Merge group, click **Use Existing List**

☐ In the Select Data Source dialog box, navigate to the location of the Word table, click it, then click **Open**

☐ Follow the steps in bullets 3-7 of Perform a Mail Merge Ribbon Method on page WDX-136

Task Pane Method

☐ Click the **Mailings tab**, click the **Start Mail Merge button** in the Start Mail Merge group, then click **Step by Step Mail Merge Wizard**

☐ In the Mail Merge task pane, click the **Letters option button** (or another type of document you are working on), then click **Next: Starting document**

☐ In Step 2 of 6, click the **option button** next to the description of your starting document; if you select Start from a template or Start from an existing document, follow the onscreen directions to navigate to the file you want to use, click it, then click **OK** or **Open**; then click **Next: Select recipients**

☐ In Step 3 of 6, click the **Use an existing list option button**, click **Browse** to open the Select Data Source dialog box, navigate to the location of the Word table, click it, then click **Open**

☐ Follow the steps in bullets 5-7 of Perform A Mail Merge Task Pane Method on page WDX-136

CREATE LABELS AND FORMS

Prepare Data by Editing the Recipients List

Ribbon Method

☐ After a recipient list has been created or selected, click the **Edit Recipient List button** in the Start Mail Merge group to open the Mail Merge Recipients dialog box

☐ Insert and remove checkmarks beside records to include or exclude them from the merge

☐ To edit data in a record, click the **data source filename** in the Data Source box, click the **Edit button** to open the Edit Data Source dialog box, make necessary changes, then click **OK**

☐ To add a new record, click the **data source filename** in the Data Source box, click the **Edit button** to open the Edit Data Source dialog box, shown in Figure WDX 4-5, click the **New Entry button** to insert a blank record, type the data for the new record, then click **OK**

Figure WDX 4-5   Edit Data Source dialog box

Click to add
a new record

Click to delete
a record

Prepare Data by Sorting the Recipients List

Ribbon Method

☐ After a recipient list has been created or selected, click the **Edit Recipient List button** in the Start Mail Merge group to open the Mail Merge Recipients dialog box

☐ Click the **list arrow** next to the field you want to sort by, shown in Figure WDX 4-6, then click **Sort Ascending** or **Sort Descending**

Figure WDX 4-6   Mail Merge Recipients dialog box

Click list arrow
to sort by field

☐ In the Refine recipient list section of the dialog box, click **Sort** to open the Filter and Sort dialog box shown in Figure WDX 4-7

☐ In the Sort Records tab, click the **Sort by list arrow** and choose a field to sort records by, then click the **Ascending** or **Descending option button**

☐ Specify additional fields to sort by, if necessary, then click **OK**

Figure WDX 4-7   **Filter and Sort dialog box**

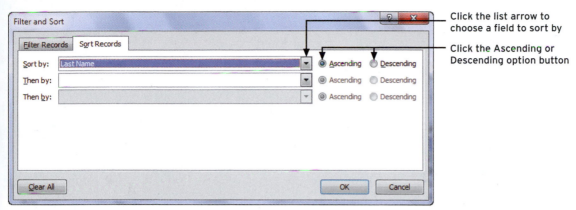

Prepare Data by Filtering Records

Ribbon Method

☐ After a recipient list has been created or selected, click the **Edit Recipient List button** in the Start Mail Merge group to open the Mail Merge Recipients dialog box

☐ In the Refine recipient list section of the dialog box, click **Filter** to open the Query Options (or Filter and Sort depending on the data source) dialog box shown in Figure WDX 4-8

☐ In the Filter Records tab, click the **Field list arrow** and choose a field, click the **Comparison list arrow** and choose the appropriate option, then type the appropriate word in the Compare to box

☐ Specify additional filters, if necessary, then click **OK**

Figure WDX 4-8   **Query Options dialog box**

Create Mailing Labels

Ribbon Method

☐ Click the **Mailings tab**, then click the **Labels button** in the Create group

☐ In the Envelopes and Labels dialog box, shown in Figure WDX 4-9, click the **Labels tab**, type the **address** in the Address text box

☐ In the Print section, choose the appropriate options, then click the **Options button**

☐ In the Labels Options dialog box, shown in Figure WDX 4-10, enter appropriate information, then click **OK** as needed to exit the dialog boxes

Figure WDX 4-9 Envelopes and Labels dialog box

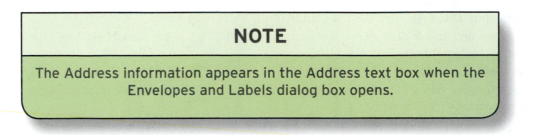

Figure WDX 4-10 Label Options dialog box

Shortcut Method

□ Select the recipient's address in a document, then follow the steps in the Create Mailing Labels Ribbon Method on the previous page

---

NOTE

The Address information appears in the Address text box when the Envelopes and Labels dialog box opens.

Create Envelope Forms

Ribbon Method

☐ Click the **Start Mail Merge button** in the Start Mail Merge group, then click **Envelopes**

☐ In the Envelope Options dialog box shown in Figure WDX 4-11, enter appropriate options in the Envelope Options tab, click the **Printing Options tab** to specify printing options, then click **OK**

☐ Follow the steps in bullets 2–6 of the Perform a Mail Merge Ribbon Method on page WDX-136

Figure WDX 4-11   Envelope Options dialog box

Task Pane Method

☐ Click the **Mailings tab**, click the **Start Mail Merge button** in the Start Mail Merge group, then click the **Step by Step Mail Merge Wizard**

☐ In the Mail Merge task pane, click the **Envelopes option button**, then click **Next: Starting document**

☐ In Step 2 of 6, click the **option button** next to the description of your starting document, click **Envelope options** to open the Envelope Options dialog box, enter appropriate options, click **OK**, then click **Next: Select Recipients**

☐ Follow the steps in bullets 4–7 of the Perform a Mail Merge Task Pane Method on page WDX-136

Create Label Forms

Ribbon Method

☐ Click the Mailings tab, click the **Start Mail Merge button** in the Start Mail Merge group, then click **Labels**

☐ In the Label Options dialog box, enter appropriate options, then click **OK**

☐ Click the **Table Tools Layout tab**, then click **View Gridlines** in the Table group to display gridlines

☐ Click the Mailings tab, click the **Select Recipients button** in the Start Mail Merge group, click **Type New List** to display the New Address List dialog box, click **Use Existing List** to use a list that was created previously, or click **Select from Outlook Contacts**, then create the list or navigate to the file, select the file, then click **OK**

☐ Position the insertion point where you want to insert a field on the labels document, then use the buttons in the Write & Insert Fields group to insert fields on the first label

☐ Click the **Update Labels button** in the Write & Insert Fields group to populate the labels in the document with data from the recipient list

☐ Click the **Preview Results button** in the Preview Results group

☐ Click the **Finish & Merge button** in the Finish group, then click **Edit Individual Documents** to create a merged file that you can edit, click **Print Documents** to send the merged document directly to the printer, or click **Send E-mail Messages** to create e-mail messages

☐ Select appropriate options in the dialog box that opens, then click **OK**

☐ If desired, save the merged document with a meaningful name

☐ If desired, save the label form with a meaningful name

> ### NOTE
> You can insert a piece of clip art onto a label, then copy it to the other labels on the page, save it and reuse it.

Task Pane Method

☐ Click the **Mailings tab**, click the **Start Mail Merge button** in the Start Mail Merge group, then click **Step by Step Mail Merge Wizard**

☐ In the Mail Merge task pane, click the **Labels option button**, then click **Next: Starting document**

☐ In Step 2 of 6, click the **option button** next to the description of the starting document, click **Label options** to open the Label Options dialog box, enter appropriate options, click **OK**, then click **Next: Select recipients**

☐ In Step 3 of 6, click the **option button** next to the recipient list you want to use, then follow the onscreen directions to create the list or navigate to and open an existing list, then click **Next: Arrange your labels**

☐ In Step 4 of 6, insert merge fields in the first label, click the **Update all labels button** to copy the layout of the first label to the other labels, then click **Next: Preview your labels**

☐ In Step 5 of 6, use the **arrow buttons** in the task pane to preview your labels, make changes if necessary, then click **Next: Complete the merge**

☐ In Step 6 of 6, click **Print** to send the merged document directly to a printer or click **Edit individual labels** to create a merge file that you can edit before printing

☐ If desired, save the merged label document with a meaningful name

☐ If desired, save the label form with a meaningful name

REVIEW QUESTIONS

FILL IN THE BLANK

Complete the following sentences by writing the correct word or words in the blanks provided.

1. You can _____ a recipient list in ascending or descending order.

2. If you are using a Word or Excel table as a data source, make sure the first row is reserved for _____.

3. A _____ is used to refine a recipient list by specifying the data meet a certain criteria.

4. You can create one _____ or an entire sheet with the same address.

5. When creating labels, it is helpful to show the _____.

MULTIPLE CHOICE

Select the best response for the following statements.

1. The _____ button allows you to add a new record to a data source.
   - A. Delete
   - B. New Entry
   - C. New Record
   - D. Filename

2. Ask and Fill-in are options on the _____ button.
   - A. Edit Recipient List
   - B. Rules
   - C. Start Mail Merge
   - D. Insert Merge Field

3. The _____ button allows you to edit the data source.
   - A. Select Recipients
   - B. Rules
   - C. Edit Recipient List
   - D. Finish & Merge

4. When creating labels, you need to use the _____ button to copy the layout of the first label to the remaining labels on the page.
   - A. Rules
   - B. Greeting Line
   - C. Preview Results
   - D. Update Labels

5. A(n) _____ cannot be used as a data source for a mail merge operation.
   - A. Clip Art graphic
   - B. Outlook Contacts List
   - C. Access table
   - D. Excel table

PROJECTS

Project WDX 4-1

1. Open the data file **Project WDX 4-1.docx**.

2. Save the document as Africa Tour Letter.docx.

3. Start a mail merge for the letter and choose **africatourlist.accdb** from the data files for this objective as the data source.

4. Edit the recipient list. In the Data Source box, select the africatourlist.accdb filename, then click the **Edit** button.

5. Click the checkbox beside John Kane and Sheela Word to remove those two recipients from the merge.

6. Sort the list in ascending order by last name.

7. Using the default formats, insert an **Address Block**, a **Greeting Line**, and the **First Name** field in the letter as shown in Figure WDX 4-12.

Figure WDX 4-12   **Letter with mail merge fields**

8. Insert a blank line after Travel Guide, and insert an If...Then...Else rule using the data in Figure WDX 4-13.

Figure WDX 4-13   **Insert Word Field: IF dialog box**

9. Click the **Preview Results** button.

10. Finish the merge. Choose to edit individual letters.

11. Scroll through the document to view the letters.

12. Save the document as **Africa Tour Merge Letters.docx** and close it. Save and close Africa Tour Letter.

Project WDX 4-2

1. Open the Word table data source file **Project WDX 4-2a**.

2. Add the following record to the table:

Jason	Brown	1	Miss Blandford

3. Save the file as **gtlist.docx** and close it.

4. Open **Project WDX 4-2b**.

5. Save the file as **GT Letter.docx**.

6. Start a mail merge for the letter and choose **gtlist.docx** that you saved in step 3, as the data source.

7. Filter the list to merge only the records for Miss Young's class.

8. Using the default formats, insert the fields shown in Figure WDX 4-14.

Figure WDX 4-14   Letter with mail merge fields

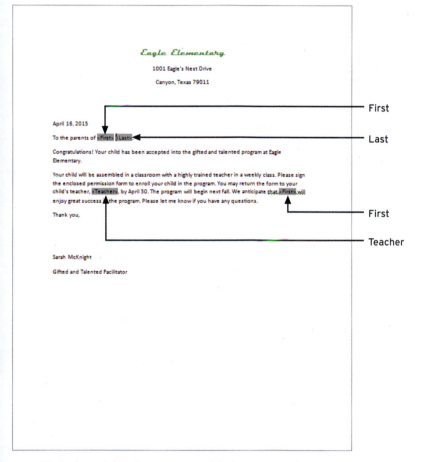

9. Click the **Highlight Merge Fields button** in the Write & Insert Fields group.

10. Finish the merge. Choose to edit individual letters.

11. Save the document as **GT Merge Letters.docx** and close it. Save and close GT Letter.docx.

Project WDX 4-3

1. Create a new document and start a mail merge for labels using the Avery US Letter 18160 Address Labels.

2. On the Table Tools Layout tab, click **View Gridlines** in the Table group.

3. Use the **EagleGTList.docx** as the data source, and insert fields in the first label as shown in Figure WDX 4-15.

Figure WDX 4-15   Label with mail merge fields

4. Click the Mailings tab, then click the **Update Labels button** in the Write & Insert Fields group.

5. Preview the merge.

6. Finish and merge to a new document.

7. Save the label document as **GT Labels.docx** and close it.

8. Close the label form without saving.

CRITICAL THINKING

Activity WDX 4-1

Use your school's name and address to create a single label. Create an entire sheet of the same label using your choice of label format. Include the school logo. Save the label form.

Activity WDX 4-2

Write an e-mail message to merge and send to 3-5 students in your class. Insert a first name and last name field and any other fields of your choice to personalize the message.

WORD EXPERT OBJECTIVE 5: MANAGING MACROS AND FORMS

APPLY AND MANIPULATE MACROS

Record a Macro

Ribbon Method

☐ Click the **View tab**, click the **Macros button arrow** in the Macros group, then click **Record Macro**

☐ In the Record Macro dialog box, shown in Figure WDX 5-1, type a name for the macro in the **Macro name box**, select a location to store the macro, type a description, then click **Keyboard**

☐ In the Customize Keyboard dialog box, shown in Figure WDX 5-2, position the insertion point in the **Press new shortcut key text box**, press the keys on the keyboard that you want to assign to the macro, then click the **Assign button**

☐ Click the **Close button** (the pointer changes to a Record Macro pointer 🖥) to begin recording

☐ Type the text and/or apply the formatting that you want to include in the macro

☐ Click the **View tab**, click the **Macros button arrow** in the Macros group, then click **Stop Recording**

Figure WDX 5-1   Record Macro dialog box

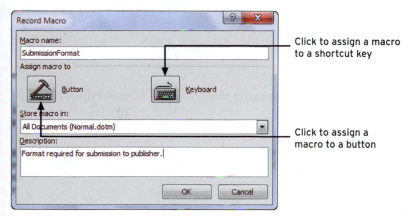

Figure WDX 5-2   Customize Keyboard dialog box

OR
- ☐ Click the **Developer tab**, then click the **Record Macro button** in the Code group
- ☐ Follow the steps in bullets 2-5 of Record a Macro Ribbon Method on the previous page
- ☐ Click the **Developer tab**, then click the **Stop Recording button** in the Code group

Shortcut Method
- ☐ Click the **Record Macro button** [icon] on the status bar
- ☐ Follow the steps in bullets 2-5 of Record a Macro Ribbon Method on the previous page
- ☐ Click the **Stop Recording button** [icon] on the status bar

Run a Macro

Ribbon Method
- ☐ Click the **View tab**, click the **Macros button arrow** in the Macros group, then click **View Macros**
- ☐ In the Macros dialog box, shown in Figure WDX 5-3, click the name of the macro you want to run in the Macro name box, then click the **Run button**

  OR
- ☐ Click the **Developer tab**, then click the **Macros button** in the Code group
- ☐ In the Macros dialog box, click the name of the macro you want to run in the Macro name box, then click the **Run button**

Shortcut Method
- ☐ Press the shortcut keys that you assigned to the macro

  OR
- ☐ Click **[Alt][F8]** to display the Macros dialog box
- ☐ Click the name of the macro that you want to run in the Macro name box, then click the **Run button**

Figure WDX 5-3   **Macros dialog box**

Delete a Macro

Ribbon Method
- ☐ Click the **View tab**, click the **Macros button arrow** in the Macros group, then click **View Macros**
- ☐ In the Macros dialog box, click the name of the macro that you want to delete, then click the **Delete** button

  OR
- ☐ Click the **Developer tab**, then click the **Macros button** in the Code group
- ☐ In the Macros dialog box, click the name of the macro that you want to delete, then click the **Delete button**

Shortcut Method
□ Press **[Alt][F8]** to display the Macros dialog box
□ Click the name of the macro that you want to delete in the Macro name box, then click the **Delete button**

Apply Macro Security
Ribbon Method
□ Click the **File tab**, then click **Options** to display the Word Options dialog box
□ Click **Trust Center** in the left pane, then click the **Trust Center Settings button**
□ In the Trust Center dialog box, click **Macro Settings** in the left pane, choose appropriate options in the right pane, as shown in Figure WDX 5-4, then click **OK**
    OR
□ Click the **Developer tab**, then click the **Macro Security button** to display the Trust Center dialog box
□ Choose appropriate options in the right pane, then click **OK**

Figure WDX 5-4   Trust Center dialog box

APPLY AND MANIPULATE MACRO OPTIONS

Run a Macro When a Document is Opened
Ribbon Method
□ Click the **View tab**, click the **Macros button arrow** in the Macros group, then click **Record Macro**
□ In the Record Macro dialog box, type **AutoOpen in the Macro name text box**, select **All Documents (Normal. dotm)** as the location to store the macro, then type a description
□ Click the **OK button** (the pointer changes to a Record Macro pointer) to begin recording
□ Type the text and/or apply the formatting or other commands that you want to include in the macro
□ Click the **View tab**, click the **Macros button arrow** in the Macros group, then click **Stop Recording**
□ To test the macro, use the **File tab** and **Open command** to open an existing document

Run a Macro When a Button is Clicked
Ribbon Method
☐ Click the **View tab**, click the **Macros button arrow** in the Macros group, then click **Record Macro**

☐ In the Record Macro dialog box, type a name for the macro in the Macro Name box, select a location to store the macro, type a description, then click the **Button button**

☐ In the Word Options dialog box, click **Customize Ribbon** in the left pane. Click the **Choose command from list arrow**, click **Macros**, then click the name of the macro in the list

☐ In the Main Tabs section, click a tab such as **View**, click the **New Group button**, then click the **Add button**, shown in Figure WDX 5-5

☐ Right-click **New Group (Custom)** and click **Rename** to display the Rename dialog box

☐ Select an icon, type a new name in the Display name box, click **OK**, then click **OK** again

☐ Type the text and/or apply the formatting or other commands that you want to include in the macro

☐ Click the **View tab**, click the **Macros button arrow** in the Macros group, then click **Stop Recording**

☐ To run the macro, click the macro button you just added

Figure WDX 5-5   Word Options dialog box

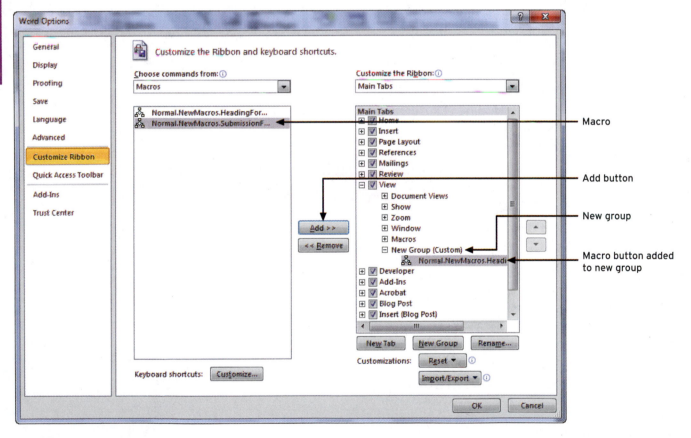

OR

☐ Click the **Developer tab**, then click the **Record Macro button**

☐ Follow the steps in bullets 2-7 in the Run a Macro When a Button is Clicked Ribbon Method

☐ Click the **Developer tab**, then click the **Stop Recording button**

☐ To run the macro, click the macro button you just added

Display the Developer Tab
Ribbon Method
- ☐ Click the **File tab**, click **Options** to open the Word Options dialog box, then click **Customize Ribbon** in the left pane
- ☐ In the right pane, click the **Developer check box** as shown in Figure WDX 5-6, then click **OK**

Figure WDX 5-6   Word Options dialog box

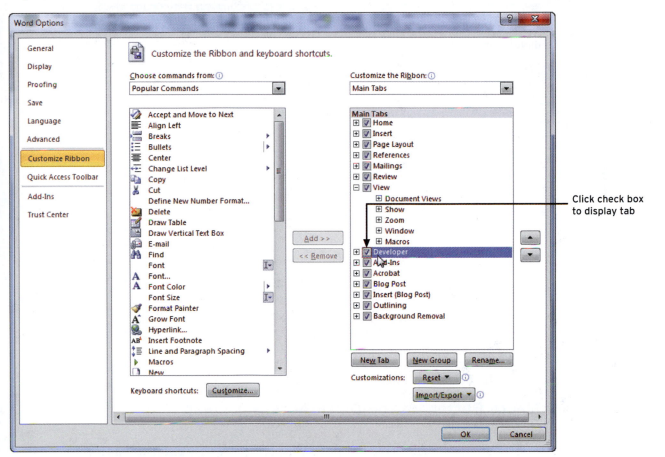

Assign a Macro to a Command Button
Ribbon Method
- ☐ If the Developer tab is not displayed, follow the steps in bullets 1-2 under Display the Developer Tab Ribbon Method
- ☐ Position the insertion point in the location where you want the command button to appear
- ☐ Click the **Developer tab**, click **Legacy Tools list arrow** in the Controls group, then click **Command button** to insert the command button
- ☐ Right-click the command button and click **View Code** from the shortcut menu
- ☐ In the window, type the name of the macro in the blank line, as shown in Figure WDX 5-7, make sure Click appears in the list arrow
- ☐ Click the **Close button** on the Microsoft Visual Basic for Applications window
- ☐ On the **Developer tab**, click the **Design Mode button** in the Controls group to turn it off
- ☐ Click the **File tab**, then click **Save As** to open the Save As dialog box
- ☐ Type a name in the file name box, click the **Save as Type list arrow** and click **Word Macro-Enabled Document**, then click **Save**
- ☐ To run the macro, click the **command button** in the document

> ## NOTE
>
> To change the label on a command button, right-click the command button, click **Command ButtonObject**, click **Edit**, then type a new name for the button.

Figure WDX 5-7 **Code dialog box**

Create a Custom Macro Button on the Quick Access Toolbar

Ribbon Method

- ☐ Click the **View tab**, click the **Macros button arrow** in the Macros group, then click **Record Macro**
- ☐ In the Record Macro dialog box, type a name for the macro in the Macro Name box, select a location to store the macro, type a description, then click the **Button button**
- ☐ In the Word Options dialog box, select the macro name in the left pane, then click the **Add button**, shown in Figure WDX 5-8, to move it to the right pane under Customize Quick Access Toolbar
- ☐ Click the **OK button** (the pointer changes to a Record Macro pointer ⬚) to begin recording
- ☐ Type the text and/or apply the formatting that you want to include in the macro
- ☐ Click the **View tab**, click the **Macros button** in the Macros group, then click **Stop Recording**
- ☐ To run the macro, click the **Macro button** ⬚ on the Quick Access Toolbar

Figure WDX 5-8   Word Options dialog box

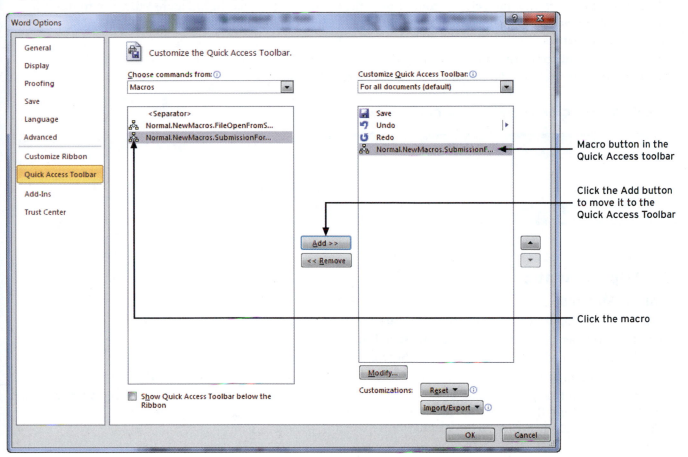

OR

☐ Click the **Developer tab**, then click the **Record Macro button** in the Code group

☐ Follow the steps in bullets 2-5 under Create a Custom Macro Button on the Quick Access Toolbar on the previous page

☐ Click the **Stop Recording button** 🔲 in the Code group

☐ To run the macro, click the **Macro button** 🔀 on the Quick Access Toolbar

Shortcut Method

☐ Click the **Record Macro button** 🔳 on the status bar

☐ Follow the steps in bullets 2-5 under Create a Custom Macro Button on the Quick Access Toolbar on the previous page

☐ Click the **Stop Recording button** 🔲 on the status bar

☐ To run the macro, click the **Macro button** 🔀 on the Quick Access Toolbar

CREATE FORMS

Insert a Form Using the Controls Group

Ribbon Method

☐ Create a new document or template or open an existing template or document

☐ If the Developer tab is not displayed, follow the steps in bullets 1-2 under Display the Developer Tab Ribbon Method on page WDX-155

☐ Click the **Developer tab**, click **Design Mode**

- [ ] **Position the insertion point** where you want to insert a control
- [ ] **Click the Developer tab**, then click a control from the Controls group, shown in Figure WDX 5-9 to insert it
- [ ] **Click the Developer tab**, then click **Properties** in the Controls group, to open a dialog box where you can set or change properties
- [ ] **Insert and edit the properties** for all controls on the form, then save the document
- [ ] **Follow the steps** in Lock a Form Ribbon Method to lock the form

Figure WDX 5-9   Controls group on the Developer tab

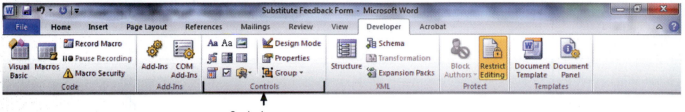

Controls group

Add Help Content to Form Fields

Ribbon Method

- [ ] **Click the Developer tab**, click the **Design Mode button** to turn on Design Mode
- [ ] **On the Developer tab**, click the **Legacy Tools list arrow** 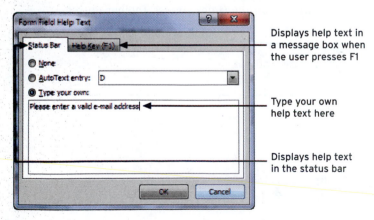, then insert a field from the Legacy Forms section
- [ ] **On the Developer tab**, click the **Properties button**
- [ ] **In the Text Form Field** (or other field type) Options dialog box, click the **Add Help Text button**
- [ ] **In the Form Field Help Text dialog box**, click the **Status Bar tab**, click the **AutoText entry option button** and **click an entry** from the list or click the **Type your own option button** and type your own text, as shown in Figure WDX 5-10, then click **OK** to display the help text in the status bar

  OR

- [ ] **In the Form Field** Help Text dialog box, click the **Help Key (F1) tab**, click the **AutoText entry option button and click** an entry from the list or click the **Type your own option button** and type your own text, then click **OK** to display the help text when the F1 key is pressed
- [ ] **Save the form**, click the **Design Mode button** in the Controls group to turn off Design Mode
- [ ] **Follow the steps** in Lock a Form Ribbon Method to lock the form
- [ ] **Click in the form field**, then depending on where you inserted the Help text look for it on the left side of the status **bar or press F1** to open a message box with the Help text

Figure WDX 5-10   Form Field Help Text dialog box

Displays help text in a message box when the user presses F1

Type your own help text here

Displays help text in the status bar

NOTE

Another way to add instructional text to a field or control is to type the text as the default or placeholder text that is replaced when the user types in their data.

Link a Form to a Database
Ribbon Method

- ☐ Open the form, saved by a user
- ☐ Click the **File tab**, click **Options**, then click **Advanced**
- ☐ Scroll down to the section titled Preserve fidelity when sharing this document and click the **Save form data as delimited text file check box**, then click **OK**
- ☐ Click **Save** to save the document again, then click **OK** in the File Conversion warning message box
- ☐ In the Save As dialog box, the Plain Text file format is selected, type a new name for the document if desired, then click **Save**
- ☐ Open a new blank database in Access. Click the **External Data tab**, then click the **Text File button** in the Import & Link group
- ☐ In the Get External Data – Text File dialog box, click the **Browse button** to navigate to the Plain Text file you just saved, select it, click **Open**, click the **Link to the data source by creating a linked table option**, then click **OK**
- ☐ Select options and follow the steps in the Link Text Wizard until finished
- ☐ Double-click the name of the table in the left pane to view the data in the fields on the right

Lock a Form
Ribbon Method

- ☐ Select the control you want to lock, then click the **Properties button** in the Controls group
- ☐ In the Content Control Properties dialog box, shown in Figure WDX 5-11, click the appropriate option in the Locking section, then click **OK**
- ☐ Repeat the steps in bullet 2 for each control that you want to lock

Figure WDX 5-11   Content Control Properties dialog box

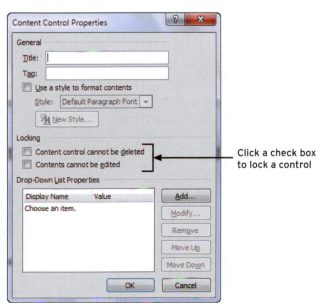

OR

☐ Click the **Developer tab**, then click the **Design Mode button** in the Controls group to turn off Design Mode

☐ Click the **Developer tab**, then click the **Restrict Editing button** in the Protect group

☐ In the Restrict Formatting and Editing task pane, click the **Allow only this type of editing in the document check box** in the Editing restrictions section, click the list arrow and choose **Filling in forms**, as shown in Figure WDX 5-12

☐ Click **Yes, Start Enforcing Protection**

☐ In the Start Enforcing Protection dialog box, click **OK** to start enforcement without protecting the document with a password

OR

☐ To password protect the document, type a password, press **[Tab]**, type the password again, then click **OK**

Figure WDX 5-12   Restrict Formatting and Editing dialog box

OR

☐ Click the **Home tab**, click the **Select list button** in the Editing group, then click **Select All**

☐ Click the **Developer tab**, then click the **Group button** in the Controls group, then click **Group**

MANIPULATE FORMS

Unlock a Form

Ribbon Method

☐ Select the control you want to unlock, then click the **Properties button** in the Controls group

☐ In the Content Control Properties dialog box, click the appropriate option in the Locking section to remove the checkmark, then click **OK**

☐ Repeat the steps in bullet 2 for each control that you want to unlock

OR

☐ In the Restrict Formatting and Editing task pane, click the **Stop Protection button**

☐ If necessary, enter the password and click **OK**

OR

☐ Select the form

☐ Click the **Developer tab**, click the **Group button** in the Controls group, then click **Ungroup**

Add Fields to a Form

Ribbon Method

☐ Position the insertion point where you want to insert a field

☐ Click the **Developer tab**, click the **Legacy Tools list arrow** 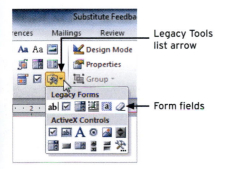 in the Controls group, then click an option from the Legacy Forms section of the gallery, shown in Figure WDX 5-13

Figure WDX 5-13   Legacy Tools list arrow and gallery

Remove Fields from a Form

Ribbon Method

☐ Select the form field or control

☐ Click the **Home tab**, then click the **Cut button** ✂ in the Clipboard group

Shortcut Method

☐ Select the form field

☐ Press the **Delete** key

OR

☐ Right-click a form field, then choose **Remove Content Control** or **Cut** from the shortcut menu

Word

REVIEW QUESTIONS

TRUE/FALSE

Circle T if the statement is true or F if the statement is false.

T   F   1. You can assign keyboard shortcuts to a macro.

T   F   2. Macros cannot be deleted.

T   F   3. You can add help text to a form field so the user can press F1 to view it.

T   F   4. [Alt][F8] stops recording a macro.

T   F   5. You can lock individual controls on a form.

MATCHING

Match the correct term in Column 2 to its description in Column 1.

Column 1	Column 2
_____ 1. A command that begins the process of creating a macro.	A. Record Macro button
_____ 2. A command used to specify options for a control.	B. Stop Recording button
_____ 3. A toggle button used for creating forms.	C. Restrict Editing button
_____ 4. Completes the process of creating a macro.	D. Properties button
_____ 5. A command used to lock or protect a form.	E. Design Mode button

PROJECTS

Project WDX 5-1

1. Open the data file **Project WDX 5-1.docx**.

2. Save the document as Newsletter.docx

3. Select the first paragraph of text.

4. Start recording a new macro named SubmissionFormat. In the Record Macro dialog box, type **Format required for submission to publisher** in the description.

5. Assign Alt+F as the keyboard shortcut keys to run the macro.

6. Perform the following formatting on the selected paragraph.

   - Indent the first line .5"
   - Use the Line Spacing Options command to apply double line spacing with 6 point spacing before the paragraph and 10 point spacing after the paragraph
   - Justify the paragraph
   - Change the font to Garamond, 11 point

7. Stop recording the macro.

8. Select the next paragraph of text and run the macro using the shortcut keys you assigned.

9. Select the remaining text and apply the macro.

10. Select the Purpose heading.

11. Start recording a new macro named HeadingFormat. In the description section of the Record Macro dialog box, type **Format required for headings**.

12. Assign a button to the macro and assign it to the Quick Access Toolbar.

Word

13. Perform the following formatting on the selected heading.
    - Change the font to Garamond, 18 point
    - Change the text to uppercase

14. Use the macro button in the Quick Access Toolbar to apply the macro to the remaining heading and the title.

15. Save and close the document.

Project WDX 5-2

1. Download the Substitute feedback form located in the Academic forms category of the Forms folder in the New section of Backstage view.

2. Save the document as **Substitute Feedback Form.docx**. (Click OK to save the document in the new format.)

3. Display the Restrict Formatting and Editing task pane and click the Stop Protection button.

4. Delete the text form field beside Today's date and insert a Date Picker Content Control. Lock the content control so that it cannot be deleted.

5. Select Contact Information (phone/e-mail) and type **Phone:**

6. Below Phone, type **E-mail Address:** and insert a Text Form Field from the Legacy Tools list arrow beside it.

7. Add the following status bar Help text to the e-mail address form field: Please enter a valid e-mail address.

8. Use the Restrict Formatting and Editing task pane to protect the document. Set Editing Restrictions to filling in forms, then start enforcing protection without a password.

9. Save and close the document.

CRITICAL THINKING

Activity WDX 5-1

Create a macro that will type your name at the top of the page in every document that is opened.

Activity WDX 5-2

Open the Substitute Feedback Form.docx document and save it with a new name. Fill out the form and save the document. Link the form data to an Access table.

Microsoft Excel 2010 Certification Prep

Getting Started with Excel 2010

The Excel Microsoft Office Specialist (MOS) exams assume a basic level of proficiency in Excel. This section is intended to help you reference these basic skills while you are preparing to take the Excel MOS exams.

> ☐ Starting and exiting Excel
> ☐ Viewing the Excel window
> ☐ Using the Ribbon
> ☐ Opening, saving, and closing workbooks
> ☐ Navigating in the worksheet window
> ☐ Using views
> ☐ Using keyboard KeyTips
> ☐ Getting Help

START AND EXIT EXCEL

Start Excel

Mouse Method

☐ Click the **Start button** 🟦 on the Windows taskbar
☐ Point to **All Programs**
☐ Click **Microsoft Office**, then click **Microsoft Excel 2010**
  OR
☐ Double-click the **Microsoft Excel program icon** 🅧 on the desktop to open the Excel window, shown in Figure EX GS-1

Exit Excel

Ribbon Method

☐ Click the **File tab**, then click **Exit**
  OR
☐ Click the **Close button** ❎ on the Excel program window title bar

Shortcut Method

☐ Press **[Alt][F4]**

VIEW THE EXCEL WINDOW

Figure EX GS-1   Excel Window

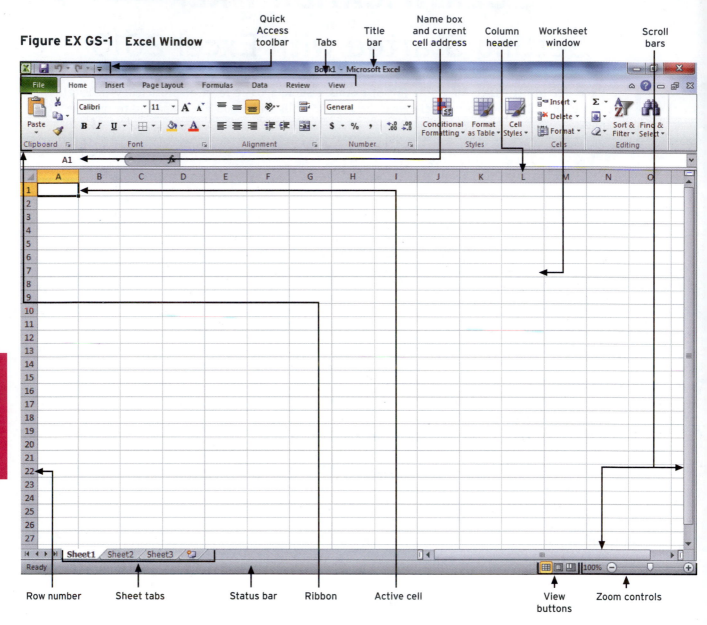

Excel

USE THE RIBBON

Display the Ribbon

Ribbon Method
☐ Double-click any tab

Shortcut Method
☐ Right-click any tab, then click **Minimize the Ribbon** to deselect it

Hide the Ribbon

Ribbon Method
☐ Double-click the active tab

Shortcut Method
☐ Right-click any tab, then click **Minimize the Ribbon** to select it

Customize the Quick Access Toolbar

Ribbon Method
☐ Right-click any Quick Access toolbar button
☐ To remove that button, click **Remove from Quick Access Toolbar**
☐ To add or remove a button, click **Customize Quick Access Toolbar**, click a command in the left or right column of the dialog box, then click **Add** or **Remove**

Reposition the Quick Access Toolbar

Ribbon Method
☐ Right-click any Quick Access toolbar button
☐ Click **Show Quick Access Toolbar Below the Ribbon**

OPEN, SAVE, AND CLOSE WORKBOOKS

Open a New Workbook

Ribbon Method
☐ Click the **File tab**, then click **New**
☐ Click the **Blank workbook icon** in the center pane, if necessary, then click the **Create button** in the right pane

Shortcut Method
☐ Press **[Ctrl][N]**

Open an Existing Workbook

Ribbon Method
☐ Click the **File tab**, then click **Open**
☐ In the Open dialog box, shown in Figure EX GS-2, navigate to the drive and folder where the file is stored
☐ Click the file you want, then click **Open**

Excel

Shortcut Method

□ Press **[Ctrl][O]**

□ Follow the steps in bullets 2–3 of the Open an Existing Workbook Ribbon Method on the previous page

Figure EX GS-2   Open dialog box

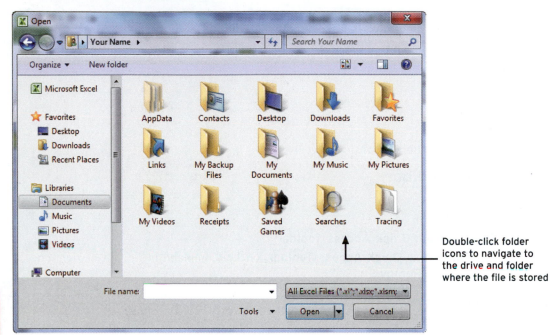

Double-click folder icons to navigate to the drive and folder where the file is stored

Use Save As

Ribbon Method

□ Click the **File tab**, then click **Save As**

□ In the Save As dialog box shown in Figure EX GS-3, navigate to the drive and folder where you want to store the workbook

□ Type an appropriate **file name** in the File name text box, then click **Save**

Shortcut Method

□ Press **[F12]**

□ Follow the steps in bullets 2–3 of the Use Save As Ribbon Method above

Excel

Figure EX GS-3   Save As dialog box

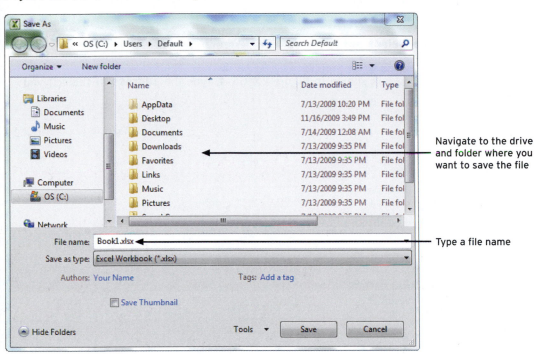

Save an Existing Workbook
Ribbon Method
☐ Click the **File tab**, then click **Save**

OR

☐ Click the **Save button** on the Quick Access toolbar

Shortcut Method
☐ Press **[Ctrl][S]**

Close a Workbook
Ribbon Method
☐ Click the **File tab**, then click **Close**

☐ If prompted to save the file, click **Save** or **Don't Save** as appropriate

OR

☐ Click the **Close Window button** in the document window

☐ If prompted to save the file, click **Save** or **Don't Save** as appropriate

Shortcut Method
☐ Press **[Ctrl][W]** or **[Alt][F4]**

☐ If prompted to save the file, click **Save** or **Don't Save** as appropriate

NAVIGATE IN THE WORKSHEET WINDOW

Ribbon Method

□ Click the **Home tab**, then click the **Find & Select button** in the Editing group

□ Click **Go To**

□ In the Reference text box in the Go To dialog box shown in Figure EX GS-4, type the **address** of the cell you want to go to, then click **OK**

Figure EX GS-4   Go To dialog box

Type the address of the cell you want to go to

Shortcut Method

□ Press **[Ctrl][G]**

□ In the Reference text box in the Go To dialog box shown in Figure EX GS-4, type the **address** of the cell you want to go to, then click **OK**

OR

□ Use Table EX GS-1 as a reference to navigate through the worksheet using keyboard shortcuts

Table EX GS-1   Navigation Keyboard Shortcuts

Keys	Moves the insertion point
[Ctrl][Home]	To the beginning of the worksheet (cell A1)
[Ctrl][End]	To the last cell in the worksheet area that contains data
[Page Up]	One screen up
[Page Down]	One screen down
[Alt][Page Up]	One screen to the left
[Alt][Page Down]	One screen to the right

Mouse Method

To change the view without moving the insertion point, do one of the following:

□ Drag the **scroll box** in a scroll bar to move within the worksheet

□ Click above the vertical scroll box in a scroll bar to move up a screen

□ Click below the vertical scroll box in a scroll bar to move down a screen

□ Click to the left of the horizontal scroll box in a scroll bar to move one screen to the left

□ Click to the right of the horizontal scroll box in a scroll bar to move one screen to the right

☐ Click the **up scroll arrow** in a scroll bar to move up one row

☐ Click the **down scroll arrow** in a scroll bar to move down one row

☐ Click the **left scroll arrow** in a scroll bar to move one column to the left

☐ Click the **right scroll arrow** in a scroll bar to move one column to the right

USE KEYBOARD KEYTIPS

Display KeyTips

☐ Press **[Alt]** to display the KeyTips (squares containing numbers or letters) on the active tab on the Ribbon and on the Quick Access toolbar as shown in Figure EX GS-5

☐ Press the letter or number for a tab to open a tab, then press the letter or number for the specific command on the active tab to perform the command

☐ Press additional letters or numbers as needed to complete the command sequence

☐ If two letters appear, press each one in order

☐ For some commands you have to click an option from a gallery or menu to complete the command sequence

☐ The KeyTips turn off automatically at the end of the command sequence

Figure EX GS-5   KeyTips

Hide KeyTips

☐ Press **[Alt]**

GET HELP

Ribbon Method

☐ Click the **Microsoft Excel Help button** 🔵 on the Ribbon

☐ Use Table EX GS-2 as a reference to select the most appropriate way to search for help using the Excel Help window, shown in Figure EX GS-6

OR

☐ Point to any button on the Ribbon, then read the ScreenTip text

☐ If you see "Press F1 for more help." at the bottom of the ScreenTip, continue pointing to the button, then press **[F1]** to see targeted help on that button in the Excel Help window

Shortcut Method

☐ Press **[F1]**

☐ Use Table EX GS-2 as a reference to select the most appropriate way to search for help using the Excel Help window, shown in Figure EX GS-6

Figure EX GS-6   **Excel Help window**

Table EX GS-2   **Microsoft Excel Help Window Options**

Option	To use
Browse Excel Help	Click a link representing a topic you want to read about; click **subtopics** that appear until you see help text for the topic
Back	Click to return to the previously displayed information
Forward	Click to go forward in the sequence of previously displayed information
Stop	Click to stop searching on a topic
Refresh	Click to refresh the Help window content
Home	Click to return to the original Help window
Print	Click to print the current page
Change Font Size	Click to enlarge or shrink the Help text
Show Table of Contents	Click to show the Table of Contents pane, showing topic links you can click; becomes the Hide Table of Contents button
Keep On Top	Click to keep Help window on top as you work; becomes the Not On Top button, which you click to leave the Help window open behind the current window as you work
Search	Type a topic for which you want Help in the search box, then click the Search button
Search button list arrow	Click the list arrow, then click the area you want Help from, such as Content from Office.com, All Excel, or Excel Help

REVIEW QUESTIONS

FILL IN THE BLANK

Complete the following sentences by writing the correct word or words in the blanks provided.

1. One way to start Excel is to double-click the Microsoft Excel program icon on the _____.

2. To hide the Ribbon, double-click the active _____.

3. To display the Go To dialog box, click the _____ tab, click the Find & Select button in the Editing group, then click Go To.

4. Pressing Ctrl + Home will move the insertion point to cell _____.

5. _____ are numbers or letters that display over commands on the Ribbon that indicate how to perform Ribbon commands using the keyboard.

MATCHING

Match the correct term in Column 2 to its description in Column 1.

Column 1	Column 2
_____ 1. Save As	A. Alt
_____ 2. Open a New Workbook	B. F1
_____ 3. Exit Excel	C. F12
_____ 4. Display KeyTips	D. Alt + F4
_____ 5. Get Help	E. Ctrl + N

PROJECTS

Project EX GS-1

1. Open Excel.

2. Open a new workbook.

3. Reposition the Quick Access Toolbar below the Ribbon.

4. Customize the Quick Access Toolbar by adding a button for a commonly used command.

5. Display the KeyTips.

6. Use the KeyTips to open the Go To dialog box.

7. Use the Go To dialog box to navigate to cell Z94.

8. Use a keyboard shortcut to move the insertion point to the beginning of the worksheet.

9. Reposition the Quick Access Toolbar above the Ribbon and remove the button that you added.

10. Close the workbook without saving.

Project EX GS-2

1. Open the **Project EX GS-2.xlsx** data file. Save the file as Sales Report.xlsx.

2. Save the file as Sales Report.xlsx.

3. Hide the Ribbon.

4. Use a keyboard shortcut to navigate to the end of the worksheet area containing data.

5. Use the Go To dialog box to navigate to cell A1.

Excel

6. Move the insertion point one screen down.

7. Change the view one screen to the right without moving the insertion point.

8. Move the insertion point to the beginning of the worksheet.

9. Display the Ribbon.

10. Save and close the workbook.

11. Exit Excel.

CRITICAL THINKING

Activity EX GS-1

Open the Excel Help window. Search for the video titled "Getting Started with Excel 2010" and watch it. Browse through Help to see all the material available for you to learn more about using Excel. What other Excel videos and training courses are available? Refer to Table EX GS-2 as a reference if you need help using the Excel Help window.

Activity EX GS-2

With the Excel Help window open, search to find out what's new in Microsoft Office Excel 2010. Open a new blank workbook and explore each tab on the Ribbon to familiarize yourself with where the commands are located. What is Microsoft Office Backstage view? Use Excel Help to find out more about this new feature for managing your files and the data about them.

Excel

EXCEL OBJECTIVE 1: MANAGING THE WORKSHEET ENVIRONMENT

NAVIGATE THROUGH A WORKSHEET

Use Hot Keys

Shortcut Method

□ Press key or combination of keys to use a keyboard shortcut to move the insertion point

□ Use Table EX 1-1 as a reference to navigate through a worksheet using hot keys

Table EX 1-1   Navigation Keyboard Shortcuts

Hot keys	Moves the insertion point
[Ctrl][Home]	To the beginning of the worksheet (cell A1)
[Ctrl][End]	To the last cell in the worksheet area that contains data
[Page Up]	One screen up
[Page Down]	One screen down
[Alt][Page Up]	One screen to the left
[Alt][Page Down]	One screen to the right

Use the Name Box

Mouse Method

□ Click the **name box** above column A to highlight the cell reference of the active cell

□ Type the cell reference of the desired destination

□ Press **[Enter]**

PRINT A WORKSHEET OR WORKBOOK

Print only Selected Worksheets

Ribbon Method

□ Click the **File tab**, then click **Print** to display the print options, as shown in Figure EX 1-1

□ In the Settings section, click the first down arrow, select **Print Active Sheets**, then click **Print**

Print an Entire Workbook

Ribbon Method

☐ Click the **File tab**, then click **Print** to display the print options, as shown in Figure EX 1-1

☐ In the Settings section, click the first down arrow, select **Print Entire Workbook**, then click **Print**

Figure EX 1-1   Print options

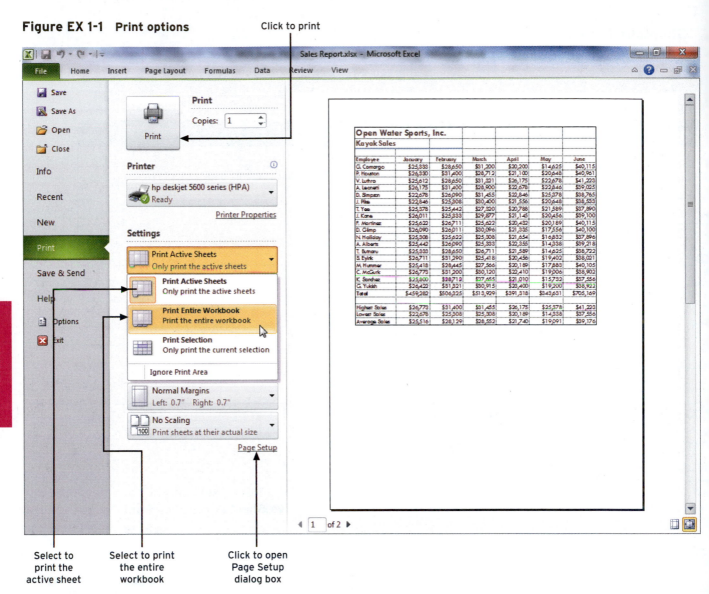

Click to print

Select to print the active sheet

Select to print the entire workbook

Click to open Page Setup dialog box

Construct Headers and Footers

Ribbon Method

☐ Click the **Insert tab**, then click the **Header & Footer button** 🖼 in the Text group to display the Header & Footer Tools Design tab, shown in Figure EX 1-2

☐ Click in the left, center, or right header section and type text, or click one of the buttons in the Header & Footer Elements group

☐ Click an option in the Options group, if desired

☐ Click the **Go to Footer button** 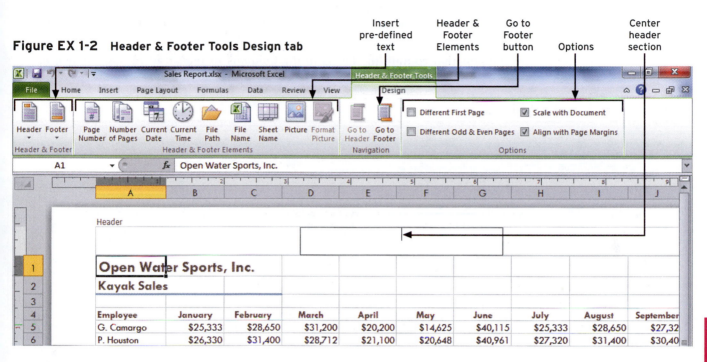 in the Navigation group

☐ Click a footer section and type text, or click one of the buttons in the Header & Footer Elements group

☐ Click in the body of the worksheet to close the Header & Footer Tools Design tab

Figure EX 1-2   Header & Footer Tools Design tab

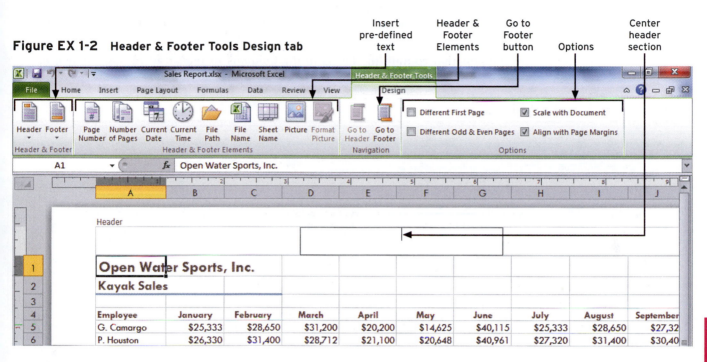

Scale Worksheet Printouts

Ribbon Method

☐ Click the **File tab**, then click **Print**

☐ In the Settings section, click the last down arrow, select a scaling option, then click **Print**

Excel

Print Titles

Ribbon Method

☐ Click the **Page Layout tab**, then click **Print Titles**  in the Page Setup group to display the Sheet tab of the Page Setup dialog box

☐ Type the reference of the rows that contain the labels in the Rows to repeat at top box, shown in Figure EX 1-3 AND/OR

☐ Type the reference of the columns that contain the labels in the Columns to repeat at left box, shown in Figure EX 1-3

Figure EX 1-3   **Page Setup dialog box**

Type the reference of the rows that contain labels to be printed

Type the reference of the columns that contain labels to be printed

Set up the Worksheet Page for Printing

Ribbon Method

☐ Click the **File tab**, then click **Print**

☐ At the bottom of the Settings section, click the **Page Setup link** (see Figure EX 1-1)

☐ In the Page Setup dialog box, shown in Figure EX 1-3, click the Page, Margins, Header/Footer, or Sheet tabs to select options

Set a Print Area

Ribbon Method

☐ Select the worksheet area you want to print

☐ Click the **Page Layout tab**, then click the **Print Area button** in the Page Setup group

☐ Click **Set Print Area** to print only that worksheet area

Print Gridlines

Ribbon Method

☐ Click the **Page Layout tab**, then click the **Print check box** under Gridlines in the Sheet Options group

---

PERSONALIZE THE ENVIRONMENT BY USING BACKSTAGE

Manipulate the Quick Access Toolbar

Ribbon Method

☐ Click the **Customize Quick Access Toolbar button** ▾ on the Quick Access Toolbar
☐ Choose an option from the menu, as shown in Figure EX 1-4

Figure EX 1-4   Quick Access Toolbar and menu

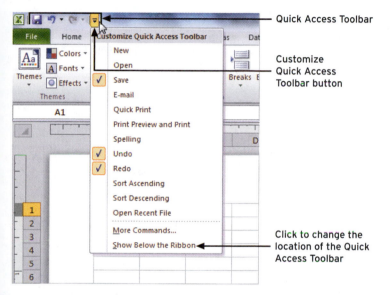

Customize a Tab

Ribbon Method

☐ Right-click a **Ribbon tab**, then click **Customize the Ribbon** to display the Customize Ribbon page of the Excel Options dialog box, as shown in Figure EX 1-5
☐ Click the **New Tab button**
☐ Click the **Rename button** to rename

Customize a Group

Ribbon Method

□ Right-click a Ribbon tab, then click **Customize the Ribbon** to display the Customize Ribbon page of the Excel Options dialog box, as shown in Figure EX 1-5

□ Click the **New Group button**

□ Click the **Rename button** to rename

□ Click a command, then click the **Add** (or **Remove**) **button** to choose buttons for the group

Figure EX 1-5   Customize Ribbon page of Excel Options dialog box

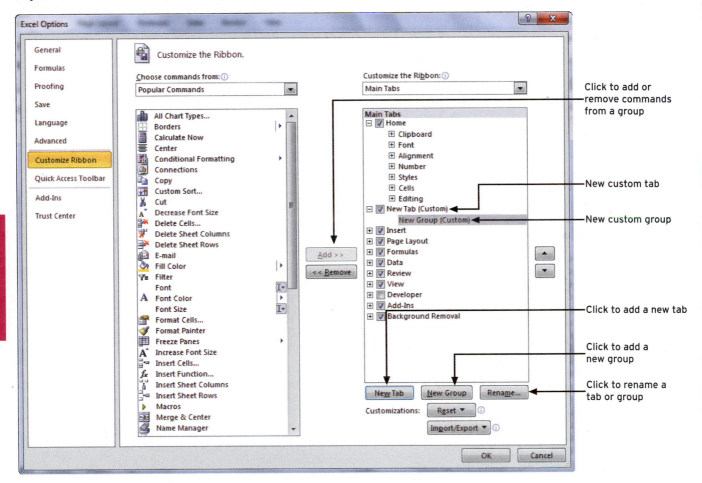

Manipulate Excel Default Settings (Excel Options)

Ribbon Method

□ Click the **File tab**, then click **Options** to display the Excel Options dialog box

□ Click a category on the left, change options on the right, then click the **OK button**

Manipulate Workbook Properties (Document Panel)

Ribbon Method

□ Click the **File tab**, then click **Info**

□ In the right pane, click the **Show All Properties link**

□ Click to change a document property, as shown in Figure EX 1-6

Figure EX 1-6 Info In Backstage view

Workbook properties

Click to manage versions

Manage Versions

Ribbon Method

☐ Click the **File tab**, then click **Info**

☐ Click the **Manage Versions button**, then click **Recover Unsaved Workbooks**, as shown in Figure EX 1-6

AutoSave

Ribbon Method

☐ Click the **File tab**, then click **Options**

☐ Click **Save**

☐ Select the **Save AutoRecover information every x minutes** check box and specify how often you want the program to save your data

REVIEW QUESTIONS

TRUE/FALSE

Circle T if the statement is true or F if the statement is false.

T   F   1. To move the insertion point to the last cell in the worksheet area that contains data, press [Ctrl] [Home].

T   F   2. There are three header sections—left, center, and right.

T   F   3. The option to print titles is located in the Sheet tab of the Page Setup dialog box.

T   F   4. To display the Excel Options dialog box, click the File tab, then click Options.

T   F   5. You cannot specify how often you want Excel to automatically save your data.

MULTIPLE CHOICE

Select the best response for the following statements.

1. The name box is located _____ .
   - A. in the Excel Options dialog box
   - B. above the Quick Access Toolbar
   - C. in the Page Setup dialog box
   - D. above column A

2. To display the print option, click the _____ tab, then click Print.
   - A. File
   - B. Home
   - C. Page Layout
   - D. View

3. Which of the following is NOT a tab in the Page Setup dialog box?
   - A. Margins
   - B. Header/Footer
   - C. Print
   - D. Sheet

4. To set a print area, you must first _____ .
   - A. select the worksheet area you want to print
   - B. open the Page Setup dialog box
   - C. add the Print button to the Quick Access Toolbar
   - D. create a worksheet header

5. To display the Customize Ribbon page of the Excel Options dialog box, _____ a tab and click Customize the Ribbon.
   - A. click
   - B. double-click
   - C. right-click
   - D. point to

Excel

PROJECTS

Project EX 1-1

1. Open the data file **Project EX 1-1.xlsx**.

2. Save the file as **Dev Schedule**.

3. Move the Quick Access Toolbar below the Ribbon.

4. Use the name box to navigate to cell E18.

5. Use hot keys to navigate to the beginning of the worksheet (cell A1).

6. Create a header with the current date in the center section.

7. Create a footer with the file name in the left section.

8. Choose to print gridlines.

9. Set the print area for the range A5:E16.

10. Print the entire workbook.

11. Move the Quick Access Toolbar above the Ribbon.

12. Save and close the workbook.

Project EX 1-2

1. Open the data file **Project EX 1-2.xlsx**.

2. Save the file as **Swim Team**.

3. Add this title to the workbook properties: **CSHS Swim Team.**

4. Scale the Midland worksheet to fit on one page.

5. Choose to print only the selected (Midland) worksheet.

6. Use the Manage Version feature to see if there are any unsaved workbooks that you could recover if you needed to.

7. Save and close the workbook.

CRITICAL THINKING

Activity EX 1-1

There are many elements and options you can use to create a header or footer, including adding a predefined header or footer to a worksheet. Open a blank worksheet and experiment with creating headers and footers by inserting the various elements located in the Header & Footer Elements group of the Header & Footer Tools Design tab. In the Header & Footer group, click the Header or Footer button and practice inserting predefined text in the left, center, or right sections to create a header or footer that you think would be useful.

Activity EX 1-2

Search for the article and video in Excel Help that explain how to customize the Ribbon. If lab guidelines allow, practice creating a custom tab with at least one custom group that includes five commands that you frequently use.

Excel

EXCEL OBJECTIVE 2: CREATING CELL DATA

CONSTRUCT CELL DATA

Use Paste Special to Paste Formats, Formulas, Values, Comments, or Validation

Ribbon Method

☐ Select the cell(s) you want to cut or copy

☐ Click the **Home tab**, then click the **Copy button** or the **Cut button** in the Clipboard group

☐ Click the cell where you want to paste the cut or copied cells, click the **Paste button list arrow** in the Clipboard group, then click **Paste Special**

☐ In the Paste Special dialog box, shown in Figure EX 2-1, select an option in the Paste section, then click **OK**

Figure EX 2-1   Paste Special dialog box

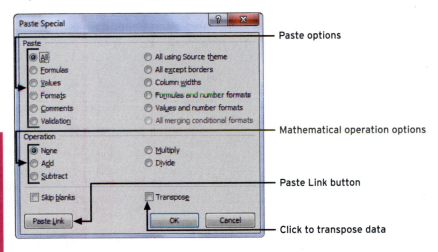

— Paste options

— Mathematical operation options

— Paste Link button

— Click to transpose data

Preview Paste Button Menu Icons

Ribbon Method

☐ Select the cell(s) you want to cut or copy

☐ Click the **Home tab**, then click the **Copy button** or the **Cut button** in the Clipboard group

☐ Click the cell where you want to paste the cut or copied cells, click the **Paste button list arrow** in the Clipboard group

☐ Click an option on the Paste Button menu, using Table EX 2-1 as a guide

Table EX 2-1   Paste Button menu

Icon	Paste option
	Paste
	Formulas
	Formulas & Number Formatting
	Keep Source Formatting

(continued)

Table EX 2-1   Paste Button menu (continued)

Icon	Paste option
	No Borders
	Keep Source Column Widths
	Transpose
	Values
	Values & Number Formatting
	Values & Source Formatting
	Formatting
	Paste Link
	Picture
	Linked Picture

Use Paste Special to Transpose Rows or Columns

Ribbon Method

☐ Select the cell(s) you want to cut or copy
☐ Click the **Home tab**, then click the **Copy button** or the **Cut button** in the Clipboard group
☐ Click the cell where you want to paste the cut or copied cells, click the **Paste button list arrow** in the Clipboard group, then click **Paste Special**
☐ In the Paste Special dialog box, click the **Transpose check box**, shown in Figure EX 2-1, then click **OK**

Use Paste Special to Perform Mathematical Operations

Ribbon Method

☐ Select the cell(s) you want to cut or copy
☐ Click the **Home tab**, then click the **Copy button** or the **Cut button** in the Clipboard group
☐ Click the cell where you want to paste the cut or copied cells, click the **Paste button list arrow** in the Clipboard group, then click **Paste Special**
☐ In the Paste Special dialog box, shown in Figure EX 2-1, select an option in the Operation section using Table EX 2-2 as a guide, then click **OK**

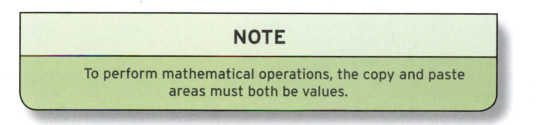

NOTE

To perform mathematical operations, the copy and paste areas must both be values.

Excel

Table EX 2-2 Operation options in the Paste Special dialog box

Operation	Description
None	Paste without a mathematical operation
Add	Add the values in the copy area to the values in the paste area
Subtract	Subtract the values in the copy area from the values in the paste area
Multiply	Multiply the values in the paste area by the values in the copy area
Divide	Divide the values in the paste area by the values in the copy area

Paste Data as a Link

Ribbon Method

□ Select the cell(s) you want to cut or copy

□ Click the **Home tab**, then click the **Copy button** 📋 or the **Cut button** ✂ in the Clipboard group

□ Click the cell where you want to paste the cut or copied cells, click the **Paste button list arrow** 📋▾ in the Clipboard group, then click **Paste Special**

□ In the Paste Special dialog box, click the **Paste Link button**, shown in Figure EX 2-1

Cut Cells

Ribbon Method

□ Select the cell(s) to cut

□ Click the **Home tab**, then click the **Cut button** ✂ in the Clipboard group

Shortcut Method

□ Select the cell(s) to cut

□ Right-click the selected cell(s), then click **Cut**

OR

□ Select the cell(s) to cut

□ Press **[Ctrl][X]**

Move Cells

Mouse Method

□ Select the cell(s) to move

□ Place the mouse pointer over any edge of the selected range until the pointer becomes ⛶

□ Drag the selected range to the desired location, then release the mouse button

Select Cell Data

Mouse Method

□ Select, or highlight, cell(s) by clicking the mouse, using Table EX 2-3 as a guide

Table EX 2-3 Selecting cells using the mouse

To select	Do this
A single cell	Click the cell
A range of cells	Click the first cell in the range (upper-left corner) and drag to the last cell in the range (lower-right corner) or Click the first cell in the range and then press and hold Shift and click the last cell in the range
Nonadjacent cells or ranges	Press and hold Ctrl as you click to select additional cells or click and drag to select additional ranges

(continued)

Excel

Table EX 2-3   Selecting cells using the mouse (continued)

To select	Do this
An entire row	Click the row heading
An entire column	Click the column heading
All cells on the worksheet	Click the Select All button in the upper-left corner of the workbook window

APPLY AUTOFILL

Copy Data Using AutoFill

Ribbon Method

☐ Drag to select **data** in one or more adjacent cells, then continue dragging to include the range you want to copy to in the selection

☐ Click the **Home tab**, click the **Fill button** 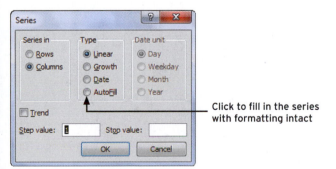 in the Editing group, then click **Down**, **Right**, **Up**, or **Left**

Mouse Method

☐ Drag to select one or more adjacent cells

☐ Point to the selected range's **fill handle** until the pointer changes to a black cross pointer

☐ Drag the **fill handle** horizontally or vertically to copy the data to the range you choose

Shortcut Method

☐ Click the cell whose value or formula you want to copy

☐ Press **[Shift][↓]** or **[Shift][→]** as necessary to select the fill range

☐ Press **[Ctrl][D]** to fill the range down or **[Ctrl][R]** to fill the range to the right

Fill a Series With or Without Formatting

Ribbon Method

☐ Drag to select two or more cells in a series you have started and continue dragging to include the range you want to fill, or select one cell containing the starting content in an AutoFill series, as described in Table EX 2-4, and the range you want to fill

☐ Click the **Home tab**, click the **Fill button** in the Editing group, then click **Series**

☐ In the Series dialog box, shown in Figure EX 2-2, click the **AutoFill option button** in the Type section, then click **OK** to fill in the series with formatting intact

Figure EX 2-2   **Series dialog box**

Click to fill in the series with formatting intact

Mouse Method

☐ Select two or more cells in a series you have started, or click one cell containing the starting content in an AutoFill series, as described in Table EX 2-4

☐ Point to the cell's **fill handle** until the pointer changes to a black cross

☐ Drag the **fill handle** horizontally or vertically to automatically fill in the appropriate values
☐ Click the **Auto Fill Options button** , shown in Figure EX 2-3, then click **Fill Series**, **Fill Formatting Only**, or **Fill Without Formatting**

Figure EX 2-3   Auto Fill Options menu

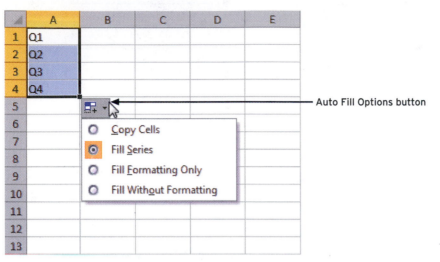

Shortcut Method

☐ Click two or more **cells** in a series you have started, or click one **cell** containing the starting content in an AutoFill series, as described in Table EX 2-4
☐ Point to the cell's **fill handle** until the pointer changes to a black cross
☐ Click and hold the **right mouse button**, then drag in the direction you want to fill
☐ On the shortcut menu, click **Fill Series**, **Fill Formatting Only**, or **Fill Without Formatting**

Table EX 2-4   AutoFill Series

To fill	Enter and select	Drag to display
Months	January	February, March, April...
Quarters	Q1	Q2, Q3, Q4
Years	2015, 2016	2017, 2018, 2019...
Times	8:00	9:00, 10:00, 11:00...
Text + Numbers	Student 1, Student 2	Student 3, Student 4, Student 5...
Numeric sequence	1, 3	5, 7, 9...

APPLY AND MANIPULATE HYPERLINKS

Create a Hyperlink in a Cell

Ribbon Method

☐ Select the appropriate cell
☐ Click the **Insert tab**, then click the **Hyperlink button** in the Links group
☐ In the Insert Hyperlink dialog box, shown in Figure EX 2-4, specify the appropriate options using Table EX 2-5 as a reference, then click **OK**

Figure EX 2-4 Insert Hyperlink dialog box

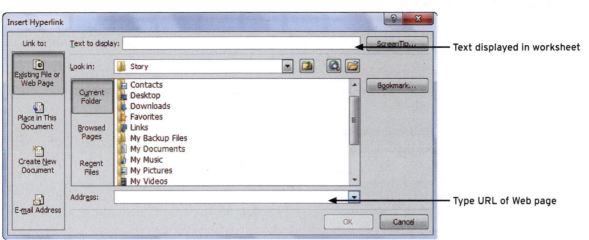

Shortcut Method

☐ Select the appropriate cell

☐ Press **[Ctrl][K]**

☐ In the Insert Hyperlink dialog box, specify the appropriate options using Table EX 2-5 as a reference, then click **OK**

Table EX 2-5 Creating Hyperlinks Using the Insert Hyperlink Dialog Box

To link to	Instructions
Another document	Click **Existing File or Web Page**, navigate to the appropriate folder, click the **file name** in the list, then click **OK**
A Web page	(*Note*: Make sure you are connected to the Internet) Click **Existing File or Web Page**, click the **Address text box**, type the URL, then click **OK**
Another place in the document	Click **Place in This Document**, select a **location** in the Or select a place in this document list, then click **OK**
A new document	Click **Create New Document**, name the document and verify the drive and folder, choose to edit it now or later, then click **OK**
An e-mail address	Click **E-mail Address**, type the **address** and any other text to display, then click **OK**

Modify Hyperlinks

Shortcut Method

☐ Right-click the **hyperlink**, then click **Edit Hyperlink** on the shortcut menu

☐ In the Edit Hyperlink dialog box, make modifications, then click **OK**

Modify Hyperlinked Cell Attributes

Ribbon Method

☐ Right-click the **hyperlink**, then click **Format Cells** on the shortcut menu

☐ In the Format Cells dialog box, modify cell attributes, then click **OK**

Remove a Hyperlink

Shortcut Method

☐ Right-click the **hyperlink**, then click **Remove Hyperlink** on the shortcut menu

REVIEW QUESTIONS

TRUE/FALSE

Circle T if the statement is true or F if the statement is false.

T   F   1. The Divide operation in the Paste Special dialog box divides the values in the copy area by the values in the paste area.

T   F   2. You can use the Paste Special dialog box to transpose columns or rows.

T   F   3. Click the row heading to select an entire row.

T   F   4. You can only fill a series down or to the right.

T   F   5. You can use the Insert Hyperlink dialog box to link to an e-mail address.

MULTIPLE CHOICE

Select the best response for the following statements.

1. The Copy and Cut buttons are located on the _____ tab.
    A. Home
    B. Insert
    C. Page Layout
    D. Data

2. Which is the shortcut method for cutting cells?
    A. [Ctrl][C]
    B. [Ctrl][P]
    C. [Ctrl][X]
    D. [Ctrl][V]

3. To select all cells in the worksheet, click the Select All button located _____.
    A. on the right side of the status bar
    B. on the Insert tab
    C. on the File tab
    D. in the upper-left corner of the workbook window

4. The Fill button is located on the Home tab in the _____ group.
    A. Editing
    B. Cells
    C. Alignment
    D. Clipboard

5. If you enter and select the numeric sequence 1, 3 then you can drag to display _____.
    A. 2, 4...
    B. 5, 7, 9...
    C. 2013, 2014 ...
    D. Student 1, Student 3, Student 5 ...

PROJECTS

Project EX 2-1

1. Open the data file Project EX 2-1.xlsx.

2. Save the file as Jewelry Sales.

3. In cell B3, create a hyperlink with *http://www.desertspringsjewelry.com* as the display text and the address.

4. Select cell B6 and use AutoFill to fill the series down to cell B9, preserving the cell format.

5. In cell B3, modify the hyperlink display text to *desertspringsjewelry.com*.

6. In cell B3, modify the hyperlinked cell attributes to be 12 point, italicized, and grey.

7. Move the value in cell E7 to cell F9.

8. Use Paste Special to copy the value in cell C9 to cell E7.

9. Use Paste Special to copy the formula in cell C10 to cell F10.

10. Use Paste Special to copy the format in cell E6 to the range F6:F10.

11. Save and close the workbook.

CRITICAL THINKING

Activity EX 2-1

The Paste Special dialog box allows you to copy or move worksheet items in a variety of ways. Table EX 2-2 lists some of the options. Use Help to learn more about using the other options in the Paste Special dialog box. In a separate document, list each option in the Paste Special dialog box and what it does. Save the document as Paste Special.

Activity EX 2-2

Create a new Excel worksheet. Use each of the options in the Insert Hyperlink dialog box to link a cell, range, chart, or graphic to another place in the document, another document, a new document, a Web page, or an e-mail address. Test each link to be sure it works and make modifications as necessary. Close the worksheet without saving.

Excel

Excel (vertical, left margin)

EXCEL OBJECTIVE 3: FORMATTING CELLS AND WORKSHEETS

APPLY AND MODIFY CELL FORMATS

Align Cell Content

Ribbon Method

☐ Select the cell(s) to format

☐ Click the **Home tab**, click an alignment button in the Alignment group, using Figure EX 3-1 as a guide

Figure EX 3-1   Alignment group on the Home tab

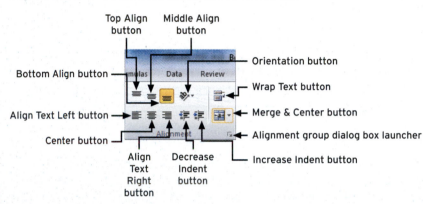

Apply a Number Format

Ribbon Method

☐ Select the cell(s) to format

☐ Click the **Home tab**, then click a button in the Number group, using Table EX 3-1 as a guide

Table EX 3-1   Number Format Options on the Home Tab

Icon	Number format	Example
$	Accounting Number Format	$ 10,000.00
%	Percent Style	Displays .06 as 6%
,	Comma Style	10,000.00
Increase Decimal icon	Increase Decimal	Changes 5.0 to 5.00
Decrease Decimal icon	Decrease Decimal	Changes 5.0 to 5

OR

☐ Click the **Home tab**, then click the **Number group dialog box launcher** ▣

☐ In the Format Cells dialog box, shown in Figure EX 3-2, click a category and select options on the Number tab using Table EX 3-2 as a guide

Figure EX 3-2   Number tab of Format Cells dialog box

Categories of number formats

Table EX 3-2   Number Tab Categories in the Format Cells Dialog Box

Category	Description
General	No number format
Number	General number format with or without decimal places or comma separators
Currency	General number format with currency symbols ($, €, etc.)
Accounting	Currency format but aligns currency symbols and decimal points
Date	Various month, day, and year formats
Time	Various hour, minute, and date formats
Percentage	Number multiplied by 100 and displayed with %
Fraction	Fractions in various formats (halves, quarters, etc.)
Scientific	Scientific format such as displaying 5500 as 5.50€+03
Text	Numbers treated as text, exactly as entered
Special	Zip code, phone number, or social security number formats
Custom	Special number, date, and time formats that user customizes

Wrapping Text in a Cell
Ribbon Method
□ Select the cell(s) to format
□ Click the **Home tab**, then click the **Wrap Text button** 📋 in the Alignment group, shown in Figure EX 3-1

Use Format Painter

Ribbon Method

☐ Select the cell whose formatting you want to copy

☐ Click the **Home tab,** then click the Format Painter button 🖌 in the Clipboard group

☐ Click the cell(s) to which you want to apply the formatting

---

NOTE

To apply the formatting to more than one cell or range, double-click the Format Painter button so that it stays active. When you are finished, click the Format Painter button again or press Esc.

MERGE OR SPLIT CELLS

Merge or Unmerge Cells

Ribbon Method

☐ Select the cells to merge or the merged cell to be split

☐ Click the **Home tab**, then click the **Merge and Center list arrow** 🔽 in the Alignment group

☐ Click an option, using Table EX 3-3 as a reference

Table EX 3-3   Merge Options

Icon	Option	Action
	Merge & Center	Merges selected cells and centers content in the newly merged cell
	Merge Across	Merges cells in a range horizontally only
	Merge Cells	Merges content across selected cell range
	Unmerge Cells	Removes merge and restores column or row structure

---

CREATE ROW AND COLUMN TITLES

Print Row and Column Headings

Ribbon Method

☐ Click the **Page Layout tab**, then select the **Print checkbox** in the Headings section of the Sheet Options group

Print Rows or Columns to Repeat with Titles

Ribbon Method

☐ Click the **Page Layout tab**, then click **Print Titles** 🖼 in the Page Setup group to display the Sheet tab of the Page Setup dialog box

☐ Type the reference of the rows that contain the labels in the Rows to repeat at top box
  AND/OR

☐ Type the reference of the columns that contain the labels in the Columns to repeat at left box

Configure Headers/Footers to Print Only on Odd or Even Pages

Ribbon Method

☐ Click the **Page Layout tab**, then click the **Page Setup group dialog box launcher** ▣

☐ In the Page Setup dialog box, click the **Header/Footer tab**, select the Different odd and even pages checkbox shown in Figure EX 3-3, then click **OK**

Figure EX 3-3   Header/Footer tab of Page Setup dialog box

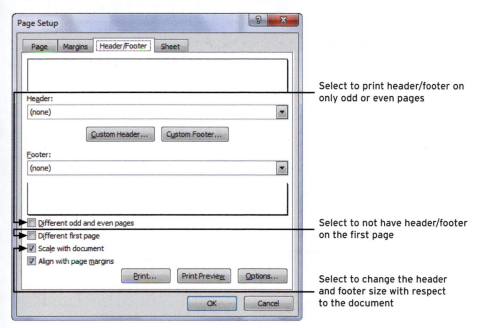

Select to print header/footer on only odd or even pages

Select to not have header/footer on the first page

Select to change the header and footer size with respect to the document

Configure Headers/Footers to Skip the First Worksheet Page

Ribbon Method

☐ Click the **Page Layout tab**, then click the **Page Setup group dialog box launcher** ▣

☐ In the Page Setup dialog box, click the **Header/Footer tab**, select the Different first page checkbox shown in Figure EX 3-3, then click **OK**

HIDE OR UNHIDE ROWS AND COLUMNS

Hide a Column or Row (or Series of Columns or Rows)

Ribbon Method

☐ Click a cell in the row or column to hide, select a range of cells spanning the rows or columns to hide, select an entire row or column, or select two or more rows or columns

☐ Click the **Home tab**, then click the **Format button** in the Cells group

☐ Point to **Hide & Unhide**, then click **Hide Rows** or **Hide Columns**

Unhide a Column or Row (or Series of Columns or Rows)

Ribbon Method

☐ Drag to select two cells, one on either side of the hidden row(s) or column(s)

☐ Click the **Home tab**, then click the **Format button** in the Cells group

☐ Point to **Hide & Unhide**, then click **Unhide Rows** or **Unhide Columns**

Excel

MANIPULATE PAGE SETUP OPTIONS FOR WORKSHEETS

Configure Page Orientation

Ribbon Method

☐ Click the **Page Layout tab**, then click the **Orientation button** [icon] in the Page Setup group and click either **Portrait** or **Landscape**

Manage Page Scaling

Ribbon Method

☐ Click the **Page Layout tab**, then click the **Page Setup group dialog box launcher** [icon]

☐ On the Page tab of the Page Setup dialog box, choose options in the Scaling section, shown in Figure EX 3-4, then click **OK**

Figure EX 3-4   Page tab of Page Setup dialog box

Page scaling options

Configure Page Margins

Ribbon Method

☐ Click the **Page Layout tab**, then click the **Margins button** [icon] in the Page Setup group

☐ Click **Normal, Wide,** or **Narrow**

OR

☐ Click **Custom Margins** to open the Page Setup dialog box

Change Header and Footer Size

Ribbon Method

☐ Click the **Page Layout tab**, then click the **Page Setup group dialog box launcher** ⬓
☐ Click the **Header/Footer tab** of the Page Setup dialog box, shown in Figure EX 3-3
☐ Select the **Scale with document** checkbox, then click **OK**

CREATE AND APPLY CELL STYLES

Apply Cell Styles

Ribbon Method

☐ Click the cell(s) to format
☐ Click the **Home tab**, click the **Cell Styles button** 🖾 in the Styles group, then click a style in one of the groups

Construct New Cell Styles

Ribbon Method

☐ Click the cell(s) to format
☐ Click the **Home tab**, click the **Cell Styles button** 🖾 in the Styles group, then click **New Cell Style**
☐ In the Style dialog box, shown in Figure EX 3-5, type a **name** in the Style name text box, then click **Format**
☐ Choose settings on the tabs of the Format Cells dialog box, then click **OK**
☐ Unselect any check box to not include that style, then click **OK**
☐ Click the **Cell Styles button** in the Styles group, then click the custom style in the Custom group to apply it

Figure EX 3-5   Style dialog box

Style	?	X

Style name: Style 1

Format...

Style Includes (By Example)
☑ Number   _(* #,##0.00_);_(* (#,##0.00);_(* "-"??_);_(@_)
☑ Alignment   General, Bottom Aligned
☑ Font   Calibri (Body) 11, Text 1
☑ Border   No Borders
☑ Fill   No Shading
☑ Protection Locked

OK   Cancel

REVIEW QUESTIONS

FILL IN THE BLANK

Complete the following sentences by writing the correct word or words in the blanks provided.

1. To wrap text in a cell, click the Home tab, then click the Wrap Text button in the _____ group.

2. The _____ option on the Merge and Center list arrow menu removes cell merge and restores column or row structure.

3. To print row and column headings, click the _____ tab, then select the Print checkbox in the Headings section of the Sheet Options group.

4. You can manage page scaling on the _____ tab of the Page Setup dialog box.

5. To apply cell styles, click the _____ tab, click the Cell Styles button in the Styles group, then click a style in one of the groups.

MATCHING

Match each number format category in Column 2 to its description in Column 1.

Column 1	Column 2
_____ 1. General	A. No number format
_____ 2. Number	B. Number multiplied by 100 and displayed with %
_____ 3. Accounting	C. Zip code, phone number, or social security number formats
_____ 4. Percentage	D. Currency format but aligns currency symbols and decimal points
_____ 5. Special	E. General number format with or without decimal places or comma separators

PROJECTS

Project EX 3-1

1. Open the data file **Project EX 3-1.xlsx**.

2. Save the file as **Attendance**.

3. Select cells A1:E2 and then merge and center the contents.

4. With the new merged cell still selected, apply the Title cell style.

5. Select columns D and E and then hide them.

6. Center-align the headings in cells F1:Y1.

7. Apply the Heading 4 cell style to cells F1:I1.

8. Use the Format Painter to copy the format of cells F1:I1 to cells J1:Y1.

9. Select cells A4:A20 and change the number format to Text.

10. Change the page orientation to Landscape.

11. Change the margins to the Narrow option.

12. Change the page scaling so the entire worksheet fits on one page.

13. Save and close the workbook.

Project EX 3-2

1. Open the data file **Project EX 3-2.xlsx**.

2. Save the file as **LostArt Photos**.

3. Select cells A1:C1 and unmerge them.

4. Unhide row 6.

5. Select cell C3 and wrap the text.

6. Select cells A3:C3 and middle-align the contents.

7. Select cells C4:C15 and center the contents.

8. Set the option to print row and column headings.

9. Save, print, and close the workbook.

CRITICAL THINKING

Activity EX 3-1

Follow the directions in this objective to create a new cell style that you think would look good as the style for your school name. Create the style using any formatting options that you like—including number, alignment, font, border, and fill. Name the style with your initials. Then create a worksheet, type the name of your school in cell A1, and apply the new cell style from the Custom section of the Cell Styles menu. Save the worksheet as My Style.

Excel

Excel Objective 4: Managing Worksheets and Workbooks

Create and Format Worksheets

Select One or More Worksheets

Ribbon Method

☐ Select one or more worksheets, using Table EX 4-1 as a reference

Table EX 4-1   Select worksheets

To select	Do this
One worksheet	Click the worksheet tab
Two or more adjacent worksheets	Click the first worksheet tab, press and hold down **[Shift]**, then click the tab of the last worksheet that you want to select
Two or more nonadjacent worksheets	Click the first worksheet tab, then press and hold down **[Ctrl]** while you click the tab(s) of the other worksheet(s) that you want to select
All worksheets in a workbook	Right-click a worksheet tab, then click **Select All Sheets** on the shortcut menu, shown in Figure EX 4-1

Group Worksheets

☐ To enter or edit data on several worksheets at a time, group them by selecting multiple worksheets using Table EX 4-1 as a reference

> **NOTE**
>
> **[Group]** is displayed in the title bar at the top of the worksheet when multiple worksheets are selected.

Insert One or More Worksheets

Ribbon Method

☐ Click the **Home tab**, click the **Insert list arrow** in the Cells group, then click **Insert Sheet**

> **NOTE**
>
> To insert multiple worksheets at the same time, press and hold down **[Shift]** and then select the same number of existing worksheet tabs that you want to insert.

Shortcut Method

☐ Click the **Insert Worksheet icon** to the right of the sheet tabs

OR

□ Press **[Shift] [F11]**

OR

□ Right-click the **sheet tab** to the right of where you want the new one to appear

□ Click **Insert** on the shortcut menu, shown in Figure EX 4-1

□ In the Insert dialog box, click the **Worksheet icon** on the General tab if necessary, then click **OK**

Figure EX 4-1   Sheet tab shortcut menu

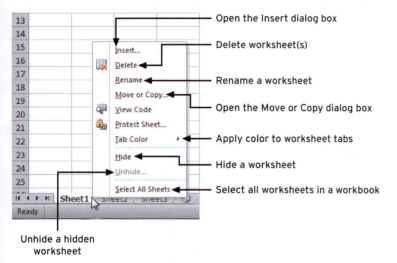

Open the Insert dialog box

Delete worksheet(s)

Rename a worksheet

Open the Move or Copy dialog box

Apply color to worksheet tabs

Hide a worksheet

Select all worksheets in a workbook

Unhide a hidden worksheet

Delete One or More Worksheets

Ribbon Method

□ Select the worksheet(s) that you want to delete

□ Click the **Home tab**, click the **Delete list arrow** in the Cells group, then click **Delete Sheet**

□ Click **Delete** in the message box to confirm the deletion, if necessary

Shortcut Method

□ Right-click the **sheet tab** to delete, then click **Delete** on the shortcut menu, shown in Figure EX 4-1

□ Click **Delete** in the message box to confirm the deletion, if necessary

Move or Copy Worksheets within a Workbook

Ribbon Method

□ Click the **Home tab**, click the **Format button** in the Cells group, then, in the Organize Sheets section, click **Move or Copy Sheet**

□ In the Move or Copy dialog box, shown in Figure EX 4-2, select the location to move or copy the worksheet in the Before sheet section

□ Click the **Create a copy check box** to copy the worksheet rather than move it if desired

□ Click **OK**

Figure EX 4-2   Move or Copy dialog box

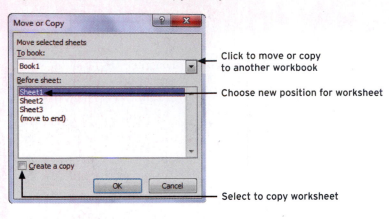

Click to move or copy
to another workbook

Choose new position for worksheet

Select to copy worksheet

Shortcut Method

☐ Right-click the **sheet tab** of the worksheet to move or copy, then click **Move or Copy** on the shortcut menu, shown in Figure EX 4-1

☐ Follow the steps in bullets 2–4 of the Move or Copy Worksheets within a Workbook Ribbon Method on the previous page

OR

☐ Position the pointer over the **sheet tab** to be moved or copied

☐ Use the sheet tab pointer to drag the tab to the appropriate location in the workbook, then release the mouse button

☐ Press **[Ctrl]** and use the drag and copy pointer to drag a worksheet copy to the desired location

Move or Copy Worksheets to Another Workbook

Ribbon Method

☐ Open the source and destination workbooks

☐ In the source workbook, click the **sheet tab** of the sheet you want to move

☐ Click the **Home tab**, click the **Format button** in the Cells group, then, under Organize Sheets, click **Move or Copy Sheet**

☐ In the Move or Copy dialog box, shown in Figure EX 4-2, click the **To book list arrow**, then click the destination workbook name

☐ Click the **Create a copy check box** to copy the worksheet rather than move it if desired

☐ Click **OK**

Mouse Method

☐ Open the source and destination workbooks

☐ Click the **View tab**, click the **Arrange All button** in the Window group.

☐ In the Arrange Windows dialog box, shown in Figure EX 4-3, click the **Tiled option button**, then click **OK**

☐ Drag to move (or press **[Ctrl]** while dragging to copy) the source worksheet to the destination workbook window

Figure EX 4-3   Arrange Windows dialog box

Excel

Rename Worksheets

Mouse Method
□ Double-click a **sheet tab**
□ Type a new worksheet **name**, then press **[Enter]**

Shortcut Method
□ Right-click a **sheet tab**, then click **Rename** on the shortcut menu, shown in Figure EX 4-1
□ Type a new worksheet **name**, then press **[Enter]**

Apply Color to Worksheet Tabs

Shortcut Method
□ Right-click the **sheet tab** to change
□ Point to **Tab Color** on the shortcut menu shown in Figure EX 4-1, then click a theme color or a standard color, or click **More Colors** to select a color from the Colors dialog box

Hide a Worksheet

Shortcut Method
□ Right-click any **worksheet tab**
□ Click **Hide** on the shortcut menu, shown in Figure EX 4-1

Unhide a Hidden Worksheet

Shortcut Method
□ Right-click any **sheet tab**
□ Click **Unhide** on the shortcut menu, shown in Figure EX 4-1
□ In the Unhide dialog box, shown in Figure EX 4-4, click the **sheet** you want to unhide, then click **OK**

Figure EX 4-4 **Unhide dialog box**

Select which sheet to unhide

MANIPULATE WINDOW VIEWS

Split Window Views

Ribbon Method
□ Click the cell below and to the right of where you want to split the worksheet
□ Click the **View tab**, then click the **Split button** in the Window group to split the worksheet horizontally and vertically
□ To remove the splits, click the **Split button** in the Window group again

Mouse Method

☐ Point to the split box ▯ to the right of the horizontal scroll bar or the split box ⊟ above the vertical scroll bar until the pointer becomes a horizontal split pointer or a vertical split pointer

☐ Drag left, right, up, or down, releasing the mouse button when the split bar is in the appropriate location

☐ To remove a split, double-click either **split bar**, or double-click the **intersection** of the horizontal and vertical split bars to remove both

Arrange Window Views

Ribbon Method

☐ With two or more workbooks open, click the **View tab**, then click the **Arrange All button** in the Window group

☐ Using Table EX 4-2 as a reference, click an option button in the Arrange Windows dialog box, shown in Figure EX 4-3, then click **OK**

Table EX 4-2   Arrange Windows Dialog Box Options

Click this option button	To
Tiled	Arrange workbooks in blocks so all are visible at once
Horizontal	Arrange workbooks horizontally, one above another
Vertical	Arrange workbooks vertically, one next to another
Cascade	Arrange workbooks on top of each other, with title bars visible

Open a New Workbook with Contents From the Current Worksheet

Ribbon Method

☐ Click the **File tab**, click **New**, then in the Available Templates section click **New from existing**

☐ In the New from Existing Workbook dialog box, browse to the workbook you want to open and click **Create New**

MANIPULATE WORKBOOK VIEWS

Change Worksheet Views

☐ Refer to Table EX 4-3 to change worksheet views

Table EX 4-3   Worksheet Views

View	What you see	Ribbon method	Status bar method
Normal view	Worksheet without headers, footers, or some graphics; does not show worksheet as it would appear as printed	Click the **View tab**, then click the **Normal button** in the Workbook Views group	Click the **Normal button** ▦ on the status bar
Page Layout view	Worksheet with headers, footers or some graphics; does not show worksheet as it would appear as printed	Click the **View tab**, then click the **Page Layout button** in the Workbook Views group	Click the **Page Layout button** ▣ on the status bar
Page Break Preview	Similar to Normal view, except with blue lines indicating page breaks; drag a page break using the vertical, horizontal, and diagonal resize pointers	Click the View tab, then click the **Page Break Preview button** in the Workbook Views group	Click the **Page Break Preview button** ▣ on the status bar

(continued)

Table EX 4-3 Worksheet Views (continued)

View	What you see	Ribbon method	Status bar method
Custom views	Saved views	Click the View tab, then click the **Custom Views button** in the Workbook Views group	None
Full screen	Worksheet, title bar, sheet tabs, and scroll bars only	Click the View tab, then click the **Full Screen button** in the Workbook Views group	None

REVIEW QUESTIONS

FILL IN THE BLANK

Complete the following sentences by writing the correct word or words in the blanks provided.

1. To select two or more adjacent worksheets, click the first worksheet tab, press and hold down _____, then click the tab of the last worksheet that you want to select.

2. To delete a worksheet, click the _____ tab, click the Delete list arrow in the Cells group, then click Delete Sheet.

3. To display the Move or Copy dialog box, right-click the _____ of the worksheet to move or copy, then click Move or Copy on the shortcut menu.

4. To rename a worksheet, double-click a sheet tab, type a new worksheet name, then press _____.

5. To remove splits from a worksheet, click the View tab, then click the Split button in the _____ group.

MATCHING

Match each window view option in Column 1 to its description in Column 2.

Column 1	Column 2
_____ 1. Tiled	A. Tab on which the Arrange All button in the Windows group is located
_____ 2. View	B. Arrange workbooks on top of each other with title bars visible
_____ 3. Horizontal	C. Arrange workbooks in blocks so all are visible at once
_____ 4. Vertical	D. Arrange workbooks next to each other
_____ 5. Cascade	E. Arrange workbooks one above another

PROJECTS

Project EX 4-1

1. Open the data file **Project EX 4-1.xlsx**.

2. Save the file as **Test Grades**.

3. Switch to Page Layout workbook view.

4. Select Sheet2 and Sheet3 and delete them.

5. Create a copy of the Winter worksheet.

6. Rename the copy of the worksheet (Winter (2)) **Spring**.

7. Insert a new worksheet and rename it **Fall**.

Excel

8. Move the Spring worksheet so it is between the Winter and Fall worksheets.

9. Hide the Fall worksheet.

10. Apply a blue color to the Winter worksheet tab and a green color to the Spring worksheet tab.

11. Switch to Page Break Preview workbook view.

12. Switch back to Normal workbook view.

13. Unhide the Fall worksheet.

14. Save and close the workbook.

CRITICAL THINKING

Activity EX 4-1

Create four new blank workbooks. In the Window group of the View tab, click the Arrange All button to display the Arrange All dialog box. Select an option, and then click OK. Repeat the process with each option in the dialog box. Notice how the worksheets are arranged for each different option. When would each view option be helpful when you have multiple workbooks open? Close the workbooks without saving.

Activity EX 4-2

With a partner, learn more about creating a custom view. What kinds of specific display settings and print settings can you save? Work together to create and save a custom view. Next, practice applying your custom view to a worksheet. When you are finished, delete the custom view.

EXCEL OBJECTIVE 5: APPLYING FORMULAS AND FUNCTIONS

CREATE FORMULAS

Use Basic Operators

Mouse Method

☐ Click the cell where you want the formula result to appear

☐ Type **=**

☐ Click the cell containing the first value you want to include

☐ Type an operator, using Table EX 5-1 as a reference

☐ Click the cell containing the second value you want to include

☐ Enter operators and other cells as necessary

☐ Press **[Enter]**

Keyboard Method

☐ Click the cell where you want the formula result to appear

☐ Type **=**

☐ Type the cell address or use the keyboard arrow keys to navigate to the cell containing the first value you want
to include

☐ Type an operator, using Table EX 5-1 as a reference

☐ Type the cell address or use the keyboard arrow keys to navigate to the cell containing the second value you
want to include

☐ Press **[Enter]**

Table EX 5-1   Arithmetic operators

Operator	Operation	Example	Description
+ (plus sign)	Addition	A7+D9	Adds the values in cells A7 and D9
– (minus sign)	Subtraction	A7–D9	Subtracts the value in D9 from the value in A7
* (asterisk)	Multiplication	A7*D9	Multiplies the value in A7 by the value in D9
/ (forward slash)	Division	A7/D9	Divides the value in A7 by the value in D9
% (percent sign)	Percent	A7*25%	Calculates 25% of the value in A7
^ (caret)	Exponentiation	A7^4	Raises the value in A7 to the fourth power

Revise Formulas

Mouse Method

☐ Select the cell containing the formula

☐ Type your changes in the formula bar

☐ Press **[Enter]**

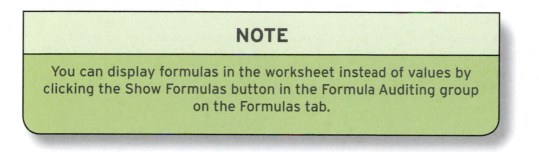

NOTE

You can display formulas in the worksheet instead of values by
clicking the Show Formulas button in the Formula Auditing group
on the Formulas tab.

ENFORCE PRECEDENCE

Order of Evaluation

Ribbon Method

- ☐ Enter a formula containing more than one arithmetic operator, using Table EX 5-2 as a reference for the sequence that Excel uses to calculate the value

Table EX 5-2   Order of evaluation

Order of evaluation	Arithmetic operator
1	Percent (%)
2	Exponentiation (^)
3	Multiplication (*) or division (/), evaluated from left to right
4	Addition (+) or subtraction (-), evaluated from left to right

Precedence Using Parentheses

Ribbon Method

- ☐ Enter a formula containing more than one arithmetic operator, using Table EX 5-2 as a reference for the sequence that Excel uses to calculate the value
- ☐ Change the default order in which calculations occur in the formula by placing parentheses around the expressions to be calculated first

Precedence of Operators for Percent vs. Exponentiation

Ribbon Method

- ☐ Enter a formula containing the percent (%) and exponentiation (^) operators, using Table EX 5-2 as a reference for the sequence that Excel uses to calculate the value

APPLY CELL REFERENCES IN FORMULAS

Use Figure EX 5-1 as a reference for using relative and absolute references in formulas

Use Relative References

Shortcut Method

- ☐ Click the appropriate cell, then click the formula bar and type **=**, or type **=** directly in the cell
- ☐ To insert a cell reference in the formula, type the cell address you want to reference in the formula bar or in the cell that contains the formula, or click the cell you want to reference
- ☐ Complete the formula using appropriate operators, values, and additional cell references, then click the **Enter button** ✔ on the formula bar

Use Absolute References

Shortcut Method

- ☐ Click a cell where you want to enter a formula, then enter the formula in the formula bar or type the formula directly in the cell
- ☐ In the formula bar, select the cell reference that you want to make an absolute reference
- ☐ Press **[F4]**, then verify that the cell reference now reads **$A$1** (where A1 is the cell address)
- ☐ Press **[Enter]** or **[Tab]**

Use Mixed References in Formulas

Shortcut Method

☐ Click a cell where you want to enter a formula, then enter the formula in the formula bar or type the formula directly in the cell

☐ In the formula bar, select the cell reference that you want to make into a mixed reference

☐ Press **[F4]** until the cell reference reads **A$1** or **$A1** (where A1 is the cell address)

☐ Press **[Enter]** or **[Tab]**

Figure EX 5-1   Relative, absolute, and mixed cell references

Formula copied from cell B11 to cell C11; relative cell reference has changed to reflect column C

	A	B	C
1	**Tax Reserve Projections**		
2			
3			
4	**Tax Rate**	**0.2**	
5			
6	Customer	Quarter 1	Quarter 2
7	Jesse's Plumbing	3500	2500
8	Tyler Music School	4000	5000
9	Café Renee	2000	1000
10	NLH Auto Mechanics	1400	2000
11		=SUM(B7:B10)	=SUM(C7:C10)
12			
13			Assuming a tax rate of
14	Tax Reserve Q1	=$B$4*B11	=$B$4
15	Tax Reserve Q2	=$B$4*C11	=$B$4
16			
17			

Formulas contain mixed references: first reference is absolute, second reference is relative

Relative cell reference

Absolute cell references with dollar signs always refer to cell B4, no matter where the reference is copied

APPLY CONDITIONAL LOGIC IN A FORMULA

Create a Formula with Values That Match Conditions

Ribbon Method

☐ Click the cell where you want the formula result to appear

☐ Click the **Formulas tab**, then click the **Insert Function button** in the Function Library group (or click the **Insert Function button** 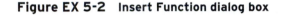 on the formula bar)

☐ In the Insert Function dialog box, shown in Figure EX 5-2, select the appropriate function using Table EX 5-3 as a reference, then click **OK**

☐ In the Function Arguments dialog box, shown in Figure EX 5-3, specify the appropriate settings or the appropriate cells if necessary, then click **OK**

OR

☐ Click the **Formulas tab** click the **Logical button** in the Function Library group, then click the function name in the drop-down menu, using Table EX 5-3 as a reference

☐ In the Function Arguments dialog box, shown in Figure EX 5-3, specify the appropriate settings or the appropriate cells if necessary, then click **OK**

Figure EX 5-2   Insert Function dialog box

Figure EX 5-3   Function Arguments dialog box

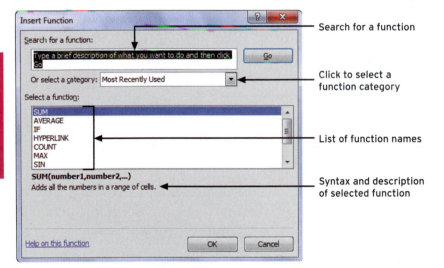

Table EX 5-3   Functions for Conditional Logic

Function	Example	Results
IF	=IF(logical_test,value, if_true value_if_false)	Performs the logical test, then returns (displays) a value if it is true or false, such as whether a budget is within limits
AND	=AND(A1>10,B1>25)	Checks two or more conditions; if all are true, then returns TRUE; if one of the conditions is not true, then returns FALSE
OR	=OR(A1>10,B1>25)	Checks two or more conditions; if any are true, then returns TRUE; if all of the conditions are not true, then returns FALSE
NOT	=NOT(A1=25)	Checks the condition; and reverses the TRUE result and reports FALSE
IFERROR	=IFERROR(Formula, "ERRORMESSAGE")	Checks a formula for correctness; if it would result in an Excel error message (such as #DIV/0!), it displays your ERRORMESSAGE text instead of the Excel error

Edit Defined Conditions in a Formula
Mouse Method
□ Double-click the cell containing the defined conditions in the formula
□ Type your changes in the formula bar, in the cell, or click the **Insert Function button** on the formula bar to make changes in the Function Arguments dialog box, shown in Figure EX 5-3
□ Press [**Enter**]

Use a Series of Conditional Logic Values in a Formula
Ribbon Method
□ Follow the steps in bullets 1-3 of the Create a Formula with Values that Match Conditions Ribbon Method on the previous page
□ In the Function Arguments dialog box, shown in Figure EX 5-3, enter a function in the argument box that you want, then click **OK**

> **NOTE**
>
> Nested functions use a function as one of the arguments of another function. You can nest up to 64 levels of functions.

APPLY NAMED RANGES IN FORMULAS

Define Ranges in Formulas
Ribbon Method
□ Select the range, including any row or column labels
□ Click the **Formulas tab**, shown in Figure EX 5-4, then click the **Create from Selection button** in the Defined Names group
□ In the Create Names from Selection dialog box, shown in Figure EX 5-5, click the appropriate check box to use as the range name, then click **OK**

Excel

Figure EX 5-4   Formulas tab

Name cell
ranges

Insert a
named range
in a formula

Display or
hide formulas

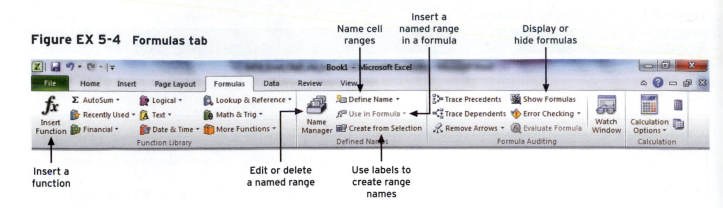

Insert a
function

Edit or delete
a named range

Use labels to
create range
names

Figure EX 5-5   Create Names from Selection dialog box

Shortcut Method

☐ Select the range, including any row or column labels

☐ Click the **Formulas tab**, shown in Figure EX 5-4, then press **[Ctrl][Shift][F3]**

☐ In the Create Names from Selection dialog box, shown in Figure EX 5-5, click the appropriate check box to use as the range name, then click **OK**

Edit Ranges in Formulas

Ribbon Method

☐ Click the **Formulas tab**, shown in Figure EX 5-4, then click the **Name Manager button** in the Defined Names group

☐ In the Name Manager dialog box, shown in Figure EX 5-6, click the name of the range you want to edit

☐ Edit the cell range in the Refers to text box

☐ Click **Close**, then click **Yes** in the dialog box to confirm your changes

Figure EX 5-6   Name Manager dialog box

Shortcut Method

☐ Click the **Formulas tab**, then press **[Ctrl][F3]**

☐ Follow the steps in bullets 2–4 of the Edit Ranges in a Formula Ribbon Method on the previous page

Rename a Named Range

Ribbon Method

☐ Click the **Formulas tab**, shown in Figure EX 5-4, then click the **Name Manager button** in the Defined Names group

☐ In the Name Manager dialog box, shown in Figure EX 5-6, click the name of the range you want to edit, then click **Edit**

☐ In the Edit Name dialog box, shown in Figure EX 5-7, rename the named range in the Name box

☐ Click **OK**

Figure EX 5-7   Edit Name dialog box

APPLY CELL RANGES IN FORMULAS

Enter a Cell Range Definition in the Formula Bar

Ribbon Method

☐ Click in the cell where the formula will appear

☐ Begin typing the formula, then when you need to insert the range name, click the **Formulas tab**, shown in Figure EX 5-4

☐ Click the **Use in Formula button** in the Defined Names group, then click the range name in the drop-down menu

☐ Complete the formula as appropriate

OR

☐ Click in the cell where the formula will appear

☐ Begin typing the formula, then when you need to insert the range name, click the **Formulas tab**

☐ Click the **Use in Formula button** in the Defined Names group, click **Paste Names**, then in the Paste Name dialog box, shown in Figure EX 5-8, double-click the range name

☐ Complete the formula as appropriate

Figure EX 5-8   Paste Name dialog box

Shortcut Method

☐ Click the cell where the formula will appear

☐ As you type the formula in the cell, type the first letter of the range name, and use **[↓]** to select the range name that appears in the drop-down menu

☐ Press **[Tab]**, then type the rest of the formula and press **[Enter]**

Define a Cell Range

Mouse Method

☐ Click the first cell in the range (in the upper-left corner) and drag to the last cell in the range (in the lower-right corner)

Keyboard Method

☐ Click the first cell in the range and then press and hold **Shift** and click the last cell in the range

REVIEW QUESTIONS

TRUE/FALSE

Circle T if the statement is true or F if the statement is false.

T   F   1. When Excel calculates the value of a formula containing more than one arithmetic operator, addition and subtraction are last in the order of evaluation.

T   F   2. When a formula contains more than one arithmetic operator, you can change the default order in which calculations occur by placing parentheses around the expressions to be calculated first.

T   F   3. $A$1 is a relative cell reference.

T   F   4. You cannot use a function as one of the arguments of another function.

T   F   5. To define a cell range using the keyboard method, click the first cell in the range and then press and hold Shift and click the last cell in the range.

MULTIPLE CHOICE

Select the best response for the following statements.

1. When creating a formula, what is the first thing you type in a cell?
   A. ? (question mark)
   B. : (colon)
   C. + (addition sign)
   D. = (equal sign)

2. Which operation has an asterisk (*) as an operator?
   A. Multiplication
   B. Division
   C. Percent
   D. Exponentiation

3. Which function performs the logical test, then returns (displays) a value if it is true or false, such as whether a budget is within limits?
   A. IF
   B. AND
   C. OR
   D. NOT

4. The Defined Names group is located on the _____ tab.
   A. Home
   B. Insert
   C. Formulas
   D. Data

5. Which expression raises the value in A7 to the fourth power?
   A. A7*4
   B. A7^4
   C. A7+4
   D. A7=4

PROJECTS

Project EX 5-1

1. Open the data file **Project EX 5-1.xlsx**.

2. Save the file as **Tea Invoice**.

3. In cell E11, enter a formula to multiply the value in cell C11 by the value in cell D11.

4. Use the AutoFill feature to copy the formula in cell E11 to the range E12: E15.

5. In cell E18, use the Sum command to get a total for the range E11:E17.

6. In cell E19, create a formula that calculates 7% sales tax on the value in cell E18. (*Hint:* Use the formula =7%*E18.)

7. In cell E20, type 7.95.

8. In cell E21, enter a formula with absolute references that totals the values of the cells in the range E18:E20.

9. Only sales totaling more than $300 qualify for a discount. In cell C23, create a formula using the OR function with E21>300 as the argument. (*Hint:* Use the Function Arguments dialog box.)

10. Save and close the workbook.

CRITICAL THINKING

Activity EX 5-1

Visit Web sites of companies that sell cell phone plans. Create a worksheet containing information about at least three different options—including the price of the cell phone, cost of the cell plan per month, how many minutes are included, cost of features such as text messaging, and any additional charges. Use a formula to determine the best plan for your budget. Use functions to determine the highest price plan, the lowest price plan, and the average price of the plans.

Activity EX 5-2

With a partner, open the Insert Function dialog box. Browse through all the various categories and familiarize your-selves with the various functions available in each one. Click a function to see the description displayed below it. Choose one that you want to know more about and click the Help on this function link to get more information. Learn as much as possible about it. Present your findings to the class and include a worksheet you have created that demonstrates the use of the function.

Activity EX 5-3

In Excel, you can create a defined name that you assign to a cell or range of cells and then use the defined name as a reference in formulas. Use Excel Help to learn the different ways you can define a name for a range, how to use defined names in a formula, and how to use the Name Manager to create, edit, delete, or find names in workbook. Open an existing workbook, and then create at least one defined name for a range of cells and use the defined name in a formula.

EXCEL OBJECTIVE 6: PRESENTING DATA VISUALLY

CREATE CHARTS BASED ON WORKSHEET DATA

Ribbon Method
- ☐ Select the data range you want to use to create a chart
- ☐ Click the **Insert tab**, click a chart type button in the Charts group, using Table EX 6-1 as a guide, then click a chart subtype from the drop-down menu

Table EX 6-1 Common Chart Types

Chart type	Icon	Used to show
Column		Relative amounts for one or multiple values at different points in time (displays vertically)
Line		Growth trends over time
Pie		Proportions or percentages of parts to a whole
Bar		Relative amounts for one or multiple values at different points in time (displays horizontally)
Area		Differences between several sets of data over time
Scatter		Values that are not in categories and where each data point is a distinct measurement

APPLY AND MANIPULATE ILLUSTRATIONS

Insert an Illustration
Ribbon Method
- ☐ Click the **Insert tab**, then click an illustration button in the Illustrations group, using Table EX 6-2 as a guide

Table EX 6-2 Illustrations group options

Illustration	Description
Picture	Digital photographs or images stored on your computer or network
Clip Art	A collection of predesigned art, including movies, drawings, sounds, or stock photography
Shapes	Ready-made shapes, such as rectangles and circles, arrows, lines, flowchart symbols, and callouts
SmartArt	A predesigned diagram made up of shapes containing text that illustrate a concept or an idea
Screenshot	A picture of a computer screen or part of a screen, such as a button

Move an Illustration
Mouse Method
- ☐ Click an illustration, then position the pointer over an edge until a four-arrow pointer appears
- ☐ Click and drag the illustration to a new location, then release the mouse button

Resize an Illustration
Ribbon Method
- ☐ Select an illustration, then on the **Drawing Tools Format tab**, click the **Shape Height** or **Shape Width text box** in the Size group
- ☐ Type a new height or width, then press **[Enter]**

Mouse Method

☐ Click a picture, then position the pointer over a corner sizing handle
☐ Drag the sizing handle to resize the chart

Rotate an Illustration

Ribbon Method

☐ Select an illustration, then on the **Drawing Tools Format tab**, click the **Rotate button** in the Arrange group
☐ Choose a rotation option from the menu

Mouse Method

☐ Click a picture, then position the pointer over the rotation handle
☐ Drag the rotation handle in the direction you want to rotate the graphic

Modify Clip Art

Ribbon Method

☐ Click a clip art image, click the **Picture Tools Format tab**, then, using Table EX 6-3 as a reference, click an option and adjust its settings

Table EX 6-3   Picture Tools Format tab options

Format tab group	Options
Adjust	Brightness, Contrast, Recolor, Compress Pictures, Change Picture, Reset Picture
Picture Styles	Predesigned picture formats; Picture Shape, Picture Border, Picture Effects
Arrange	Bring to Front, Send to Back, Selection Pane, Align, Group, Rotate
Size	Crop, Shape Height, Shape Width

Modify SmartArt

Ribbon Method

☐ Select a SmartArt object, then click the **SmartArt Tools Design tab**
☐ In the SmartArt Styles group, click the **More button**, then click a **style**
  OR
☐ Click the **Change Colors button**, then click a new color scheme if desired

Modify Shape

Ribbon Method

☐ Select a shape object, then click the **Drawing Tools Format tab**, shown in Figure EX 6-1
☐ Use the options available to modify the shape

Figure EX 6-1   **Drawing Tools Format tab**

Modify Screenshots

Ribbon Method

☐ Select a screenshot object, then click the **Picture Tools Format tab**
☐ Use the options available to modify the screenshot

CREATE AND MODIFY IMAGES BY USING THE IMAGE EDITOR

Sharpen or Soften an Image

Ribbon Method

☐ Select an image

☐ On the Picture Tools Format tab, click the **Corrections button** in the Adjust group

☐ Choose an option from the Soften and Sharpen section of the menu

   OR

☐ Click **Picture Corrections Options** to display the Format Picture dialog box, shown in Figure EX 6-2, and make adjustments in the Soften and Sharpen section

Figure EX 6-2 Format Picture dialog box

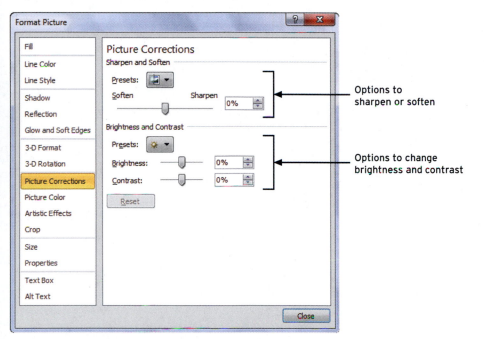

Change Image Brightness

Ribbon Method

☐ Select an image

☐ On the Picture Tools Format tab, click the **Corrections button** in the Adjust group

☐ Choose an option from the Brightness and Contrast section of the menu

   OR

☐ Click **Picture Corrections Options** to display the Format Picture dialog box, shown in Figure EX 6-2, and make adjustments in the Brightness and Contrast section

Change Image Contrast

Ribbon Method

☐ Select an image

☐ On the Picture Tools Format tab, click the **Corrections button** in the Adjust group

☐ Choose an option from the Brightness and Contrast section of the menu

   OR

☐ Click **Picture Corrections Options** to display the Format Picture dialog box, shown in Figure EX 6-2, make adjustments in the Brightness and Contrast section

Use Picture Color Tools

Ribbon Method

☐ Select an image

☐ On the Picture Tools Format tab, click the **Color button** in the Adjust group

☐ On the Color menu, shown in Figure EX 6-3, choose a color option

Figure EX 6-3   Color menu

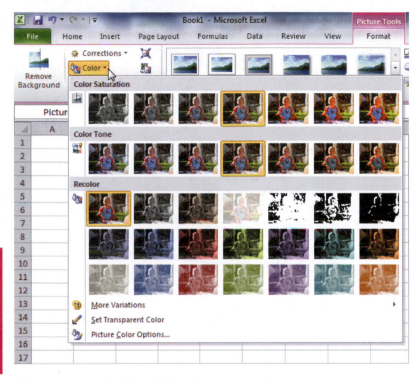

Change Artistic Effects on an Image

Ribbon Method

☐ Select an image

☐ On the Picture Tools Format tab, click the **Artistic Effects button** in the Adjust group

☐ On the menu, choose an artistic effects option

APPLY SPARKLINES

Use Line Chart Types

Ribbon Method

☐ Select the data range you want to use to create a chart

☐ Click the **Insert tab**, then click the **Line button** in the Charts group, shown in Figure EX 6-4

☐ Click a **2-D** or **3-D** line chart type

Figure EX 6-4 Insert tab

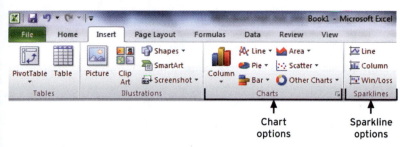

Chart
options

Sparkline
options

Use Column Chart Types

Ribbon Method

☐ Select the data range you want to use to create a chart

☐ Click the **Insert tab**, then click the **Column button** in the Charts group, shown in Figure EX 6-4

☐ Click column chart type

Use Win/Loss Chart Types

Ribbon Method

☐ Select the data range you want to use to create a chart

☐ Click the **Insert tab**, then click the **Win/Loss button** in the Sparklines group, shown in Figure EX 6-4

☐ In the Create Sparklines dialog box, shown in Figure EX 6-5, choose the data range and location range, then click **OK**

Figure EX 6-5 Create Sparklines dialog box

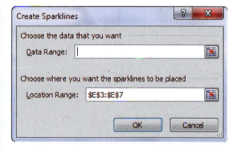

NOTE

Sparklines are miniature charts that are embedded in the
background of a single cell, displaying a graphic representation
of the data in a small space and helping to spot patterns or data
trends that otherwise might be hard to see.

Create a Sparkline Chart

Ribbon Method

☐ Select the data range you want to use to create a chart

☐ Click the **Insert tab**, then click a button in the Sparklines group, shown in Figure EX 6-4

☐ In the Create Sparklines dialog box, shown in Figure EX 6-5, choose the data range and location range, then click **OK**

Customize a Sparkline

Ribbon Method

☐ Select one or more sparklines

☐ Use the buttons on the Sparkline Tools Design tab, shown in Figure EX 6-6, to customize the sparkline style, show or hide data markers in a line sparkline, control how a sparkline handles empty cells in a range, or clear selected sparklines

Figure EX 6-6 **Sparkline Tools Design tab**

Show or hide data
marker options

Format a Sparkline

Ribbon Method

☐ Select one or more sparklines

☐ Use the buttons on the Sparkline Tools Design tab, shown in Figure EX 6-6, to edit sparkline data, change the type of sparkline, or format a sparkline

Show or Hide Data Markers

Mouse Method

☐ Select a sparkline

☐ On the Sparkline Tools Design tab, shown in Figure EX 6-6, select any of the check boxes to show individual markers (such as high, low, negative, first, or last), or select the Markers check box to show all markers

REVIEW QUESTIONS

MATCHING

Match each illustration in Column 1 to its description in Column 2.

Column 1	Column 2
_____ 1. Picture	A. A collection of predesigned art, including movies, drawings, sounds, or stock photography
_____ 2. Clip Art	
_____ 3. Shapes	B. A picture of a computer screen or part of a screen, such as a button
_____ 4. SmartArt	C. Digital photographs or images stored on your computer or network
_____ 5. Screenshot	D. Ready-made objects, such as rectangles and circles, arrows, lines, flowchart symbols, and callouts
	E. A predesigned diagram made up of shapes containing text that illustrate a concept or an idea

MULTIPLE CHOICE

Select the best response for the following statements.

1. Which chart type shows proportions or percentages of parts to a whole?
   A. column
   B. line
   C. pie
   D. bar

2. Which chart type is used to show growth trends over time?
   A. line
   B. bar
   C. area
   D. scatter

3. Which Picture Tools Format tab group contains the Crop, Shape Height, and Shape Width options?
   A. Adjust
   B. Pictures Styles
   C. Arrange
   D. Size

4. Which illustration modification can NOT be made in the Adjust group on the Picture Tools Format tab?
   A. contrast
   B. size
   C. brightness
   D. color

5. To create a sparkline chart, select the data you want to use, then click a button in the Sparklines group on the _____ tab.
   A. Home
   B. Insert
   C. Data
   D. View

PROJECTS

Project EX 6-1

1. Open the data file **Project EX 6-1.xlsx**.

2. Save the file as **First Quarter**.

3. Select range A4:D8 and create a 2-D Clustered Column chart.

4. Move the chart so that it is below the data on the worksheet (with the upper left corner in cell A9).

5. Search for clip art with the keyword "**tea**" and insert one that you like.

6. Resize the clip art so that it is approximately 1" high.

7. Move the clip art so that it is to the right of the company name (with the upper left corner in cell E1).

8. Change the color of the clip art to a grayscale, if it is not already.

9. Save and close the workbook.

Project EX 6-2

1. Open a new, blank worksheet.

2. Save the file as **Tea Types**.

3. Insert a **Hierarchy List** SmartArt graphic.

4. Replace the first [Text] bullet placeholder on the left with **Black**.

5. Replace the second [Text] bullet placeholder underneath it with **Irish Breakfast**.

6. Replace the third [Text] bullet placeholder underneath it with **Earl Grey**.

7. Add another shape after Earl Grey with **Darjeeling** as the text.

8. Continue adding to the SmartArt graphic until it looks like Figure EX 6-7.

9. Change the SmartArt style to **Subtle Effect**.

10. Save and close the workbook.

Figure EX 6-7   Tea Types SmartArt

CRITICAL THINKING

Activity EX 6-1

Create a worksheet that shows the number of hours each day that you spend doing various activities—sleeping, eating, attending school, doing homework, hanging out with friends, and so on. Create a pie chart to illustrate the data. Insert a picture of yourself and modify it by softening, sharpening, changing the brightness or contrast, using the picture color tools, or changing the artistic effect. Save the file as **My Time**.

Activity EX 6-2

Search for the training course in Excel Help titled *Sparklines: Use tiny charts to show data trends*, and complete it. Then create a worksheet that shows some kind of data trend (i.e. your grades in this class or the temperature in your city this week) and create sparklines to represent the data. Save the workbook as **Sparklines**.

Excel Objective 7: Sharing Worksheet Data with Other Users

Share Spreadsheets by using Backstage

Send a Worksheet via E-Mail

Ribbon Method

☐ Open the workbook you want to send

☐ Click the **File tab**, then click **Save & Send**

☐ Click **Send Using E-mail**, then click one of the options on the right, as shown in Figure EX 7-1

☐ An e-mail message will open in Microsoft Outlook with your workbook attached

☐ Type the recipient's e-mail address in the To box, type a message, and then click **Send**

Figure EX 7-1   Send Using E-mail options on the File tab

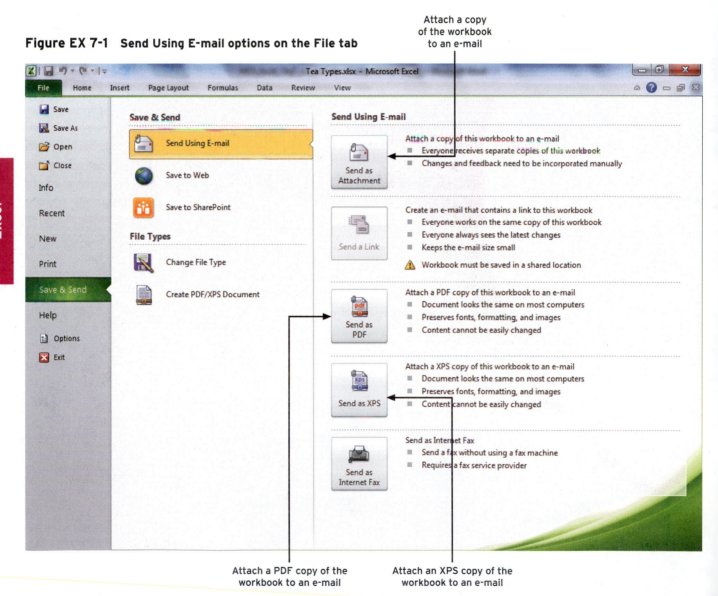

Attach a copy of the workbook to an e-mail

Attach a PDF copy of the workbook to an e-mail

Attach an XPS copy of the workbook to an e-mail

Send a Worksheet via Skydrive

Ribbon Method

☐ Open the workbook you want to send

☐ Click the **File tab**, then click **Save & Send**

☐ Click **Save to Web**

☐ Click the **Sign In button**, shown in Figure EX 7-2, to sign in to Windows Live

☐ Enter your Windows Live ID credentials in the dialog box

☐ Once you are connected, you can make your file accessible from any computer using Windows Live SkyDrive, a free online storage service from Microsoft, shown in Figure EX 7-3

NOTE

If you don't have a Windows Live ID, click the *Sign up for Windows Live* link.

Figure EX 7-2   Save to Web options on File tab

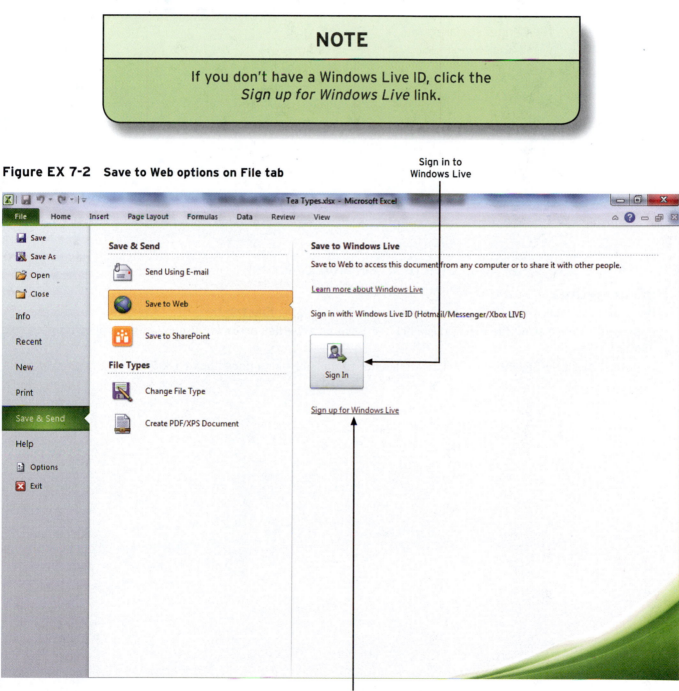

Sign in to
Windows Live

Click to sign up
for Windows Live

Figure EX 7-3 Windows Live

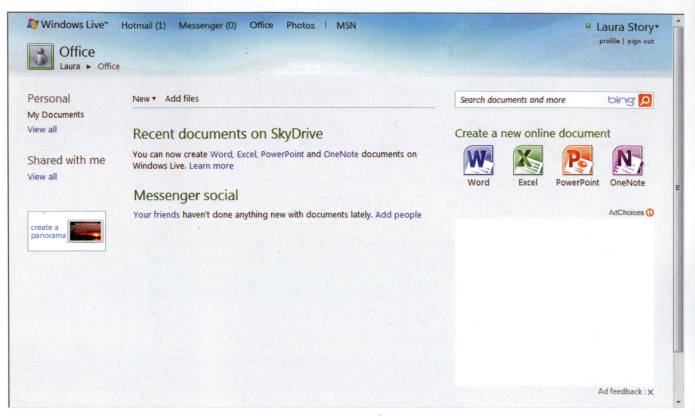

Change the File Type to a Different Version of Excel

Ribbon Method

☐ Open the workbook you want to save to another format, click the **File tab** then click **Save As**

☐ Enter a file location and file name, then click the **Save as type list arrow** to display a list, as shown in Figure EX 7-4

☐ Choose a format, using Table EX 7-1 as a reference to some of the options, then click **Save**

Figure EX 7-4   **Document type options in Save As dialog box**

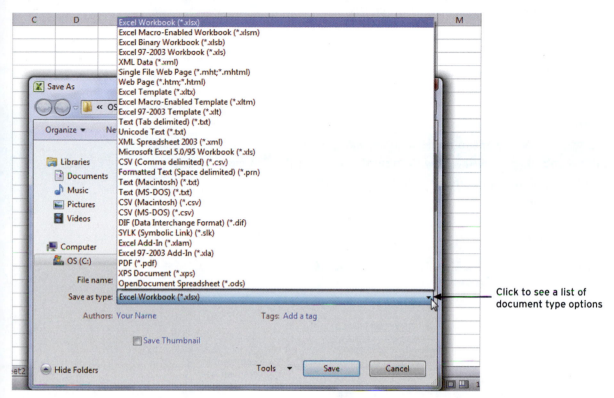

Click to see a list of document type options

Table EX 7-1   Document type options in Save As dialog box

Option	To save a workbook...
Excel Macro-Enabled Workbook (*.xlsm)	With macros that you can enable for use
Excel template (*.xltx)	As a template that you can use to create duplicate workbooks with the same design and content
PDF (*.pdf)	In the Portable Document Format that can be easily opened by people with Adobe Acrobat Reader on their computer
Single File Web Page (*.mht, *.mhtml)	As a page that you can place on the World Wide Web, with the page and all supporting files and graphics in one file
Web Page (*.htm, *.html)	As a page that you can place on the World Wide Web, with the page in one .htm file and all supporting files and graphics in a separate folder
Text (Tab delimited) (*.txt)	As a file that can be opened in most word processors and spreadsheets, and that has tabs in place of column breaks
XML Data (*.xml)	In XML format, which allows it to be used by others to extract only the information they need

Save as a PDF or XPS

Ribbon Method

☐ Click the **File tab,** click **Save & Send**, click **Create PDF/XPS Document** in the File Types section, then click the **Create PDF/XPS button**

☐ In the Publish as PDF or XPS dialog box, select a location, type a file name, and choose a document type

☐ If you want to open the file immediately after saving it, select the **Open file after publishing** check box (this check box is available only if you have a PDF reader installed on your computer)

□ Next to **Optimize for**, select **Standard (publishing online and printing)** or **Minimum size (publishing online)**

□ Click **Options**, select publishing options, then click **OK**

□ Click **Publish**

MANAGE COMMENTS

Insert Comments

Ribbon Method

□ Select the cell to which you want to attach a comment

□ Click the **Review tab**, then click the **New Comment button** in the Comments group

□ In the comment box, shown in Figure EX 7-5, type the appropriate text

□ Click outside the comment box

Figure EX 7-5   **Comment box**

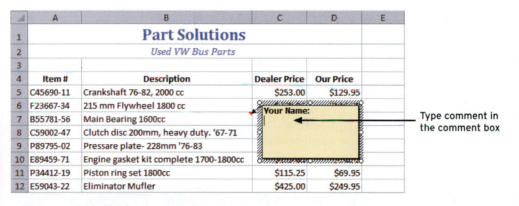

Shortcut Method

□ Right-click the cell to which you want to attach a comment

□ Click **Insert Comment** on the shortcut menu

□ Follow the steps in bullets 3–4 of the Insert Comments Ribbon Method above

View Comments

Ribbon Method

□ Click the **Review tab**, then click a cell marked with a comment (a red triangle in the upper-right corner of the cell)

□ Click the **Show/Hide Comment button** in the Comments group; the comment remains displayed when you click other cells

Shortcut Method

□ Point to a cell containing the comment, then read the comment that appears

   OR

□ Right-click a cell marked with a comment (a red triangle in the upper-right corner of the cell), then click **Show/ Hide Comments** on the shortcut menu

Edit Comments

Ribbon Method

□ Click a cell marked with a comment (a red triangle in the upper-right corner of the cell)

□ Click the **Review tab**, then click the **Edit Comment button** in the Comments group

□ Modify the comment

□ Click outside the comment box

Shortcut Method

□ Right-click a cell marked with a comment (a red triangle in the upper-right corner of the cell), then click **Edit Comment** on the shortcut menu

□ Follow the steps in bullets 3–4 of the Edit Comments Ribbon Method on the previous page

Delete Comments

Ribbon Method

□ Click the cell marked with a comment (a red triangle in the upper-right corner of the cell)

□ Click the **Review tab**, then click the **Delete Comment button** in the Comments group

Shortcut Method

□ Right-click the cell marked with a comment (a red triangle in the upper-right corner of the cell), then click **Delete Comment** on the shortcut menu

REVIEW QUESTIONS

TRUE/FALSE

Circle T if the statement is true or F if the statement is false.

T   F   1. To send a worksheet via e-mail, click the Insert tab, then click E-mail.

T   F   2. SkyDrive is a version of Excel with macros that you can enable for use.

T   F   3. The Comments commands are located on the Insert menu.

T   F   4. XML data is in a format that allows it to be used by others to extract only the information they need.

T   F   5. To delete a comment, you can right-click the cell, then click Delete Comment on the shortcut menu.

MULTIPLE CHOICE

Select the best response for the following statements.

1. The Save & Send command is located on which tab?

    A. File

    B. Home

    C. Review

    D. View

2. The free service from Microsoft that allows you to share documents online is Windows Live _____.

    A. DocShare

    B. CloudConnect

    C. SkyDrive

    D. OnStore

3. Which document type option would you use to create duplicate workbooks with the same design and content?

    A. (*.xlsm)

    B. (*.xltx)

    C. (*.pdf)

    D. (*.xml)

4. To insert a comment, click the Review tab, then click the _____ button in the Comments group.

    A. Insert Comment

    B. New Comment

    C. Comment

    D. Create Comment

5. A cell with a comment is indicated by a _____.

    A. green triangle in the upper-right corner

    B. green outline around the cell

    C. red triangle in the upper-right corner

    D. red outline around the cell

PROJECTS

Project EX 7-1

1. Open the data file **Project EX 7-1.xlsx**.

2. Save the file as **Expenses**.

3. View the comment in cell D6.

4. In cell B6, insert a comment that reads **Include mileage log**.

5. In cell I7, insert a comment that reads **Indicate whether client should be billed**.

6. Edit the comment in cell B6 by adding **Mileage rate is 55 cents per mile**.

7. Delete the comment in cell D6.

8. Create a PDF/XPS document named **Expenses.pdf**. Choose to open the file after publishing. Optimize for standard publishing online and printing.

9. Save and close the workbook.

CRITICAL THINKING

Activity EX 7-1

Open the **Expenses** worksheet that you saved in Project EX 7-1.

Save the file in each of the following formats:

    a. A single file Web page named **Expenses Web.mht**. Choose to save (publish) all the items on Sheet1.

    b. A macro-enabled workbook named **Expenses Macro.xlsm**.

    c. A workbook that is compatible with Excel 97-2003 named **Expenses Retro.xls**. Use the Compatibility Checker to determine which features are incompatible with a previous version. Choose to continue saving even if some formatting is not supported.

    d. A template named **Expenses Template.xltx**.

Activity EX 7-2

So that the expenses reimbursement worksheet is easily accessible online, save the Expenses.xlsx file to Windows Live SkyDrive (check with your instructor first). Send the link to a classmate and ask your classmate to view the worksheet in his or her browser. Save and close the workbook.

Excel

Excel Objective 8: Analyzing and Organizing Data

Filter Data

Define and Apply a Filter

Ribbon Method

- ☐ Click inside the list range
- ☐ Click the **Data tab**, then click the **Filter button** ▼ in the Sort & Filter group, shown in Figure EX 8-1
- ☐ Click the list arrow at the top of the column on which you want to filter
- ☐ Click **(Select All)** to remove all check marks
- ☐ Click the check boxes for the items you want to display
- ☐ Click **OK**

Shortcut Method

- ☐ Click inside the list range, then press **[Ctrl][Shift][L]**
- ☐ Follow the steps in bullets 3–6 of the Define and Apply a Filter Ribbon Method above
  OR
- ☐ Right-click in a cell that contains the value, color, font color, or icon on which you want to filter
- ☐ Point to **Filter**, then click **Filter by Selected Cell's Value** (or **Color**, **Font Color**, or **Icon**)

Figure EX 8-1   Sort & Filter group on Home tab

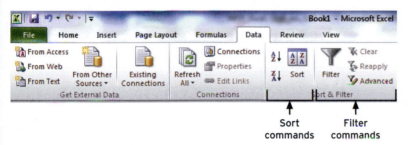

Remove a Filter

Ribbon Method

- ☐ Click in the filtered list range
- ☐ Click the **Data tab**, then click the **Clear button** 🗙 in the Sort & Filter group, shown in Figure EX 8-1, to clear the filter but keep the filter arrows
  OR
- ☐ Click the **Data tab**, then click the **Filter button** in the Sort & Filter group to deselect the button and remove the filter arrows

Filter Lists Using AutoFilter

Ribbon Method

- ☐ Click inside the list range
- ☐ Click the **Data tab**, then click the **Filter button** ▼ in the Sort & Filter group, shown in Figure EX 8-1
- ☐ Click the **list arrow** at the top of the column on which you want to filter
- ☐ Use the Search box to enter text or numbers on which to search, shown in Figure EX 8-2
  OR
- ☐ Select and clear check boxes for the items you want to display, shown in Figure EX 8-2

OR

☐ Use advanced criteria by selecting a filter from the submenu, shown in Figure EX 8-2

Figure EX 8-2   Filter lists using AutoFilter

Sort Data

Use Sort Options

Ribbon Method

☐ Click inside the list range

☐ Click the **Data tab**, then click the **Sort button** 📊 in the Sort & Filter group

☐ In the Sort dialog box, shown in Figure EX 8-3, click the **Sort by list arrow**, then click the column on which to sort

☐ Select appropriate value in the Sort On list, including Values, Cell Color, Font Color, or Cell Icon

☐ Select appropriate value in the Order list, then click **OK**

☐ To sort within the groupings you created, click **Add Level**, then select another column on which to sort and specify Sort On and Order values

☐ Continue adding levels as necessary, then click **OK**

Figure EX 8-3   Sort dialog box

Shortcut Method

☐ Right-click a cell value on which you want to sort
☐ Point to **Sort**, then click the appropriate option

APPLY CONDITIONAL FORMATTING

Apply Conditional Formatting to Cells

Ribbon Method

☐ Select a cell range to format conditionally
☐ Click the **Conditional Formatting button** in the Styles group on the Home tab
☐ Point to a conditional formatting category, then click a category option, using Table EX 8-1 as a reference

Table EX 8-1   Conditional Formatting Options

Formatting category	Options	Displays
Highlight Cells Rules	Greater Than, Less Than, Between, Equal To, Text that Contains, A Date Occurring, Duplicate Values	Colored text and fills, or custom formats
Top/Bottom Rules	Top 10 Items, Top 10%, Bottom 10 Items, Bottom 10%, Above Average, Below Average	Colored text and fills, or custom formats
Data Bars	Gradient Fill, Solid Fill	Colored data bars in a cell where the length of the data bar represents the value in the cell
Color Scales	12 built-in types	Gradients in a range of cells where the shade represents the value in the cell
Icon Sets	Directional, Shapes, Indicators, Ratings	Icons from a set where each icon represents a value in the cell

Use the Rule Manager to Apply Conditional Formats

Ribbon Method

☐ Select a data range
☐ Click the **Conditional Formatting button** in the Styles group on the Home tab, then click **New Rule**
☐ In the New Formatting Rule dialog box, shown in Figure EX 8-4, click a **rule type** in the Select a Rule Type section
☐ In the Edit the Rule Description section, specify the values that you want formatted

Excel

☐ Click the **Format button** in the Edit the Rule Description section, then specify a format in the Format Cells dialog box

☐ Click **OK** to close the Format Cells dialog box, then click **OK** again to close the New Formatting Rule dialog box

Figure EX 8-4   New Formatting Rule dialog box

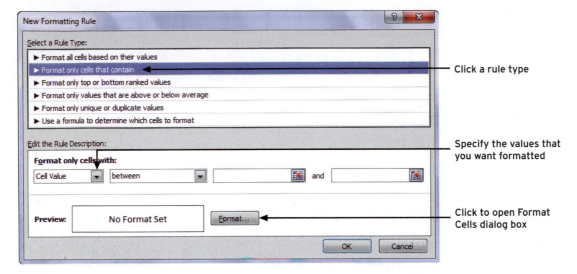

Use the IF Function to Apply Conditional Formatting

Ribbon Method

☐ Click the **cell** where you want the formula result to appear

☐ Click the **Formulas tab**, then click the **Logical button** in the Function Library group (or click the **Insert Function button** f_x on the formula bar), then click IF

☐ In the Function Arguments dialog box, specify the logical test and the values if true or false, then click **OK**

Clear Rules

Ribbon Method

☐ Click any worksheet cell

☐ Click the **Conditional Formatting button** in the Styles group on the Home tab, point to **Clear Rules**, then click **Clear Rules from Selected Cells** or **Clear Rules from Entire Sheet**

OR

☐ Click any worksheet cell

☐ Click the **Conditional Formatting button** in the Styles group on the Home tab, then click **Manage Rules**

☐ In the Conditional Formatting Rules Manager dialog box, shown in Figure EX 8-5, click the **Show formatting rules for list arrow**, then click **This Worksheet**

☐ Click the rule to delete, click **Delete Rule** or press **[Delete]**, then click **OK**

Figure EX 8-5   Conditional Formatting Rules Manager dialog box

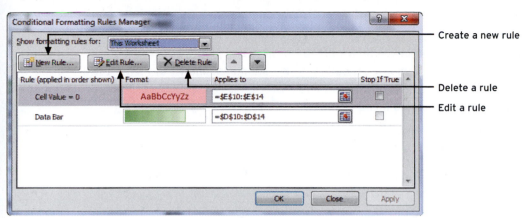

Create a new rule

Delete a rule

Edit a rule

Use Icon Sets

Ribbon Method

☐ Select a cell range to format conditionally

☐ Click the **Conditional Formatting button** in the Styles group on the Home tab

☐ Point to **Icon Sets** on the menu and then choose an option on the submenu, shown in Figure EX 8-6

Figure EX 8-6   Icon Sets conditional formatting menu

Use Data Bars

Ribbon Method

☐ Select a cell range to format conditionally

☐ Click the **Conditional Formatting button** in the Styles group on the Home tab

☐ Point to **Data Bars** on the menu and then choose an option on the submenu, shown in Figure EX 8-7

Figure EX 8-7   Data Bars conditional formatting menu

REVIEW QUESTIONS

MULTIPLE CHOICE

Select the best response for the following statements.

1. Pressing [Ctrl][Shift][L] is the shortcut method for _____.

   A. filtering

   B. sorting

   C. applying conditional formatting

   D. using the Rules Manager

2. Which of the following is NOT a method of filtering lists using AutoFilter?

   A. Use the Search box to enter text or numbers on which to search

   B. Select and clear check boxes for the items you want to display

   C. Use advanced criteria by selecting a filter from the submenu

   D. Specify the logical test and the values if true or false

3. Which conditional formatting category contains the options Greater Than, Less Than, Between, Equal To, Text that Contains, A Date Occurring, and Duplicate Values?

    A. Highlight Cells Rules

    B. Top/Bottom Rules

    C. Data Bars

    D. Color Scales

4. The Conditional Formatting button is located in the Styles group on the _____ tab.

    A. Home

    B. Insert

    C. Page Layout

    D. Data

5. To use the IF function, click the Formulas tab, then click the _____ button in the Function library group?

    A. Financial

    B. Logical

    C. Text

    D. Date & Time

FILL IN THE BLANK

Complete the following sentences by writing the correct word or words in the blanks provided.

1. The Filter button is located in the Sort & Filter group on the _____ tab.

2. When filtering, there is a list _____ at the top of each column.

3. In the _____ dialog box, you can select sort options including Values, Cell Color, Font Color, or Cell Icon.

4. Directional, Shapes, Indicators, and Ratings are options in the _____ conditional formatting category.

5. To clear a rule in the Conditional Formatting Rules Manager dialog box, click the rule then click _____.

PROJECTS

Project EX 8-1

1. Open the data file **Project EX 8-1.xlsx**.

2. Save the file as **Baseball Stats**.

3. Sort the players by Games from smallest to largest.

4. Sort the players by At Bats from largest to smallest.

5. Filter the data to show only the players with less than 25 hits.

6. Clear the filter.

7. Filter the data to show only the players with greater than four home runs (HR).

8. Clear the filter.

9. Filter the data to show only the players whose position is outfield (OF).

10. Clear the filter and remove the filter arrows.

11. Sort the players by name in alphabetic order from A to Z.

12. Save and close the workbook.

Project EX 8-2

1. Open the data file **Project EX 8-2.xlsx**.

2. Save the file as **Desert Springs**.

3. For the range D5:G8, create a new conditional formatting rule so the values that are less than $300 are displayed in Light Red Fill with Dark Red Text.

4. For the same range, create a conditional formatting rule that highlights all cells that are greater than $700 with Green Fill with Dark Green Text.

5. For the range H5:H8, apply a Gradient Fill Blue Data Bar conditional formatting.

6. For the same range, apply Directional 4 Arrows (Colored) Icon Sets conditional formatting.

7. Use the Rules Manager Delete to delete the Cell Value < 300 conditional formatting rule.

8. For the ranges D5:G8, create a new conditional formatting rule so the values ranking in the bottom 10% are displayed in Yellow Fill with Dark Yellow Text.

9. Use an AutoFilter to filter data in column H so that only values greater than $2,000 are displayed.

10. Remove the filter.

11. Save and close the worksheet.

CRITICAL THINKING

Activity EX 8-1

Search for the video in Excel Help titled *Apply conditional formatting* and watch it. What are the benefits of conditional formatting? How can conditional formatting help you answer specific questions about your data? What is the difference between color scales, data bars, and icon sets—and when would you format cells using each one?

Excel

EXCEL EXPERT OBJECTIVE 1: SHARING AND MAINTAINING WORKBOOKS

APPLY WORKBOOK SETTINGS, PROPERTIES, AND DATA OPTIONS

Set Advanced Properties

Ribbon Method

☐ Click the **File tab**, then click **Info**

☐ On the right side, click **Properties**, then click **Advanced Properties**, shown in Figure EXX 1-1

☐ In the dialog box, make changes to properties using the General, Summary, Statistics, Contents, and Custom tabs

Figure EXX 1-1   Set advanced properties

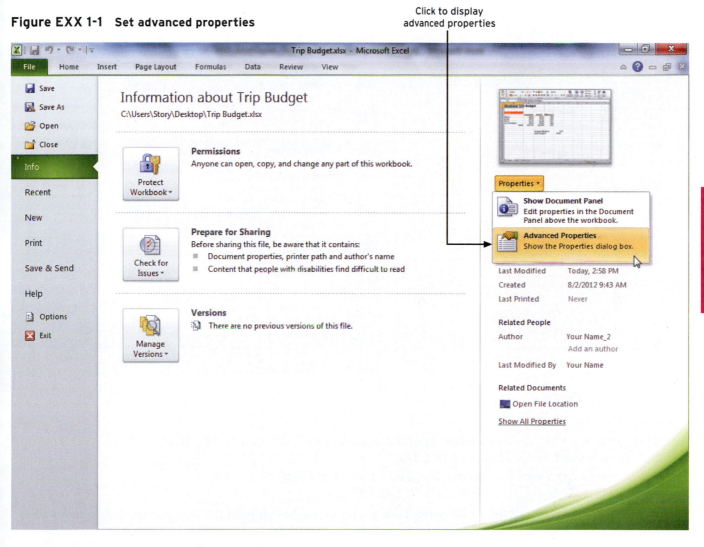

Save a Workbook as a Template

Ribbon Method

☐ Click the **File tab**, then click **Save & Send**

☐ In the center pane, click **Change File Type**, then click **Template (*xltx)**, then click the **Save As button**, shown in Figure EXX 1-2

☐ In the Save As dialog box, choose a location, type a filename, and then click **Save**

Figure EXX 1-2   Save a workbook as a template

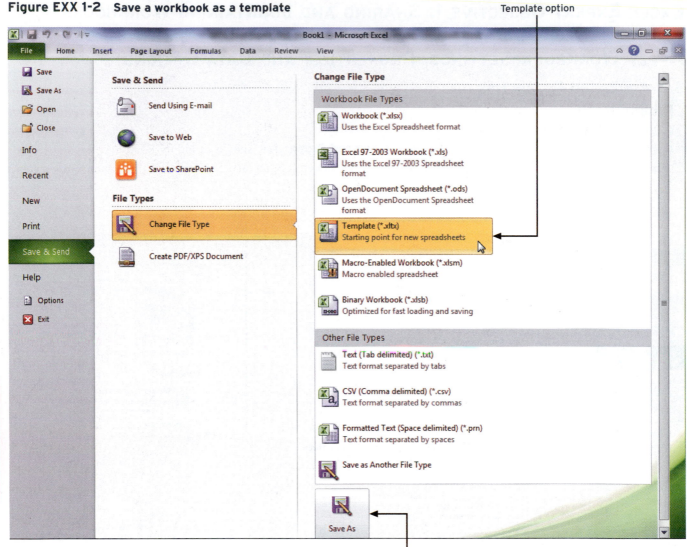

Import XML Data

Ribbon Method

- ☐ On the Data tab, click the **From Other Sources button** in the Get External Data group, and then click **From XML Data Import**, shown in Figure EXX 1-3
- ☐ Select a file in the Select Data Source dialog box, then click **Open**
  OR
- ☐ Click the **New Source button** in the Select Data Source dialog box to open the Data Connection Wizard and connect to the data source you want

Figure EXX 1-3 Import XML data

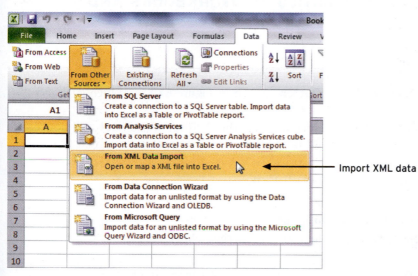

Import XML data

Export XML Data

Ribbon Method

☐ Click the **File tab**, then click **Save As**

☐ In the Save As dialog box, click the **Save as type list arrow**, click **XML Data (*xml)**, shown in Figure EXX 1-4, then click **Save**

Figure EXX 1-4 Export XML data

XML data option

APPLY PROTECTION AND SHARING PROPERTIES TO WORKBOOKS AND WORKSHEETS

Protect the Current Sheet

Ribbon Method

□ Click the **File tab**, click **Info**, click the **Protect Workbook button**, shown in Figure EXX 1-5, then click **Protect Current Sheet**

□ In the Protect Sheet dialog box, shown in Figure EXX 1-6, click to select the **Protect worksheet and contents of locked cells check box** if necessary, then type a password in the Password to unprotect sheet text box

□ Click **OK**

□ In the Confirm Password dialog box, retype the password, then click **OK**

OR

□ Click the **Review tab**, then click the **Protect Sheet button** in the Changes group

□ Follow the steps in bullets 2–4 of the Protect the Current Sheet Ribbon Method above

OR

□ Click the **Home tab**, click the **Format button** in the Cells group, then click **Protect Sheet**

□ Follow the steps in bullets 2–4 of the Protect the current sheet Ribbon Method above

Shortcut Method

□ Right-click a sheet tab, then click **Protect Sheet** on the shortcut menu

□ Follow the steps in bullets 2–4 of the first Protect the Current Sheet Ribbon Method above

Figure EXX 1-5   Protection options

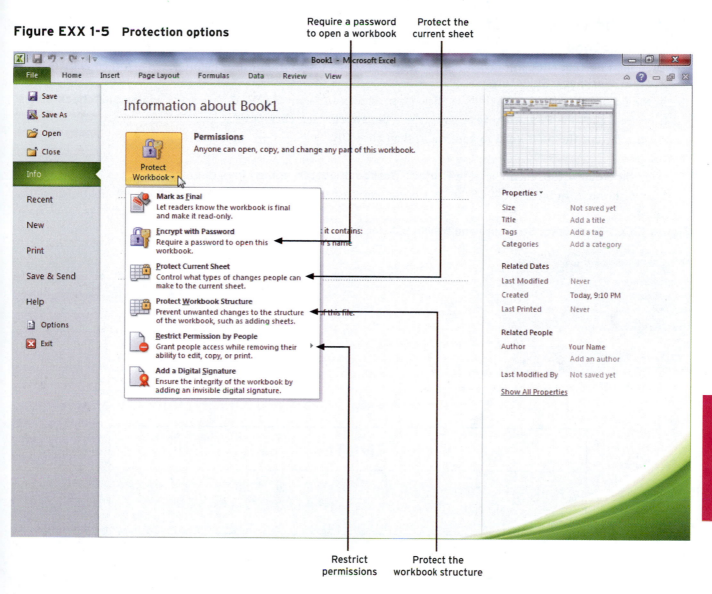

Require a password
to open a workbook

Protect the
current sheet

Restrict
permissions

Protect the
workbook structure

Figure EXX 1-6   Protect Sheet dialog box

Protect the Workbook Structure

Ribbon Method

☐ Click the **File tab**, click **Info**, click the **Protect Workbook button**, shown in Figure EXX 1-5, then click **Protect Workbook Structure**

☐ In the Protect Structure and Windows dialog box, shown in Figure EXX 1-7, select the appropriate **check boxes**

☐ If desired, click the **Password text box**, type a **password**, then click **OK**

☐ If desired, type the **password** to confirm it, then click **OK**

OR

☐ Click the **Review tab**, then click the **Protect Workbook button** in the Changes group

☐ Follow the steps in bullets 2–4 of the Protect the Workbook Structure Ribbon Method above

Figure EXX 1-7   Protect Structure and Windows dialog box

NOTE

In order to set workbook permissions you must be using the Information Rights Management (IRM) service.

Restricting Permissions

Ribbon Method

☐ Click the **File tab**, click **Info**, click the **Protect Workbook button**, shown in Figure EXX 1-5, then click **Restrict Permission by People**

☐ Click **Unrestricted Access**, **Restricted Access**, or **Manage Credentials** on the submenu

Require a Password to Open a Workbook

Ribbon Method

☐ Click the **File tab**, click **Info**, click the **Protect Workbook button**, shown in Figure EXX 1-5, then click **Encrypt with Password**

☐ In the Encrypt Document dialog box, shown in Figure EXX 1-8, type a password, then click **OK**

☐ Type the password again in the Confirm Password dialog box, then click **OK**

Figure EXX 1-8   **Encrypt Document dialog box**

MAINTAIN SHARED WORKBOOKS

Merge Workbooks

Ribbon Method

□ To add the Compare and Merge Workbooks command to the Quick Access Toolbar, click the **File tab**, then click **Options**, then click **Quick Access Toolbar**

□ Click the **Choose commands from list arrow**, then click **All Commands**, shown in Figure EXX 1-9

□ In the list, click **Compare and Merge Workbooks**, click **Add**, and then click **OK**

□ Open the copy of the shared workbook into which you want to merge the changes

□ On the Quick Access Toolbar, click **Compare and Merge Workbooks**, and save the workbook if prompted

□ In the Select Files to Merge Into Current Workbook dialog box, click a copy of the workbook that contains the changes that you want to merge, and then click **OK**

Figure EXX 1-9   **Add command to Quick Access Toolbar**

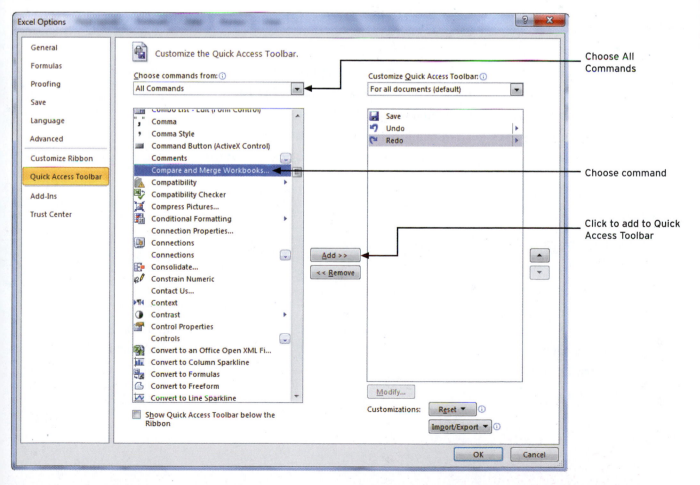

Set Track Changes Options

Ribbon Method

☐ Click the **Review tab**, click the **Track Changes button** in the Changes group, then click **Highlight Changes**

☐ In the Highlight Changes dialog box, click to select the **Track changes while editing check box**, shown in Figure EXX 1-10

☐ Select the appropriate check boxes to choose the When, Who, and Where options that you want

☐ Make sure the **Highlight changes on screen check box** is selected, then click **OK**

☐ In the message box, click **OK**

Figure EXX 1-10   Highlight Changes dialog box

REVIEW QUESTIONS

TRUE/FALSE

Circle T if the statement is true or F if the statement is false.

T   F   1. You can protect the current worksheet using the File tab, Review tab, or Home tab.

T   F   2. You can require a password to open a workbook in the Set Password dialog box.

T   F   3. The Compare and Merge Workbooks command is located on the Data tab.

T   F   4. You can set options to track changes in the Highlight Changes dialog box.

T   F   5. In order to set workbook permissions you must be using the Information Rights Management (IRM) service.

MATCHING

Match each location in Column 2 to its task in Column 1.

Column 1	Column 2
_____ 1. Set advanced properties	A. File tab, Info
_____ 2. Save a workbook as a template	B. File tab, Options
_____ 3. Import XML data	C. File tab, Save & Send
_____ 4. Add a command to the Quick Access Toolbar	D. Review tab, Changes group
_____ 5. Track Changes	E. Data tab, Get External Data group

PROJECTS

Project EXX 1-1

1. Open the data file **Project EXX 1-1.xlsx**.

2. Save the file as **Swim Meet**.

3. Begin tracking workbook changes. Save the workbook when prompted.

4. In cell H5, change the word "Free" to "Freestyle."

5. In cell D9, change the word "Average" to "Time."

6. In cell I17, change the time "58.39" to "58.09."

7. Stop tracking the changes to the workbook. Remove the workbook from shared use when prompted.

8. Protect the workbook structure.

9. Save the workbook as a template named **Swim Meet Template.xltx**.

10. Save and close the workbook.

CRITICAL THINKING

Activity EXX 1-1

Open a workbook and set a password that is required to open it. Write down the password and store it in a secure place. Close the workbook and then open it up again, using the password you just created. Use Excel Help or the Internet to read about what makes a strong password. Was the password you created a strong one?

Activity EXX 1-2

Open a workbook and begin the process of restricting permission. When prompted, learn more about the Information Rights Management Service and then sign up for this service using Windows Live ID. Restrict permission to the workbook by enabling a specific user to change the workbook. Save and close the workbook.

EXCEL EXPERT OBJECTIVE 2: APPLYING FORMULAS AND FUNCTIONS

AUDIT FORMULAS

Trace Formula Precedents

Ribbon Method

☐ Click a cell that contains a formula

☐ Click the **Formulas tab**, shown in Figure EXX 2-1, then click the **Trace Precedents button** in the Formula Auditing group

☐ Double-click one of the **blue arrows** to navigate between the cell containing the formula and the precedent cells

Figure EXX 2-1   Formula Auditing group on Formulas tab

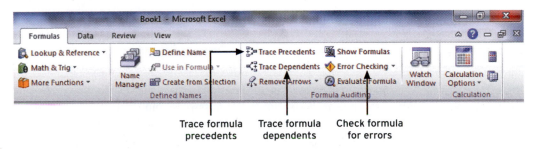

Trace Formula Dependents

Ribbon Method

☐ Click a cell that is referenced in a formula

☐ Click the **Formulas tab**, then click the **Trace Dependents button** in the Formula Auditing group, shown in Figure EXX 2-1

☐ Double-click one of the **blue arrows** to navigate between the cells

Trace and Locate Errors, Invalid Data, and Invalid Formulas

Ribbon Method

☐ Click the cell that shows an error, using Table EXX 2-1 as a reference

☐ Click the **Formulas tab**, click the **Error Checking button arrow** in the Formula Auditing group, shown in Figure EXX 2-1, then click **Trace Error**

☐ Make edits to the formula in the formula bar

Table EXX 2-1   Common Cell Errors

Error	Means
#DIV/0!	Value is divided by zero
#NAME?	Excel does not recognize text
#N/A	Value is not available for the formula
#NULL!	When a formula specifies an intersection of two areas that do not intersect
#NUM!	Invalid formula number(s)
#REF!	Invalid cell reference
#VALUE!	Operand or argument is incorrect

Remove All Tracer Arrows

Ribbon Method

□ Click the **Formulas tab**, then click the **Remove Arrows button** in the Formula Auditing group, shown in Figure EXX 2-1

Correct Errors in Formulas

Ribbon Method

□ Click the **Formulas tab**, then click the **Error Checking button** in the Formula Auditing group, shown in Figure EXX 2-1

□ In the Error Checking dialog box, shown in Figure EXX 2-2, click the appropriate button, using Table EXX 2-2 as a reference, fix or view the error as prompted, then click **OK**

□ Click the **Next** and **Previous buttons** to navigate through the errors

Figure EXX 2-2   **Error Checking dialog box**

Click the Previous and Next buttons to navigate through the errors

Table EXX 2-2   Error Checking Dialog Box Options

Button	Action
Help on this error	Opens the Microsoft Excel Help Window and displays an article about this type of function or formula
Show Calculation Steps	Opens the Evaluate Formula dialog box
Ignore Error	Moves to the next error without modifying the current error
Edit in Formula Bar	Activates the cell containing the error in the formula bar

MANIPULATE FORMULA OPTIONS

Set Iterative Calculation Options

Mouse Method

□ Click the **File tab**, click **Options**, and then click **Formulas**

□ In the Calculation options section of the Excel Options dialog box, shown in Figure EXX 2-3, select the **Enable iterative calculation check box**

□ To set the maximum number of times that Excel will recalculate, type the number of iterations in the Maximum Iterations box (The higher the number of iterations, the more time that Excel needs to calculate a worksheet.)

□ In the Maximum Change box, type the smallest value required for iteration to continue (The smaller the number, the more precise the result and the more time that Excel needs to calculate a worksheet.)

Excel

Figure EXX 2-3   Calculation options

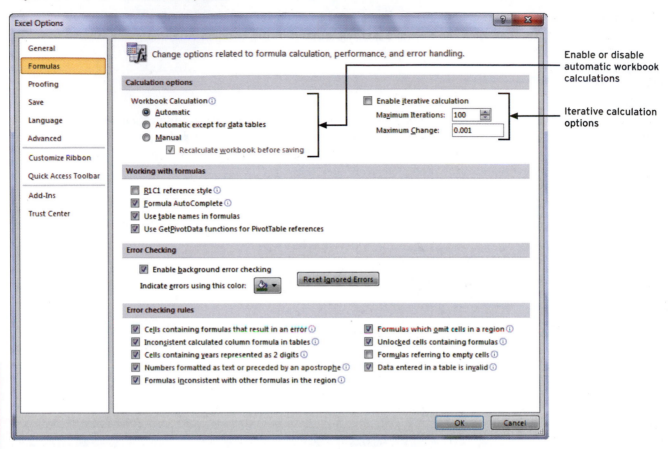

Enable or disable automatic workbook calculations

Iterative calculation options

Enable or Disable Automatic Workbook Calculation

Mouse Method

☐ Click the **File tab**, click **Options**, and then click **Formulas**

☐ In the Calculation options section of the Excel Options dialog box, shown in Figure EXX 2-3, select the **Automatic** or **Manual** options

Ribbon Method

☐ On the Formulas tab, in the Calculation group, click the **Calculation Options button**, and then click **Automatic** or **Manual**

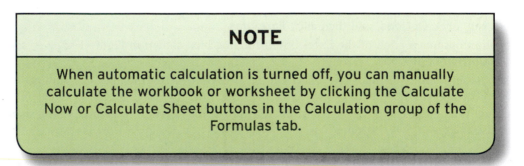

NOTE

When automatic calculation is turned off, you can manually calculate the workbook or worksheet by clicking the Calculate Now or Calculate Sheet buttons in the Calculation group of the Formulas tab.

PERFORM DATA SUMMARY TASKS

Use an Array Formula

Ribbon Method

☐ Click the cell where you want the formula result to appear

☐ Enter the formula, beginning with an equal sign (=)

☐ Press **CTRL+SHIFT+ENTER** to enter the formula (Excel will surround your array formula with braces { })

Use a SUMIFS Function

Ribbon Method

☐ Verify that your worksheet has a range to search and numerical values to summarize

☐ Click in the cell that will contain the conditional formula result

☐ Type =, then type a conditional function and arguments, using the syntax SUMIFS(sum_range, criteria_range1, criteria1, criteria_range2, criteria2...)

> ## NOTE
>
> For example, *=SUMIFS(D1:D50, E1:E5,">2",E1:E5,"<5")* tells Excel to add the amounts from the range D1:D50, for instances where the amounts in E1:E5 are between 2 and 5.

APPLY FUNCTIONS IN FORMULAS

Find and Correct Errors in Functions

Ribbon Method

☐ Click the **Formulas tab**, then click the **Error Checking button** in the Formula Auditing group

☐ In the Error Checking dialog box, shown in Figure EXX 2-2, click the **Edit in Formula Bar** button to fix the error in the formula bar

☐ Click the **Next** and **Previous buttons** to navigate through the errors and fix as needed, then click **OK**

Applying Arrays to Functions

Ribbon Method

☐ Click the cell(s) where you want the formula result to appear

☐ Enter the formula, beginning with an equal sign (=), and using any of Excel's built-in functions, such as the examples in Table EXX 2-3

☐ Press **CTRL+SHIFT+ENTER** to enter the formula (Excel will surround your array formula with braces { })

Table EXX 2-3   Examples of functions using arrays

Function	Syntax	Description
COLUMNS	COLUMNS(array)	Returns the number of columns in an array
LOOKUP	LOOKUP(lookup_value, array)	Look in the first row or column of an array for the specified value and return a value from the same position in the last row or column of the array
INDEX	INDEX(array, row_num, [column_num])	Returns a value or the reference to a value from within a table or range
ROWS	ROWS(array)	Returns the number of rows in an array
SUMPRODUCT	SUMPRODUCT(array1, [array2], [array3], ...)	Multiplies corresponding components in the given arrays, and returns the sum of those products

Use Statistical Functions

Ribbon Method

☐ On the Formulas tab, in the Function Library group, click **More Functions**, shown in Figure EXX 2-4, click **Statistical** on the menu, then click a function on the submenu

☐ In the Function Arguments dialog box, specify the appropriate settings or the appropriate cells if necessary, then click **OK**

Use Date and Time Functions

Ribbon Method

☐ On the Formulas tab, in the Function Library group, click **Date & Time**, shown in Figure EXX 2-4, then click a function on the menu

☐ In the Function Arguments dialog box, specify the appropriate settings or the appropriate cells if necessary, then click **OK**

Use Financial Functions

Ribbon Method

☐ On the Formulas tab, in the Function Library group, click **Financial**, shown in Figure EXX 2-4, then click a function on the menu

☐ In the Function Arguments dialog box, specify the appropriate settings or the appropriate cells if necessary, then click **OK**

Use Text Functions

Ribbon Method

☐ On the Formulas tab, in the Function Library group, click **Text**, shown in Figure EXX 2-4, then click a function on the menu

☐ In the Function Arguments dialog box, specify the appropriate settings or the appropriate cells if necessary, then click **OK**

Cube Functions

Ribbon Method

☐ On the Formulas tab, in the Function Library group, click **More Functions**, shown in Figure EXX 2-4, click **Cube** on the menu, then click a function on the submenu

☐ In the Function Arguments dialog box, specify the appropriate settings or the appropriate cells if necessary, then click **OK**

Figure EXX 2-4   **Formula Auditing group on Formulas tab**

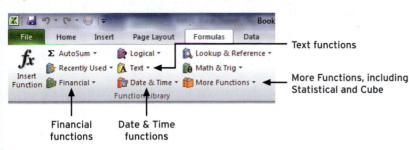

REVIEW QUESTIONS

TRUE/FALSE

Circle T if the statement is true or F if the statement is false.

T   F   1. When tracing formula precedents, you can double-click one of the blue arrows to navigate between the cell containing the formula and the precedent cells.

T   F   2. When you click the Show Calculation Steps button in the Error Checking dialog box, it opens the Evaluate Formula dialog box.

T   F   3. You can set iterative calculation options in the Excel Options dialog box.

T   F   4. When you enter an array formula, Excel surrounds the formula with quotation marks (" ").

T   F   5. The Function Library group is located on the Insert tab.

MATCHING

Match each description in Column 2 to its error value in Column 1.

Column 1	Column 2
_____ 1. #DIV/0!	A. Invalid cell reference
_____ 2. #NAME?	B. When a formula specifies an intersection of two areas that do not intersect
_____ 3. #NULL!	C. Value is divided by zero
_____ 4. #REF!	D. Operand or argument is incorrect
_____ 5. #VALUE!	E. Excel does not recognize text

PROJECTS

Project EXX 2-1

1. Open the data file **Project EXX 2-1.xlsx**.

2. Save the file as **Project Estimate**.

3. Click cell D3 and trace the error.

4. Trace the error for cells D8 and D10.

5. Remove all tracer arrows.

Excel

6. Open the Error Checking dialog box.

7. Correct the error in cell D3 by deleting the word **hours** from cell B3.

8. Resume the error checking, and correct the formula in cell D5 by copying the formula from the cell above.

9. Resume the error checking, and correct the error in cell D8 by editing the formula in the formula bar to read =C8*B8.

10. Resume the error checking and correct the error in cell D10 by editing the formula in the formula bar to read =C10*B10.

11. Click **OK** when the error check is complete to close the Error Checking dialog box.

12. Save and close the workbook.

Project EXX 2-2

1. Open the data file **Project EXX 2-2.xlsx**.

2. Save the file as **Water Use**.

3. In cell B1, enter a function that inserts the current date. (Hint: Use the TODAY function.)

4. In cells B4:B14, enter the estimated total number of times you have (or plan to) participate in the activity for the given week.

5. Select cells D4:D14 and enter an array formula in the formula bar that calculates the total weekly gallons of water used for each activity. (Hint: =B4:B14*C4:C14)

6. Press CTRL+SHIFT+ENTER to enter the array formula and make the calculations.

7. In cell D15, enter an array formula using the SUM function that calculates the total gallons of water used for the week. (Hint: =SUM(B4:B14*C4:C14))

8. Press CTRL+SHIFT+ENTER to enter the array formula and make the calculation.

9. Disable automatic workbook calculations.

10. Enable iterative calculation with maximum iterations of 100 and maximum change of 0.001.

11. Save and close the workbook.

CRITICAL THINKING

Activity EXX 2-1

With a partner, choose one of the following function categories: Statistical, Date & Time, Financial, Text, or Cube. Choose five functions in your category and use Excel Help or other resources to find out more about each function. Create a worksheet that lists your five functions, including the name, description, and syntax of each, along with an example of how it would be used. Present your worksheet to the class and demonstrate the use of the function.

EXCEL EXPERT OBJECTIVE 3: PRESENTING DATA VISUALLY

APPLY ADVANCED CHART FEATURES

Use Trendlines

Ribbon Method

☐ On an unstacked, 2-D, area, bar, column, line, stock, xy (scatter), or bubble chart, click the data series to which you want to add a trendline

☐ On the Chart Tools Layout tab, in the Analysis group, click the **Trendline button** to display the menu, shown in Figure EXX 3-1

☐ Click a predefined option or click **More Trendline Options** to open the Format Trendline dialog box

Figure EXX 3-1   Trendline menu

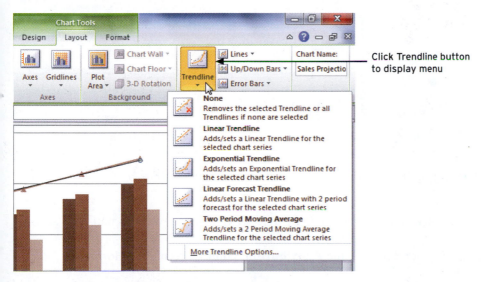

Use a Secondary Vertical Axis

Ribbon Method

☐ In a 2-D chart, click the data series that you want to plot on a secondary vertical axis

☐ On the Chart Tools Format tab, in the Current Selection group, click the **Format Selection button** to display the Format Data Series dialog box, shown in Figure EXX 3-2

☐ In the Plot Series On section, select **Secondary Axis**, then click **Close**

Figure EXX 3-2   **Format Data Series dialog box**

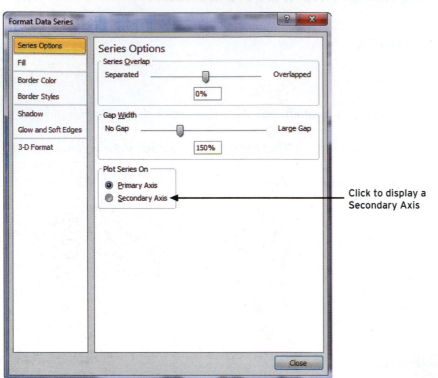

Click to display a
Secondary Axis

Use a Secondary Horizontal Axis

Ribbon Method

☐ In a 2-D chart that already has a secondary vertical axis, click the data series that you want to plot on a secondary horizontal axis

☐ On the Chart Tools Layout tab, in the Axes group, click the **Axes button**, point to Secondary Horizontal Axis, then click the display option that you want

Use Chart Templates

Ribbon Method

☐ Click the **File tab**, then click **New**

☐ In the Office.com Templates section, click the **More button** if necessary, click the **Charts and diagrams** folder, then click the **Business charts** folder to display templates, shown in Figure EXX 3-3

☐ Select the template you want, then click the **Download button**

Figure EXX 3-3   Chart templates

Use Sparklines
Ribbon Method
- Select the data range you want to use to create a chart
- Click the **Insert tab**, then click a button in the Sparklines group
- In the Create Sparklines dialog box, shown in Figure EXX 3-4, choose the data range and location range, then click **OK**

Figure EXX 3-4 Create Sparklines dialog box

APPLY DATA ANALYSIS

Use Automated Analysis Tools

Ribbon Method

- ☐ Select the cell(s) in which you want to restrict the data entered
- ☐ Click the **Data tab**, then click the **Data Validation button** in the Data Tools group
- ☐ In the Data Validation dialog box, shown in Figure EXX 3-5, click the **Allow list arrow**, then click a validation option, using Table EXX 3-1 as a guide
- ☐ If desired, click the **Input Message tab** and type a message title and the text you want the user to see when selecting the cell
- ☐ If desired, click the **Error Alert tab** and choose an error alert style, title, and text

Figure EXX 3-5 Data Validation dialog box

Table EXX 3-1   Data Validation Criteria Options

Criteria	Use to	Next action
Any value	Allow user to input any value	Click **OK**
Whole number, Decimal, Date, Time, or Text length	Limit data to a range you specify	Select a data option, such as "between," enter minimum and maximum values, then click **OK**
List	Limit data to a list of entries you specify	Enter a list of allowable entries separated by commas in the Source text box, then click **OK**
Custom	Limit data to a formula	Enter a formula in the you specify Formula text box, then click **OK**

Perform What-If Analysis

Ribbon Method

□ Click the Data tab, then click the **What-If Analysis button** in the Data Tools group to display the menu, shown in Figure EXX 3-6

□ Click a What-If Analysis option, using Table EXX 3-2 as a guide

Figure EXX 3-6   What-If Analysis menu

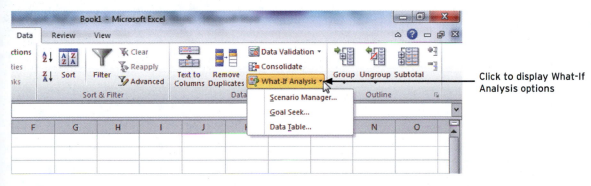

Click to display What-If Analysis options

Table EXX 3-2   What-If Analysis Options

Option	Use to	Clicking opens
Scenario Manager	Create and save different groups of values, or scenarios, and switch between them	Scenario Manager dialog box
Goal Seek	Find the right input when you know the result you want	Goal Seek dialog box
Data Table	See the results of many different possible inputs at the same time	Data Table dialog box

APPLY AND MANIPULATE PIVOTTABLES

Create a PivotTable Report

Ribbon Method

□ Select the cells that contain the data you want to use in the PivotTable report

□ On the Insert tab, in the Tables group, click the **PivotTable button**

□ In the Create PivotTable dialog box, shown in Figure EXX 3-7, make sure that Select a table or range is selected, and then in the Table/Range box, verify the range of cells

□ Choose the location where you want the PivotTable report to be placed, then click **OK**

Figure EXX 3-7   Create PivotTable dialog box

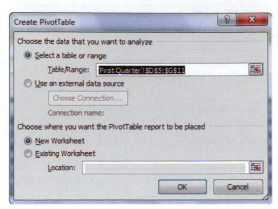

Manipulate PivotTable Data

Ribbon Method

☐ In the PivotTable Field List, right-click a field name in the field section and then select Add to Report Filter, Add to Column Labels, Add to Row Labels, or Add to Values, shown in Figure EXX 3-8

Mouse Method

☐ In the PivotTable Field List, select a field name in the field section and then drag it to the Report Filter, Column Labels, Row Labels, or Values area, shown in Figure EXX 3-8

Figure EXX 3-8   PivotTable Field List

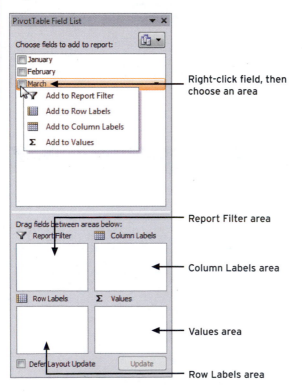

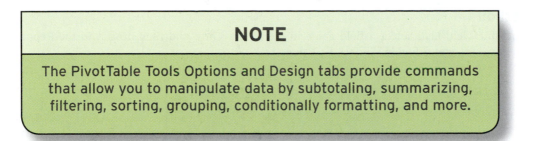

> **NOTE**
>
> The PivotTable Tools Options and Design tabs provide commands that allow you to manipulate data by subtotaling, summarizing, filtering, sorting, grouping, conditionally formatting, and more.

Use the Slicer to Filter and Segment Your PivotTable Data in Multiple Layers

Ribbon Method

☐ Click anywhere in the PivotTable report for which you want to create a slicer

☐ On the PivotTable Tools Options tab, in the Sort & Filter group, click the **Insert Slicer button**

☐ In the Insert Slicers dialog box, shown in Figure EXX 3-9, select the check box of the PivotTable fields for which you want to create a slicer, then click **OK**

☐ In each slicer, click the items on which you want to filter

Figure EXX 3-9   Insert Slicers dialog box

APPLY AND MANIPULATE PIVOTCHARTS

Create a PivotChart

Ribbon Method

☐ Select the cells that contain the data you want to use in the PivotChart

☐ On the Insert tab, in the Tables group, click the **PivotTable button arrow**, then click **PivotChart**

☐ In the Create PivotTable with PivotChart dialog box, make sure that Select a table or range is selected, and then in the Table/Range box, verify the range of cells

☐ Choose the location where you want the PivotTable and PivotChart to be placed, then click **OK**

☐ Build the PivotChart by choosing fields from the PivotTable field list

Manipulate PivotChart Data

Ribbon Method

☐ In the PivotTable Field List, right-click a field name in the field section and then select Add to Report Filter, Add to Axis Fields (Categories), Add to Legend Fields (Series), or Add to Values

Mouse Method

☐ In the PivotTable Field List, select a field name in the field section and then drag it to the Report Filter, Axis Fields (Categories), Legend Fields (Series), or Values area

---

NOTE

The PivotChart Tools Design, Layout, Format, and Analyze tabs provide commands that allow you to work with your PivotChart.

Analyzing PivotChart Data

Ribbon Method

☐ Click the **PivotChart Tools Analyze tab**, shown in Figure EXX 3-10, and click a command, using Table EXX 3-3 as a reference

Figure EXX 3-10   PivotChart Tools Analyze group

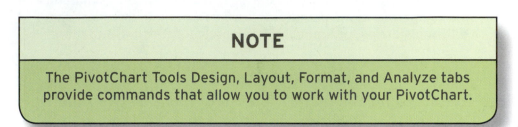

Table EXX 3-3   PivotChart Tools Analyze commands

Command	Use to
Expand Entire Field	Expand all items of the active field
Collapse Entire Field	Collapse all items of the active field
Insert Slicer	Insert a slicer to filter data interactively
Refresh	Update all the information that is coming from a data source
Clear	Clear the PivotChart so that you can choose different data to analyze
Field List	Show or hide the field list, allowing you to add or remove fields
Field Buttons	Show or hide Report Filter, Legend, Axis, or Value fields

---

DEMONSTRATE HOW TO USE THE SLICER

Choose Data Sets from External Data Connections

Ribbon Method

☐ On the Insert tab, in the Filter group, click the **Insert Slicer button**

☐ In the Existing Connections dialog box, click the **Browse for More button**

☐ In the Select Data Source dialog box, choose an existing external data source or click the **New Source button** and go through the Data Connection Wizard, shown in Figure EXX 3-11, to connect to a remote data source

☐ In the Select Data Source dialog box, click **Open**

☐ In the Existing Connections dialog box, select a connection, then click **Open**

Figure EXX 3-11   Data Connection Wizard

REVIEW QUESTIONS

FILL IN THE BLANK

Complete the following sentences by writing the correct word or words in the blanks provided.

1. To download a chart template, first click the File tab, then click _____, select a template, then click the Download button.

2. The Settings, Input Message, and Error Alert tabs are located in the _____ dialog box.

3. The What-If Analyis option called _____ allows you to find the right input when you know the result you want.

4. The PivotTable _____ has Report Filter, Column Labels, Row Labels, and Values areas.

5. The _____ Wizard is used to connect to a remote data source when inserting a slicer.

MATCHING

Match each Ribbon location in Column 2 to its button in Column 1.

Column 1	Column 2
_____ 1. Trendline button	A. Insert tab, Tables group
_____ 2. What-If Analysis button	B. Chart Tools Layout tab, Analysis group
_____ 3. PivotTable button	C. Chart Tools Format tab, Current Selection group
_____ 4. Insert Slicer button	D. Data tab, Data Tools group
_____ 5. Format Selection button	E. Insert tab, Filter group

PROJECTS

Project EXX 3-1

1. Open the data file **Project EXX 3-1.xlsx**.

2. Save the file as **First Quarter**.

3. Add a linear trendline to the March data series on the chart.

4. Plot the Total data series on a secondary vertical axis and change the chart type to Line with Markers.

5. In cells C10:E10 create a Line sparkline using the data in cells C4:E9.

6. In cell C13, open the Data Validation dialog box and enter the following:

   Settings tab

   Allow: **Text length**

   Data: **less than or equal to**

   Maximum: **3**

   Input Message tab

   Input message: **Enter your initials**

   Error Alert tab

   Style: **Stop**

   Error message: **Limited to three characters**

7. Perform a Goal Seek What-If Analysis that determines how much Altman would have to sell in March to have a total of $600,000. (Hint: In the Goal Seek dialog box, set cell F4 to a value of 600,000 by changing cell E4.)

8. Click **OK** to close the Goal Seek Status dialog box.

9. Save and close the workbook.

CRITICAL THINKING

Activity EXX 3-1

Download a chart template that is of interest to you and customize it with your own data. For example, you can download a family tree, fitness progress chart, rain chart, or a loan tree. Share your chart template with the class and explain how it was (or wasn't) helpful for your purpose.

Activity EXX 3-2

Search Excel Help for the video titled *Create a PivotTable report* and watch it to see how you can use PivotTable reports to analyze your data. Open or create a worksheet and practice creating PivotTable reports, and using the slicer to filter and segment your PivotTable data in multiple layers.

EXCEL EXPERT OBJECTIVE 4: WORKING WITH MACROS AND FORMS

CREATE AND MANIPULATE MACROS

Display the Developer Tab

Ribbon Method

☐ Click the **File tab**, click **Options** to open the Excel Options dialog box, then click **Customize Ribbon** in the left pane

☐ In the Main Tabs list in the right pane, click the **Developer check box**, then click **OK** to display the Developer tab, shown in Figure EXX 4-1

Figure EXX 4-1   Developer tab

![Developer tab ribbon]

Record an Action Macro

Ribbon Method

☐ Click the **View tab**, click the **Macros button arrow** in the Macros group, then click **Record Macro**

☐ In the Record Macro dialog box, shown in Figure EXX 4-2, type a name for the macro in the Macro name box, choose a shortcut key, select a location to store the macro, type a description, then click **OK**

☐ Type the text and/or apply the formatting that you want to include in the macro

☐ Click the **View tab**, click the **Macros button arrow** in the Macros group, then click **Stop Recording**

Figure EXX 4-2   Record Macro dialog box

![Record Macro dialog box]

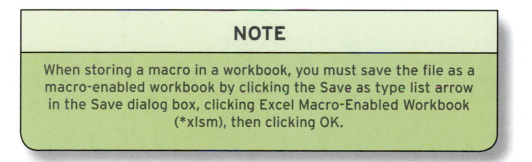

NOTE

When storing a macro in a workbook, you must save the file as a macro-enabled workbook by clicking the Save as type list arrow in the Save dialog box, clicking Excel Macro-Enabled Workbook (*.xlsm), then clicking OK.

OR

☐ Click the **Developer tab**, then click the **Record Macro button** in the Code group

☐ Follow the steps in bullets 2-3 of Record an Action Macro Ribbon Method on the previous page

☐ Click the **Developer tab**, then click the **Stop Recording button** in the Code group

Shortcut Method

☐ Click the **Record Macro button** 🖼 on the status bar

☐ Follow the steps in bullets 2-3 of Record an Action Macro Ribbon Method on the previous page

☐ Click the **Stop Recording button** 🖼 on the status bar

Run a Macro

Ribbon Method

☐ Click the **View tab**, click the **Macros button arrow** in the Macros group, then click **View Macros**

☐ In the Macro dialog box, shown in Figure EXX 4-3, click the name of the macro you want to run in the Macro name box, then click the **Run button**

OR

☐ Click the **Developer tab**, then click the **Macros button arrow** in the Code group

☐ In the Macro dialog box, shown in Figure EXX 4-3, click the name of the macro you want to run in the Macro name box, then click the **Run button**

Shortcut Method

☐ Press the shortcut keys that you assigned to the macro

OR

☐ Press **[Alt][F8]** to display the Macro dialog box, shown in Figure EXX 4-3

☐ Click the name of the macro that you want to run in the Macro name box, then click the **Run button**

Figure EXX 4-3 **Macro dialog box**

Run a Macro When a Workbook is Opened

Ribbon Method

☐ On the Developer tab, in the Code group, click **Record Macro**

☐ In the Record Macro dialog box, shown in Figure EXX 4-2, in the Macro name box, type **Auto_Open**

☐ Select a shortcut key, select the workbook where you want to store the macro, type a description, and click **OK**

☐ Perform the actions that you want to record

☐ On the Developer tab, in the Code group, click **Stop Recording**

☐ To test the macro, use the **File tab** and **Open command** to open an existing workbook

Run a Macro When a Button is Clicked

Ribbon Method

☐ On the Developer tab, in the Controls group, click **Insert** and then, under Form Controls, click **Button**

☐ Click the worksheet location where you want the upper-left corner of the button to appear

☐ In the Assign Macro dialog box, shown in Figure EXX 4-4, assign a macro to the button, and then click **OK**

☐ To run the macro, click the macro button you just added

Figure EXX 4-4   Assign Macro dialog box

Assign a Macro to a Command Button

Ribbon Method

☐ If the Developer tab is not displayed, follow the steps in bullets 1-2 under Display the Developer Tab Ribbon Method

☐ Click the **Developer tab**, click the **Insert button** in the Controls group, then under ActiveX Controls, click **Command Button (ActiveX Control)**

☐ Click the worksheet location where you want the upper-left corner of the button to appear

☐ Right-click the command button and click **View Code** from the shortcut menu

☐ In the Microsoft Visual Basic for Applications window, type the name of the macro in the blank line of the Code dialog box, shown in Figure EXX 4-5, and make sure Click appears in the list arrow

☐ Click the **Close button** ❌ on the Microsoft Visual Basic for Applications window

☐ On the **Developer tab**, click the **Design Mode button** in the Controls group to turn it off

☐ Click the **File tab**, then click **Save As** to open the Save As dialog box

☐ Type a name in the file name box, click the **Save as type list arrow** and click **Excel Macro-Enabled Workbook (*xlsm)**, then click **Save**

☐ To run the macro, click the **command button** in the document

> ### NOTE
>
> To change the label on a command button, right-click the command button, click **Command ButtonObject**, click **Edit**, then select the label and type a new name for the button.

Excel

Figure EXX 4-5   Microsoft Visual Basic for Applications

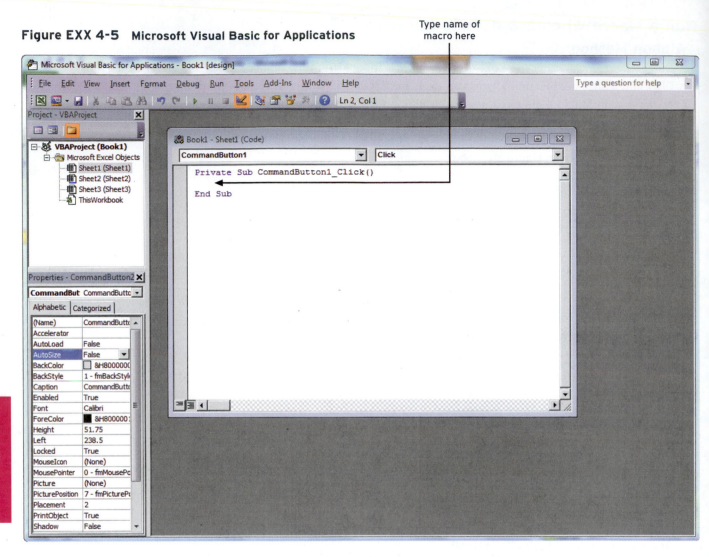

Create a Custom Macro Button on the Quick Access Toolbar

Ribbon Method

☐ Click the **File tab**, then click **Options**

☐ In the Excel Options dialog box, shown in Figure EXX 4-6, click **Quick Access Toolbar** in the left pane, then click **Macros** in the Choose commands from menu

☐ Select the macro name in the center pane, then click the **Add button** to move it to the right pane under Customize Quick Access Toolbar

☐ Click the **OK** button

☐ To run the macro, click the **Macro button** on the Quick Access Toolbar

Figure EXX 4-6   Excel Options dialog box

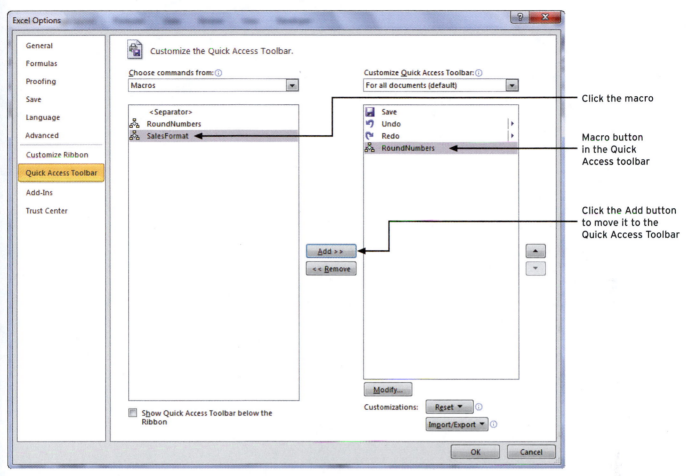

Excel

Apply Modifications to a Macro
Ribbon Method
- [ ] On the View tab, in the Macros group, click the **Macros button arrow** then click **View Macros**
- [ ] In the Macro dialog box, select the macro to which you want to apply modifications, then click **Options**
- [ ] In the Macro Options dialog box, make changes to the shortcut key or description, then click **OK**
    OR
- [ ] In the Macro dialog box, select the macro to which you want to apply modifications, then click **Edit**
- [ ] In the Microsoft Visual Basic for Applications window, make changes in the Code dialog box
- [ ] Click the **Close button**  on the Microsoft Visual Basic for Applications window

INSERT AND MANIPULATE FORM CONTROLS

Insert Form Controls
Ribbon Method
- [ ] If the Developer Tab is not displayed, follow the steps in bullets 1-2 under Display the Developer tab Ribbon Method
- [ ] Click the **Developer Tab**, then click **Design Mode** in the Controls group
- [ ] Click the **Developer Tab**, click the **Insert button** in the Controls group, then click a control in the Form Controls section of the menu, shown in Figure EXX 4-7, to insert it
- [ ] Click the worksheet location where you want the control to appear

Figure EXX 4-7   Insert menu

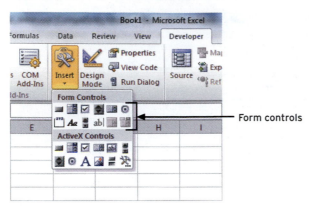

Form controls

Set Form Properties

Ribbon Method

☐ If the Developer Tab is not displayed, follow the steps in bullets 1-2 under Display the Developer Tab Ribbon Method

☐ Click the **Developer Tab**, then click **Properties** in the Controls group, to open the Properties dialog box, shown in Figure EXX 4-8, where you can set or change properties

Figure EXX 4-8   Properties dialog box

Properties	
Sheet1 Worksheet	
Alphabetic	Categorized
(Name)	Sheet1
DisplayPageBreaks	False
DisplayRightToLeft	False
EnableAutoFilter	False
EnableCalculation	True
EnableFormatConditio	True
EnableOutlining	False
EnablePivotTable	False
EnableSelection	0 - xlNoRestrictions
Name	Sheet1
ScrollArea	
StandardWidth	8.43
Visible	-1 - xlSheetVisible

REVIEW QUESTIONS

TRUE/FALSE

Circle T if the statement is true or F if the statement is false.

T   F   1. Press [Alt][F8] to run a macro.

T   F   2. You can assign keyboard shortcut keys to a macro.

T   F   3. The Developer tab is always displayed on the Ribbon.

T   F   4. You can create a custom macro button on the Quick Access Toolbar.

T   F   5. To access the Code dialog box, click the File tab, then click Options.

FILL IN THE BLANK

Complete the following sentences by writing the correct word or words in the blanks provided.

1. To display the Developer tab, click the _____ tab, click Options to open the Excel Options dialog box, then click Customize Ribbon in the left pane.

2. To run a macro, click the _____ tab, click the Macros button arrow in the Macros group, then click View Macros.

3. To assign a macro to a command button, click the _____ tab, click the Insert button in the Controls group, then under ActiveX Controls, click Command Button (ActiveX Control).

4. To insert form controls, click the _____ tab, then click Design Mode in the Controls group.

5. To set form properties, click the _____ tab, then click Properties in the Controls group.

PROJECTS

Project EXX 4-1

1. Open the data file **Project EXX 4-1.xlsx**.

2. Save the workbook as a macro-enabled file (*.xlsm) named **State Water**.

3. Select cells D3:D8.

4. Start recording a new macro.

5. In the Record Macro dialog box, name the macro PercentFormat, assign **Ctrl +p** as the keyboard shortcut keys to run the macro, and type **Format percentage of water** in the description.

6. Perform the following formatting on the selected cells.
   - Change the Number format to Percentage with one decimal place
   - Apply Gradient Fill Blue Data Bars
   - Apply bold formatting

7. Stop recording the macro.

8. Select cells D11:D14 and run the macro using the shortcut keys you assigned.

9. Select cells D17:D19 and apply the macro.

10. Save and close the workbook.

11. If lab guidelines allow, create a custom macro button on the Quick Access Toolbar.

CRITICAL THINKING

Activity EXX 4-1

Search Excel Help for the video *Create a simple macro in Excel* and watch it. How can you use macros to do repetitive tasks for you? Make a list of ten ways that Excel macros could be used to help automate tasks that you perform.

Activity EXX 4-2

Create a macro that will type your name and the current date in the header of every workbook that is opened.

Excel

MICROSOFT ACCESS 2010 CERTIFICATION PREP

Getting Started with Access 2010

The Access Microsoft Office Specialist (MOS) exam assumes a basic level of proficiency in Access. This section is intended to help you reference these basic skills while you are preparing to take the Access MOS exam.

☐ Starting and exiting Access
☐ Viewing the Getting Started with Microsoft Office Access window
☐ Opening a database
☐ Viewing the database window
☐ Using the Navigation Pane
☐ Using the Ribbon
☐ Saving and closing objects and databases
☐ Using keyboard KeyTips
☐ Getting Help

START AND EXIT ACCESS

Start Access

Shortcut Method

☐ Click the **Start button** on the Windows taskbar
☐ Point to **All Programs**
☐ Click **Microsoft Office**, then click **Microsoft Access 2010**
   OR
☐ Double-click the **Microsoft Access 2010 program icon** on the desktop

Exit Access

Ribbon Method

☐ Click the **File tab**, then click **Exit**

Shortcut Method

☐ Click the **Close button** on the Access program window title bar

VIEW THE GETTING STARTED WITH MICROSOFT OFFICE ACCESS WINDOW

When you first start Access, Backstage view appears as shown in Figure AC GS-1.

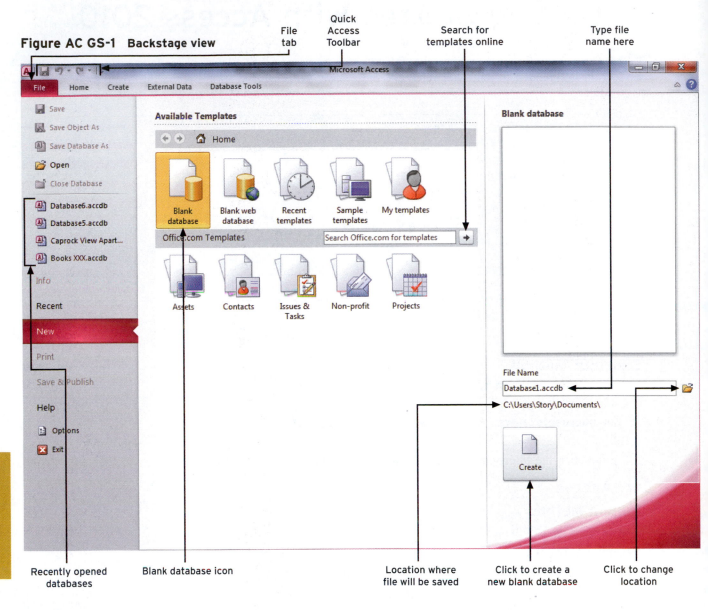

Figure AC GS-1   Backstage view

Recently opened databases

Blank database icon

Location where file will be saved

Click to create a new blank database

Click to change location

OPEN A DATABASE

Open an Existing Database

Ribbon Method

☐ Click the **File tab**, then click **Open**

☐ In the Open dialog box shown in Figure AC GS-2, navigate to the appropriate drive and folder

☐ Click the file you want, then click **Open**

   OR

☐ Click the **File tab**, click **Recent**, then click the file you want in the Recent Databases list

Figure AC GS-2   Open dialog box

Click icons to navigate to the drive and folder where the file is stored

VIEW THE DATABASE WINDOW

The Access program window appears as shown in Figure AC GS-3.

Access

Figure AC GS-3 **Access program window**

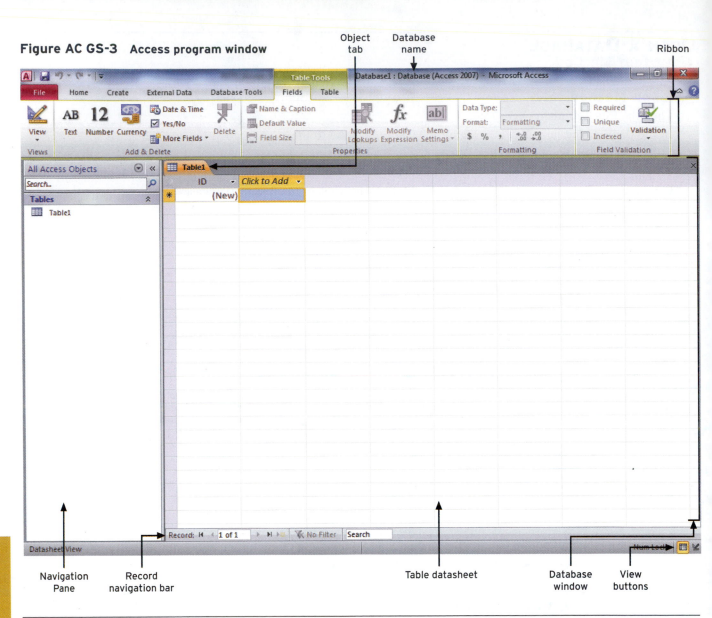

USE THE NAVIGATION PANE

Open an Object

Shortcut Method

☐ Double-click the object in the Navigation Pane

OR

☐ Right-click the object in the Navigation Pane, then click **Open**

Open an Object in Design View or Layout View

Ribbon Method

☐ Double-click the object in the Navigation Pane

☐ Click the **View button arrow** in the Views group on the Home tab, then click **Design View** or **Layout View**, as appropriate

Shortcut Method

☐ Right-click the object in the Navigation Pane, then click **Design View** or **Layout View**

Open and Close the Navigation Pane

Shortcut Method
□ Click the **Shutter Bar Open/Close button** ≪

Change the View of Objects in the Navigation Pane

Shortcut Method
□ Click the **Navigation Pane arrow button** ⊙, click a **Navigate To Category option**, then click a **Filter By Group option**

USE THE RIBBON

Change Tabs

Ribbon Method
□ Click the name of a tab, such as Home, Create, External Data, or Database Tools, or the name of a contextual tab, such as Table Tools Fields

Open and Close the Ribbon

Shortcut Method
□ Right-click a blank area of the Ribbon, then click **Minimize the Ribbon**
OR
□ Click the Quick Access toolbar arrow, then click **Minimize the Ribbon**
OR
□ Double-click a Ribbon tab

Open a Dialog Box or Task Pane

Ribbon Method
□ Click the **launcher icon** in a group on a tab, such as the Clipboard group on the Home tab

---

SAVE AND CLOSE OBJECTS AND DATABASES

Save an Object

Ribbon Method
□ With the object open in the database window, click the **File tab**, then click **Save**

Shortcut Method
□ Click the **Save button** 🖫 on the Quick Access toolbar

Save an Object with a Different Name

Ribbon Method
□ Click the **File tab**, then click **Save Object As**
□ In the Save As dialog box shown in Figure AC GS-4, enter a name for the object, then click **OK**

Figure AC GS-4   **Save As dialog box (for object)**

Type a name for the object

Save a Database

Ribbon Method

□ Click the **File tab**, then click **Save**

NOTE

Access automatically saves changes you make to database settings, so you rarely need to save a database. However, you should save changes to a database object before you close it.

Save a Database with a Different Name, Location, or Format

Ribbon Method

□ Save and close all open database objects
□ Click the **File tab**, then click **Save Database As**
□ In the Save As dialog box, enter a database name, navigate to the appropriate drive and folder, if necessary, then click **Save**

Close an Object

Shortcut Method

□ Click the **Close object button** ☒
OR
□ Click the **Close Window button** if the window is maximized; otherwise, click the **Close button** on the object's title bar

Close a Database

Ribbon Method

□ Save and close all database objects
□ Click the **File tab**, then click **Close Database**
OR
□ Click the **Close button** on the object's title bar

USE KEYBOARD KEYTIPS

Display KeyTips

Shortcut Method

□ Press **[Alt]** to display the KeyTips for each command on the active tab of the Ribbon and on the Quick Access toolbar, as shown in Figure AC GS-5
□ Press the letter or number for the specific command for the active tab on the Ribbon
□ Press additional letters or numbers as needed to complete the command sequence
□ If two letters appear, press each one in order; for some commands you will find that you have to click an option from a gallery or menu to complete the command sequence
□ The KeyTips turn off automatically at the end of the command sequence

Hide KeyTips

Shortcut Method

☐ Press **[Alt]** to hide the KeyTips for each Ribbon command

Figure AC GS-5 KeyTips

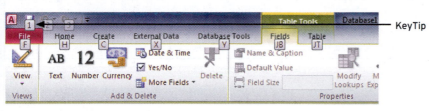

KeyTip

GET HELP

Ribbon Method

☐ Click the **Microsoft Access Help button**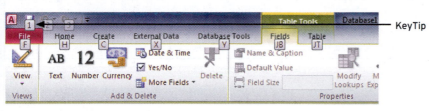

☐ Use Table Access-1 as a reference to select the most appropriate way to get help using the Access Help window shown in Figure AC GS-6

Shortcut Method

☐ Press **[F1]**

☐ Use Table Access GS-1 as a reference to select the most appropriate way to get help using the Access Help window shown in Figure AC GS-6

Figure AC GS-6   Access Help window

Access

Table AC GS-1   Access Help Window Options

Option	To use
Type words to search for	Type one or more keywords, click the **Search button arrow**, click the Help source you want to search, click **Search**, then click a topic in the search results
Browse Access Help	Click a topic category, then click a topic
Table of Contents	Click the **Show Table of Contents button** on the Help window toolbar, click a topic category in the Table of Contents pane, then click a topic

REVIEW QUESTIONS

FILL IN THE BLANK

Complete the following sentences by writing the correct word or words in the blanks provided.

1. One way to start Access is to double-click the Microsoft Access program icon on the _____.

2. To open a dialog box or task pane using the Ribbon, click the _____ icon in a group on a tab.

3. To open an existing database, click the _____ tab, click Recent, then click the file you want in the Recent Databases list.

4. Use the _____ dialog box to save a database with a different name, location, or format.

5. _____ are numbers or letters that display over commands on the Ribbon that indicate how to perform Ribbon commands using the keyboard.

MATCHING

Match the correct term in Column 2 to its location in Column 1.

Column 1	Column 2
_____ 1. Start button	A. Navigation pane
_____ 2. Exit	B. Title bar
_____ 3. Shutter Bar Open/Close button	C. File tab
_____ 4. Save button	D. Windows taskbar
_____ 5. Close database button	E. Quick Access toolbar

PROJECTS

Project AC GS-1

1. Open Access.

2. Open the AC GS-1.accdb data file.

3. Save the database as Aquatic Center.

4. Open the Navigation Pane, if it is not already displayed.

5. Hide the Ribbon.

6. Change the view of objects in the Navigation Pane to display them by object type.

7. Open the Classes: Table object.

8. Display the Ribbon.

9. Save the table as Kids Classes.

10. Display the Home tab.

11. Use KeyTips to display the Kids Classes table in Design View.

12. Close the Kids Classes table.

13. Close the database and exit Access.

CRITICAL THINKING

Activity AC GS-1

Open the Access Help window. Search for the video titled "Getting Started with Access 2010" and watch it. What other Access videos and training courses are available? Browse through Help to see all the material available for you to learn more about using Access. Refer to Table Access GS-1 as a reference if you need help using the Access Help window.

Activity AC GS-2

With the Access Help window open, search to find out what's new in Microsoft Office Access 2010. Open a new blank database and explore each tab on the Ribbon to familiarize yourself with where the commands are located in the new interface. Use Access Help to find out more about Microsoft Office Backstage view, the new feature for managing your files and the data about them.

ACCESS OBJECTIVE 1: MANAGING THE ACCESS ENVIRONMENT

CREATE AND MANAGE A DATABASE

Use Save Object As

Ribbon Method

☐ Select an object in the Navigation Pane

☐ Click the **File tab**, then click **Save Object As**

☐ In the Save As dialog box, enter a name for the object, then click **OK**

Use Open

Ribbon Method

☐ Click the **File tab**, then click **Open**

☐ In the Open dialog box, navigate to the database you want to open, then click the database to select it, then click **Open**

Use Save and Publish

Ribbon Method

☐ Click the **File tab**, then click **Save & Publish**

☐ Choose an option, as shown in Figure AC 1-1

Figure AC 1-1 Save & Publish options

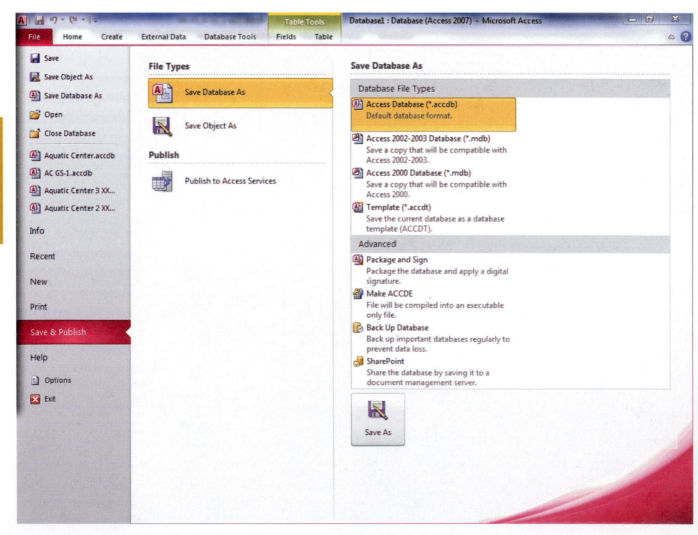

Use Compact & Repair Database
Ribbon Method
☐ Save and close all objects in the database

☐ Click the **File tab**, click **Info**, then click the **Compact & Repair Database button**, shown in Figure AC 1-2
OR

☐ Click the **File tab**, click **Options**, click **Current Database**, click the **Compact on Close check box**, click **OK**, then close the database

Figure AC 1-2   **Info options**

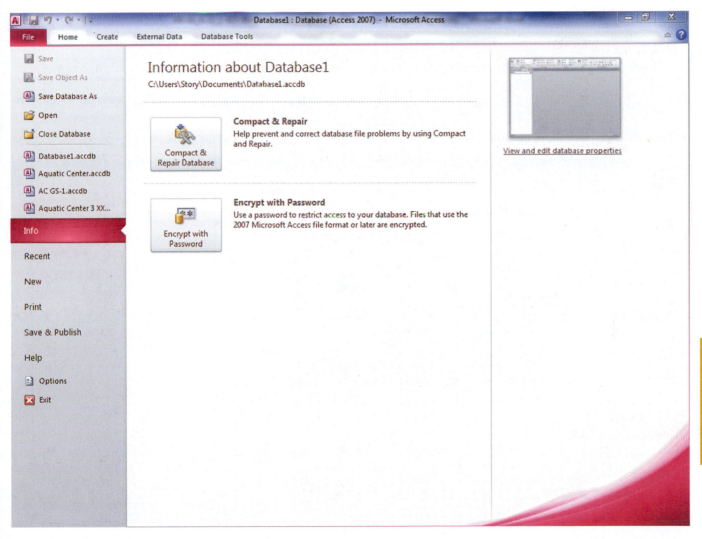

Use Encrypt with Password Commands
Ribbon Method
☐ Click the **File tab**, then click **Open**

☐ In the Open dialog box, click the **Open arrow button**, then click **Open Exclusive**

☐ Click the **File tab**, click **Info**, then click the **Encrypt with Password button**, shown in Figure AC 1-2

☐ In the Set Database Password dialog box, shown in Figure AC 1-3, type the password, type it again to verify the password, then click **OK**

Figure AC 1-3 Set Database Password dialog box

Create a Database from a Template

Ribbon Method

☐ Click the **File tab**, then click **New**

☐ Click the template you want to use, shown in Figure AC 1-4

☐ Change the database name in the File Name text box, if necessary, then specify where you want to save the database

☐ Click **Create** if you selected an installed template; click **Download** if you selected an online template

Figure AC 1-4 Template options

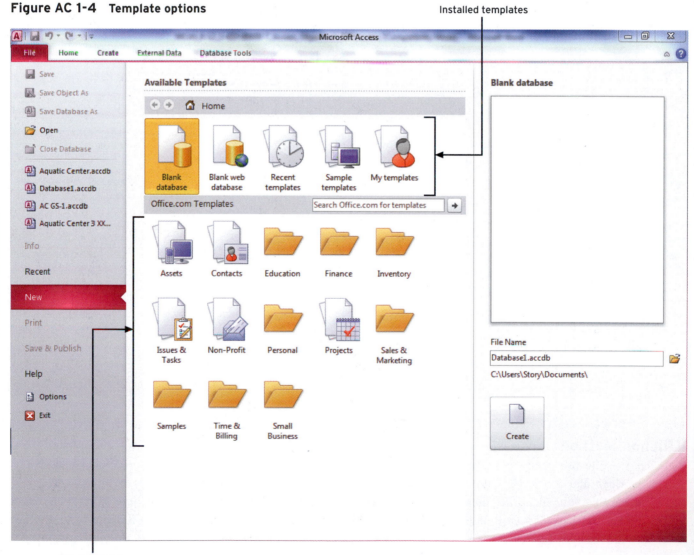

Set Access Options
Ribbon Method
☐ Click the **File tab**, then click **Options**
☐ In the Access Options dialog box, shown in Figure AC 1-5, click an option on the left, set the options you want, then click **OK**

Figure AC 1-5   **Access Options dialog box**

CREATE AND MANAGE A DATABASE

Rename Objects
Ribbon Method
☐ Right-click the table name in the Navigation Pane
☐ Click **Rename** on the shortcut menu, shown in Figure AC 1-6
☐ Type a new table name, then press **Enter**

NOTE

You can only rename an object when it is closed.

Figure AC 1-6   Object shortcut menu

Delete Objects

Ribbon Method

- ☐ Right-click the object name in the Navigation Pane
- ☐ Click **Delete** on the shortcut menu, shown in Figure AC 1-6
- ☐ Click **Yes** to confirm the deletion

Set Navigation Options

Shortcut Method

- ☐ Click the **Navigation Pane arrow button**  to display the Navigation Pane menu, shown in Figure AC 1-7
- ☐ Click a **Navigate To Category option** and/or click a **Filter By Group option**

Figure AC 1-7   Navigation Pane menu

APPLY APPLICATIONS PARTS

Use Blank Forms

Ribbon Method

☐ Click the **Create tab**, click the **Application Parts button**, then click a **Blank Forms option**, shown in Figure AC 1-8

Figure AC 1-8   Application Parts menu

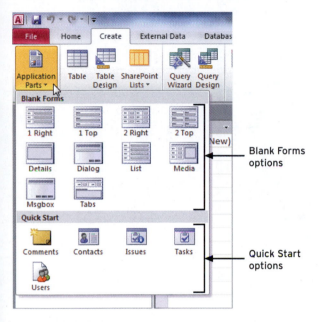

Use Quick Start

Ribbon Method

☐ Click the **Create tab**, click the **Application Parts button**, then click a **Quick Start option**, shown in Figure AC 1-8
☐ In the Create Relationship dialog box, shown in Figure AC 1-9, specify a relationship, click **Next**, and then click **Create**

Figure AC 1-9   Create Relationship dialog box

Use User Templates

Ribbon Method

☐ Click the **File tab**, click **New**, then click an Office.com Templates option or double-click a folder to display user template options, shown in Figure AC 1-10

Figure AC 1-10   User templates

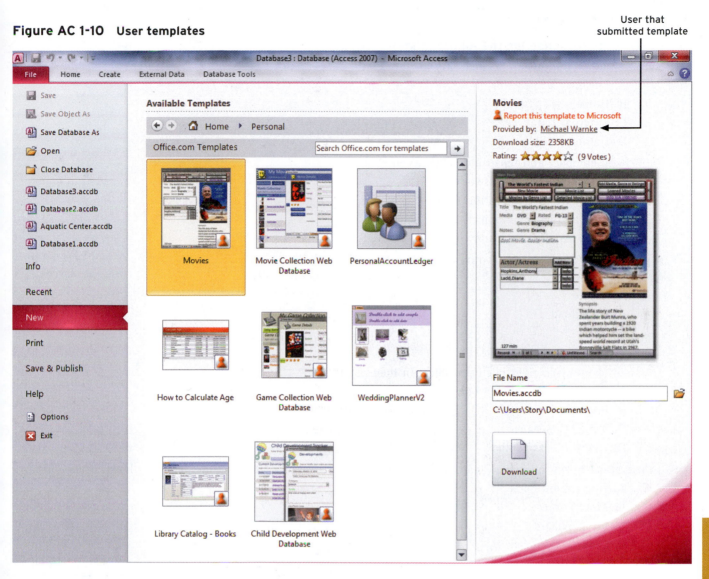

REVIEW QUESTIONS

TRUE/FALSE

Circle T if the statement is true or F if the statement is false.

T F 1. To use the Save Object As command, click the File tab, click Save Object As, enter a name for the object in the Save As dialog box, then click OK.

T F 2. Set Database Password is a Save & Publish option.

T F 3. You can only rename an object when it is closed.

T F 4. The Navigation Pane menu includes Navigation to Category options and Filter By Group options.

T F 5. Quick Start options are located in the Access Options dialog box.

MULTIPLE CHOICE

Select the best response for the following statements.

1. Save & Publish options are located on the _____ tab.
   - A. File
   - B. Home
   - C. External Data
   - D. Database Tools

2. Before you compact and repair a database, you should _____.
   - A. encrypt it with a password
   - B. configure the Navigation Pane
   - C. save and close all objects in the database
   - D. apply Application Parts

3. If you are creating a database from a template, you will click the _____ button if you selected an online template.
   - A. Create
   - B. Download
   - C. Add
   - D. Import

4. To rename an object, right-click the object in the _____ and click Rename.
   - A. Access Options dialog box
   - B. File tab
   - C. Navigation Pane
   - D. Quick Access Toolbar

5. To use blank forms, click the Create tab, click the _____ button, then click a Blank Forms option.
   - A. Application Parts
   - B. More Forms
   - C. Form Wizard
   - D. Options

PROJECTS

Project AC 1-1

1. Use the Open dialog box to open the data file **Project AC 1-1.accdb**.

2. Save the file as **Animal Shelter** and enable the content, if necessary.

3. Select the **New Owner: Table** in the Navigation Pane and save it as a new table titled **Potential Donors: Table**.

4. Select the **Animals: Table** in the Navigation Pane and rename it **Pets: Table**.

5. Select the New Owner Query in the Navigation Pane and delete it.

6. Open the Access Options dialog box, click each category to see what options are available, then cancel the dialog box.

7. Select the **Object Type** option in the Navigate to Category section of the Navigation Pane menu.

8. Use a Quick Start Application Part to create a Comments table with no relationship specified.

9. Select the **Tables** option in the Filter by Group section of the Navigation Pane menu.

10. Compact and repair the database.

11. Save and close the workbook.

CRITICAL THINKING

Activity AC 1-1

Create a database using an installed template and notice what database objects it contains. If lab guidelines allow, download an online database template as well and notice what database objects it contains.

Activity AC 1-2

Click the File tab, then click Save & Publish and view the options available. One of the advanced options is Back Up Database. Use Access Help or another resource to learn more about how to back up a database and why it is important to do so regularly to prevent data loss.

Activity AC 1-3

Open a database in Exclusive mode and set a password that is required to open it. Write down the password and store it in a secure place. Close the database and then open it up again, using the password you just created. Use Access Help or the Internet to read about what makes a strong password. How could you improve the strength of your password?

ACCESS OBJECTIVE 2: BUILDING TABLES

CREATE TABLES

Create Tables in Design View

Ribbon Method

☐ Click the **Create tab**, then click the **Table Design button** in the Tables group

☐ For each field you want in the table, type the field name in the Field Name column, then press **[Enter]**

☐ To specify the type of data for a field, click the **Data Type list arrow**, shown in Figure AC 2-1, then click the appropriate data type for the field, using Table AC 2-1 as a reference

☐ To set properties for data that is entered in a field, click the appropriate property text box in the Field Properties pane, shown in Figure AC 2-1, then specify and modify the property for that field using Table AC 2-2 as a reference

☐ Click the field you want to define as the primary key, then click the **Primary Key button** in the Tools group on the Table Tools Design tab, shown in Figure AC 2-2

Figure AC 2-1   **Table in Design View**

Figure AC 2-2   **Table Tools Design tab**

Click to designate Primary Key

Table AC 2-1   Data Types

Data Type	Purpose
Text	Stores text and/or numbers up to 255 characters; most common data type
Number	Stores numeric data that can be used in mathematical calculations
Currency	Stores monetary data displayed with dollar sign
Date & Time	Stores dates and/or times
Yes/No	Stores True/False, Yes/No, or On/Off values; used when only two values can be chosen
Lookup & Relationship	Displays a list of values from which a user can choose
Rich Text	Stores rich-formatted text in a Memo field
Memo	Stores text and/or numbers up to 65,535 characters; used for larger amounts of text
Attachment	Stores any supported file type, such as images, documents, and charts
Hyperlink	Stores links such as Web addresses
Calculated Field	Displays a value that is calculated from other data in the same table

Table AC 2-2   Selected Field Properties

Field property	Can be used to	Used for data type(s)
Field Size	Set the maximum size for data stored in a field set	Text, Number, and AutoNumber
Format	Customize the way numbers, dates, times, and text are displayed and printed, or use special symbols to create custom formats, such as to display information in all uppercase	Text, Memo, Date/Time, AutoNumber, Yes/No, Hyperlink, and Number
Decimal Places	Specify the number of decimal places that are displayed, but not how many decimal places are stored	Number and Currency
New Values	Specify whether an AutoNumber field is incremented or assigned a random value	AutoNumber
Input Mask	Make data entry easier and to control the values users can enter in a text box control, such as (___) ___-____ for a phone number	Text and Date
Caption	Provide helpful information to the user through captions on objects in various views	All fields
Default Value	Specify a value that is entered in a field automatically when a new record is added; (for example, in an Address table you can set the default value for the State field to Massachusetts); when a new record is added to the table, you can either accept this value or enter a new state	All fields except AutoNumber or OLE object

(continued)

Access

Table AC 2-2   Selected Field Properties (continued)

Field property	Can be used to	Used for data type(s)
Validation Rule	Specify requirements for data entered into a record, field, or control	All fields except AutoNumber or OLE object
Validation Text	Specify a message to be displayed when the user enters data that violates the Validation Rule property	All fields where a Validation Rule is specified
Required	Specify whether a value is required in a field	All fields except AutoNumber
Allow Zero Length	Allow users to enter a zero-length string ("")	Text and Memo
Indexed	Set a single-field index that will speed up queries on the indexed fields, as well as sorting and grouping operations	Text, Number, Date/Time, Currency, AutoNumber, Yes/No, Hyperlink, and Memo
Smart Tags	Specify that certain data be marked as a Smart Tag	Text, Currency, Number, Date/Time, AutoNumber, and Hyperlink

CREATE AND MODIFY FIELDS

Insert a Field

Ribbon Method

- ☐ In Datasheet View, click the **Click to Add** column header and then select a data type (see Table AC 2-1)
- ☐ With the field name selected, type a field name, then press **[Enter]**

  OR

- ☐ Open a table in Design View, then enter a field name in a blank row of the Field Name column
- ☐ Click in the Data Type column, click the **Data Type list arrow**, then select a data type (see Table AC 2-1)
- ☐ Click the **Save button** 🖫 on the Quick Access toolbar

Delete a Field

Ribbon Method

- ☐ In Datasheet View, right-click the field name, then click **Delete Field** on the shortcut menu, shown in Figure AC 2-3
- ☐ Click **Yes** in the dialog box to permanently delete the field

  OR

- ☐ In Design View, right-click the row selector for the field name you want to delete, then click **Delete Rows** on the shortcut menu
- ☐ Click **Yes** in the dialog box to permanently delete the field

Access

Figure AC 2-3 **Field shortcut menu**

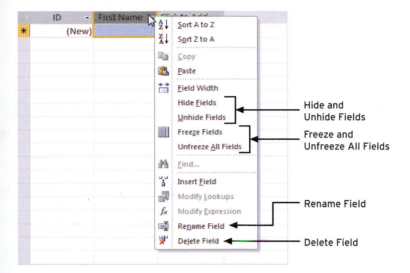

Rename a Field
Ribbon Method
☐ In Datasheet View, right-click the field name, then click **Rename Field** on the shortcut menu, shown in Figure AC 2-3
☐ With the field name selected, type a new field name, then press **[Enter]**
   OR
☐ In Design View, select the field name in the Field Name column, type a new field name, then press **[Enter]**

Hide or Unhide Fields
Ribbon Method
☐ In Datasheet View, right-click the field name, then click **Hide Fields or Unhide Fields** on the shortcut menu, shown in Figure AC 2-3

Freeze or Unfreeze Fields
Ribbon Method
☐ In Datasheet View, right-click the field name, then click **Freeze Fields or Unfreeze All Fields** on the shortcut menu, shown in Figure AC 2-3

Modify Data Types
Ribbon Method
☐ In Design View, click the arrow in the Data Type field and click a data type on the menu

Modify the Field Description
Ribbon Method
☐ In Design View, click the Description box for a field and type or edit a description that will be displayed in the status bar when you select this field on a form

Modify Field Properties
Ribbon Method
☐ In Datasheet View, click a field name header, then click an option in the Properties group on the Table Tools Fields tab
   OR
☐ In Design View, click a field row selector, then make changes in the Field Properties pane, shown in Figure AC 2-1

SORT AND FILTER RECORDS

Use Find

Ribbon Method

□ Open a table in Datasheet View or a form in Form View

□ Click the **Find button** in the Find group on the Home tab

□ In the Find and Replace dialog box, shown in Figure AC 2-4, enter the value you want to find in the Find What text box

□ To search using wildcards, enter the value using * (asterisk) to stand for any number of characters and ? (question mark) to stand for a single character

□ To specify additional criteria, click the **Look In list arrow**, then select a field name; click the **Match list arrow**, then select which part of the field you want to search; click the **Search list arrow**, then select the direction you want to search

□ Click **Find Next**

Figure AC 2-4   **Find and Replace dialog box**

Shortcut Method

□ Open a table in Datasheet View or a form in Form View

□ Press **[Ctrl][F]**

□ Follow the steps in bullets 3–6 of the Use Find Ribbon Method above

Use Sort

Ribbon Method

□ Open a table or query in Datasheet View

□ Click any value in the field you want to sort

□ In the Sort & Filter group on the Home tab, shown in Figure AC 2-5, click the **Ascending button** or the **Descending button**

□ To remove the sort, click the **Clear All Sorts button** in the Sort & Filter group on the Home tab

Shortcut Method

□ Open a table or query in Datasheet View

□ Click the **column heading list arrow** for the field you want to sort

□ Click a sort option, such as Sort Smallest to Largest or Sort Newest to Oldest, then click **OK**

□ To remove the sort, click **Clear filter from *field***, where field is the name of the field, then click **OK**

Figure AC 2-5   **Sort & Filter group**

Sort & Filter group

Use AutoFilter
Ribbon Method
□ Open the table or query in Datasheet View

□ Click a value in the field you want to filter

□ Click the **Filter button** in the Sort & Filter group on the Home tab, shown in Figure AC 2-5, to display the AutoFilter menu

□ Click a field value for which you want to filter, then click **OK**

   OR

□ Click a field value for which you want to filter, point to **Data type Filters**, where *Data type* is the data type for the field, click a filter option, as shown in Figure AC 2-6, such as Equals, enter a value, then click **OK**

□ To remove the filter, click the **column heading list arrow** for the field, click **Clear filter from field**, where *field* is the name of the field

Figure AC 2-6   **Data Type filter fields**

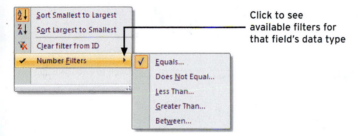

Click to see available filters for that field's data type

Shortcut Method
□ Open the table or query in Datasheet View

□ Click the **column heading list arrow** for the field you want to filter to display the AutoFilter menu

□ Click a field value for which you want to filter, then click **OK**

   OR

□ Click a field value for which you want to filter, point to **Data type Filters**, where *Data type* is the data type for the field, click a filter option, as shown in Figure AC 2-6, such as Equals, enter a value, then click **OK**

□ To remove the filter, right-click the field, then click **Clear filter from field**, where *field* is the name of the field

Filter Records Using Filter by Selection
Ribbon Method
□ Open a table or query in Datasheet View or a form in Form View

□ Click the field that contains criteria that you want to apply as a filter to the rest of the data

□ Click the **Selection button arrow** in the Sort & Filter group on the Home tab, shown in Figure AC 2-5, click a filter option

□ To remove the filter, click the field, then click the **Toggle Filter button** in the Sort & Filter group on the Home tab

Shortcut Method

☐ Open a table or query in Datasheet View or a form in Form View

☐ Right-click the field that contains criteria that you want to apply as a filter, then click a filter option for the current value

OR

☐ Point to **Data type Filters**, where *Data type* is the data type for the field, click a filter option, such as Equals, enter a value, then click **OK**

☐ To remove the filter, right-click the field, then click **Clear filter from *field***, where *field* is the name of the field

Filter Records Using Filter By Form

Ribbon Method

☐ Open a table or query in Datasheet View or a form in Form View

☐ Click the field that contains criteria that you want to apply as a filter to the rest of the data

☐ Click the **Advanced button arrow** in the Sort & Filter group on the Home tab, shown in Figure AC 2-5, then click **Filter By Form**

☐ In the form, shown in Figure AC 2-7, click the cell that contains the value that you want all records in the filter results to contain, then type the criteria using Table AC 2-3 as a reference, or click the cell by which to filter, click the **list arrow**, then click the value by which to filter

☐ To filter by additional criteria, click the **Or tab**, shown in Figure AC 2-7, then enter additional criteria

☐ Click the **Toggle Filter button** in the Sort & Filter group on the Home tab

Figure AC 2-7   Filter by Form

Click to choose value by which to filter

Click the Or tab to filter by additional criteria

Table AC 2-3 Comparison Operators

Operator	Description	Expression	Meaning
<	Less than	<"Cassidy"	Names from A through Cassidy, but not Cassidy
<=	Less than or equal to	<="Delaney"	Names from A through, and including, Delaney
>	Greater than	>450	Numbers greater than 450
>=	Greater than or equal to	>=450	Numbers greater than or equal to 450
<>	Not equal to	<>"Malone"	Any name except for Malone
OR	Needs to meet 1 of 2 criteria	"Murphy" OR "Malone"	Only names Murphy or Malone
AND	Needs to meet both of 2 criteria	>="Cassidy" AND <="Murphy"	All names between and including Cassidy and Murphy

Create and Apply Advanced Filters

Ribbon Method

☐ Open a table or query in Datasheet View or a form in Form View

☐ Click the field that contains criteria that you want to apply as a filter to the rest of the data

☐ Click the **Advanced button arrow** in the Sort & Filter group on the Home tab, shown in Figure AC 2-5, then click **Advanced Filter/Sort**

☐ Double-click each field you want in the filter to add it to the filter design grid

☐ Click the **Criteria cell** for each field, then type the criteria you want each record in the filter results to meet, using Table AC 2-3 as a reference

☐ Click the **Sort cell** for each field, click the **list arrow**, then click **Ascending** or **Descending** as appropriate

☐ Click the **Toggle Filter button** in the Sort & Filter group on the Home tab

SET RELATIONSHIPS

Define Primary Keys

Ribbon Method

☐ Open a table in Design View

☐ Click the field you want to set as the primary key

☐ Click the **Primary Key button** in the Tools group on the Table Tools Design tab, shown in Figure AC 2-2

Shortcut Method

☐ Open a table in Design View

☐ Right-click the field you want to set as the primary key, then click **Primary Key**

NOTE

When you create a table in Datasheet view, Access automatically creates a primary key for you and assigns it the AutoNumber data type.

Access

Use Primary Keys to Create a One-to-Many Relationship Between Tables

Ribbon Method

☐ Open a database that contains two tables for which you want to establish a one-to-many relationship

☐ Click the **Database Tools tab**, then click the **Relationships button** in the Relationships group

☐ If necessary, click the **Show Table button** in the Relationships group on the Relationship Tools Design tab

☐ In the Show Table dialog box, shown in Figure AC 2-8, double-click the object(s) you want to relate, then click **Close**

☐ In the Relationships window, shown in Figure AC 2-9, create a one-to-many relationship by dragging the "one" field (usually the primary key) from its field list to the "many" field (usually the foreign key) in another field list

Figure AC 2-8   Show Table dialog box

Figure AC 2-9   Relationships window

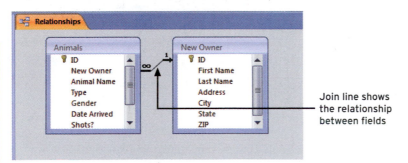

☐ In the Edit Relationships dialog box, shown in Figure AC 2-10, click **Create**

☐ Close and save the Relationships window

Figure AC 2-10   Edit Relationships dialog box

Create a One-to-One Relationship Between Tables
Ribbon Method
- □ Open a database that contains two tables for which you want to establish a one-to-one relationship
- □ Click the **Database Tools tab**, then click the **Relationships button** in the Relationships group
- □ If necessary, click the **Show Table button** in the Relationships group on the Relationship Tools Design tab
- □ In the Show Table dialog box, shown in Figure AC 2-8, double-click the object(s) you want to relate, then click **Close**
- □ In the Relationships window, shown in Figure AC 2-9, create a one-to-one relationship by dragging the "one" field (usually the primary key) from its field list to the "one" field (usually the primary key) in another field list
- □ In the Edit Relationships dialog box, shown in Figure AC 2-10, click **Create**
- □ Close and save the Relationships window

Edit Relationships
Ribbon Method
- □ Click the **Database Tools tab**, then click the **Relationships button** in the Relationships group
- □ In the Relationships window, shown in Figure AC 2-9, click the **join line** for the relationship you want to modify, then click the **Edit Relationships button** in the Tools group on the Relationship Tools Design tab
  OR
- □ Double-click the **join line** for the relationship you want to modify
- □ In the Edit Relationships dialog box, shown in Figure AC 2-10, make the appropriate modifications, then click **OK**

IMPORT DATA FROM A SINGLE DATA FILE

Import Source Data Into a New Table
Ribbon Method
- □ Click the **External Data tab**, then click a **source button** (ex. Excel, Access, Text File, etc.) in the Import & Link group
- □ In the Get External Data dialog box, as shown in Figure AC 2-11 (which uses data from an Excel spreadsheet), click **Browse** to navigate to the appropriate drive and folder, click the file you want to import, then click **Open**
- □ Click the **Import the source data into a new table in the current database option button**
- □ Click **OK**
- □ Follow the instructions in the Import Wizard dialog boxes, as shown in Figure AC 2-12 (which uses data from Excel spreadsheet), then click **Finish**
- □ Click **Close**

Figure AC 2-11   Get External Data dialog box

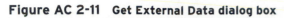

Get External Data - Excel Spreadsheet

Select the source and destination of the data

Specify the source of the data.

File name: C:\Users\Your Name\Documents\   Browse...

Specify how and where you want to store the data in the current database.

○ **Import the source data into a new table in the current database.**
   If the specified table does not exist, Access will create it. If the specified table already exists, Access might overwrite its contents with the imported data. Changes made to the source data will not be reflected in the database.

○ **Append a copy of the records to the table:** Contacts ▾
   If the specified table exists, Access will add the records to the table. If the table does not exist, Access will create it. Changes made to the source data will not be reflected in the database.

○ **Link to the data source by creating a linked table.**
   Access will create a table that will maintain a link to the source data in Excel. Changes made to the source data in Excel will be reflected in the linked table. However, the source data cannot be changed from within Access.

OK   Cancel

Choose this option to append records to a table

Choose this option to link the data

Figure AC 2-12   Import Spreadsheet Wizard dialog box

Import Spreadsheet Wizard

Your spreadsheet file contains more than one worksheet or range. Which worksheet or range would you like?

○ Show Worksheets
○ Show Named Ranges

Sheet1
Sheet2
Sheet3

Sample data for worksheet 'Sheet1'.

	First Name	Last Name	Address	City	State	ZIP
1	First Name	Last Name	Address	City	State	ZIP
2	Judy	Lew	345 Spring Hill	Bozeman	MT	65331
3	Bjorn	Rettig	89 North Street	Jackson Hole	WY	90907
4	Mike	Tiano	12 Third Avenue	Denver	CO	45211
5	Karin	Zimprich	6789 Cypress Lane	Seattle	WA	74284

Cancel   < Back   Next >   Finish

Append Records to an Existing Table

Ribbon Method

☐ Click the **External Data tab**, then click a **source button** (ex. Excel, Access, Text File, etc.) in the Import & Link group

☐ In the Get External Data dialog box, as shown in Figure AC 2-11 (which uses an Excel spreadsheet), click **Browse** to navigate to the appropriate drive and folder, click the file you want to import, then click **Open**

☐ If you want to add the records to an existing table in the database, click the **Append a copy of the records to the table option button**, click the **list arrow**, then select a table

☐ Click **OK**

☐ Follow the instructions in the Import Wizard dialog boxes, as shown in Figure AC 2-12 (which uses an Excel spreadsheet), then click **Finish**

☐ Click **Close**

Import Data as a Linked Table

Ribbon Method

☐ Click the **External Data tab**, then click the **Excel button** in the Import & Link group

☐ In the Get External Data dialog box, shown in Figure AC 2-11, click **Browse** to navigate to the appropriate drive and folder, click the file you want to import, then click **Open**

☐ Click the **Link to the data source by creating a linked table option button**

☐ Click **OK**

☐ Follow the instructions in the Link Spreadsheet Wizard dialog boxes, then click **Finish**

☐ Click **Close**

REVIEW QUESTIONS

FILL IN THE BLANK

Complete the following sentences by writing the correct word or words in the blanks provided.

1. The shortcut method for opening the _____ dialog box is [Ctrl][F].

2. To remove all sorts, click the _____ button in the Sort & Filter group on the Home tab.

3. To create and apply advanced filters on a table or query, open it in _____ view.

4. Tables you choose in the Show Table dialog box will be displayed in the _____ window.

5. To append records to an existing table, click the _____ tab, then click a source button (ex. Excel, Access, Text File) in the Import & Link group.

Matching

Match each purpose in Column 2 to its data type in Column 1.

Column 1	**Column 2**
_____ 1. Text	A. Stores monetary data displayed with a dollar sign
_____ 2. Yes/No	B. Most common data type
_____ 3. Currency	C. Stores data that can be used in mathematical calculations
_____ 4. Number	D. Displays a list of values from which a user can choose
_____ 5. Lookup & Relationship	E. Used when only two values can be chosen

Projects

Project AC 2-1

1. Open the data file **AC 2-1.accdb**.

2. Save the file as **Business Startup**.

3. Using the data file **Vendors.xlsx**, import the data into a new table called Vendors. (*Hint: The first row contains column headings. You do not need to specify information about the fields you are importing. Let Access add the primary key. Do not save the import steps.*)

4. Open the Vendors table in the database to verify that the data has been imported.

5. Using the data file **Webmasters.xlsx**, link to the data source by creating a linked table called Webmasters. (*Hint: The first row contains column headings.*)

6. Open the linked Webmasters table to verify the data source has been linked.

7. Using the data file **Associations.txt**, import the data into a new table called Associations. (*Hint: Tab delimiters separate the fields. You don't need to specify information about the fields. Let Access add the primary key. Do not save the import steps.*)

8. Save and close all database objects.

9. Close the database.

Project AC 2-2

1. Create a new blank database named **Voter Registration**.

2. Use Design View to create a custom table named *Voters*.

3. Create the following new fields and assign the corresponding data type to each one:
   - Voter Name—Text
   - Date of Birth—Date/Time
   - Precinct—Number
   - Signed—Attachment
   - Pre-Registered?—Yes/No

4. Rename the Signed field as Signature Card.

5. Delete the Pre-Registered? field.

6. Hide the Signature Card field.

7. Modify the Voter Name field properties to be required and have a maximum field size of 50.

8. Save and close the database.

CRITICAL THINKING

Activity AC 2-1

Open the database that you created in Project AC 2-2 and save the database as **Classroom Voters**. Use information about classmates to create at least ten records (or make up the information). Sort or filter voters by the following criteria:

- Sort voters from youngest to oldest.
- Sort voters by name in descending order.
- Sort voters by precinct in ascending order.
- Filter voters to show only those in your precinct.
- Filter voters to show only those born in the same month as you.
- Save and close the database.

Activity AC 2-2

Open the data file **Swim Classes.accdb** and display the Relationships window. What is the primary key for each table? How are the tables related? Is each relationship one-to-many or one-to-one? How can you tell? Close the database without saving.

ACCESS OBJECTIVE 3: BUILDING FORMS

CREATE FORMS

Use the Form Wizard

Ribbon Method

☐ In the Navigation Pane, click an object on which you want to base a form

☐ Click the **Create tab** then click the **Form Wizard button** in the Forms group, shown in Figure AC 3-1

☐ In the Form Wizard dialog box, shown in Figure AC 3-2, select the data source in the Tables/Queries drop down menu

☐ Choose the fields you want on your form by clicking a field name in the Available Fields box to select it, then clicking the **Add field button** to move it to the Selected Fields list box

☐ Click the **Next > button** and choose a layout

☐ Click the **Next > button**, type a title, choose to open the form or continue to work on it by modifying its design, then click the **Finish button**

Figure AC 3-1   Forms group on Create tab

Forms options

Figure AC 3-2   Form Wizard

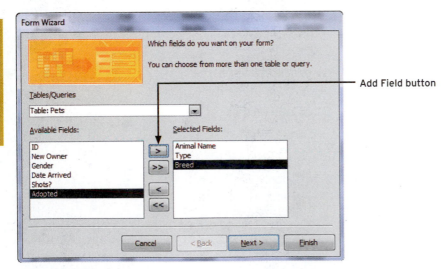

Add Field button

Create a Blank Form

Ribbon Method

☐ In the Navigation Pane, click an object on which you want to create a form

☐ Click the **Create tab** then click the **Blank Form button** in the Forms group, shown in Figure AC 3-1

☐ If necessary, click the **Add Existing Fields button** in the Tools group on the Form Layout Tools Design tab to open the Field List

☐ If necessary, click **Show all tables** in the **Field List**

☐ Expand the list of tables and fields as necessary to display the fields you want to add to the form

☐ Drag one or more fields from the Field List to the appropriate location on the form

☐ Click the **Save button** 💾 on the Quick Access toolbar, type an appropriate name for the form in the Save As dialog box, then click **OK**

Use Form Design Tools
Ribbon Method

☐ In the Navigation Pane, click an object on which you want to base a form

☐ Click the **Create tab** then click the **Form Design button** in the Forms group, shown in Figure AC 3-1

☐ Use the tools on the Form Design Tools Design, Arrange, and Format tabs to create a form

Create Navigation forms
Ribbon Method

☐ In the Navigation Pane, click an object on which you want to base a form

☐ Click the **Create tab** then click the **Navigation button** in the Forms group, shown in Figure AC 3-1

☐ Click an option on the Navigation menu, shown in Figure AC 3-3

Figure AC 3-3   Navigation form options

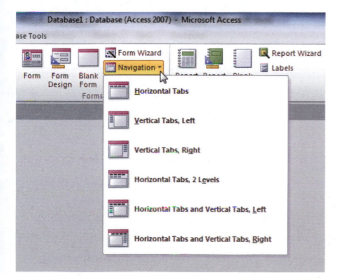

NOTE

There are other tools that you can use to create different types of forms, by clicking the More Forms button in the Forms group on the Create tab.

APPLY FORM DESIGN OPTIONS

Apply a Theme

Ribbon Method

☐ Open a form in Layout View or Design View, click the **Themes button** in the Themes group on the Form Layout (Design) Tools Design tab, then click an option on the Themes menu, shown in Figure AC 3-4

Figure AC 3-4   Themes menu

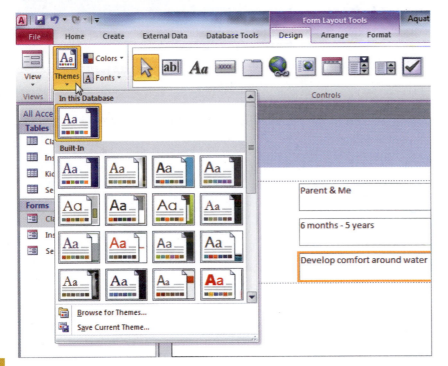

Add Bound Controls

Ribbon Method

☐ Open a form in Design View
☐ Click a button in the Controls group on the Form Design Tools Design tab or click the **More button** to display additional control options, shown in Figure AC 3-5
☐ Click a control, then click where you want to place the control on the form

Figure AC 3-5   Controls menu

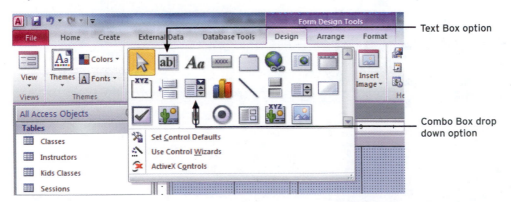

Format Header/Footer

Ribbon Method

☐ Open a form in Design View or Layout View

☐ In the Header/Footer group on the Form Design (Layout) Tools Design tab, shown in Figure AC 3-6, click a button to insert a logo, title, or the date and time

Figure AC 3-6   Header / Footer and Tools groups

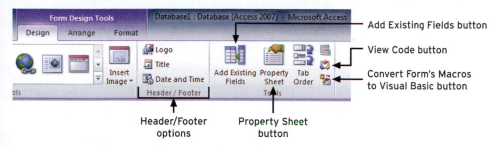

View Code

Ribbon Method

☐ Open a form in Design View

☐ In the Tools group on the Form Design Tools Design tab, click the **View Code button**, shown in Figure AC 3-6

Convert Macros to Visual Basic

Ribbon Method

☐ Open a form in Design View

☐ In the Tools group on the Form Design Tools Design tab, click the **Convert Form's Macros to Visual Basic button**, shown in Figure AC 3-6

☐ In the Convert form macros dialog box, click **Convert**

View Property Sheet

Ribbon Method

☐ Open a form in Design View or Layout View

☐ In the Tools group on the Form Design (Layout) Tools Design tab, click the **Property Sheet button**, shown in Figure AC 3-6

Add Existing Fields

Ribbon Method

☐ Open a form in Design View or Layout View

☐ In the Tools group on the Form Design (Layout) Tools Design tab, click the **Add Existing Fields button**, shown in Figure AC 3-6

☐ Click a field in the *Fields available for this view:* list and drag it to the form

APPLY FORM ARRANGE OPTIONS

Insert Rows or Columns

Ribbon Method

☐ Open a form in Layout View

☐ Select a cell adjacent to where you want to add the new column or row

☐ On the Form Layout Tools Arrange tab, in the Rows & Columns group, click the **Insert Above button** or **Insert Below button**, shown in Figure AC 3-7, to insert a new row above or below the current row

OR

☐ On the Form Layout Tools Arrange tab in the Rows & Columns group, click the **Insert Left button** or **Insert Right button**, shown in Figure AC 3-7, to insert a new column to the left or right of the current column

Figure AC 3-7   Form Layout Tools Arrange tab

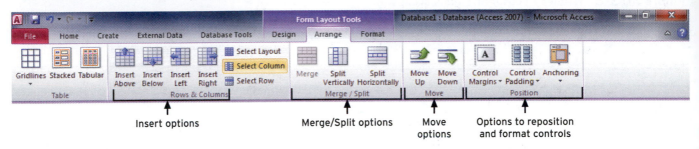

Merge Cells

Ribbon Method

☐ Open a form in Layout View

☐ Select the first cell that you want to merge, hold down the **Shift key**, and select the other cell(s) that you want to merge

☐ On the Form Layout Tools Arrange tab, in the Merge/Split group, click the **Merge button**, shown in Figure AC 3-7

Split Cells

Ribbon Method

☐ Open a form in Layout View

☐ Select the cell that you want to split

☐ On the Form Layout Tools Arrange tab, in the Merge/Split group, click the **Split Vertically button**, shown in Figure AC 3-7, to create a new row in the structure of the layout

OR

☐ On the Form Layout Tools Arrange tab in the Merge/Split group, click the **Split Horizontally button**, shown in Figure AC 3-7, to create a new column in the structure of the layout

Move Table

Ribbon Method

☐ Open a form in Layout View and select a table

☐ On the Form Layout Tools Arrange tab, in the Move group, click the **Move Up button** or **Move Down button**

Reposition/Format Controls

Ribbon Method

☐ Open a form in Layout View

☐ On the Form Layout Tools Arrange tab, in the Position group, click the **Control Margins button** and select an option on the menu

OR

☐ On the Form Layout Tools Arrange tab, in the Position group, click the **Control Padding button** and select an option on the menu

OR

☐ On the Form Layout Tools Arrange tab, in the Position group, click the **Anchoring button** and select an option on the menu

APPLY FORM FORMAT OPTIONS

Reformat Font in Form

Ribbon Method

- ☐ In the Selection group of the Form Layout Tools Format tab, shown in Figure AC 3-8, click the **Select All button** or click the **Object list arrow** and select a form control or label
- ☐ In the Font group of the Form Layout Tools Format tab, shown in Figure AC 3-8, click the font attributes you want to apply

Figure AC 3-8   Form Layout Tools Format tab

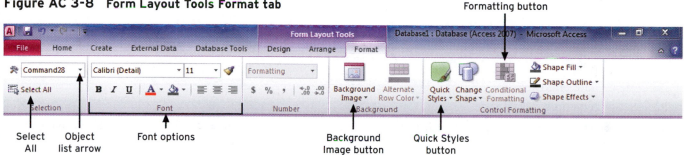

Apply Background Image to Form

Ribbon Method

- ☐ In the Background group of the Form Layout Tools Format tab, click the **Background Image button**, shown in Figure AC 3-8, then click **Browse**
- ☐ In the Insert Picture dialog box, select the picture file you want to use, then click the **Open button**

Apply Quick Styles to Controls in Form

Ribbon Method

- ☐ In the Selection group of the Form Layout Tools Format tab, shown in Figure AC 3-8, click the **Object list arrow** and select a form control
- ☐ In the Control Formatting group of the Form Layout Tools Format tab, click the **Quick Styles button**, shown in Figure AC 3-8, then click an option on the menu

Apply Conditional Formatting in Form

Ribbon Method

- ☐ In the Selection group of the Form Layout Tools Format tab, shown in Figure AC 3-8, click the **Object list arrow** and select a form control
- ☐ In the Control Formatting group of the Form Layout Tools Format tab, click the **Conditional Formatting button**, shown in Figure AC 3-8
- ☐ In the Conditional Formatting Rules Manager dialog box, click **New Rule**
- ☐ In the New Formatting Rule dialog box, select a rule type and edit the rule description, then click **OK**

REVIEW QUESTIONS

MULTIPLE CHOICE

Select the best response for the following statements.

1. Which of the following is NOT a contextual tab for modifying forms in Layout View or Design View?
   A. Design
   B. Create
   C. Arrange
   D. Format

2. Which of the following is NOT an option that can be inserted using the buttons in the Header/Footer group?
   A. logo
   B. title
   C. date and time
   D. hyperlink

3. When selecting cells to merge, hold down the _____ key, and select the other cell(s) that you want to merge.
   A. Shift
   B. Alt
   C. Ctrl
   D. Tab

4. Which is NOT an option for repositioning/formatting controls in the Position group on the Arrange tab?
   A. Add Existing Fields
   B. Control Margins
   C. Control Padding
   D. Anchoring

5. The Forms group options are located on the _____ tab.
   A. Home
   B. Create
   C. External Data
   D. Database Tools

MATCHING

Match each Ribbon location in Column 2 to its button command in Column 1.

Column 1	Column 2
_____ 1. Form Wizard	A. Format tab, Control Formatting group
_____ 2. View Code	B. Arrange tab, Position group
_____ 3. Insert Above	C. Design tab, Tools group
_____ 4. Quick Styles	D. Create tab, Forms group
_____ 5. Anchoring	E. Arrange tab, Rows & Columns group

Access

PROJECTS

Project AC 3-1

1. Open the data file **Project AC 3-1.accdb**.

2. Save the file as **Baseball Cards**.

3. Use the Form Wizard to create a form named *Wizard Form* using the Item, Card Year, and Description fields, with a columnar layout.

4. In Layout View, change the theme to **Angles**.

5. View the Property Sheet.

6. Insert the date and time into the header.

7. Insert the data file **baseball.png** as the background image.

8. Close the Property Sheet.

9. Change the font color of the Card Year field to **Orange, Accent 2**.

10. Select the Description field and anchor it in the **Bottom Right** position on the form.

11. Save the changes and close the form.

CRITICAL THINKING

Activity AC 3-1

Use Access Help to search for the *Introduction to form and report layouts* video and watch it. Take turns with a classmate demonstrating to each other how to do each of the following on a form, or practice on your own:

- Add controls to a layout
- Resize a row or column
- Delete a control from a layout
- Delete a row or column from a layout
- Move a control in a layout
- Merge cells
- Split cells

Activity AC 3-2

Open a database that you have worked on and create a form that you can use to enter data into one of the tables. Which type of form did you create and why? View the form in Layout View, and use the buttons on the Format Layout Tools Format, Design, and Arrange tabs to modify the design of the form to your liking.

ACCESS OBJECTIVE 4: CREATING AND MANAGING QUERIES

CONSTRUCT QUERIES

Create Select Query

Ribbon Method

☐ Open a database and select the table on which you want to base the query

☐ Click the **Create tab**, then click the **Query Wizard button** in the Queries group

☐ In the New Query dialog box, click **Simple Query Wizard**, then click **OK**

☐ In the Simple Query Wizard dialog box, shown in Figure AC 4-1, choose the fields you want in your query, then click **Next >**

☐ Type a title for your query and choose to open the query or modify the query's design, then click **Finish**

Figure AC 4-1   **Simple Query Wizard dialog box**

> # NOTE
>
> When you save a query, you are actually saving the design of the query, not the query results. When you run a query, you perform the query with the most recent data, and give instructions to display the record and fields in your original query design.

Create Make Table Query

Ribbon Method

☐ Follow the steps in the Create Select Query Ribbon Methods above to create a query

☐ Switch to Design View, if necessary

☐ To preview the new table before you create it, click the **View button arrow** in the Results group on the Query Tools Design tab, then click **Datasheet View**

☐ Return to Design View, make any necessary changes, then click the **Make Table button** in the Query Type group on the Query Tools Design tab, shown in Figure AC 4-2

☐ In the Make Table dialog box, shown in Figure AC 4-3, enter or select the name of the table you want to make

☐ To create the table in the current database, click the **Current Database option button**; to create a table in a different database, click the **Another Database option button**, then type the path of the database where you want to make the new table or click **Browse** to locate the database, then click **OK** to close the Make Table dialog box

☐ Click the **Run button** in the Results group on the Query Tools Design tab, shown in Figure AC 4-2

☐ Click **Yes**

Figure AC 4-2   Query Tools Design tab

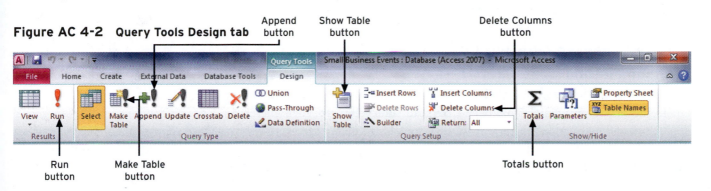

Figure AC 4-3   Make Table dialog box

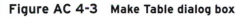

Create Append Query

Ribbon Method

☐ Follow the steps in the Create Select Query Ribbon Methods above and on the previous page to create a query

☐ Switch to Design View, if necessary

☐ To preview the records before you append them, click the **View button arrow** in the Results group on the Query Tools Design tab, shown in Figure AC 4-2, then click **Datasheet View**

☐ Return to Design View, make any necessary changes, then click the **Append button** in the Query Type group on the Query Tools Design tab, shown in Figure AC 4-2

☐ In the Append dialog box, shown in Figure AC 4-4, enter or select the name of the table to which you want to append records

☐ To add records to the table in the current database, click the **Current Database option button**; to add records to a table in a different database, click the **Another Database option button**, then type the path of the database where you want to append records or click **Browse** to locate the database, then click **OK** to close the Append dialog box

☐ Click the **Run button** in the Results group on the Query Tools Design tab, shown in Figure AC 4-2

☐ Click **Yes**

Figure AC 4-4   Append dialog box

Create Crosstab Query

Ribbon Method

☐ Click the **Create tab**, then click the **Query Wizard button** in the Queries group

☐ In the New Query dialog box, click **Crosstab Query Wizard**, then click **OK**

☐ Follow the instructions in the Crosstab Query Wizard dialog boxes, shown in Figure AC 4-5, then click **Finish**

Figure AC 4-5   Crosstab Query Wizard dialog box

MANAGE SOURCE TABLES AND RELATIONSHIPS

Use the Show Table Command

Ribbon Method

☐ Open a query in Design View

☐ Click the **Show Table button** in the Query Setup group on the Query Tools Design tab, shown in Figure AC 4-2

☐ In the Show Table dialog box, double-click the table you want to add to the query

Shortcut Method

☐ Open a query in Design View

☐ Right-click a blank area of the query window, then click **Show Table**

☐ In the Show Table dialog box, double-click the table you want to add to the query

Use Remove Table Command

Shortcut Method

☐ Open a query in Design View

☐ Right-click the title bar of the field list for the table you want to remove, then click **Remove Table**

Create Ad Hoc Relationships

Ribbon Method

☐ Open a query in Design View

☐ Click the **Show Table button** in the Query Setup group on the Query Tools Design tab, shown in Figure AC 4-2

☐ In the Show Table dialog box, double-click the tables you want to add to the query

☐ Click the field in one table and drag it to a field in another table to create an ad hoc relationship, represented by a thin line

Shortcut Method

☐ Open a query in Design View

☐ Right-click a blank area of the query window, then click **Show Table**

☐ In the Show Table dialog box, double-click the tables you want to add to the query

☐ Click the field in one table and drag it to a field in another table to create an ad hoc relationship, represented by a thin line

MANIPULATE FIELDS

Add Field

Ribbon Method

☐ Click the **Create tab**, then click the **Query Design button** in the Queries group

☐ In the Show Table dialog box, double-click each object you want to query, then click **Close**

☐ Add a field to the query by dragging the field from the field list to the Field column in the query design grid, shown in Figure AC 4-6

Figure AC 4-6   Add fields to a query

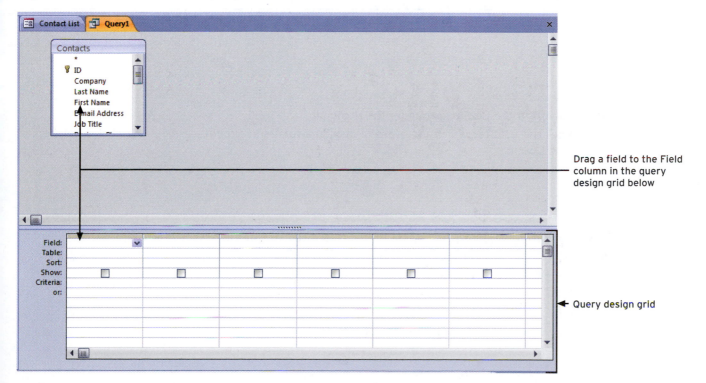

Drag a field to the Field column in the query design grid below

← Query design grid

Access

Remove Field

Ribbon Method

☐ In the query design grid, place the insertion point in the column of the field you want to remove

☐ In the Query Setup group on the Query Tools Design tab, click the **Delete Columns button**, shown in Figure AC 4-2

Rearrange Fields

Ribbon Method

☐ In the query design grid, click the header of the field column to select it

☐ Click the header of selected (black) column and drag it to a new position, indicated by a thick black line, as shown in Figure AC 4-7

Figure AC 4-7   Rearrange fields

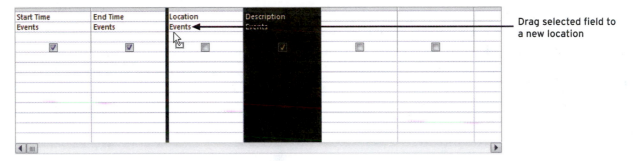

Drag selected field to a new location

Use Sort and Show Options

Ribbon Method

☐ In the query design grid, click a Sort cell and then click the down arrow

☐ In the menu, click **Ascending** or **Descending**

   OR

☐ In the query design grid, click the **checkbox** in a Show cell to select or deselect it

---

CALCULATE TOTALS

Use the Total Row

Ribbon Method

☐ Open a table in Datasheet View

☐ Click the **Totals button** in the Records group on the Home tab

☐ In the Total row, click the field for which you want to display a total, click the list arrow, then click a calculation, such as **Sum** or **Count**

Use Group By

Ribbon Method

☐ Open the query in Design View

☐ Click the **Totals button** in the Show/Hide group on the Query Tools Design tab, shown in Figure AC 4-2

☐ Click **Group By** in the Total row for the field, click the **Group By list arrow**, then click the appropriate aggregate function, using Table AC 4-1 as a reference

Shortcut Method

☐ Open the query in Design View

☐ Right-click a field in the query design grid, then click **Totals**

☐ Click **Group By** in the Total row for the field, click the **Group By list arrow**, then click the appropriate aggregate function, using Table AC 4-1 as a reference

Table AC 4-1   Aggregate Functions

Function	Used to calculate the	Used for field types
Sum	Total value	Number, Date/Time, Currency, and AutoNumber
Avg	Average value	Number, Date/Time, Currency, and AutoNumber
Min	Lowest value in a field	Text, Number, Date/Time, Currency, and AutoNumber
Max	Highest value in a field	Text, Number, Date/Time, Currency, and AutoNumber
Count	Number of values in a field (not counting null values)	Text, Memo, Number, Date/Time, Currency, AutoNumber, Yes/No, and OLE Object
StDev	Standard deviation of values	Number, Date/Time, Currency, and AutoNumber
Var	Variance of values	Number, Date/Time, Currency, and AutoNumber

GENERATE CALCULATED FIELDS

Perform calculations using the Zoom box and Expression Builder

Ribbon Method

☐ Open a query in Design View

☐ Click the first blank field in the query design grid, type the heading for the calculated field, then type **:** (colon)

☐ Click the **Builder button** in the Query Setup group on the Query Tools Design tab, shown in Figure AC 4-2

☐ In the Expression Builder dialog box, shown in Figure AC 4-8, use the expression elements and common operators to build the expression, then click **OK**, or type the exact expression

☐ In the expression, use arithmetic operators (+, -, /, *), comparison operators (=, <, >, <=, >=, < >), and logical operators (And, Or, Not, Like) as necessary to create the calculation

Figure AC 4-8   Expression Builder

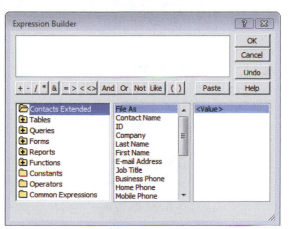

Shortcut Method

☐ Open a query in Design View

☐ Click the first blank field in the query design grid, type the heading for the calculated field, then type **:** (colon)

☐ Enter an expression, enclosing the field names in brackets

OR

□ Right-click the field, click **Zoom**, type the expression, enclosing field names in brackets, then click **OK**
  OR

□ Right-click the first blank field in the query design grid, click **Build**, use the Expression Builder dialog box, shown in Figure AC 4-8, to create an expression, then click **OK**

□ In the expression, use arithmetic operators (+, -, /, *), comparison operators (=, <, >, <=, >=, < >), and logical operators (And, Or, Not, Like) as necessary to create the calculation

REVIEW QUESTIONS

TRUE/FALSE

Circle T if the statement is true or F if the statement is false.

T   F   1. The Make Table dialog box has options for selecting the current database or another database.

T   F   2. Crosstab Query Wizard is an option in the New Query dialog box.

T   F   3. Tables cannot be removed from a query in Design View.

T   F   4. Sort and Show options are found in the query design grid.

T   F   5. The Sum aggregate function is used to calculate the highest value in a field.

FILL IN THE BLANK

Complete the following sentences by writing the correct word or words in the blanks provided.

1. To create a select query, click the Create tab, then click the Query Wizard button in the _____ group.

2. To use the Totals row, open a table in Datasheet View, click the Totals button in the _____ group on the Home tab.

3. To use Group By, open the query in Design View, click the Totals button in the _____ group on the Query Tools Design tab.

4. To remove a field, click the Delete Columns button in the _____ group on the Query Tools Design tab.

5. To create a Make Table query, click the Make Table button in the _____ group on the Query Tools Design tab.

PROJECTS

Project AC 4-1

1. Open the data file AC 4-1.accdb.

2. Save the file as **Rental Houses**.

3. Use Design View to create a query that includes the Address, Monthly Rent, and Property Manager from the Zone 2 table named Zone 2 Design Query.

4. Use the Simple Query Wizard to create a simple detail query that includes all fields from the Zone 1 table except the ID field, named Zone 1 Simple Query, and open the query to view the information.

5. Use the Zone 1 Simple Query to create a Make Table query named Zone 1 Backup. Close the Zone 1 Simple Query and do not make changes to the table design.

6. Open the Zone 1 Simple Query in Design View and use the Show Table command to add the Zone 2 table.

7. Create an ad hoc relationship between the Property Manager fields in both tables.

8. Use the Remove Table command to remove the Zone 2 table from the query.

9. Use the Sort option to sort the Monthly Rent in Ascending order, then run the query.

10. Save the design of the Zone 1 Simple Query and close the database.

Project AC 4-2

1. Open the data file AC 4-2.accdb.

2. Save the file as **Sports Cards**.

3. Use the Simple Query Wizard to create a simple query including all the fields from the Baseball table except the CurrentPrice field and name it Baseball Query.

4. Filter for all the records where the manufacturer is Fleer and then delete those records (Hint: record ID 3, 8, 10, 12, and 19).

5. Filter the query to show only those records where the Manufacturer is Topps. Save the filter as a query named Filter Query and close it.

6. Close the Baseball Query without saving the changes to the design.

7. Create a query that includes the Card Year, Description, PurchasePrice, and CurrentPrice fields.

8. Create a calculated field with the following expression: Increase: [CurrentPrice] - [PurchasePrice] and run the query. Save it as Increase Query and close it.

9. Open the Baseball Query and create a sum query for the PurchasePrice field, a minimum query for the Card Year field, and a count query for the Rookie Card field.

10. Close the query and save the changes.

11. Open the Increase query and create a maximum query for the Current Price field and an average query for the Increase field.

12. Close the query and save the changes.

13. Save and close all database objects and close the database.

CRITICAL THINKING

Activity AC 4-1

Using expressions in Access is similar to using formulas in Excel. Expressions—or query criteria—allow you to limit the number of records included in the results. There are many different expressions ranging from simple to complex, and the ones you will use vary by data type. Use Access Help to look up examples of query criteria to familiarize yourself with all the various kinds of expressions that you can use to get the results you want. Practice by opening a database, creating a query, and using different criteria to return different records.

Activity AC 4-2

Open the **Caprock View Apartments.accdb** database. With a partner, take turns providing requirements for an apartment you might want to rent. For example, you might want to rent a two-bedroom apartment that has a washer and dryer. Or, you might want to rent something for less than $1,600 per month. Take turns with your partner to create a query to determine which apartments meet the other's requirements.

Access

ACCESS OBJECTIVE 5: DESIGNING REPORTS

CREATE REPORTS

Create a Blank Report

Ribbon Method

☐ In the Navigation Pane, click an object on which you want to create a report

☐ Click the **Create tab**, then click the **Blank Report button** in the Reports group, shown in Figure AC 5-1

☐ If necessary, click the **Add Existing Fields button** in the Tools group on the Report Layout Tools Design tab to open the Field List

☐ If necessary, click **Show all tables** in the Field List

☐ Expand the list of tables and fields as necessary to display the fields you want to add to the report

☐ Drag one or more fields from the Field List to the appropriate location on the report

☐ Click the **Save button** 🖫 on the Quick Access toolbar, type an appropriate name for the report in the Save As dialog box, then click **OK**

Figure AC 5-1   Reports group on Create tab

Reports options

> **NOTE**
>
> You can double-click a field name in the Field List to quickly add it to the report and align it precisely with other fields.

Use Report Design Tools

Ribbon Method

☐ Click the **Create tab**, shown in Figure AC 5-1, then click the **Report Design button** in the Reports group

☐ On the Report Design Tools Design tab, click the **Property Sheet button** in the Tools group, if necessary, to open the Property Sheet

☐ In the Property Sheet, click the **Selection type list arrow**, if necessary, then click **Report**

☐ Click the **Data tab**

☐ To base the report on an existing database object, click the **Record Source list arrow**, then click the object's name

OR

☐ To base the report on a new query, click the **Build button** ⋯ in the Record Source property, create the query, then save and close the query

☐ On the Report Design Tools Design tab, click the **Add Existing Fields button** in the Tools group to open the Field List

☐ Drag one or more fields from the Field List to the appropriate location on the report, using Table AC 5-1 as a reference

☐ Click the **Save button** 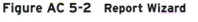 on the Quick Access toolbar, type an appropriate name for the report in the Save As dialog box, then click **OK**

Table AC 5-1   Report Sections

Section	Information that can appear here	Location in printed report
Report Header	Report title, company graphics, graphic line to separate the title	Only on the first page of the report, at the top of the page
Page Header	Page numbers, author information, a date field below the report header	On the top of every page
Group Header	Text boxes for the grouped records	Before each record group
Detail	Text boxes for the fields in the table or query that the report is based on	For each record
Group Footer	Any calculations for a group of records	After each group of records
Page Footer	Page numbers, author information, a date field	On the bottom of each page
Report Footer	Summary information or calculations for all of the records and groups in the report	Only on the last page of the report, at the bottom of the page

Use the Report Wizard

Ribbon Method

☐ Click the **Create tab**, shown in Figure AC 5-1, then click the **Report Wizard button** in the Reports group

☐ Follow the instructions in the Report Wizard dialog boxes, shown in Figure AC 5-2, specifying the fields, grouping levels, sort order, layout, style, and title to create the report, then click **Finish**

Figure AC 5-2   Report Wizard

APPLY REPORT DESIGN OPTIONS

Apply a Theme

Ribbon Method

☐ Open a report in Design View or Layout View, click the **Themes button** in the Themes group on the Report Design (Layout) Tools Design tab, as shown in Figure AC 5-3, then click an option on the Themes menu

Figure AC 5-3   Report Design Tools Design tab

Grouping & Totals options

Header/Footer options

Add Total Report Records

Ribbon Method

☐ Open a report in Layout View or Design View

☐ On the Design tab, click the **Totals button** in the Grouping & Totals group, shown in Figure AC 5-3

☐ On the Totals menu, click the option you want to use

Add Group Report Records

Ribbon Method

☐ Open a report in Layout View or Design View

☐ On the Design tab, click the **Group & Sort button** in the Grouping & Totals group, shown in Figure AC 5-3, to open the Group, Sort, and Total pane, shown in Figure AC 5-4

☐ In the Group, Sort, and Total pane, click **Add a group**

☐ Click the field you want to use as the group header

Figure AC 5-4   Group, Sort, and Total pane

Shortcut Method

☐ Open a report in Layout View

☐ Right-click the field on which you want to group the records, then click **Group on field**, where *field* is the field name

Add Bound/Unbound Controls

Ribbon Method

☐ Open a report in Design View

☐ Click a button (i.e. Text Box, Hyperlink, List Box, Chart, Insert Page Break) in the Controls group on the Report Design Tools Design tab, shown in Figure AC 5-3, then click where you want to place the control

Insert Page Numbers in the Header/Footer

Ribbon Method

☐ Open a report in Design View or Layout View

☐ On the Report Design (Layout) Tools Design tab, click the **Page Numbers button** in the Header/Footer group, shown in Figure AC 5-3

☐ In the Page Numbers dialog box, choose format, position, and alignment options, then click **OK**

Insert a Logo in the Header/Footer

Ribbon Method

☐ Open a report in Design View or Layout View

☐ On the Report Design (Layout) Tools Design tab, click the **Logo button** in the Header/Footer group, shown in Figure AC 5-3

☐ In the Insert Picture dialog box, browse to locate the logo file, then click **OK**

☐ Click and drag to reposition the logo where you want

Reorder Tab Function

Ribbon Method

☐ Open a report in Design View

☐ Click the **Tab Order button** in the Tools group on the Report Design Tools Design tab, shown in Figure AC 5-3

☐ In the Tab Order dialog box, click to select a row, then drag to move the row to desired tab order

---

APPLY REPORT ARRANGE OPTIONS

Use the Table Functions

Ribbon Method

☐ Open a report in Design View or Layout View

☐ Click a button (i.e. Insert, Merge, Split) in the Rows & Columns or Merge/Split group on the Report Design (Layout) Tools Arrange tab, shown in Figure AC 5-5

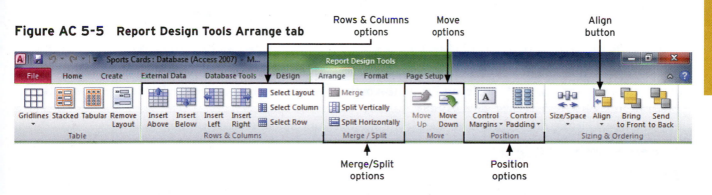

Figure AC 5-5   Report Design Tools Arrange tab

Move Table

Ribbon Method

☐ Open a report in Design View or Layout View

☐ Click the **Move Up button** or **Move down button** in the Move group on the Report Design (Layout) Tools Arrange tab, shown in Figure AC 5-5

Reposition/Format Records

Ribbon Method

☐ Open a report in Design View or Layout View

☐ Click the **Controls Margins button** or **Control Padding button** in the Position group on the Report Design (Layout) Tools Arrange tab, shown in Figure AC 5-5, then click an option on the menu

Align Report Outputs to Grid

Ribbon Method

☐ Open a report in Design View

☐ Click the **Align button** in the Sizing & Ordering group on the Report Design Tools Arrange tab, shown in Figure AC 5-5, then click an option on the menu

---

APPLY REPORT FORMAT OPTIONS

Rename Label in a Report

Ribbon Method

☐ In the Selection group of the Report Design (Layout) Tools Format tab, click the **Object list arrow**, shown in Figure AC 5-6, then click a label

☐ Double-click the text in the selected label (outlined in orange)

☐ Type a new label to rename it and press **Enter**

Figure AC 5-6   Report Design Tools Format tab

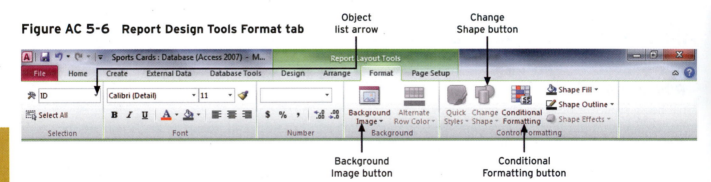

Apply Background Image to Report

Ribbon Method

☐ In the Background group of the Report Design (Layout) Tools Format tab, click the **Background Image button**, shown in Figure AC 5-6, then click **Browse**

☐ In the Insert Picture dialog box, select the picture file you want to use, then click **OK**

Change Shape in Report

Ribbon Method

☐ In the Selection group of the Report Design (Layout) Tools Format tab, click the **Object list arrow**, shown in Figure AC 5-6, and select a button control

☐ In the Control Formatting group of the Form Design (Layout) Tools Format tab, click the **Change Shape button**, shown in Figure AC 5-6, then click an option on the menu

Apply Conditional Formatting in Report

Ribbon Method

☐ In the Selection group of the Report Design (Layout) Tools Format tab, click the **Object list arrow**, shown in Figure AC 5-6, and select a form control

☐ In the Control Formatting group of the Form Layout Tools Format tab, click the **Conditional Formatting button**, shown in Figure AC 5-6

☐ In the Conditional Formatting Rules dialog box, click **New Rule**

☐ In the New Formatting Rule dialog box, select a rule type and edit the rule description, click **OK**, and then click **OK** again to close the Conditional Formatting Rules dialog box as well

APPLY REPORT PAGE SETUP OPTIONS

Change Page Size

Ribbon Method

☐ Open a report in Design View or Layout View

☐ Click the **Page Size button** in the Page Size group on the Report Design (Layout) Tools Page Setup tab, shown in Figure AC 5-7 and click an option on the menu

Figure AC 5-7   Report Design Tools Page Setup tab

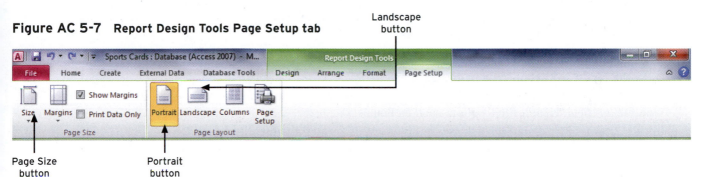

Change Page Orientation

Ribbon Method

☐ Open a report in Design View or Layout View

☐ Click the **Portrait button** or the **Landscape button** in the Page Layout group on the Report Design Tools Page Setup tab, shown in Figure AC 5-7 and click an option on the menu

SORT AND FILTER RECORDS FOR REPORTING

Use the Find Command

Ribbon Method

☐ Open a report in Report View or Layout View

☐ Click the **Find button** in the Find group on the Home tab

☐ In the Find dialog box, enter the value you want to find in the Find What text box

☐ To search using wildcards, enter the value using * (asterisk) to stand for any number of characters and ? (question mark) to stand for a single character

☐ To specify additional criteria, click the **Look In list arrow**, then select a field name; click the **Match list arrow**, then select which part of the field you want to search; click the **Search list arrow**, then select the direction you want to search

☐ Click **Find Next**

Use Sort Command

Ribbon Method

☐ Open a report in Layout View

☐ Click any value in the field you want to sort

☐ In the Sort & Filter group on the Home tab, click the **Ascending button** or the **Descending button**

☐ To remove the sort, click the **Remove Sort button** in the Sort & Filter group on the Home tab

Shortcut Method

☐ Open a report in Layout View

☐ Right-click any value in the field you want to sort

☐ Click a sort option, such as Sort Smallest to Largest or Sort Newest to Oldest

Use Filter Commands

Ribbon Method

☐ Open the report in Layout View or Design View

☐ Click a field value for which you want to filter, then click the **Filter button** in the Sort & Filter group on the Home tab

☐ Point to **_Data type_ Filters**, where _Data type_ is the data type for the field, click a filter option, such as Equals

☐ In the Custom Filter dialog box, shown in Figure AC 5-8 enter a value, then click **OK**

☐ To remove the filter, click the **Remove Filter (Toggle filter) button** in the Sort & Filter group on the Home tab

Shortcut Method

☐ Open the report in Layout View or Design View

☐ Right-click a field value for which you want to filter, point to **_Data type_ Filters**, where _Data type_ is the data type for the field, click a filter option, such as Equals

☐ In the Custom Filter dialog box, shown in Figure AC 5-8 enter a value, then click **OK**

☐ To remove the filter, right-click the field, then click **Clear filter from _field_**, where _field_ is the name of the field

Figure AC 5-8   Custom Filter dialog box

Use View Types

Ribbon Method

☐ On the Home tab, in the Views menu, click the **View button arrow**

☐ Click an option on the View menu, shown in Figure AC 5-9

Figure AC 5-9   View menu

REVIEW QUESTIONS

MULTIPLE CHOICE

Select the best response for the following statements.

1. Where does the report footer appear?
   A. Only on the first page of the report, at the top of the page
   B. On the top of every page
   C. Before each record group
   D. Only on the last page of the report, at the bottom of the page

2. The Report Wizard button is located in the Reports group on the _____ tab.
   A. Home
   B. Create
   C. Design
   D. Database Tools

3. Selected labels or controls are outlined in _____.
   A. blue
   B. green
   C. orange
   D. black

4. When searching using wildcards, enter the value using a(n) _____ to stand for a single character.
   A. ? (question mark)
   B. ! (exclamation point)
   C. & (ampersand)
   D. ^ (caret)

5. Which option is not on the View menu in the Views group on the Home tab?
   A. Report
   B. Arrange
   C. Layout
   D. Design

MATCHING

Match each location in Column 2 to its button in Column 1.

Column 1	Column 2
_____ 1. Control Margins	A. Design tab, Grouping & Totals group
_____ 2. Tab Order	B. Design tab, Headers/Footers group
_____ 3. Totals	C. Design tab, Tools group
_____ 4. Landscape	D. Arrange tab, Position group
_____ 5. Page Numbers	E. Page Setup tab, Page Layout group

PROJECTS

Project AC 5-1

1. Open the data file **Project AC 5-1.accdb**.

2. Save the file as **Education Conference**.

3. Use the Report Wizard to create a report based on the Presenters table that includes the First Name, Last Name, and Room fields, with no grouping levels, sort by last name in ascending order, Tabular layout, and title it **Room Assignments**.

4. In Layout view, apply the Composite theme.

5. Rename the Room field label to **Room Number**.

6. Insert a logo using the **globe.png** data file and position it to the right of the report title.

7. Apply conditional formatting to the Room Number field values that formats with bold and red cells where the field value is greater than or equal to 300.

8. Sort the report by room number in ascending order.

9. Filter the report to show only the records where the room is on the first floor (between 100 and 199).

10. Remove the filter and clear all sorts.

11. Save and close the workbook.

Project AC 5-2

1. Open the data file **Project AC 5-2.accdb**.

2. Save the file as **Windy Ridge**.

3. Create a blank report with Cabin Name, Bedrooms, and Weekly fields and save it as **Cabins**.

4. Add the **cabin.png** data file as a background image on the report.

5. In the Cabin Name field, set the Control Padding option to **Medium**.

6. Change the Page Size option to **Legal** (8.5" × 14").

7. Use the Find command to look in the current document and match any part of the field to find each occurrence of the word "Trail," then close the Find dialog box.

8. Change the report orientation to **Landscape**.

9. Sort the Bedrooms field in descending order.

10. Filter to show only those cabins with a weekly rent of less than or equal to $1,000.

11. Remove the filter and clear all sorts.

12. Save and close the Cabins report, then save and close the workbook.

CRITICAL THINKING

Activity AC 5-1

Search Access Help for the video titled *Use conditional formatting on reports* and watch it. How can conditional formatting help you see patterns or relationships in the data that might be hard to spot otherwise? Open a database and create a report. Practice adding some simple conditional formatting to highlight certain ranges of values on the report.

MICROSOFT POWERPOINT 2010 CERTIFICATION PREP

Getting Started with PowerPoint 2010

The Microsoft Office Specialist 2010 (MOS) PowerPoint exam assumes a basic level of proficiency in PowerPoint. This section is intended to help you reference these basic skills while you are preparing to take the PowerPoint MOS exam.

□ Starting and exiting PowerPoint
□ Viewing the PowerPoint window
□ Using the Ribbon
□ Changing views
□ Using task panes
□ Using keyboard KeyTips
□ Creating, opening, and closing presentations
□ Navigating in the PowerPoint window
□ Saving presentations
□ Getting Help

START AND EXIT POWERPOINT

Start PowerPoint

Mouse Method

□ Click the **Start button** on the Windows taskbar
□ Point to **All Programs**
□ Click **Microsoft Office**, then click **Microsoft PowerPoint 2010**

　OR

□ Double-click the **Microsoft PowerPoint program icon** on the desktop

Exit PowerPoint

Ribbon Method

□ Click the **File tab**, then click **Exit**

　OR

□ Click the **Close button** on the program window title bar

Shortcut Method

□ Press **[Alt][F4]**

VIEW THE POWERPOINT WINDOW

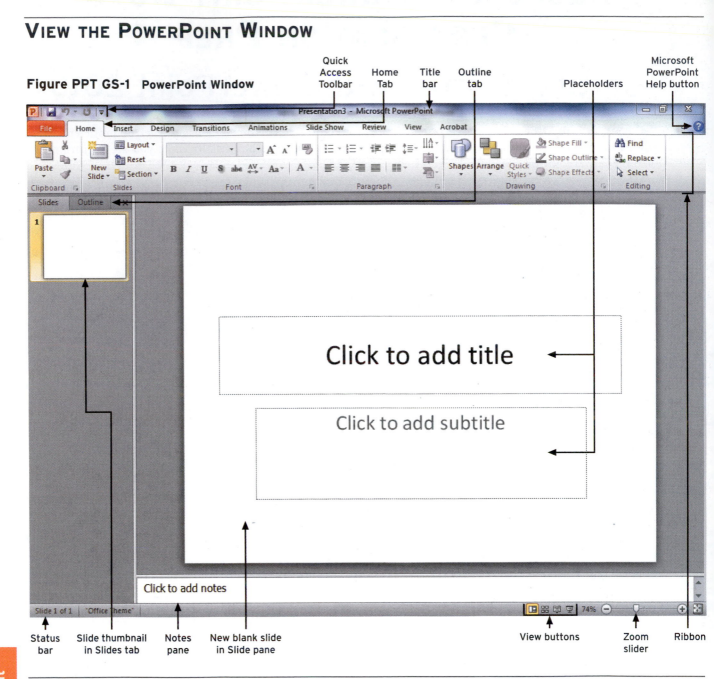

Figure PPT GS-1   PowerPoint Window

USE THE RIBBON

Display the Ribbon

Ribbon Method

☐ Double-click any tab

   OR

☐ Right-click any tab, then click **Minimize the Ribbon** to deselect it

Shortcut Method

☐ Press **[Ctrl][F1]**

Hide the Ribbon

Ribbon Method

□ Double-click the active tab

   OR

□ Right-click any tab, then click **Minimize the Ribbon**

Shortcut Method

□ Press **[Ctrl][F1]**

CHANGE VIEWS

Ribbon Method

□ Click the **View tab** on the Ribbon, then click the desired button in the Presentation Views group or the Master Views group, shown in Figure PPT GS-2 to switch to one of the following views: **Normal**, **Slide Sorter**, **Notes Page**, **Reading View**, **Slide Master**, **Handout Master**, or **Notes Master**

Figure PPT GS-2   View tab

Shortcut Method

□ Click the **Normal button** 🖼, **Slide Sorter button** 🖼, **Reading View button** 🖼, or **Slide Show button** 🖼 on the status bar to switch to Normal, Slide Sorter, Reading View, or Slide Show view

   OR

□ Press and hold **[Shift]**, then click the **Normal button** 🖼 on the status bar to switch to Slide Master view

□ Press and hold **[Shift]** then click the **Slide Sorter button** 🖼 on the status bar to switch to Handout Master view

---

USE TASK PANES

Display Task Panes

Ribbon Method

□ See Table PPT GS-1 for a list of task panes and the Ribbon commands that open them

   OR

□ To open the Clip Art task pane, click the **Clip Art button** 🖼 in a content placeholder

Close Task Panes

Ribbon Method

□ See Table PPT GS-1 for a list of task panes and the Ribbon commands that close them

Shortcut Method

□ Click the **Close button** ✖ on the task pane title bar

   OR

□ Click the **Task Pane Options button** ▼ on the task pane title bar, then click **Close**

Table PPT GS-1 Task Panes

Task pane	Click to open or close the task pane
Clip Art	**Clip Art button** in the Images group on the Insert tab
Research	**Research button** in the Proofing group on the Review tab
Animation Pane	**Animation Pane button** in the Advanced Animation group on the Animations tab
Reuse Slides	**New Slide button arrow** in the Slides group on the Home tab, then click **Reuse Slides**
Selection and Visibility	**Arrange button** in the Drawing group on the Home tab, then click **Selection Pane** OR **Selection Pane button** in the Arrange group on the Drawing Tools Format tab

USE KEYBOARD KEYTIPS

Display KeyTips

- ☐ Press **[Alt]** to display the KeyTips for each command on the active tab on the Ribbon and on the Quick Access toolbar, as shown in Figure PPT GS-3
- ☐ Press the letter or number shown in the KeyTip for a command to perform the command
- ☐ Press additional letters or numbers as needed to complete the command sequence
- ☐ If two letters appear, press each one in order
- ☐ For some commands, you have to click an option from a gallery or menu to complete the command sequence
- ☐ The KeyTips turn off automatically at the end of the command sequence

Figure PPT GS-3 KeyTips

KeyTip

Hide KeyTips

- ☐ Press **[Alt]**

CREATE, OPEN, AND CLOSE PRESENTATIONS

Create a New Presentation

Ribbon Method

- ☐ Click the **File tab**, then click **New**
- ☐ Choose the appropriate options in the Available Templates and Themes section of Backstage view

Shortcut Method

- ☐ Press **[Ctrl][N]**

Open an Existing Presentation

Ribbon Method

- ☐ Click the **File tab**, then click **Open**
- ☐ In the Open dialog box, shown in Figure PPT GS-4, navigate to the appropriate drive and folder
- ☐ Click the presentation file you want, then click **Open**

Figure PPT GS-4   Open dialog box

Navigate to the drive and
folder where the file is stored

Shortcut Method

☐ Press **[Ctrl][O]**

☐ In the Open dialog box, navigate to the appropriate drive and folder

☐ Click the presentation file you want, then click **Open**

Close a Presentation

Ribbon Method

☐ Click the **File tab**, then click **Close**

☐ If prompted to save the presentation, click **Save** or **Don't Save** as appropriate

OR

☐ Click the **Close button** [X] on the title bar

☐ If prompted to save the presentation, click **Save** or **Don't Save** as appropriate

Shortcut Method

☐ Press **[Ctrl][W]** or **[Alt][F4]**

☐ If prompted to save the presentation, click **Save** or **Don't Save** as appropriate

NAVIGATE IN THE POWERPOINT WINDOW

Use Table PPT GS-2 as a reference to navigate in the PowerPoint window.

Table PPT GS-2   Keyboard Navigation Techniques

Press these keys	To move the insertion point
[Ctrl][Home] or **[Home]** or **[End]**	To the beginning or end of the currently selected **[Ctrl][End]** textbox
	To the beginning or end of the line of text in a selected text box or text placeholder
	OR
	To the first or last slide on the Outline or Slides tab or in Slide Sorter view (if no object is selected on the slide)
[PgDn] or **[PgUp]**	Down or up one slide at a time
[Tab] or **[Shift][Tab]**	Between objects on a slide
[Ctrl][Right Arrow] or **[Ctrl][Left Arrow]**	One word to the right or left
[Ctrl][Enter]	To the next title or body text placeholder; if it is the last placeholder on a slide, a new slide with same layout will be inserted

SAVE PRESENTATIONS

Save an Existing Presentation with the Same File Name

Ribbon Method

☐ Click the **Save button** 🖫 on the Quick Access toolbar

   OR

☐ Click the **File tab**, then click **Save**

Shortcut Method

☐ Press **[Ctrl][S]**

Use Save As

Ribbon Method

☐ Click the **File tab**, then click **Save As**

☐ In the Save As dialog box, shown in Figure PPT GS-5, navigate to the drive and folder where you want to store the presentation

☐ Type an appropriate presentation name in the File name text box, then click **Save**

Figure PPT GS-5   Save As dialog box

Shortcut Method

☐ Press **[F12]**

☐ Follow the steps in bullets 2–3 of the Use Save As Ribbon Method on the previous page

---

GET HELP

Ribbon Method

☐ Click the **Microsoft PowerPoint Help button** ⦸ on the Ribbon to display the PowerPoint Help window, shown in Figure PPT GS-6

☐ Use Table PPT GS-3 as a reference to select the most appropriate way to search for help in the PowerPoint Help window

Figure PPT GS-6   PowerPoint Help window

Shortcut Method

☐ Press **[F1]**

☐ Use Table PPT GS-3 as a reference to select the most appropriate way to search for help in the PowerPoint Help window

Table PPT GS-3   PowerPoint Help Window Options

Option	To use
Getting started with PowerPoint 2010	Click a link representing a topic you want to read about; click subtopics that appear until you see help text for the topic
Browse PowerPoint 2010 support	Click a link representing a topic you want to read about; click subtopics that appear until you see help text for the topic
Back button	Click to return to the previously displayed information
Forward button	Click to go forward in the sequence of previously displayed information
Stop button	Click to stop searching on a topic
Refresh button	Click to refresh the Help window content
Home button	Click to return to the PowerPoint Help window
Print button	Click to print the current page
Change Font Size button	Click to enlarge or shrink the help text

(continued)

PowerPoint

Table PPT GS-3   PowerPoint Help Window Options (continued)

Option	To use
Show Table of Contents	Click to show the Table of Contents pane, showing topic links you can click
Keep on Top	Click to keep the Help window on top as you work; button becomes the Not On Top button, which you click to let the Help window go behind the current window as you work
Type words to search for box	Type a word, then click the Search button
Search button list arrow	Click the list arrow, then click the area, such as Content from Office.com, All PowerPoint, or PowerPoint Help
Microsoft Office Search help using Bing	Type a word, then click the Search button or Type a word, then click the link downloads, images, or templates to search for those items on Office.com

REVIEW QUESTIONS

FILL IN THE BLANK

Complete the following sentences by writing the correct word or words in the blanks provided.

1. Double-click the active tab to _____ the Ribbon.

2. To open a new document, click the File Tab, then click _____.

3. The Microsoft PowerPoint Help button is usually located in the top _____ corner of the window.

4. Press _____ to display the KeyTips for any active tab.

5. The Slide Sorter button is located on the _____ tab.

MATCHING

Match the correct term in Column 2 to its description in Column 1.

Column 1	Column 2
_____ 1. Move down one slide at a time	A. [Alt][F4]
_____ 2. Exit PowerPoint	B. [Ctrl][S]
_____ 3. Navigate to the last slide of a presentation	C. [PgDn]
_____ 4. Navigate to the beginning of the presentation	D. [Home]
_____ 5. Save an existing presentation	E. [End]

PROJECTS

Project PPT GS-1

1. Open PowerPoint.

2. Open a new presentation.

3. Display the KeyTips.

4. Use the KeyTips to display the View tab.

5. Display the Home tab.

6. Hide the Ribbon.

7. Display the Ribbon.

8. Display the PowerPoint Help window.

9. Type **help** in the textbox, then press **Enter**.

10. Close the PowerPoint Help window.

11. Close the presentation without saving it.

Project PPT GS-2

1. Open PowerPoint.

2. Open the **Project PPT GS-2.pptx** data file.

3. Display the View tab.

4. Display the presentation in Slide Sorter view.

5. Display the presentation in Normal view.

6. Display the Insert tab.

7. Open the ClipArt task pane.

8. Close the ClipArt task pane.

9. Press **Page Down** to go to slide 2.

10. Press **End** to go to the end of the presentation (slide 20).

11. Press **Home** to go to slide 1.

12. Save the presentation as **Introduction.pptx**, then close the document.

13. Exit PowerPoint.

CRITICAL THINKING

Activity PPT GS-1

Open the PowerPoint Help window. Search for the video *Getting Started – Exploring the Ribbon* and watch it. What other PowerPoint videos and training options are available? Browse through Help to see all the material available to help you learn more about using PowerPoint. Refer to Table PowerPoint PPT GS-3 as a reference while using the PowerPoint Help window.

Activity PPT GS-2

Open the **Activity PPT GS-2.pptx** data file and view it as a slide show. Start familiarizing yourself with PowerPoint by clicking on each tab on the Ribbon and viewing the available commands.

POWERPOINT OBJECTIVE 1: MANAGING THE POWERPOINT ENVIRONMENT

ADJUST VIEWS

Use the Ribbon to Adjust Views

Ribbon Method

☐ Click the **View tab**, then click the desired button in the Presentation Views group or the Master Views group, shown in Figure PPT 1-1 to switch to one of the following views: **Normal**, **Slide Sorter**, **Notes Page**, **Reading View**, **Slide Master**, **Handout Master**, or **Notes Master** (See Table PPT 1-1.)

Figure PPT 1-1   View tab

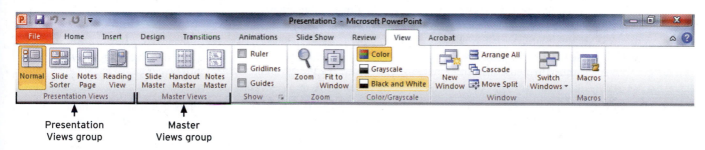

Presentation Views group   Master Views group

OR

☐ Click the **Slide Show tab**, shown in Figure PPT 1-2, then click the desired button in the Start Slide Show group to start a slide show in Slide Show view

NOTE

Slide masters control the layout and design of the slides, handouts, and notes. When you make a change to a master, the change affects every slide in the presentation.

Slide Show tab

Figure PPT 1-2   Slide Show tab

PowerPoint

Table PPT 1-1   Adjust PowerPoint Views

View	What you see	Ribbon Method	Shortcut Method (Status Bar)
Normal view	Displays the screen in three sections: the Outline and Slides tabs in the left pane, the Slide pane on the right, and the Notes pane below the Slide pane	Click the **Normal button** in the Presentation Views group on the View tab	Click the **Normal button** 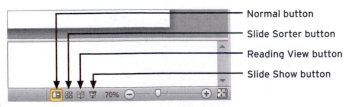
Slide Sorter view	Displays thumbnail versions of all slides in a presentation	Click the **Slide Sorter button** in the Presentation Views group on the View tab	Click the **Slide Sorter button**
Notes Page view	Allows you to enter and edit notes on a full screen instead of just in the small Notes pane at the bottom of Normal view	Click the **Notes Page button** in the Presentation Views group on the View tab	
Reading view	Used to view a presentation within a window instead of filling the entire screen	Click the **Reading View button** in the Presentation Views group on the View tab	Click the **Reading View button**
Slide Master view	Displays the slide masters for the presentation	Click the **Slide Master button** in the Master Views group on the View tab	Press and hold Shift, then click the **Normal View button**
Handout Master view	Allows you to change the design and layout of handout masters	Click the **Handout Master button** in the Master Views group on the View tab	Press and hold **Shift**, then click the **Slide Sorter button**
Notes Master view	Allows you to change the design and layout of notes	Click the **Notes Master button** in the Master Views group on the View tab	
Slide Show view	Plays a slide show	Click the **From Beginning button** or **From Current Slide button** in the Start Slide Show group on the Slide Show tab	Click the **Slide Show button**

Use the Status Bar to Adjust Views

Shortcut Method

☐ Click the **Normal button**, **Slide Sorter button**, **Reading View button**, or **Slide Show button** on the status bar, shown in Figure PPT 1-3 to switch to Normal, Slide Sorter, Reading View, or Slide Show view

  OR

☐ Press and hold **[Shift]**, then click the **Normal button** on the status bar to switch to Slide Master view

☐ Press and hold **[Shift]** then click the **Slide Sorter button** on the status bar to switch to Handout Master view

Figure PPT 1-3   View buttons on the status bar

Normal button

Slide Sorter button

Reading View button

Slide Show button

MANIPULATE THE POWERPOINT WINDOW

Create a New Window

Ribbon Method

☐ Click the **View tab**, then click **New Window button** in the Window group, shown in Figure PPT 1-4, to open a new window containing the current document

Figure PPT 1-4   Window group on the View tab

Arrange All Windows

Ribbon Method

☐ Click the **View tab**, then click the **Arrange All button** in the Window group

☐ To view only one document, click the **Maximize button** on the title bar of that document

Cascade Windows

Ribbon Method

☐ Click the **View tab,** then click the **Cascade button** in the Window group to cascade all the open PowerPoint windows

Move Splitter Bars

Ribbon Method

☐ Click the **View tab**, then click the **Move Split button** in the Window group

☐ Use the arrow keys on the keyboard to move the split bars, then press **Enter**

OR

☐ Drag the **Resize Pane Vertical pointer** ╬ or **Resize Pane Horizontal pointer** ╪ to move the bars that split up the screen

Switch Windows

Ribbon Method

☐ Open two or more PowerPoint windows on your screen

☐ Click the **View tab**, then click the **Switch Windows button arrow** in the Window group

☐ Click the title of the window you want to view

CONFIGURE THE QUICK ACCESS TOOLBAR

Show the Quick Access Toolbar (QAT) Below the Ribbon

Ribbon Method

☐ Click the **Customize Quick Access Toolbar button** on the Ribbon, then click **Show Below the Ribbon** as shown in Figure PPT 1-5

PowerPoint

□ To show the Quick Access Toolbar above the ribbon, click the **Customize Quick Access Toolbar button** , then click **Show Above the Ribbon**

Figure PPT 1-5   Customize Quick Access Toolbar button and menu

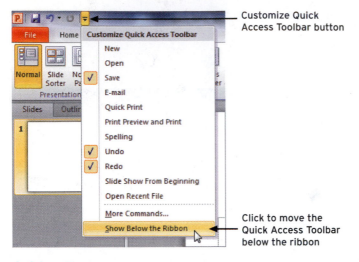

Add a Button to the Quick Access Toolbar

□ Click the **Customize Quick Access Toolbar button** ▾ on the Ribbon, then click a button on the menu to add to the Quick Access Toolbar or click **More Commands** to open the PowerPoint Options dialog box where you can access additional commands to add to the Quick Access Toolbar

□ To remove a button from the Quick Access Toolbar, click the **Customize Quick Access Toolbar button** ▾, then click the name of the button to remove the checkmark beside it

---

CONFIGURE POWERPOINT FILE OPTIONS

Use PowerPoint Proofing

□ Click the **File tab**, click **Options** to open the PowerPoint Options dialog box, then click **Proofing** in the left pane
□ Select appropriate options, then click **OK**

Use PowerPoint Save Options

Ribbon Method

□ Click the **File tab**, click **Options**, then click **Save** in the left pane of the PowerPoint Options dialog box, shown in Figure PPT 1-6
□ Select appropriate options, then click **OK**

Figure PPT 1-6   PowerPoint Options dialog box

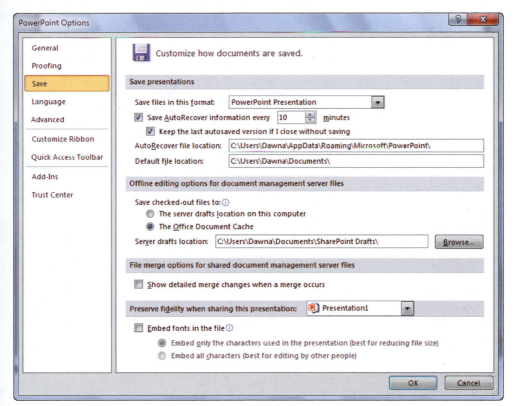

REVIEW QUESTIONS

TRUE/FALSE

Circle T if the statement is true or F if the statement is false.

T   F   1. The Cascade Windows button is located on the View tab.

T   F   2. The Slide Show button on the status bar displays the Slide Show tab.

T   F   3. The Quick Access Toolbar cannot be moved.

T   F   4. You can change spelling options in the Proofing section of the PowerPoint Options dialog box.

T   F   5. The Move Split button allows you to move splitter bars.

MATCHING

Match the button or keyboard shortcut in Column 2 to its description in Column 1.

Column 1	Column 2
_____ 1. Displays the screen in three sections.	A. Slide Master view
_____ 2. Allows you to change the design and layout of handout masters.	B. Notes Page view
_____ 3. Displays slide masters for the presentation.	C. Slide Sorter view
_____ 4. Displays thumbnail versions of all slides in a presentation.	D. Normal view
_____ 5. Allows you to enter and edit notes on a full screen.	E. Handout Master view

PROJECTS

Project PPT 1-1

1. Open the data file **Project PPT 1–1a.pptx**.

2. View the presentation in Slide Sorter view.

3. Change to Reading view and click each slide to advance the presentation. Click after the last slide to exit.

4. Change to Normal view.

5. Open the data file **Project PPT 1–1b.pptx**.

6. Use the Arrange All command to view both presentations on your screen.

7. Cascade the presentations on your screen.

8. Use the Switch Windows command to view the Presentation 1-1a.pptx.

9. Close **Presentation PPT 1–1a.pptx** without saving.

10. Move the Quick Access Toolbar below the ribbon.

11. Add the Slide Show From Beginning button to the Quick Access Toolbar.

12. Use the Slide Show From Beginning button to view the presentation. Click after the last slide to exit.

13. Move the Quick Access Toolbar above the ribbon.

14. Remove the Slide Show From Beginning button from the Quick Access Toolbar.

15. Save the presentation as **Driver Safety.pptx** and close it.

CRITICAL THINKING

Activity PPT 1-1

Open a new blank presentation. Change the default save location to a new location on your computer, and change the option to save AutoRecover information to every 5 minutes. With your teacher's permission, add two or three buttons to the Quick Access Toolbar that you think you will use often.

PowerPoint Objective 2: Creating a Slide Presentation

Construct and Edit Photo Albums

Create a New Blank Presentation

Ribbon Method

□ Click the **File tab**, then click **New**
□ Click **Blank presentation** under Available Templates and Themes in Backstage view
□ Click **Create**

Shortcut Method

□ Press **[Ctrl][N]**

Create a New Presentation from a Template

Ribbon Method

□ Click the **File tab**, then click **New**
□ Click the **Sample templates button** under Available Templates and Themes in Backstage view
□ Click the appropriate template
□ Click **Create**

OR

□ Click the **File tab**, then click **New**
□ Click **My templates** under the Available Templates and Themes in Backstage view
□ Click the appropriate template (if you haven't downloaded and installed any templates to your hard drive, the New Presentation dialog box might be empty)
□ Click **OK**

OR

□ Click the **File tab**, then click **New**
□ Click a category under **Office.com Templates** or type a keyword in the Search Office.com for templates box and click the **Start searching button**
□ Click the appropriate template or click a folder to browse available templates
□ Click **Download**

Create a New Photo Album

Ribbon Method

□ Click the **Insert tab**, click the **Photo Album button arrow** in the Images group, then click **New Photo Album** to open the Photo Album dialog box
□ In the Album Content section, click the **File/Disk button** under Insert picture from to open the Insert New Pictures dialog box
□ Navigate to the picture you want to insert, then click the **Insert button**
□ Insert additional pictures and/or select additional options from the Photo Album dialog box, shown in Figure PPT 2-1
□ Click **Create**

NOTE

To insert multiple pictures at one time from the Insert New Pictures dialog box, click the first picture to select it, press and hold [Ctrl], then click the remaining pictures.

PowerPoint

Figure PPT 2-1   Photo Album dialog box

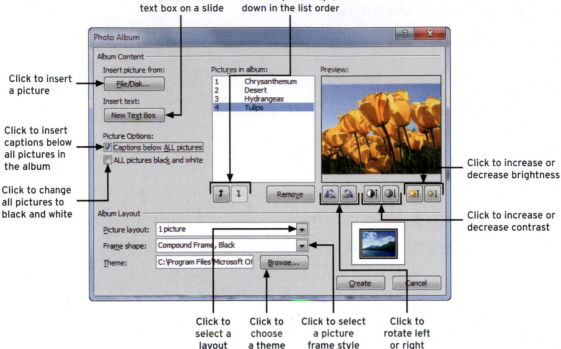

Add Captions to Pictures

Ribbon Method

- ☐ Click the **Insert tab**, then click **Photo Album button arrow** in the Images group, then click **Edit Photo Album** to open the Edit Photo Album dialog box
- ☐ In the Album Layout section, click an option from the Picture layout list other than Fit to Slide so that there will be space on the slides for a caption
- ☐ In the Album Content section under Picture Options, click the **Captions below ALL pictures check box**
- ☐ Click the **Update button**

Insert Text

Ribbon Method

- ☐ Click the **Insert tab**, then click **Photo Album button arrow** in the Images group, then click **Edit Photo Album** to open the Edit Photo Album dialog box
- ☐ In the Album Content section, click the **New Text Box button** to insert a text box on a slide in the photo album
- ☐ Click the **Update button**

Insert Images in Black and White

Ribbon Method

- ☐ Click the **Insert tab**, click the **Photo Album button arrow** in the Images group, then click **Edit Photo Album** to open the Edit Photo Album dialog box
- ☐ In the Album Content section, click the **ALL pictures black and white check box**
- ☐ Click the **Update button**

Reorder Pictures in an Album

Ribbon Method

☐ Click the **Insert tab**, click **Photo Album button arrow** in the Images group, then click **Edit Photo Album** to open the Edit Photo Album dialog box

☐ In the Album Content section under Pictures in album, click a **picture** in the list to select it

☐ Click the **Move Up button** [↑] to move the picture up to a new position in the list or click the **Move Down button** [↓] to move the picture down to a new position in the list

☐ Click the **Update button**

Adjust the Rotation, Brightness, or Contrast of an Image

Ribbon Method

☐ Click the **Insert tab**, click the **Photo Album button arrow** in the Images group, then click **Edit Photo Album** to open the Edit Photo Album dialog box

☐ In the Album Content section under Pictures in album, click a picture in the list to select it and display the preview

☐ Click the **Rotate Left button** [🔄] to rotate the picture 90 degrees to the left or click the **Rotate Right button** [🔄] to rotate the picture 90 degrees to the right

☐ Click the **Increase Contrast button** [◑] to increase contrast or click the **Decrease Contrast button** [◑] to decrease contrast

☐ Click the **Increase Brightness button** [☀] to increase the brightness or click the **Decrease Brightness button** [☀] to decrease the brightness

☐ Click the **Update button**

APPLY SLIDE SIZE AND ORIENTATION SETTINGS

Change the Orientation of Slides

Ribbon Method

☐ Click the **Design tab** on the Ribbon

☐ Click the **Slide Orientation button** in the Page Setup group

☐ Click **Landscape** or **Portrait**

Set up a Custom Size

Ribbon Method

☐ Click the **Design tab** on the Ribbon

☐ Click the **Page Setup button** in the Page Setup group

☐ In the Page Setup dialog box, shown in Figure PPT 2-2, click the **Slides sized for list arrow**

☐ Select a slide size from the Slides sized for list arrow or click the Height and Width up and down arrows to set a custom size

Figure PPT 2-2   **Page Setup dialog box**

ADD AND REMOVE SLIDES

Insert a New Slide

Ribbon Method

☐ Click the **Home tab**, then click the **New Slide button** in the Slides group to insert a slide with the same layout as the selected slide

OR

☐ Click the **Home tab**, then click the **New Slide button arrow** in the Slides group to open the layout gallery, shown in Figure PPT 2-3

☐ Click a layout in the gallery to insert a new slide with the selected layout

Figure PPT 2-3   New Slide button and Layout gallery

Shortcut Method

☐ Right-click the **selected slide thumbnail** in the Slides tab

☐ Click **New Slide** on the shortcut menu to insert a slide with the same layout as the selected slide

OR

☐ Press **[Ctrl][M]** to insert a slide with the same layout as the selected slide

Insert an Outline

Ribbon Method

☐ Create a new blank presentation

☐ In Normal view, click the **Outline tab**

☐ Type the outline, pressing **[Enter]** at the end of the line and pressing **[Tab]** to indent items

CREATE A NEW PRESENTATION FROM AN OUTLINE

Ribbon Method

☐ Create a new blank presentation

☐ Click the **Home tab**, click the **New Slide button arrow** in the Slides group, then click **Slides from Outline** to open the Insert Outline dialog box

☐ Navigate to the existing document or outline file you want to use, then click **Insert**

Reuse Slides From a Saved Presentation

Ribbon Method

☐ Click the **Home tab**, click the **New Slide button arrow** in the Slides group, then click **Reuse Slides** to open the Reuse Slides task pane shown in Figure PPT 2-4

☐ Click the **Open a PowerPoint File link** and use the Browse dialog box to navigate to a saved presentation, then click **Open**

☐ Click the **Keep source formatting check box** in the Reuse Slides task pane if you want to retain the formatting from the original presentation

☐ Click each slide thumbnail that you want to add to the existing presentation

Figure PPT 2-4   Reuse Slides task pane

Reuse Slides From a Slide Library

Ribbon Method

☐ Click the **Home tab**, click the **New Slide button arrow** in the Slides group, then click **Reuse Slides** to open the Reuse Slides task pane

☐ Click the **Open a Slide Library link** to open the Select a Slide Library dialog box

PowerPoint

□ Click the slide library that you want to use, then click **Select**
□ Click each slide thumbnail that you want to add to the existing presentation

Duplicate Selected Slides

Ribbon Method

□ Select the **slide** or **slides** to be duplicated
□ Click the **Home tab**, click the **New Slide button arrow** in the Slides group, then click **Duplicate Selected Slides**

Shortcut Method

□ Right-click the **selected slide thumbnail** in the Slides tab
□ Click **Duplicate Slide** on the shortcut menu

Delete Slides

Shortcut Method

□ Select the slide you want to delete
□ Right-click the selected slide thumbnails in the Slides tab, then click **Delete Slide** on the shortcut menu
   OR
□ Select the slide you want to delete
□ Press **[Delete]**

Delete Multiple Slides Simultaneously

Shortcut Method

□ Press and hold **[Ctrl]**, then click each slide that you want to select for deletion
□ Right-click a selected slide, then click **Delete Slide** on the shortcut menu
   OR
□ Press and hold **[Ctrl]**, then click each slide that you want to select for deletion
□ Press **[Delete]**

Include Non-Contiguous Slides in a Presentation

Ribbon Method

□ With the current presentation on your screen, open a saved presentation from which you want to cut or copy slides
□ In Normal view, press and hold **[Ctrl]**, then click each slide thumbnail that you want to cut or copy whether they are side by side or not
□ Click the **Home tab**, then click the **Cut button** ✄ or the **Copy button** 📑 in the Clipboard group
□ Switch to the current presentation, position the insertion point in the Slides tab where you want to insert the copied slides, then click the **Paste button** in the Clipboard group

FORMAT SLIDES

Add a Section

Ribbon Method

□ In Normal view, select the slide where you want to begin a section
□ Click the **Home tab**, click the **Section list arrow** in the Slides group, then click **Add Section**

Rename a Section

Ribbon Method

□ Click the **Section heading** to select it, click the **Section list arrow** in the Slides group, then click **Rename Section** to open the Rename Section dialog box
□ Type a new section name, then click the **Rename button**

Shortcut Method

☐ Right-click the **Section heading**, then click **Rename Section** from the shortcut menu to display the Rename Section dialog box

☐ Type a new section name, then click the **Rename button**

Format a Section

Ribbon Method

☐ Click a section heading to select it

☐ Click the **Design tab**, then click an option from the Themes group or click the **Background Styles list arrow** and select background formatting options to apply formatting to the entire section at once

Apply Themes

Ribbon Method

☐ In Normal view, click the **Design tab** on the Ribbon

☐ Click the **More button** ⊡ in the Themes group to open the Themes gallery, then click a thumbnail to apply the theme

Modify Themes

Ribbon Method

☐ In Normal view, click the **Design tab** on the Ribbon

☐ Click the **Colors button** in the Themes group to open the Colors gallery, as shown in Figure PPT 2-5

☐ Click a color scheme in the gallery

Figure PPT 2-5   Colors gallery

Click to choose a new color scheme for a theme

OR

☐ In Normal view, click the **Design tab** on the Ribbon

☐ Click the **Fonts button** in the Themes group to open the Fonts gallery

☐ Click a font scheme in the gallery

OR

☐ In Normal view, click the **Design tab** on the Ribbon

☐ Click the **Effects button** in the Themes group to open the Effects gallery

☐ Click an effect in the gallery

Switch to a Different Slide Layout

Ribbon Method

☐ Select the slide

☐ Click the **Home tab**, then click the **Layout button arrow** in the Slides group to open the layout gallery

☐ Click the new slide layout

Shortcut Method

☐ Right-click the slide, point to **Layout** on the shortcut menu, then click a layout from the gallery

Apply Background Formatting to a Slide

Ribbon Method

☐ Select the slide you want to format

☐ Click the **Design tab**, then click the **Background Styles list arrow** in the Background group to display a gallery of options

☐ Click an option from the gallery or click **Format Background** to open the Format Background dialog box, shown in Figure PPT 2-6

☐ Click any one of the Solid fill, Gradient fill, Picture or texture fill, or Pattern fill option buttons to display related options to customize the format of the slide background

☐ Click the **Apply to All button** to apply the formatting to the entire presentation

Shortcut Method

☐ Right-click a slide, then click **Format Background** from the shortcut menu to open the Format Background dialog box

☐ Follow the steps in bullets 4-5 of the Apply Background Formatting to a Slide Ribbon Method above

Figure PPT 2-6   Format Background dialog box

Set up Slide Footers

Ribbon Method

☐ In Normal view, click the **Insert tab**, click the **Header & Footer button** in the Text group

☐ On the Slide tab of the Header and Footer dialog box, click the **Footer check box**

☐ Type the footer text in the Footer text box

☐ Click **Apply to All**

   OR

☐ Switch to Slide Master view

☐ Click the layout thumbnail in the left pane to which you want to add a footer

☐ Click the **Footers check box** in the Master Layout group on the Slide Master tab to insert a check mark

☐ Type the footer text in the Footer placeholder on the slide in the Slide pane

ENTER AND FORMAT TEXT

Apply Text Effects

Ribbon Method

☐ Select the appropriate text

☐ Use the appropriate button or keyboard shortcut listed in Table PPT 2-1 to format text as desired

Table PPT 2-1   Text Formatting Buttons and Keyboard Shortcuts

Formatting effect	Button (in Font group on Home tab, or on Mini Toolbar)	Keyboard shortcut
Bold	**B**	[Ctrl][B]
Italic	*I*	[Ctrl][I]
Underline	<u>U</u>	[Ctrl][U]
Shadow	S	
Font Color	A ▾	

   OR

☐ Select the text

☐ Click the **Home tab** on the Ribbon, click the **Launcher** ⌕ in the Font group

☐ On the Font tab in the Font dialog box, select appropriate options

☐ Click **OK**

   OR

Shortcut Method

☐ Select the text

☐ Right-click the text, click **Format Text Effects** from the shortcut menu to open the Format Text Effects dialog box

☐ Click a category in the left pane, then specify options in the right pane

☐ Click **Close**

Change Indentation

Ribbon Method

☐ Select the **text**

☐ Click the **View tab** on the Ribbon, then click the **Ruler check box** in the Show group to display the Ruler

☐ Drag the **indent markers** ⧗ on the Ruler to adjust the position of the text on the line

Shortcut Method

☐ Select the **text**

☐ Right-click the **text** in the text box, then click **Paragraph** on the shortcut menu

☐ In the Paragraph dialog box, click the **Before text arrows** in the Indentation section

☐ Click the **Special list arrow**, then select an option if desired

☐ Click **OK**

Change Horizontal Alignment

☐ Select the **text**

☐ Use the appropriate button command or keyboard shortcut listed in Table PPT 2-2 to align the text as desired

Table PPT 2-2   Text Alignment Buttons and Keyboard Shortcuts

Alignment	Button (in Paragraph group on Home tab or on Mini Toolbar)	Keyboard shortcut
Left	☰	[Ctrl][L]
Center	☰	[Ctrl][E]
Right	☰	[Ctrl][R]
Justify	☰	[Ctrl][J]

OR

☐ Select the **text**

☐ Click the **Home tab** on the Ribbon, click the **Launcher** ⧉ in the Paragraph group

☐ In the General section of the Paragraph dialog box, click the **Alignment list arrow**, then click an **alignment option**

☐ Click **OK**

Change Line Spacing

Ribbon Method

☐ Select the **text**

☐ Click the **Home tab**, click the **Line Spacing button** ⧊ in the Paragraph group, then click the line spacing you want (1.0, 1.5, 2.0, 2.5, or 3.0) on the list

OR

☐ Select the **text**

☐ Click the **Home tab**, click the **Line Spacing button** ⧊ in the Paragraph group, then click **Line Spacing Options**

☐ On the Indents and Spacing tab of the Paragraph dialog box, shown in Figure PPT 2-7, adjust the values in the Spacing Before text box and After text box as desired

☐ Click the **Line Spacing list arrow**, select the desired spacing option, then adjust the number in the **At text box** as necessary

☐ Click **OK**

PowerPoint

Figure PPT 2-7   Paragraph dialog box

Shortcut Method

☐ Select the text, right-click the text, then click **Paragraph** on the shortcut menu

☐ Follow the steps in bullets 3–5 of the second Change Line Spacing Ribbon Method on the previous page

Set Text Direction

Ribbon Method

☐ Select the text box

☐ Click the **Home tab**, click the **Text Direction button** 〔▥〕 in the Paragraph group

☐ Click a text direction option in the gallery

Shortcut Method

☐ Select the text box

☐ Right-click the text box, then click **Format Shape**

☐ Click **Text Box** in the left pane in the Format Shape dialog box

☐ Click the **Text direction list arrow** in the Text layout section, then click a text direction option

☐ Click **Close**

Change the Formatting of Bulleted Lists

Ribbon Method

☐ Select the text, or select the text box or placeholder to format all the bullets in the list

☐ Click the **Home tab**, click the **Bullets button arrow** 〔▤〕 in the Paragraph group, then click **Bullets and Numbering** to open the Bullets and Numbering dialog box shown in Figure PPT 2-8

☐ Click a bullet style on the Bulleted tab to change the bullet style

☐ Adjust the value in the Size text box to change the bullet size

☐ Click the **Color button** 〔▨〕, then click a color to change the bullet color

☐ Click the **Picture button**, select a picture in the Picture Bullet dialog box, then click **OK** to create a picture bullet

☐ Click **OK** in the Bullets and Numbering dialog box

PowerPoint

Figure PPT 2-8   Bullets and Numbering dialog box

Shortcut Method

☐ Select the text, or select the text box or placeholder to format all the bullets in the list

☐ Right-click the selection, point to **Bullets** on the shortcut menu, then click **Bullets and Numbering**

☐ Follow the steps in bullets 3–7 of the Change the Formatting of Bulleted Lists Ribbon Method on the previous page

Format Numbered Lists

Ribbon Method

☐ Select the text, or select the text box or placeholder to format all the numbers in the list

☐ Click the **Home tab**, click the **Numbering button arrow** ▤▾ in the Paragraph group, then click **Bullets and Numbering** to open the Bullets and Numbering dialog box

☐ Click a numbering style on the Numbered tab to change the numbering style

☐ Adjust the value in the Size text box to change the number size

☐ Click the **Color button arrow** ◭▾ then click a color to change the number color

☐ Click **OK**

Shortcut Method

☐ Select the text, or select the text box or placeholder to format all the numbers in the list

☐ Right-click the selection, point to **Numbering** on the shortcut menu, then click **Bullets and Numbering**

☐ Follow the steps from the bullets 3-6 in the Format Numbered Lists Ribbon Method above

Promote and Demote Bullets and Numbering

Ribbon Method

☐ Select the appropriate item(s) in the bulleted or numbered list

☐ Click the **Home tab**, then click the **Increase List Level button** ▤ in the Paragraph group to demote the list item(s)

☐ Click the **Decrease List Level button** ▤ in the Paragraph group to promote the list item(s)

Shortcut Method

☐ Select the appropriate item(s) in the bulleted or numbered list

☐ Press **[Tab]** to demote the list item(s)

☐ Press **[Shift][Tab]** to promote the list item(s)

  OR

☐ Select the appropriate slide

☐ In the Outline tab, select the appropriate list item(s), then right-click the selection

PowerPoint

☐ Click **Promote** on the shortcut menu to promote the list item(s)

☐ Click **Demote** on the shortcut menu to demote the list item(s)

Enter text in a Placeholder

Ribbon Method

☐ Insert or select a slide with a content placeholder

☐ Click the placeholder text, and type your own text

Convert Text to SmartArt

Ribbon Method

☐ Select a bulleted list

☐ Click the **Home tab**, then click the **Convert to SmartArt Graphic button** in the Paragraph group

☐ Click a SmartArt graphic in the gallery shown in Figure PPT 2-9

Figure PPT 2-9   SmartArt graphic gallery

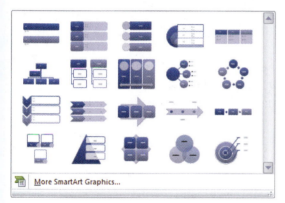

Copy and Paste Text

Ribbon Method

☐ Select the text

☐ Click the **Home tab**, then click the **Copy button** in the Clipboard group

☐ Click in the new location in the presentation where you want to copy the text

☐ Click the **Home tab**, then click the **Paste button** in the Clipboard group

Shortcut Method

☐ Select the text

☐ Right-click the selected text, then click **Copy** on the shortcut menu

☐ Right-click in the new location in the presentation where you want to copy the text, then click a **Paste option** on the shortcut menu

OR

☐ Select the text

☐ Press **[Ctrl][C]**

☐ Click in the new location in the presentation where you want to copy the text

☐ Press **[Ctrl][V]**

Use Paste Special

Ribbon Method

☐ Select the text or object

☐ Click the **Home tab**, then click the **Cut button** or **Copy button** in the Clipboard group

☐ Click in the new location in the presentation where you want to paste the text or object

☐ Click the **Home tab**, click the **Paste button arrow** in the Clipboard group, then click **Paste Special**

☐ Select the appropriate **options** in the Paste Special dialog box, shown in Figure PPT 2-10

☐ Click **OK**

Figure PPT 2-10   Paste Special dialog box

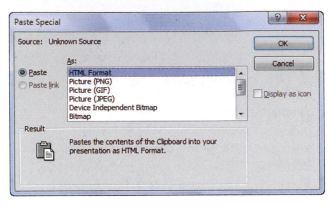

Shortcut Method

☐ Select the text or object

☐ Right-click the selected text or object, then click **Cut** or **Copy** on the shortcut menu

☐ Follow the steps in bullets 4–6 of the Use Paste Special Ribbon Method on the previous page and above

   OR

☐ Select the text or object

☐ Press **[Ctrl][X]** to cut or **[Ctrl][C]** to cut or copy the selected text or object

☐ Press **[Ctrl][Alt][V]** to open the Paste Special dialog box

☐ Select the appropriate options in the Paste Special dialog box

☐ Click **OK**

Use the Format Painter

Ribbon Method

☐ Select the text or object with the attributes that you want to copy

☐ Click the **Home tab**, then click the **Format Painter button** 🖌 in the Clipboard group

☐ Select the text or object to which you want to apply the formatting

Shortcut Method

☐ Select the text or object with the attributes that you want to copy

☐ Right-click the text or object, then click the **Format Painter button** 🖌 on the Mini Toolbar

☐ Select the text or object to which you want to apply the formatting

---

NOTE

Double-click the Format Painter button to apply the copied format to more than one selection.

PowerPoint

FORMAT TEXT BOXES

Insert a Text Box

Ribbon Method

☐ Select the slide on which you want to insert a text box

☐ Click the **Insert tab**, then click the **Text Box button** in the Text group

☐ Outside any current placeholders on the slide, click to create a text box that does not wrap the text within a shape, or drag to draw a text box that is a particular width so that the text wraps within the text box

☐ Type the desired text

OR

☐ Select the slide on which you want to insert a text box

☐ Click **Home tab**, click the **Shapes button** in the Drawing group, then click the **Text Box button**  in the Shapes gallery

☐ Follow the steps in bullets 3–4 of the Insert a Text Box Ribbon Method above

Delete a Text Box

Ribbon Method

☐ Select the text box

☐ Click the **Home tab**, then click the **Cut button** ✂ in the Clipboard group

Shortcut Method

☐ Select the text box, then press **[Delete]**

OR

☐ Right-click the text box, then click **Cut** on the shortcut menu

Apply Formatting Fills to a Text Box

Ribbon Method

☐ Select the text box

☐ Click the **Drawing Tools Format tab**, click the **Shape Fill button arrow** in the Shape Styles group to display the menu shown in Figure PPT 2-11 or click the **Home tab**, then click the **Shape Fill button arrow** in the Drawing group

☐ Click a color in the Theme Colors or Standard Colors group, or click any one of the Picture, Gradient, or Texture options to format the text box fill

Figure PPT 2-11   Shape Fill button and menu

OR

☐ Select the text box

☐ Click the **Drawing Tools Format tab**, then click the **Launcher** ⬜ in the Shape Styles group

☐ Click **Fill** in the left pane in the Format Shape dialog box, shown in Figure PPT 2-12, then adjust the options as desired to format the text box fill

☐ Click **Close**

Figure PPT 2-12 **Format Shape dialog box**

Shortcut Method

☐ Select the text box

☐ Right-click the text box, then click **Format Shape** on the shortcut menu

☐ Click **Fill** in the left pane of the Format Shape dialog box, then adjust the options as desired to format the text box fill

☐ Click **Close**

Change the Outline of a Text Box

Ribbon Method

☐ Select the text box

☐ Click the **Drawing Tools Format tab**, click the **Shape Outline button arrow** in the Shape Styles group to display the menu or click the **Home tab**, then click the **Shape Outline button arrow** in the Drawing group

☐ Click a color in the Theme Colors or Standard Colors group, or click any one of the Weight or Dashes options to format the text box border

OR

☐ Select the text box

☐ Click the **Drawing Tools Format tab**, then click the **Launcher** 🔲 in the Shape Styles group

☐ Click **Line Color** in the left pane of the Format Shape dialog box, then adjust the options as desired

☐ Click **Line Style** in the left pane, then adjust the options as desired

☐ Click **Close**

Shortcut Method

☐ Right-click the text box

☐ Click **Format Shape** on the shortcut menu

☐ Click **Line Color** in the Format Shape dialog box, then adjust the options as desired

PowerPoint

☐ Click **Line Style** in the Format Shape dialog box, then adjust the options as desired
☐ Click **Close**

Format Text Box Fill, Border, and Effects Using Quick Styles

Ribbon Method
☐ Select the text box
☐ Click **Home tab**, then click the **Quick Styles button** in the Drawing group
☐ Click a Quick Style in the gallery
   OR
☐ Select the text box
☐ Click the **Drawing Tools Format tab**, then click the **More button** ⊡ in the Shape Styles group
☐ Click a shape style in the gallery

Change the Shape of a Text Box

Ribbon Method
☐ Select the text box
☐ Click the **Drawing Tools Format tab**, click the **Edit Shape button** ⬚⁻ in the Insert Shapes group, point to **Change Shape**, then click a shape from the gallery

Apply Effects

Ribbon Method
☐ Select the text box
☐ Click the **Drawing Tools Format tab**, click the **Shape Effects button** in the Shape Styles group to display the menu shown in Figure PPT 2-13, or click the **Home tab**, then click the **Shape Effects button** in the Drawing group
☐ Point to a category of effects, then click the desired option from the submenu

Figure PPT 2-13   **Shape Effects button, menu, and submenu**

   OR
☐ Select the text box
☐ Click the **Drawing Tools Format tab**, then click the **Launcher** ◳ in the Shape Styles group

PowerPoint

☐ Click **Shadow**, **Reflection**, **Glow and Soft Edges**, **3-D Format**, or **3-D Rotation** in the left pane of the Format Shape dialog box, then adjust the options as desired

☐ Click **Close**

Shortcut Method

☐ Right-click the text box

☐ Click **Format Shape** on the shortcut menu

☐ Click **Shadow**, **Reflection**, **Glow and Soft Edges**, **3-D Format**, or **3-D Rotation** in the left pane of the Format Shape dialog box, then adjust the options as desired

☐ Click **Close**

Align Text Vertically

Ribbon Method

☐ Select the text box

☐ Click the **Home tab**, then click the **Align Text button** in the Paragraph group

☐ Click an alignment option from the menu shown in Figure PPT 2-14

Figure PPT 2-14   **Align Text button and menu**

OR

☐ Select the text box

☐ Click the **Home tab**, click the **Align Text button** in the Paragraph group, then click **More Options**

☐ In the Format Text Effects dialog box, click **Text Box** in the left pane, click the **Vertical alignment list arrow** in the Text layout section, then click an alignment

Shortcut Method

☐ Select the text box

☐ Right-click the text box, then click **Format Shape** on the shortcut menu

☐ In the Format Text Effects dialog box, click **Text Box** in the left pane, click the **Vertical alignment list arrow** in the Text layout section, then click an alignment

☐ Click **Close**

Create Columns in a Text Box

Ribbon Method

☐ Select the text box

☐ Click the **Home tab**, then click the **Columns button** in the Paragraph group

☐ Click an option on the list

Shortcut Method

☐ Right-click the text box, then click **Format Shape** on the shortcut menu

☐ Click **Text Box** in the left pane of the Format Shape dialog box

☐ Click the **Columns button** in the Internal margin section to open the Columns dialog box

□ Adjust the value in the Number text box to the number of columns desired

□ Adjust the value in the Spacing text box to the desired spacing between the columns

□ Click **OK**, then click **Close**

Set Internal Margins

Ribbon Method

□ Select the text box

□ Click the **Drawing Tools Format tab**, then click the **Launcher** ⊡ in the Shape Styles group

□ Click Text Box in the left pane of the Format Shape dialog box

□ In the Internal margin section, adjust the values in the Left, Right, Top, and Bottom text boxes

□ Click **Close**

Shortcut Method

□ Right-click the text box, then click **Format Shape** on the shortcut menu

□ Follow the steps in bullets 3–5 of the Set Internal Margins Ribbon Method above

Set the Current Text Box Formatting as the Default for New Text Boxes

Shortcut Method

□ Apply formatting to the text box

□ Right-click the text box and click **Set as Default Text Box**

Wrap Text in a Text Box

Ribbon Method

□ Select the text box

□ Click the **Drawing Tools Format tab**, then click the **Launcher** ⊡ in the Shape Styles group

□ Click Text Box in the left pane of the Format Shape dialog box

□ In the Internal margin section, click the **Wrap text in shape check box** to insert a check mark

□ Click **Close**

Shortcut Method

□ Right-click the text box, then click **Format Shape** on the shortcut menu

□ Follow the steps in bullets 3–5 of the Wrap Text in a Text Box Ribbon Method above

Adjust the Size and Position of a Text Box

Ribbon Method

□ Select the text box

□ Click the **Drawing Tools Format tab**, then click the **Launcher** ⊡ in the Shape Styles group to open the Format Shape dialog box

□ Click **Size** in the left pane, then adjust the values in the Height, Width, and Rotation text boxes in the Size and rotate section

□ Click **Position** in the left pane, then adjust the values in the Horizontal, Vertical, and From text boxes in the Position on slide section

□ Click **Close**

Shortcut Method

□ Right-click the text box, then click **Size and Position** on the shortcut menu

□ Follow the steps in bullets 3–5 of the Adjust the Size and Position of a Text Box Ribbon Method above

Use AutoFit

Ribbon Method

□ Select the text box

□ Click the **Drawing Tools Format tab**, then click the **Launcher** ⊡ in the Shape Styles group to open the Format Shape dialog box

PowerPoint

☐ Click **Text Box** in the left pane, then click one of the option buttons in the Autofit section: Do not Autofit, Shrink text on overflow, or Resize shape to fit text

☐ Click **Close**

Shortcut Method

☐ Right-click the text box, then click **Format Shape** on the shortcut menu

☐ Follow the steps in bullets 3-4 of the Use AutoFit Ribbon Method on the previous page

REVIEW QUESTIONS

FILL IN THE BLANK

Complete the following sentences by writing the correct word or words in the blanks provided.

1. The _____ button separates text in a text box into two or more parallel paths.

2. After making changes in the Edit Photo Album dialog box, click the _____ button to apply the changes.

3. Press and hold _____ to select multiple slides.

4. You can add a hanging indent to text using the _____ dialog box.

5. The _____ button has a picture of a pair of scissors on it.

MULTIPLE CHOICE

Select the best response for the following statements.

1. _____ is the keyboard shortcut for copying text.
   - A. [Ctrl][V]
   - B. [Ctrl][X]
   - C. [Ctrl][C]
   - D. [Ctrl][B]

2. The Reuse Slides command is located on the _____ button arrow.
   - A. Photo Album
   - B. New Slide
   - C. Slide Layout
   - D. Background Styles

3. You can convert a _____ to a SmartArt graphic.
   - A. Quick Style
   - B. slide show
   - C. footer
   - D. bulleted list

4. The _____ button allows you to rotate text 90 degrees.
   - A. Effects
   - B. Text Box
   - C. Text Direction
   - D. Align Text

5. Use the _____ button to promote a numbered list item.

    A. Decrease Indent

    B. Tab

    C. Increase Indent

    D. Numbering

PROJECTS

Project PPT 2-1

1. Create a new blank presentation.

2. Click the title placeholder and type **Marketing Plan**.

3. Click the subtitle placeholder, then type **Blue Yonder Airlines**.

4. Insert a new Title and Content slide.

5. Click the title placeholder, then type **Market Summary**.

6. Apply the Waveform theme to your presentation.

7. Change the background to Style 10.

8. Insert two more Title and Content slides.

9. Type Competition as the title on slide 3 and Product Definition as the title on slide 4.

10. In Normal view, delete slide 2.

11. Add a footer. Type **Your Name** in the text box.

12. Click the Don't show on title slide check box and apply the changes to all slides.

13. Select slide 3 and reuse the Projected Earnings and Projected Capital Expenditures slides from Project PPT 2-3.

14. Save the presentation as **Marketing Plan**, then close it.

Project PPT 2-2

1. Create a new blank presentation.

2. Insert a new photo album with the following elements:

    • Pictures: Chrysanthemum, Desert, Hydrangeas, and Tulips photos from the Sample Pictures folder on your computer

    • Picture layout: 1 picture with title

    • Frame shape: Compound Frame, Black

    • Theme: Austin

3. Save the presentation as **Nature Album**.

4. Make following changes to the photo album:

    • Picture layout: 1 picture

    • Move the tulips picture up to be the 2nd picture in the album

    • Add captions below ALL pictures

5. Update the file.

6. On the first slide, insert a text box below your name. Type **2015**. Change the text color to Green, Accent 1.

7. Change the theme colors to Module.

8. Save and close the presentation.

PowerPoint

Project PPT 2-3

1. Open the data file Project PPT 2-3.

2. On slide 1, select *Blue Yonder Airlines* and apply a text shadow.

3. Italicize the name and date on slide 1.

4. On slide 2, select *4th Quarter FY 2015* and apply an underline.

5. On slide 2, convert the bulleted list to a numbered list. Format the numbered list with Roman numerals.

6. On slide 6, select the last bulleted item, which begins with *Renewed commitment…* cut the item from the list, go to slide 7 and paste it under the first bulleted item.

7. On slide 9, select *Legacy holdings* and *Regulatory changes* and demote them one list level.

8. On slide 12, copy the airplane clip art and paste it to the top center of slide 1.

9. Save the presentation as **Financial Outlook** and close it.

CRITICAL THINKING

Activity PPT 2-1

Create a new presentation from the outline in the Activity PPT 2-1 data file. Notice that the information did not transfer onto the slides perfectly, but a lot of the work has been done for you. Start cleaning up the presentation by typing Outline for a Speech in the Title placeholder on slide 1, then delete slide 2. Notice that on slides 2 and 3 some of the outline items are labeled twice, such as with letters and bullets. Choose which you would like to use and make those changes throughout the rest of the presentation. Format the presentation using a theme, background format, or any other elements you learned in this lesson. Name, save, and close the file.

PowerPoint Objective 3: Working with Graphical and Multimedia Elements

Manipulate Graphical Elements

Arrange Graphical Elements

☐ Select the graphical element

☐ Refer to Table PPT 3-1 to use the commands in the Arrange group on the Picture Tools Format tab or Drawing Tools Format tab, shown in Figure PPT 3-1, or to apply the commands using the shortcut menu

Figure PPT 3-1   **Arrange group on the Picture Tools Format tab**

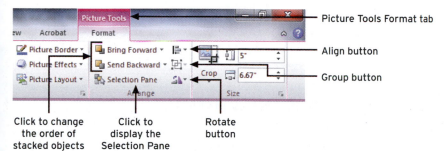

Table PPT 3-1   Arranging Graphical Elements

What You Want to Do	Ribbon Method: Arrange group on the Picture Tools Format tab or Drawing Tools Format tab	Shortcut Method
Change the order of stacked objects: move an object from the bottom to the top	Select the object, click the **Bring Forward button arrow**, then click **Bring Forward** or **Bring to Front**	Right-click the object, point to **Bring to Front** on the shortcut menu, then click **Bring to Front** or **Bring Forward** OR Right-click an object, then click the **Bring Forward button** 🔲 on the Mini Toolbar
Change the order of stacked objects: move an object from the top to the bottom	Select the object, click the **Send Backward button arrow**, then click **Send Backward** or **Send to Back**	Right-click the object, point to **Send to Back** on the shortcut menu, then click **Send to Back** or **Send Backward** OR Right-click an object, then click the **Send Backward button** 🔲 on the Mini Toolbar
Display the Selection Pane to select individual graphic elements	Click the **Selection Pane button**	
Align objects	Press and hold **[Ctrl]**, select the objects, click the **Align list arrow**, then click **Align Left**, **Align Center**, **Align Right**, **Align Top**, **Align Middle**, **Align Bottom**, **Distribute Horizontally**, or **Distribute Vertically**	
Combine two or more objects so they can be treated as one	Press and hold **[Ctrl]**, select the objects, click the **Group list arrow**, then click **Group**	Select the objects, right-click the objects, point to **Group** on the shortcut menu, then click **Group**

(continued)

Table PPT 3-1 Arranging Graphical Elements (continued)

What You Want to Do	Ribbon Method: Arrange group on the Picture Tools Format tab or Drawing Tools Format tab	Shortcut Method
Separate a grouped object	Select the object, click the **Group list arrow**, then click **Ungroup**	Right-click the object, point to **Group** on the shortcut menu, then click **Ungroup**
Change the position of an object	Select the object, click the **Rotate list arrow**, then click **Rotate Right 90°**, **Rotate Left 90°**, **Flip Vertical**, **Flip Horizontal**, or **More Rotation Options**	Right-click a picture, click the **Rotate button** on the Mini Toolbar, then click an option from the menu OR Select an object, then drag the green rotate handle

Position Graphical Elements

Ribbon Method

□ Select the graphical element
□ Click the **Picture Tools Format tab** or the **Drawing Tools Format tab** on the Ribbon
□ Click the **Launcher** in the Size group to open the Format Picture dialog box
□ Click **Position** in the left pane, then adjust the values in the Horizontal and Vertical text boxes and the From list arrows in the Position on slide section
□ Click **Close**

Shortcut Method

□ Right-click the graphical element, then click **Size and Position** on the shortcut menu
□ Follow the steps in bullets 4–5 of the Position Graphical Elements Ribbon Method above

Resize Graphical Elements

Ribbon Method

□ Select the graphical element
□ Click the **Picture Tools Format tab** or the **Drawing Tools Format tab** on the Ribbon
□ Click the **Shape Width text box** in the Size group and type a number, or click the up and down arrows to adjust the width
□ Click the **Shape Height text box** in the Size group and type a number, or click the up and down arrows to adjust the height
OR
□ Select the graphical element
□ Click the **Picture Tools Format tab** or the **Drawing Tools Format tab**, click the **Launcher** in the Size group to open the Format Picture or Format Shape dialog box, shown in Figure PPT 3-2
□ Click **Size** in the left pane, then adjust the values in the Height and Width text boxes in the Size and rotate section
□ Click **Close**

Figure PPT 3-2   Format Shape dialog box

Shortcut Method

☐ Select the graphical element

☐ Right-click the **graphical element**, click **Size and Position** or **Format Picture** on the shortcut menu to open the Format Picture dialog box

☐ Click **Size** in the left pane, then adjust the values in the Height and Width text boxes in the Size and rotate section

☐ Click **Close**

   OR

☐ Select the graphical element

☐ Drag the sizing handles to resize the object

Apply Effects to Graphical Elements

Ribbon Method

☐ Select a picture

☐ Click the **Picture Tools Format tab**, click the **Picture Effects button** in the Picture Styles group, point to a category of effects on the menu, then click an option from the submenu, as shown in Figure PPT 3-3

Figure PPT 3-3   Picture Effects button, menu, and submenu

OR

☐ Select a drawing object

☐ Click the **Drawing Tools Format tab**, click the **Shape Effects button** in the Shape Styles group, point to a category of effects on the menu, then click an option from the submenu

Apply Styles to Graphical Elements

Ribbon Method

☐ Select a picture

☐ Click the **Picture Tools Format tab**, click the **More button** 🔽 in the Picture Styles group, then click an option from the gallery

OR

☐ Select a drawing object

☐ Click the **Drawing Tools Format tab**, click the **More button** 🔽 in the Shape Styles group, then click an option from the gallery

OR

☐ Select a drawing object

☐ Click the **Home tab**, click the **Quick Styles button** in the Drawing group, then click a style in the gallery

Apply Borders to Graphical Elements

Ribbon Method

☐ Select a picture

☐ Click the **Picture Tools Format tab**, then click the **Picture Border button arrow** in the Picture Styles group

☐ Click a color in the Theme Colors or Standard Colors group, or click any one of the More Outline Colors, Weight, or Dashes options to format the picture border

OR

☐ Select a picture

☐ Click the **Picture Tools Format tab**, then click the **Launcher** 🔲 in the Picture Styles group

☐ Click **Line Color** in the left pane of the Format Shape dialog box, then adjust the options as desired

☐ Click **Line Style** in the left pane, then adjust the options as desired

☐ Click **Close**

OR

☐ Select a drawing object

☐ Click the **Drawing Tools Format tab**, then click the **Shape Outline button arrow** in the Shape Styles group

☐ Click a color in the Theme Colors or Standard Colors group, or click any one of the More Outline Colors, Weight, or Dashes options to format the object border

　OR

☐ Select a drawing object

☐ Click the **Drawing Tools Format tab**, then click the **Launcher** 🔲 in the Shape Styles group

☐ Click **Line Color** in the left pane of the Format Shape dialog box, then adjust the options as desired

☐ Click **Line Style** in the left pane, then adjust the options as desired

☐ Click **Close**

Shortcut Method

☐ Right-click a picture

☐ Click **Format Picture** on the shortcut menu

☐ Click **Line Color** in the Format Picture dialog box, then adjust the options as desired

☐ Click **Line Style** in the Format Picture dialog box, then adjust the options as desired

☐ Click **Close**

　OR

☐ Right-click a drawing object

☐ Click **Format Shape** on the shortcut menu

☐ Click **Line Color** in the Format Shape dialog box, then adjust the options as desired

☐ Click **Line Style** in the Format Shape dialog box, then adjust the options as desired

☐ Click **Close**

　OR

☐ Right-click a drawing object

☐ Click the **Shape Outline list button arrow** 🖉▾ on the Mini Toolbar

☐ Click a color in the Theme Colors or Standard Colors group, or click any one of the More Outline Colors, Weight, or Dashes options to format the object border

Insert Hyperlinks

Ribbon Method

☐ Select the graphical element

☐ Click the **Insert tab**, then click the **Hyperlink button** in the Links group to open the Insert Hyperlink dialog box, shown in Figure PPT 3-4

☐ Make the appropriate selections using Table PPT 3-2 as a reference, then click **OK**

Figure PPT 3-4   Insert Hyperlink dialog box

Shortcut Method

☐ Select the graphical element

☐ Right-click the selection, then click **Hyperlink**, or press **[Ctrl][K]**

☐ In the Insert Hyperlink dialog box, make the appropriate selections using Table PPT 3-2 as a reference, then click **OK**

Table PPT 3-2   Inserting Hyperlinks Using the Insert Hyperlink Dialog Box

To link to	Do this
An existing file	Click **Existing File or Web Page**, navigate to the appropriate drive and folder, click the filename in the list, then click **OK**
A Web page	Click **Existing File or Web Page**, click the **Address text box**, type the **URL**, then click **OK** (*Note:* Make sure you are connected to the Internet to successfully follow this link)
Another place in the document	Click **Place in This Document**, select a location in the Select a place in this document list, then click **OK**
A new document	Click **Create New Document**, name the document, verify the drive and folder, choose to edit it now or later, then click **OK**
An e-mail address	Click **E-mail Address**, type the address and any other text to display, then click **OK**

MANIPULATE IMAGES

Insert Pictures from a File

Ribbon Method

☐ Click the **Insert tab**, then click the **Picture button** in the Images group to open the Insert Picture dialog box

☐ Navigate to the file, then click the file to select it

☐ Click **Insert**

Shortcut Method

☐ Select the appropriate slide containing a content placeholder

☐ Click the **Insert Picture from File button** on the content placeholder

☐ Navigate to the file, then click the file to select it

☐ Click **Insert**

Insert Clip Art
Ribbon Method
☐ Position the insertion point in the desired location
☐ Click the **Insert tab**, then click the **Clip Art button** in the Images group
☐ In the Clip Art task pane, type the search criteria in the Search for text box, use the **Results should be list arrow** to identify the format to find, click the Include Office.com content check box if you want to search for clip art on Office.com, then click **Go**
☐ Position the pointer over the image you want to insert
☐ Click the list arrow that appears, then click **Insert**, as shown in Figure PPT 3-5, or click an image to insert it

Figure PPT 3-5   Clip Art task pane

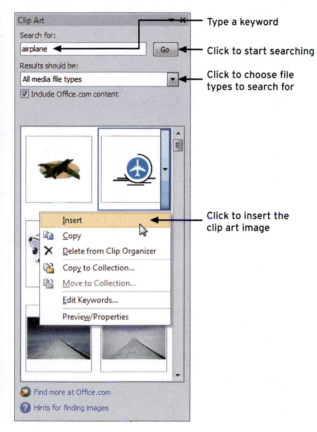

Shortcut Method
☐ Select the appropriate slide containing a content placeholder
☐ Click the **Clip Art button** in the content placeholder
☐ Follow the steps in bullets 3-5 under the Insert Clip Art Ribbon Method above

Apply Color Adjustments
Ribbon Method
☐ Select the picture
☐ Click the **Picture Tools Format tab** on the Ribbon, then click the **Color button** in the Adjust group
☐ Click an option in the gallery shown in Figure PPT 3-6

PowerPoint

Figure PPT 3-6   Color button and gallery

OR

☐ Select the picture

☐ Click the **Picture Tools Format tab** on the Ribbon, then click the **Launcher** ⬚ in the Picture Styles group

☐ In the Format Picture dialog box, click **Picture Color** in the left pane, then click a Color Saturation, Color Tone, or Recolor option

☐ Click **Close**

Apply Image Corrections

Ribbon Method

☐ Select the picture

☐ Click the **Picture Tools Format tab**, then click the **Corrections button** in the Adjust group

☐ Select an option in the gallery from the Sharpen and Soften or Brightness and Contrast sections or click **Picture Corrections Options** to open the Format Picture dialog box

OR

☐ Select the picture

☐ Click the **Picture Tools Format tab**, click the **Launcher** ⬚ in the Picture Styles group to open the Format Picture dialog box

☐ Click **Picture Corrections** in the left pane, then select options from the Sharpen and Soften or Brightness and Contrast sections

☐ Click **Close**

OR

Shortcut Method

☐ Right-click the picture on the slide, then click **Format Picture** from the shortcut menu to open the Format Picture dialog box

☐ Click **Picture Corrections** in the left pane, then select options from the Sharpen and Soften or Brightness and Contrast sections

☐ Click **Close**

Remove a Background

Ribbon Method

☐ Select the picture

☐ Click the **Picture Tools Format tab**, then click the **Remove Background button** in the Adjust group

☐ Drag the handles and marquee lines to enclose the parts of the picture you want to keep

☐ In most cases, this is all you need to do to achieve the results you want. If necessary, use the buttons on the Background Removal tab, shown in Figure PPT 3-7, to mark areas to keep or remove to achieve the desired results

☐ Click **Keep Changes**

Figure PPT 3-7   Background Removal tab

Background Removal tab

Preview

Selection handles

marquee lines

OR

☐ Select the picture

☐ Click the **Picture Tools Format tab**, then click the **Color button** in the Adjust group

☐ Click **Set Transparent Color**, then click the **Set Transparent Color pointer** ✎ on the color in the picture you want to be transparent

Crop a Picture
Ribbon Method

☐ Select the picture

☐ Click the **Picture Tools Format tab**, then click the **Crop button** in the Size group

☐ Drag one or more of the black cropping handles inward

☐ Click the **Crop button** or press **[Esc]** to remove the unwanted parts of the picture

OR

☐ Select the picture

☐ Click the **Picture Tools Format tab**, then click the **Launcher** 🔲 in the Size group to open the Format Picture dialog box

☐ Click **Crop** in the left pane, then adjust the values in the Picture position and Crop position sections

☐ Click **Close**

Shortcut Method

☐ Select the picture

☐ Right-click the picture, then click the **Crop button** 🔲 on the Mini Toolbar

☐ Drag one or more of the black cropping handles inward

☐ Click the **Crop button** or press **[Esc]** to remove the unwanted parts of the picture

OR

☐ Select the picture

☐ Right-click the picture, then click **Format Picture** on the shortcut menu to open the Format Picture dialog box

☐ Click **Crop** in the left pane, then adjust the values in the Picture position and Crop position sections

☐ Click **Close**

Compress Selected Pictures or All Pictures
Ribbon Method

☐ Select a picture

☐ Click the **Picture Tools Format tab**, then click the **Compress Pictures button** 🔲 in the Adjust group to open the Compress Pictures dialog box, shown in Figure PPT 3-8

☐ To compress only the selected picture, click the **Apply only to this picture check box** to insert a checkmark

☐ To compress all the pictures in the document, click the **Apply only to this picture check box** to remove the checkmark

☐ Click **OK**

Figure PPT 3-8   Compress Pictures dialog box

Click to compress only
the selected picture;
remove the check mark
to compress all pictures

Change a Picture

Ribbon Method

☐ Select the picture

☐ Click the **Picture Tools Format tab**, then click the **Change Picture button** in the Adjust group to open the Insert Picture dialog box

☐ Navigate to the picture you want to insert to replace the selected picture

☐ Click **Insert**

Shortcut Method

☐ Select the picture

☐ Right-click the selection, then click **Change Picture** on the shortcut menu to open the Insert Picture dialog box

☐ Navigate to the picture you want to insert to replace the selected picture

☐ Click **Insert**

Reset a Picture

Ribbon Method

☐ Select the picture

☐ Click the **Picture Tools Format tab**, then click the **Reset Picture button** in the Adjust group to open the Insert Picture dialog box

---

MODIFY WORDART AND SHAPES

Insert a Shape

Ribbon Method

☐ Click the **Home tab**, click the **Shapes button** in the Drawing group, then click a shape in the gallery or click the **Insert tab**, click the **Shapes button** in the Illustrations group, then click a shape in the gallery shown in Figure PPT 3-9

☐ Position the crosshair pointer ╀ where you want the shape to appear, then drag to create the shape and release the mouse button, or click to insert the shape in the default size

PowerPoint

Figure PPT 3-9   Shapes button and gallery

Set the Formatting of the Current Shape as the Default for Future Shapes

Ribbon Method

☐ Select the shape

☐ Right-click the shape, then click **Set as Default Shape** on the shortcut menu

Change the Fill Color or Texture

Ribbon Method

☐ Select the shape

☐ Click the **Shape Fill button arrow** in the Shape Styles group on the Drawing Tools Format tab or in the Drawing group on the Home tab

☐ Click a color in the Theme Colors or Standard Colors section, or click any one of the Picture, Gradient, or Texture options to format the shape fill

OR

☐ Select the shape

☐ Click the **Home tab**, then click the **Quick Styles button** in the Drawing group

☐ Click a style in the gallery

Shortcut Method

☐ Select the shape

☐ Right-click the shape, then click the **Shape Fill button arrow**  on the Mini Toolbar

☐ Click a color in the Theme Colors or Standard Colors section, or click any one of the Picture, Gradient, or Texture options to format the shape fill

Insert WordArt
Ribbon Method
- ☐ Select the appropriate slide
- ☐ Click the **Insert tab**, then click the **WordArt button** in the Text group
- ☐ In the WordArt gallery, shown in Figure PPT 3-10, click the appropriate **WordArt style**
- ☐ In the inserted WordArt text box, type the text you want to create as WordArt
- ☐ Drag the **WordArt object** to the appropriate location on the slide

Figure PPT 3-10   WordArt button and gallery

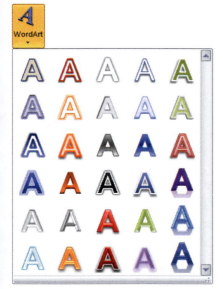

Format WordArt Text
Ribbon Method
- ☐ Select the existing WordArt object
- ☐ Click a **WordArt style** in the WordArt Styles group on the Drawing Tools Format tab, or click the **Text Fill button arrow**, **Text Outline button arrow**, or **Text Effects button** in the WordArt Styles group shown in Figure PPT 3-11, and select an appropriate formatting style

Figure PPT 3-11   WordArt Styles group

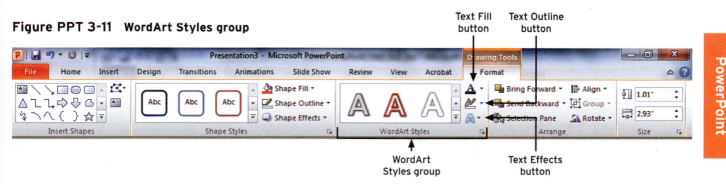

OR
- ☐ Select the existing WordArt object
- ☐ Click the **Launcher** in the WordArt Styles group on the Drawing Tools Format tab
- ☐ Adjust the options as desired in the Text Fill, Text Outline, Outline Style, Shadow, Reflection, Glow and Soft Edges, 3-D Format, 3-D Rotation, and Text Box sections of the Format Text Effects dialog box
- ☐ Click **Close**

Shortcut Method

□ Right-click the existing WordArt object, then click **Format Text Effects** on the shortcut menu

□ Follow the steps in bullets 3-4 of the second Format WordArt Text Ribbon Method on the previous page

Apply Quick Styles to WordArt

Ribbon Method

□ Select the existing WordArt object

□ Click a **WordArt style** in the WordArt Styles group on the Drawing Tools Format tab, or click the **WordArt Style More button** ⊡ then select an appropriate Quick Style from the gallery

OR

□ Select the existing WordArt object

□ Click the **Home tab** on the Ribbon, click the **Quick Styles button** in the Drawing group, then select an appropriate Quick Style from the gallery

Change WordArt Shape

Ribbon Method

□ Select the existing WordArt object

□ Click the **Drawing Tools Format tab**, click the **More button** ⊡ in the Shape Styles group, then click an appropriate shape style in the gallery

OR

□ Select the existing WordArt object

□ Click the **Shape Fill button arrow**, **Shape Outline button arrow**, or **Shape Effects button** in the Drawing group on the Home tab or in the Shape Styles group on the Drawing Tools Format tab

□ Select the desired shape fill, outline, and effects options to format the WordArt shape

Change WordArt Text Shape

Ribbon Method

□ Select the existing WordArt object

□ Click the **Drawing Tools Format tab**, then click the **Text Effects button** 🅰 in the WordArt Styles group

□ Point to **Transform**, then click an appropriate style from the Follow Path or Warp sections of the gallery, as shown in Figure PPT 3-12

PowerPoint

Figure PPT 3-12   Text Effects button and gallery

Convert WordArt to SmartArt

Ribbon Method

☐ Select the WordArt object

☐ Click the **Home tab**, click the **Convert to SmartArt button** in the Paragraph group, then click a SmartArt graphic from the gallery

Shortcut Method

☐ Select the WordArt object

☐ Right-click the WordArt object, point to **Convert to SmartArt** on the shortcut menu, then click a SmartArt graphic from the gallery

MANIPULATE SMARTART

Insert a SmartArt Graphic on a Slide

Ribbon Method

☐ Click the **Insert tab**, then click the **SmartArt button** in the Illustrations group

☐ In the Choose a SmartArt Graphic dialog box, shown in Figure PPT 3-13, click the appropriate category in the left pane, click the desired SmartArt graphic in the center pane, then click **OK**

☐ Enter and modify the text and format of the graphic as desired

Figure PPT 3-13   Choose a SmartArt Graphic dialog box

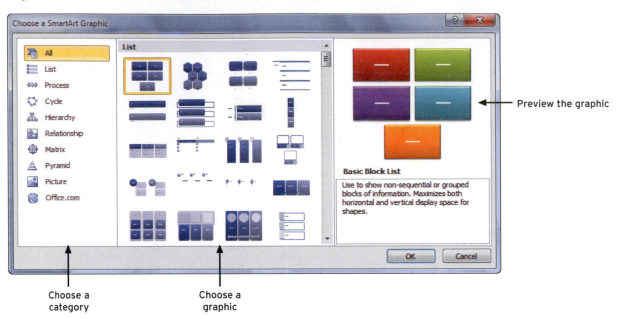

Choose a category

Choose a graphic

Preview the graphic

OR

☐ Select the appropriate slide containing a content placeholder

☐ Click the **Insert SmartArt Graphic button** 🖼 on the content placeholder

☐ Follow the steps in bullets 2–3 of the Insert a SmartArt Graphic on a Slide Ribbon Method on the previous page

Add Text to SmartArt Diagrams

Ribbon Method

☐ Select the SmartArt graphic

☐ Click each **Text placeholder**, then type the text

OR

☐ Select the SmartArt graphic

☐ Click the **SmartArt Tools Design tab** on the Ribbon, then click the **Text Pane button** in the Create Graphic group, or click the **Text Pane Control button** on the left side of the SmartArt Graphic selection box

☐ In the Text Pane, type text in the appropriate locations, then press **Enter** to insert a new bullet if desired

Shortcut Method

☐ Right-click the **SmartArt graphic** on the slide, then click **Show Text Pane** on the shortcut menu

☐ In the Text Pane, type text in the appropriate locations, then press **Enter** to insert a new bullet if desired

Add Shapes to a SmartArt Graphic

Ribbon Method

☐ Select the SmartArt graphic

☐ Click the **SmartArt Tools Design tab**, then click a shape or object in the SmartArt graphic

☐ Click the **Add Shape button** in the Create Graphic group, or click the **Add Shape button arrow** to display the menu as shown in Figure PPT 3-14, then click **Add Shape After**, **Add Shape Before**, **Add Shape Above**, **Add Shape Below**, or **Add Assistant** according to the type of SmartArt graphic and desired location for the new shape

Figure PPT 3-14   Add Shape button and menu

Shortcut Method

☐ Right-click the SmartArt graphic shape on the slide, then point to **Add Shape** on the shortcut menu

☐ Click **Add Shape After**, **Add Shape Before**, **Add Shape Above**, **Add Shape Below**, or **Add Assistant** according-ing to the type of SmartArt graphic and desired location for the new shape

Remove Shapes from a SmartArt Graphic

Ribbon Method

☐ Select the SmartArt graphic

☐ Click the **SmartArt Tools Design tab**, click the **Text Pane button** in the Create Graphic group, or click the **Text Pane Control button** on the SmartArt graphic

☐ Select the text in the Text Pane that you want to delete, then press **[Delete]**

Shortcut Method

☐ Select the SmartArt graphic

☐ Select the shape that you want to delete, then press **[Delete]**

Change SmartArt Styles

Ribbon Method

☐ Select the SmartArt graphic

☐ Click the **SmartArt Tools Design tab**, click the **More button** ⊡ in the SmartArt Styles group, then click a Quick Style in the gallery

   OR

☐ Select the SmartArt graphic, then select one or more shapes in the graphic

☐ Click the **SmartArt Tools Format tab**, click the **More button** ⊡ in the SmartArt Styles group, then click a Quick Style in the gallery

   OR

☐ Select the SmartArt graphic, one or more shapes within the graphic or text within the graphic

☐ Click the **SmartArt Tools Format tab**, click the **More button** ⊡ in the WordArt Styles group, then click a Quick Style in the gallery

Change Theme Colors in SmartArt Diagrams

Ribbon Method

☐ Select the SmartArt graphic

☐ Click the **SmartArt Tools Design tab**, click the **Change Colors button** in the SmartArt Styles group, then click a set of theme colors in the gallery

Change the Layout of SmartArt Graphics

Ribbon Method

☐ Select the SmartArt graphic

☐ Click the **SmartArt Tools Design tab**, click the **More button** ⊡ in the Layouts group, then click a new layout in the gallery

   OR

☐ Select the SmartArt graphic

☐ Click the **SmartArt Tools Design tab**, click the **More button** ⊡ in the Layouts group, then click **More Layouts** to open the Choose a SmartArt Graphic dialog box

☐ Click a SmartArt category in the left pane, click the desired new layout in the center pane, then click **OK**

Shortcut Method

☐ Right-click the SmartArt graphic on the slide, then click **Change Layout** on the shortcut menu

☐ In the Choose a SmartArt Graphic dialog box, click a SmartArt category in the left pane, click a new layout in the center pane, then click **OK**

Reorder Shapes

Ribbon Method

☐ Select the SmartArt graphic

☐ Click the **SmartArt Tools Design tab**, then click the **Right to Left button** in the Create Graphic group to switch the layout of shapes from left to right or right to left

OR

☐ Select the SmartArt graphic

☐ Click the **SmartArt Tools Design tab**, then click the **Move Selection Up button** or the **Move Selection Down button** in the Create Graphic group to move the selected shape forward or backward in the sequence

Convert a SmartArt Graphic to Text

Ribbon Method

☐ Select the SmartArt graphic

☐ Click the **SmartArt Tools Design tab**, click the **Convert button** in the Reset group, then click **Convert to Text**

Convert SmartArt to Shapes

Ribbon Method

☐ Select the SmartArt graphic

☐ Click the **SmartArt Tools Design tab**, click the **Convert button** in the Reset group, then click **Convert to Shapes**

Make Shapes Larger or Smaller

Ribbon Method

☐ Select a shape within a SmartArt graphic

☐ Click the **SmartArt Tools Format tab**, click the **Larger button** in the Shapes group to increase the size of the shape or click the **Smaller button** in the Shapes group to decrease the size of the shape

OR

☐ Select a shape within a SmartArt graphic

☐ Click the **SmartArt Tools Format tab**, then adjust the values in the Height and Width boxes in the Size group

OR

☐ Select a shape within a SmartArt graphic

☐ Drag one or more selection handles to change the size of the shape

Promote and Demote Bullet Levels

Ribbon Method

☐ Select the SmartArt graphic

☐ Click the **SmartArt Tools Design tab**, then click the **Text Pane button** in the Create Graphic group to display the Text Pane

☐ Select a bulleted item in the Text Pane, then click the **Demote button** in the Create Graphic group to decrease the level of the selection or click the **Promote button** to increase the level of the selection

EDIT VIDEO AND AUDIO CONTENT

Insert a Movie on a Slide

Ribbon Method

☐ Click the **Insert tab**, click the **Video button arrow** in the Media group, as shown in Figure PPT 3-15, then click **Video from File**

☐ In the Insert Video dialog box, navigate to the appropriate drive and folder, click the movie file you want, then click **Insert**

Figure PPT 3-15   **Video button and menu**

OR

☐ Click the **Insert tab**, click the **Video button arrow** in the Media group, then click **Clip Art Video**

☐ In the Clip Art task pane, type an appropriate **keyword** in the Search for text box, click **Go**, then click the video file you want

☐ Drag the movie thumbnail to the appropriate location on the slide

OR

☐ Insert or display a slide with a content placeholder

☐ Click the **Insert Media Clip button** 🎬 on the content placeholder

☐ In the Insert Video dialog box, navigate to the appropriate drive and folder, click the movie file you want, then click **Insert**

Insert a Sound on a Slide

Ribbon Method

☐ Click the **Insert tab**, click the **Audio button arrow** in the Media group, then click **Audio from File**

☐ In the Insert Audio dialog box, navigate to the appropriate drive and folder, click the sound file you want, then click **Insert**

☐ Drag the **sound icon** 🔊 to the appropriate location on the slide

OR

☐ Click the **Insert tab** on the Ribbon, click the **Audio button arrow** in the Media group, then click **Clip Art Audio**

☐ In the Clip Art task pane, type an appropriate keyword in the Search for text box, click **Go**, then click the sound file you want

☐ Drag the **sound icon** 🔊 to the appropriate location on the slide

Apply a Style to Video or Audio Content

Ribbon Method

☐ Select the video, click the **Video Tools Format tab**, click the **More button** ⬇ in the Video Styles group, then click a style in the gallery or click one or more of the **Video Shape**, **Video Border**, or **Video Effects buttons** in the Video Styles group and select options for formatting the video

OR

☐ Select the audio icon, click the **Audio Tools Format tab**, click the **More button** ⬇ in the Picture Styles group, then click a style in the gallery or click one or more of the **Picture Border** or **Picture Effects buttons** in the Picture Styles group and select options for formatting the audio content

Adjust Video Content

Ribbon Method

☐ Select the video content

☐ Click the **Video Tools Format tab**, then click an option in the Adjust group, shown in Figure PPT 3-16

☐ To adjust the Brightness and Contrast, click the **Corrections button**, then click an option in the gallery

☐ To apply color effects to the video, click the **Color button**, then click an option from the gallery

☐ To set the preview image for the video, click the **Poster Frame button**, then click Current Frame, Image from File, or Reset

☐ To remove all the formatting you have applied to the video, click the **Reset Design button arrow**, then choose Reset Design or Reset Design & Size

Figure PPT 3-16   **Adjust group on the Video Tools Format tab**

OR

☐ Select the video content

☐ Right-click the selection, then click **Format Video** on the shortcut menu to open the Format Video dialog box

☐ Click **Video** in the left pane, then select options from the Recolor and Brightness and Contrast sections in the right pane

☐ Click **Close**

Adjust Audio Content

Ribbon Method

☐ Select the audio content

☐ Click the **Audio Tools Format tab**, then click an option in the Adjust group

☐ To Sharpen and Soften or to adjust the Brightness and Contrast, click the **Corrections button**, then click an option in the gallery

☐ To apply color effects to the audio icon, click the **Color button**, then click a Color Saturation, Color Tone, or Recolor option from the gallery

☐ To apply artistic effects to the audio icon, click the **Artistic Effects button**, then click an option in the gallery

☐ To compress the image, click the **Compress Pictures button** 🖼, then select options from the Compress Pictures dialog box

☐ To replace the image with a new picture, click the **Change Picture button** 🖼, then navigate to the file you want to insert in the Insert Picture dialog box, then click **Insert**

☐ To remove all the formatting you have applied to the video, click the **Reset Picture button** 🖼, then choose Reset Picture or Reset Picture & Size

OR

☐ Select the audio content

☐ Right-click the selection, then click **Format Audio** on the shortcut menu to open the Format Audio dialog box

☐ Click **Picture Corrections** in the left pane, then select options from the Sharpen and Soften and Brightness and Contrast sections in the right pane

☐ Click **Picture Color** in the left pane, then select options from the Color Saturation, Color Tone, and Recolor sections in the right pane

☐ Click **Artistic Effects** in the left pane, then click the **Artistic Effects button** and choose an option from the gallery

☐ Click **Close**

Arrange Video or Audio Content

☐ Select the video or audio content

☐ Refer to Table PPT 3-1 to use the Ribbon Method or Shortcut Method to arrange video and audio content

Size Video or Audio Content

Ribbon Method

☐ Select the video or audio content

☐ Click the **Video Tools Format tab** or the **Audio Tools Format tab** on the Ribbon

☐ Click the **Shape Width text box** in the Size group and type a number, or click the up and down arrows to adjust the width

☐ Click the **Shape Height text box** in the Size group and type a number, or click the up and down arrows to adjust the height

OR

☐ Select the video or audio content

☐ Click the **Video Tools Format tab** or the **Audio Tools Format tab**, click the **Launcher** 🔲 in the Size group to open the Format Video or Format Audio dialog box

☐ Click **Size** in the left pane, then adjust the values in the Height and Width text boxes in the Size and rotate section

☐ Click **Close**

Shortcut Method

☐ Select the video or audio content

☐ Right-click the selection, then click **Size and Position** on the shortcut menu to open the Format Video or Format Audio dialog box

☐ Click **Size** in the left pane, then adjust the values in the Height and Width text boxes in the Size and rotate section

Adjust Video Playback Options

Ribbon Method

☐ Select the video content

☐ Click the **Video Tools Playback tab**, then select options in the Video Options group, as shown in Figure PPT 3-17

Figure PPT 3-17   Video Options group on the Video Tools Playback tab

Adjust Audio Playback Options

Ribbon Method

☐ Select the audio content

☐ Click the **Audio Tools Playback tab**, shown in Figure PPT 3-18, then select options in the Audio Options group

Figure PPT 3-18   Audio Options group on the Audio Tools Playback tab

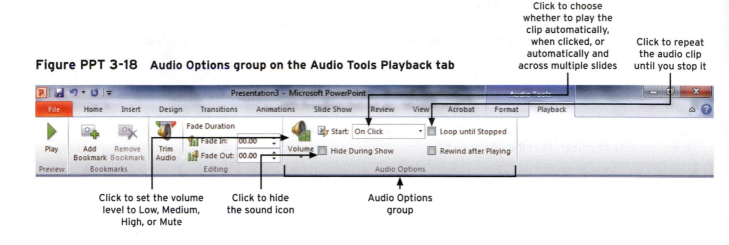

REVIEW QUESTIONS

TRUE/FALSE

Circle T if the statement is true or F if the statement is false.

T   F   1. Videos can be set to play automatically or when the mouse is clicked.

T   F   2. You cannot change the look of the audio icon.

T   F   3. The Text Pane is used to insert text in WordArt.

T   F   4. WordArt can be converted to SmartArt.

T   F   5. Shape Styles are quick styles for shapes.

MATCHING

Match the correct term in Column 2 to its description in Column 1.

Column 1	Column 2
_____ 1. Allows two or more objects to be treated as one.	A. Ungroup
_____ 2. Changes a color background of a picture to clear.	B. Group
_____ 3. Arranges the order of an object so that it is on the bottom of a stack.	C. Bring to front
_____ 4. Separates a grouped object.	D. Send to back
_____ 5. Arranges the order of an object so that it is on top of a stack.	E. Remove Background

PowerPoint

PROJECTS

Project PPT 3-1

1. Open the data file **Project PPT 3-1.pptx**.

2. Select the bulleted list on slide 5 and convert it to a SmartArt graphic using the **Vertical Picture Accent List**.

3. Click the Picture placeholder in the top rectangle and insert the Chrysanthemum picture from the Sample Pictures folder.

4. Insert the Tulips picture from the Sample Pictures folder in the bottom rectangle's placeholder.

5. Change the Color of the SmartArt graphic to **Colored Fill – Accent 2**.

6. Change the SmartArt Style to **3-D Inset**.

7. Select the top shape and add a new shape after it.

8. Delete the new shape.

9. On slide 6, click the Insert SmartArt Graphic placeholder and insert a Block Cycle SmartArt graphic from the Cycle category.

10. Type the following text (without bullets) in three of the rectangles and delete the two extra rectangles.
    - Three New Products/Services in Research and Development
    - Rollout Planned for New Division
    - Campaigns Targeting New Markets

11. Change the Color of the SmartArt graphic to **Colored Fill – Accent 2**.

12. Change the SmartArt Style to **3-D Inset**.

13. Change the layout to **Segmented Cycle**.

14. Save the presentation as **Quarterly Earnings** and close it.

Project PPT 3-2

1. Open the data file **Project PPT 3-2.pptx**.

2. Select the large blue rectangle behind the picture of the eagle and change the fill to **Blue, Accent 1, Lighter 60%**.

3. Change the black outline to ¼ point around the rectangle.

4. Select the eagle picture and change the picture style to **Simple Frame, White**.

5. Recolor the picture to **Sepia**.

6. Change the Brightness to +20% Contrast to -20%.

7. Click the Reset Picture button.

8. Draw a rectangle just a little bit bigger and on top of the eagle picture.

9. Change the fill to white.

10. Click the Send to Back button. Notice that the rectangle is all the way behind the large light blue rectangle.

11. Select the large light blue rectangle and send it to the back.

12. Select the white rectangle and the picture of the eagle and group them.

13. Flip the picture horizontally so the eagle is facing toward the words on the certificate.

14. In the Clip Art task pane, search for airplane and insert the clip art of the white airplane in a blue circle with the keywords *airplanes, airports, jets, places*.

15. Reduce the height to .7" and the width to .95".

16. Drag the clip art to the upper right corner of the slide.

17. Draw a line for a signature just above *Mary Martin, VP Human Resources*.

18. Save the presentation as **Award.pptx** and close it.

Project PPT 3-3

1. Open a new blank presentation.

2. Type **Nature** as the title and delete the subtitle placeholder.

3. Insert a Title and Content slide.

4. Click the Insert Media Clip button in the content placeholder and insert the video Wildlife from the Sample Videos library.

5. Apply the Moderate Beveled Rounded Rectangle video style.

6. Set the video to start automatically.

7. Type **Wildlife** as the title of the slide.

8. View the presentation in Slide Show view.

9. Save the presentation file as **Wildlife.pptx** and close it.

CRITICAL THINKING

Activity PPT 3-1

Create a new blank presentation. On a blank slide, insert a Hierarchy SmartArt diagram and create your family tree. Add text, choose colors and a layout of your choice, and add or remove shapes as needed. Save it with a meaningful name.

Activity PPT 3-2

Open the data file Activity PPT 3-2. Insert an appropriate audio file on one of the slides. Adjust the look of the icon and set appropriate playback options. Keep in mind the content of the presentation and the audience. Save the presentation with a meaningful name. Be prepared to share your choices with the class.

POWERPOINT OBJECTIVE 4: CREATING CHARTS AND TABLES

CONSTRUCT AND MODIFY TABLES

Insert a Table in a Slide

Ribbon Method

☐ Click the **Insert tab**, then click the **Table button** in the Tables group
☐ Drag in the grid to create the desired number of columns and rows for the table, as shown in Figure PPT 4-1

Figure PPT 4-1   Table button and menu

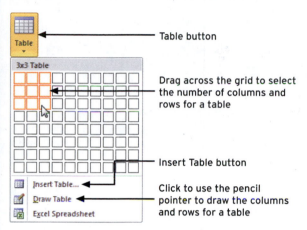

Table button

Drag across the grid to select
the number of columns and
rows for a table

Insert Table button

Click to use the pencil
pointer to draw the columns
and rows for a table

OR

☐ Click the **Insert tab**, click the **Table button** in the Tables group, then click **Insert Table**
☐ In the Insert Table dialog box, adjust the values in the Number of columns text box and the Number of rows text box to create the desired table, then click **OK**

OR

☐ Click the **Insert tab**, click the **Table button** in Tables group, then click **Draw Table**
☐ Drag the **Draw Table pencil** ✐ on the slide to draw the lines for the columns and rows in the table
☐ Use the commands in the Draw Borders group on the Table Tools Design tab to construct the table

Shortcut Method

☐ Select the slide containing a content placeholder
☐ Click the **Insert Table icon** ▦ in the content placeholder
☐ In the Insert Table dialog box, adjust the values in the Number of columns text box and the Number of rows text box to create the desired table, then click **OK**

Insert a Microsoft Excel Spreadsheet

Ribbon Method

☐ Click the **Insert tab**, click the **Table button** in the Tables group, then click **Excel Spreadsheet** to open a blank spreadsheet, as shown in Figure PPT 4-2
☐ Type data in the spreadsheet, drag the selection handles to resize the spreadsheet, and use the commands on the Ribbon as needed to format data
☐ Click outside the spreadsheet

PowerPoint

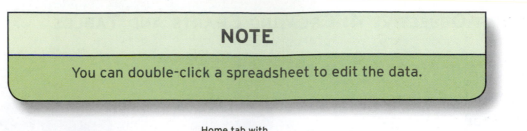

NOTE

You can double-click a spreadsheet to edit the data.

Figure PPT 4-2   Excel Spreadsheet

Home tab with
spreadsheet
formatting options

Spreadsheet

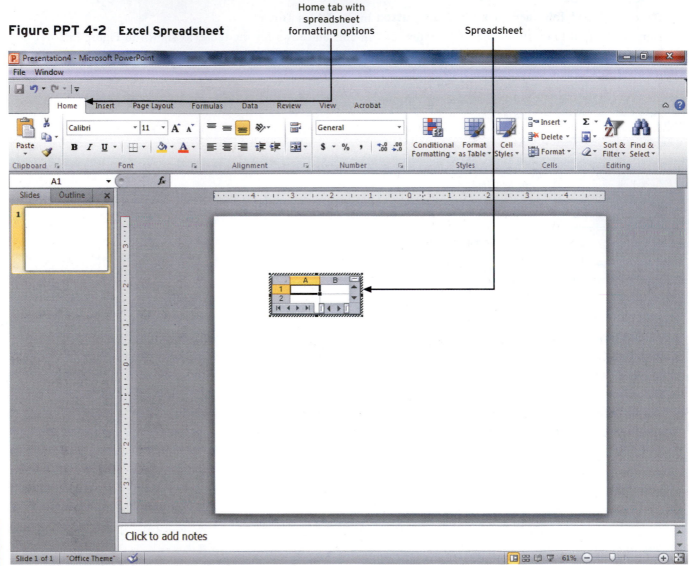

Apply Quick Styles to a Table

Ribbon Method

☐ Select the table

☐ Click the **Table Tools Design tab** on the Ribbon

☐ Click the **More button** in the Table Styles group, then click a **Quick Style** in the gallery shown in Figure PPT 4-3

Figure PPT 4-3   **Table Styles gallery**

Set Table Style Options

Ribbon Method

☐ Click in the table, click the **Table Tools Design tab**, click check boxes in the Table Style Options group, shown in Figure PPT 4-4 to apply special formatting styles to the checked options

Figure PPT 4-4   **Table Style Options group**

Add Shading

Ribbon Method

☐ Select the table

☐ Click the **Table Tools Design tab**, then click the **Shading button arrow** ![shading icon] in the Table Styles group to open the palette and menu shown in Figure PPT 4-5

☐ Click a color in the Theme Colors or Standard Colors section of the color palette, or click the No Fill, More Fill Colors, Picture, Gradient, Texture, or Table Background option to add shading

Figure PPT 4-5 Shading palette and menu

OR

☐ Select the table

☐ Click the **Home tab**, then click the **Shape Fill button** in the Drawing group

☐ Click a color in the Theme Colors or Standard Colors section of the color palette, or click the No Fill, More Fill Colors, Picture, Gradient, Texture, or Table Background option to add shading

Shortcut Method

☐ Right-click the table, then click the **Shape Fill button arrow** on the Mini Toolbar

☐ Click a color in the Theme Colors or Standard Colors section of the color palette, or click the No Fill, More Fill Colors, Picture, Gradient, or Texture option to add shading

OR

☐ Right-click the table, then click **Format Shape** on the shortcut menu

☐ In the right pane of the Format Shape dialog box, click one of the No fill, Solid fill, Gradient fill, Picture or texture fill, or Pattern fill option buttons, then adjust the options as desired

☐ Click **Close**

Add Borders

Ribbon Method

☐ Select the table

☐ Click the **Table Tools Design tab**, then click the **Borders button arrow** in the Table Styles group

☐ Click an option from the menu, shown in Figure PPT 4-6, to apply borders to the table

Figure PPT 4-6 Borders menu

No Border
All Borders
Outside Borders
Inside Borders
Top Border
Bottom Border
Left Border
Right Border
Inside Horizontal Border
Inside Vertical Border
Diagonal Down Border
Diagonal Up Border

Shortcut Method

- ☐ Right-click the table, then click the **Borders button arrow** on the Mini Toolbar
- ☐ Click an option from the menu to apply borders

Add Effects

Ribbon Method

- ☐ Select the table
- ☐ Click the **Table Tools Design tab**, then click the **Effects list arrow** in the Table Styles group
- ☐ Point to an option in the menu, then click an option in the submenu

Shortcut Method

- ☐ Right-click the table, then click the **Format Shape** on the shortcut menu
- ☐ Click **Shadow** or **Reflection** in the left pane, then adjust options in the right pane as desired to add effects
- ☐ Click **Close**

Change the Alignment of Columns and Rows

Ribbon Method

- ☐ Select the table or cells
- ☐ Click the **Table Tools Layout tab**, then click the appropriate alignment button in the Alignment group, shown in Figure PPT 4-7, to change the alignment
- ☐ Click the **Text Direction button** in the Alignment group, then click an option from the menu to change the text orientation; or click **More Options** to open the Format Text Effects dialog box and change the Text Box layout and features
- ☐ Click the **Cell Margins button** in the Alignment group, then click an option from the menu to change margins of the cells or click Custom Margins to open the Cell Text Layout dialog box where you can select custom settings for the Text layout and Internal margins

Shortcut Method

- ☐ Select the table or cells
- ☐ Right-click the selection, then click the **Align Text Left**, **Center**, or **Align Text Right** alignment button on the Mini Toolbar

Figure PPT 4-7   Table Tools Layout Tab

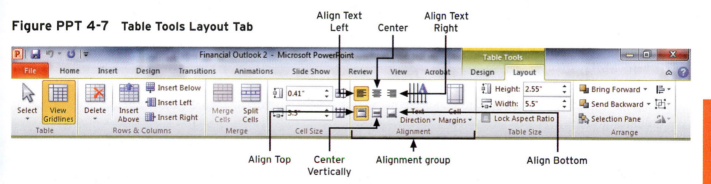

Resize Columns and Rows

Ribbon Method

- ☐ Click in the column or row, click the **Table Tools Layout tab**, then click the up and down arrows in the Table Row Height text box or the Table Column Width text box in the Cell Size group to increase or decrease the width of a column or height of a row

  OR

- ☐ Use the **Horizontal Resize pointer** or the **Vertical Resize pointer** to drag a column border left or right or a row border up or down to the desired position

Merge Table Cells

Ribbon Method

☐ Select the cells you want to merge into one cell, click the **Table Tools Layout tab**, then click the **Merge Cells button** in the Merge group

Shortcut Method

☐ Select the cells you want to merge into one cell, right-click the selection, then click **Merge Cells** on the shortcut menu

---

NOTE

A cell is the intersection of a row and column.

Split Table Cells

Ribbon Method

☐ Click the cell you want to split, click the **Table Tools Layout tab**, then click the **Split Cells button** in the Merge group
☐ In the Split Cells dialog box, enter the appropriate options, then click **OK**

Shortcut Method

☐ Select the cell you want to split, right-click, then click **Split Cells** on the shortcut menu
☐ In the Split Cells dialog box, enter the appropriate options, then click **OK**

Distribute Rows and Columns

Ribbon Method

☐ Select the rows or columns
☐ Click the **Table Tools Layout tab**, then click the **Distribute Rows button** 🎛 or the **Distribute Columns button** 🎛 in the Cell Size group to distribute the height of rows evenly among the rows or the width of columns evenly among the columns

Arrange a Table By Adding a Row

Ribbon Method

☐ Click in a table row
☐ Click the **Table Tools Layout tab**, then click the **Insert Above button** or **Insert Below button** in the Rows & Columns group
OR
☐ To insert multiple rows, select the number of rows you want to add
☐ Click the **Table Tools Layout tab**, then click the **Insert Above button** or **Insert Below button** in the Rows & Columns group to add the number of rows to the top or bottom of the selected rows

Shortcut Method

☐ Right-click in a table row
☐ Point to **Insert** on the shortcut menu, then click **Insert Rows Above** or **Insert Rows Below** from the submenu

Arrange a Table by Adding a Column

Ribbon Method

☐ Click in a table column
☐ Click the **Table Tools Layout tab**, then click the **Insert Left button** or **Insert Right button** in the Rows & Columns group

OR

☐ To add multiple columns at a time, select the number of columns you want to add
☐ Click the **Table Tools Layout tab**, then click the **Insert Left button** or **Insert Right button** in the Rows & Columns group to add the number of columns to the right or left of the selected columns

Shortcut Method

☐ Right-click in a table column
☐ Point to **Insert** on the shortcut menu, then click **Insert Columns to the Left** or **Insert Columns to the Right** from the submenu

Delete Columns and Rows

Ribbon Method

☐ Select the column(s) or row(s), click the **Table Tools Layout tab**, click the **Delete button** in the Rows & Columns group, then click **Delete Columns** or **Delete Rows**

Shortcut Method

☐ Select the column(s) or row(s), right-click the selection, then click **Delete Rows** or **Delete Columns** from the shortcut menu

OR

☐ Select the column(s) or row(s), then press **[Shift][Delete]**

INSERT AND MODIFY CHARTS

Insert a Chart on a Slide

Ribbon Method

☐ Click the **Insert tab** on the Ribbon, then click the **Chart button** in the Illustrations group
☐ In the left pane of the Insert Chart dialog box, shown in Figure PPT 4-8, click the chart type, using Table PPT 4-1 as a guide
☐ Click the thumbnail for the desired chart in the center pane, then click **OK**
☐ The screen splits into two windows: A PowerPoint window on the left with the sample chart on the slide, and an Excel window on the right with sample data in the worksheet, as shown in Figure PPT 4-9
☐ Replace the sample data in the Excel worksheet with the labels and values for your chart
☐ Click the **Close button** on the Microsoft Excel window

Figure PPT 4-8   Insert Chart dialog box

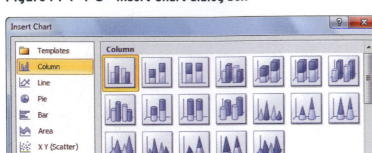

Figure PPT 4-9   Split screen

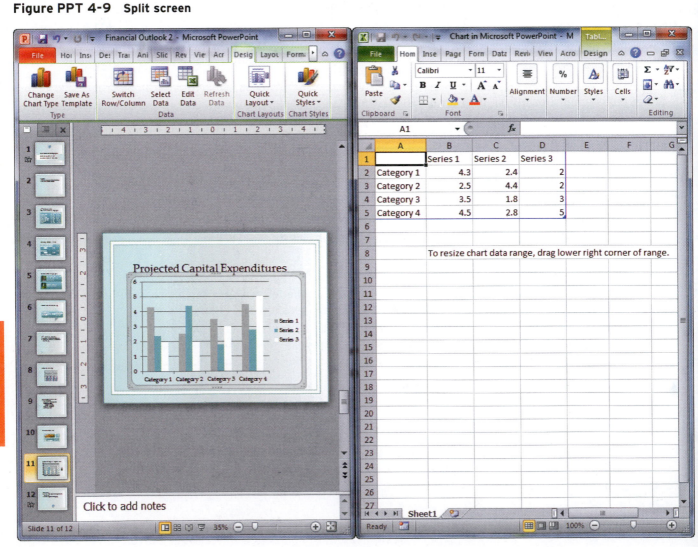

Shortcut Method

☐ Select the appropriate slide containing a content placeholder
☐ Click the **Insert Chart icon** ▥ in the content placeholder
☐ Follow the instructions in bullets 2–6 in the Insert a Chart on a Slide Ribbon Method on page PPT-69

Table PPT 4-1   Common Chart Types

Chart type	Icon	Used to show
Column	▥	Relative amounts for one or multiple values at different points in time (displays vertically)
Line	◪	Growth trends over time
Pie	◕	Proportions or percentages of parts to a whole
Bar	▤	Relative amounts for one or multiple values at different points in time (displays horizontally)
Area	◢	Differences between several sets of data over time
Scatter	⠿	Values that are not in categories and where each data point is a distinct measurement

Enter or Edit Chart Data

Ribbon Method

☐ Select the chart, click the **Chart Tools Design tab**, then click the **Edit Data button** in the Data group
☐ If necessary, resize the chart data range by dragging the lower right corner of the blue range line
☐ Click the cell where you want to enter or edit data
☐ Click the **Close button** ❌ on the Microsoft Excel window

NOTE

You don't have to save the Excel spreadsheet that contains the chart data. When you close Excel, the data is saved automatically.

Change the Chart Type

Ribbon Method

☐ Select the chart
☐ Click the **Chart Tools Design tab** on the Ribbon, then click the **Change Chart Type button** in the Type group
☐ In the left pane of the Change Chart Type dialog box, click the new chart type, click the thumbnail for the new chart in the center pane, then click **OK**

Shortcut Method

☐ Right-click the **chart**
☐ Click **Change Chart Type** in the shortcut menu
☐ In the left pane of the Change Chart Type dialog box, click the new chart type, click the thumbnail for the new chart type in the center pane, then click **OK**

Change the Chart Layout

Ribbon Method

☐ With a chart selected, click the **Chart Tools Design tab**, then click the **Quick Layout button** in the Chart Layouts group to open the Chart Layouts gallery, shown in Figure PPT 4-10
☐ Click a chart layout in the gallery

Figure PPT 4-10 **Chart Layout gallery**

Switch Row and Column

Ribbon Method

☐ Select the chart

☐ Click the **Chart Tools Design tab**, click the **Switch Row/Column button** in the Data group

OR

☐ Select the chart

☐ Click the **Chart Tools Design tab**, click the **Select Data button** in the Data group, then click the **Switch Row/Column button** in the Select Data Source dialog box

Select Data

Ribbon Method

☐ Select the chart

☐ Click the **Chart Tools Design tab**, then click the **Select Data button** in the Data group

☐ In the Select Data Source dialog box, shown in Figure PPT 4-11, select appropriate options to change the data range

☐ Click **OK**

Figure PPT 4-11 **Select Data Source dialog box**

APPLY CHART ELEMENTS

Identify Chart Elements

□ Refer to Figure PPT 4-12 to identify chart elements

Figure PPT 4-12   **Chart elements**

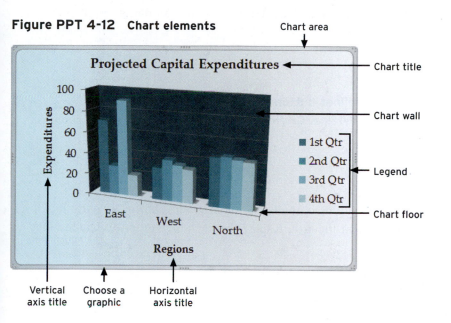

Add or Arrange the Location of Data Labels

Ribbon Method

□ With a chart selected, click the **Chart Tools Layout tab**, then click the **Data Labels button** in the Labels group

□ Click an option from the menu or click More Data Label Options to open the Format Data Labels dialog box where you can specify additional label options

Add a Chart Legend

Ribbon Method

□ Select the chart

□ Click the **Chart Tools Layout tab**, then click the **Legend button** in the Labels group

□ Click a legend style in the gallery or click **More Legend Options** to open the Format Legend dialog box and create a custom legend for the chart

Add a Chart Title

Ribbon Method

□ Select the chart

□ Click the **Chart Tools Layout tab**, then click the **Chart Title button** in the Labels group

□ Click a chart title style in the gallery or click **More Title Options** to open the Format Chart Title dialog box and create a custom title for the chart

Use Axes

Ribbon Method

□ Select the chart

□ Click the **Chart Tools Layout tab**, then click the **Axes button** in the Axes group

□ Point to **Primary Horizontal Axis** or **Primary Vertical Axis**, then click an option on the submenu

PowerPoint

Add Axis Titles

Ribbon Method

□ Select the chart

□ Click the **Chart Tools Layout tab**, then click the **Axis Titles button** in the Labels group

□ Point to **Primary Horizontal Axis Title** or **Primary Vertical Axis Title**, then click an option on the submenu

Use Gridlines

Ribbon Method

□ Select the chart

□ Click the **Chart Tools Layout tab**, then click the **Gridlines button** in the Axes group

□ Point to **Primary Horizontal Gridlines** or **Primary Vertical Gridlines**, then click an option on the submenu

Use Backgrounds

Ribbon Method

□ Select the chart

□ Click the **Chart Tools Layout tab**, click one of the buttons in the Background group, shown in Figure PPT 4-13

□ Click an option from the menu that is displayed to clear the area, display the default color, or display a dialog box with more options

Figure PPT 4-13 **Background group options**

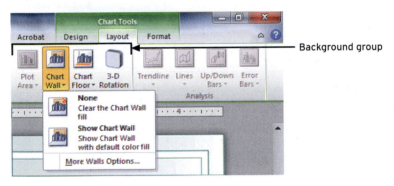

MANIPULATE CHART LAYOUTS

Select Chart Elements

Ribbon Method

□ Click in the chart

□ Click the **Chart Tools Format tab**, then click the **Chart Elements list arrow** in the Current Selection group, shown in Figure PPT 4-14

□ Click the chart element from the list that you want to format, then apply the formatting

Shortcut Method

□ Right-click a chart element, then click **Format <Chart Element>** on the shortcut menu

OR

□ Right-click a chart

□ Click the **Chart Elements list arrow** on the Mini Toolbar, click the chart element from the list that you want to format, then apply the formatting

Figure PPT 4-14 **Chart Tools Layout tab**

Chart Elements
list arrow

Format Selections

Ribbon Method

☐ Click a chart element to select it

☐ Click the **Chart Tools Format tab**, then click the **Format Selection** button in the Current Selection group to open an appropriate dialog box where you can apply formatting for the selected chart element

☐ Click the **Close button**

MANIPULATE CHART ELEMENTS

Arrange Chart Elements

Ribbon Method

☐ Click a chart or chart element

☐ Click the **Chart Tools Format tab**, click a button in the Arrange group to Bring Forward, Send Backward, Align, Group or Ungroup, or Rotate the element

Specify a Precise Position for a Chart

Ribbon Method

☐ Click the chart

☐ Click the **Chart Tools Format tab**, then click the **Launcher** 🔲 in the Size group to open the Format Chart Area dialog box

☐ Click **Position** in the left pane

☐ Adjust the values in the Horizontal, Vertical, and From boxes to position the chart at a specific location on the slide

Shortcut Method

☐ Right-click the chart, then click **Format Chart Area** on the shortcut menu to open the Format Chart Area dialog box

☐ Follow the steps in bullets 3-4 under Specify a Precise Position for a Chart Ribbon Method above

Apply Effects

Ribbon Method

☐ Select a text chart element

☐ Click the **Chart Tools Format tab**, click the **Text Effects button** 🄰 in the WordArt Styles group, point to a category on the menu, then click an option from the submenu

OR

☐ Select a text chart element

☐ Click the **Chart Tools Format tab**, click the **Launcher** 🔲 in the WordArt Styles group, to open the Format Text Effects dialog box

☐ Click a category in the left pane, then adjust options in the right pane to format text effects

☐ Click **Close**

OR

☐ Select a graphical chart element

☐ Click the **Chart Tools Format tab**, click the **Shape Effects button** in the Shape Styles group, point to a category on the menu, then click an option from the submenu

OR

☐ Select a graphical chart element

☐ Click the **Chart Tools Format tab**, click the **Launcher** ⬚ in the Shape Styles group to open a related dialog box

☐ Click a category in the left pane, then adjust options in the right pane to format effects

Shortcut Method

☐ Right-click a graphical or textual chart element

☐ Click **Format <Chart Element>** on the shortcut menu to open a related dialog box

☐ Click a category in the left pane, then adjust options in the right pane to format effects

Resize Chart Elements

Ribbon Method

☐ Select a text chart element

☐ Click the **Home tab**, click the **Font Size list arrow** in the Font group, then click an option from the list

Shortcut Method

☐ Right-click a text chart element

☐ Click the **Font Size list arrow** on the Mini Toolbar, then click an option from the list

OR

☐ Select a graphical chart element

☐ Drag one or more selection handles to resize the element

Apply Quick Styles

Ribbon Method

☐ Select the chart

☐ Click the **Chart Tools Design tab**, then click the **More button** ⬚ in the Chart Styles group

☐ Click an option in the gallery shown in Figure PPT 4-15

Figure PPT 4-15   Chart Styles gallery

OR
☐ Select a graphical chart element
☐ Click the **Chart Tools Format tab**, then click the **More button** ⊡ in the Shape Styles group
☐ Click an option in the gallery
OR
☐ Select a text chart element
☐ Click the **Chart Tools Format tab**, then click the **More button** ⊡ in the WordArt Styles group
☐ Click an option in the gallery

Apply a Border

Ribbon Method

☐ Select the chart
☐ Click the **Chart Tools Format tab**, then click the **Shape Outline button arrow** in the Shape Styles group
☐ Click a color in the Theme Colors or Standard Colors section of the color palette, or click the No Outline, More Outline Colors, Weight, or Dashes option to apply a border

Shortcut Method

☐ Right-click the chart
☐ Click the **Shape Outline button arrow** 🖌▾ on the Mini Toolbar
☐ Click a color in the Theme Colors or Standard Colors section of the color palette, or click the No Outline, More Outline Colors, Weight, or Dashes option to apply a border

Add Hyperlinks

Ribbon Method

☐ Select the chart or chart element
☐ Click the **Insert tab**, then click the **Hyperlink button** in the Links group
☐ In the Insert Hyperlink dialog box, click the option you want to link to in the Link to list, then complete the rest of the Insert Hyperlink dialog box based on the Link to option you selected
☐ Click **OK**

Shortcut Method

☐ Select the chart or chart element you want to create as a hyperlink, then press **[CTRL][K]**
☐ Follow the steps in bullets 3-4 of the Add Hyperlinks Ribbon Method above

REVIEW QUESTIONS

FILL IN THE BLANK

Complete the following sentences by writing the correct word or words in the blanks provided.

1. To replace a column chart with a line chart, click the _____ button.

2. The _____ button lets you make changes to chart data.

3. The _____ command formats the height of all rows in a table evenly.

4. The chart legend and chart title are examples of chart _____.

5. Shadows and Reflections are examples of _____.

MULTIPLE CHOICE

Select the best response for the following statements.

1. A chart is based on data in a _____.
   - A. Microsoft Excel worksheet
   - B. Microsoft PowerPoint presentation
   - C. Microsoft Access database
   - D. Microsoft Word document

2. The _____ button is used to combine multiple cells into one.
   - A. Split Cells
   - B. Merge Cells
   - C. Insert Left
   - D. Distribute Columns

3. The command to insert an Excel spreadsheet is on the _____ button on the Insert tab.
   - A. Chart
   - B. Table
   - C. Hyperlink
   - D. Picture

4. The _____ button allows you to rotate text 90 degrees.
   - A. Effects
   - B. Text Box
   - C. Text Direction
   - D. Align Text

5. Header Row and Total Row are _____.
   - A. Chart Layouts
   - B. Table Styles
   - C. Table Style Options
   - D. Quick Styles

PROJECTS

Project PPT 4-1

1. Open the file **Project PPT 4-1.pptx**.

2. Go to slide 10 and click the Table placeholder to insert a table with 3 columns and 3 rows.

3. Enter the following data in the table.

	Estimated	% Change
Revenue Growth	$14.2M	(0.5%)
Capital Expenditures	$12.5M	0.3%

4. Apply the **Themed Style 2 – Accent 2** quick style, the third option on the second row.

5. In the first row, drag the lower gridline to increase its size to approximately 1 ½" tall.

6. Select the **Estimated** heading and rotate it to 270°.

7. Select the **% Change** heading and rotate it to 270°.

8. Vertically center align both the Estimated and % Change headings.

9. In the first row, first column, insert the **Tulips** picture from the Sample Pictures folder as the fill.

10. Insert a new row below the second row and insert the following data.

EPS	$1.6M	0.7%

11. Change the width of the first column to 3.5".

12. Change the width of the second and third columns to 1".

13. Position the table in the center of the slide.

14. Save the presentation file as **Financial Outlook 2.pptx**.

Project PPT 4-2

1. Open the file **Project PPT 4-2.pptx**.

2. On slide 11, click the Insert Chart placeholder and insert a Clustered Column chart.

3. Replace the data in the sample spreadsheet with the data below.

	1st Qtr	2nd Qtr	3rd Qtr	4th Qtr
East	20.4	27.4	90	20.4
West	30.6	38.6	34.6	31.6
North	45.9	46.9	45	43.9

4. Change the chart type to **3-D Clustered Column**.

5. Change the chart style to **Style 20**.

6. Add the solid fill Dark Teal, Background 2 to the chart wall.

7. Edit the data in cell B2 (East, 1st Qtr) to **70.4**.

8. On Slide 8, add a legend to the right side of the chart using the Show Legend at Right command.

9. Add the title **2016** above the chart.

10. Change the Chart Layout to **Layout 1**.

11. Change the chart style to **Style 20**.

12. Save the presentation as **Financial Outlook 3** and close it.

CRITICAL THINKING

Activity PPT 4-1

Create a pie chart that shows how you use your time on a typical day. Be sure to account for all 24 hours in a day. Replace the sample data with your own data. Experiment, format, and change chart attributes until your chart is complete. Be prepared to present your chart to the class. Do you think you spend your time wisely? Why or why not? Save it with a meaningful name.

PowerPoint

POWERPOINT OBJECTIVE 5: APPLYING TRANSITIONS AND ANIMATIONS

APPLY BUILT-IN AND CUSTOM ANIMATIONS

Insert a Built-in Animation

Ribbon Method
- □ Select the object or text to be animated
- □ Click the **Animations tab** on the Ribbon, then click the **Animation Styles button** in the Animation group
- □ Click an option in the Entrance, Emphasis, or Exit sections of the gallery, shown in Figure PPT 5-1

Figure PPT 5-1   Animation Styles gallery

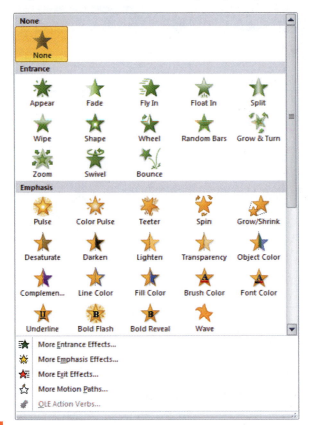

OR
- □ After applying one animation on the slide, select another object or text block to be animated
- □ Click the **Animations tab**, then click the **Add Animation button** in the Advanced Animation group
- □ Click an option in the Entrance, Emphasis, Exit, or Motion Paths sections of the gallery to apply the second animation

Create Custom Animations

Ribbon Method
- □ Select the object or text to be animated
- □ Click the **Animations tab**, click the **Animation Styles button** in the Animation group, then click an option in the gallery
- □ With the animation selected, click the **Animation Pane button** in the Advanced Animation group
- □ In the Animation Pane, right-click the animation or click the animation list arrow, as shown in Figure PPT 5-2

☐ Click an option in the menu to customize the animation or to open a dialog box with additional options for customization

Figure PPT 5-2   Animation Pane

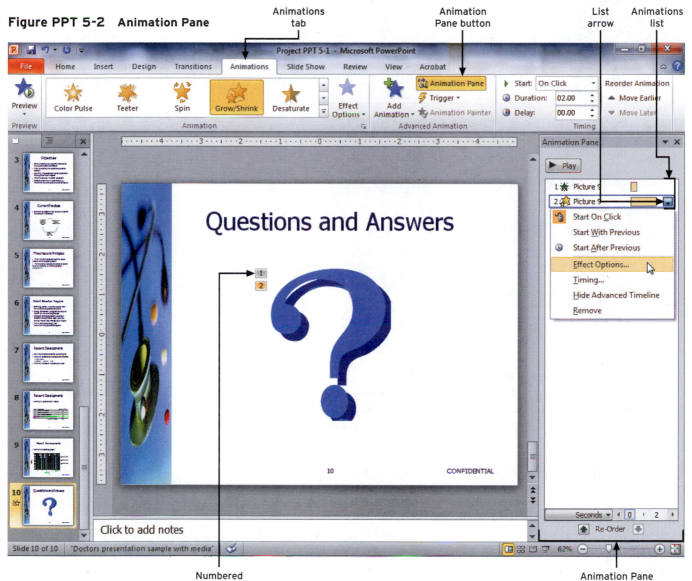

Numbered animation labels

Animation Pane

Use More Entrance

Ribbon Method

☐ Select the text or object to be animated

☐ Click the **Animations tab**, click the **Animation Styles button** in the Animation group, then click **More Entrance Effects** to open the Change Entrance Effect dialog box, shown in Figure PPT 5-3

☐ Click an option from the Basic, Subtle, Moderate, or Exciting sections

☐ Click **OK**

Figure PPT 5-3   Change Entrance Effect dialog box

Use More Emphasis

Ribbon Method

☐ Select the text or object to be animated

☐ Click the **Animations tab**, click the **Animate Styles button** in the Animation group, then click **More Emphasis Effects** to open the Change Emphasis Effect dialog box

☐ Click an option from the Basic, Subtle, Moderate, or Exciting sections

☐ Click **OK**

Use More Exit Effects

Ribbon Method

☐ Select the text or object to be animated

☐ Click the **Animations tab**, click the **Animation Styles button** in the Animation group, then click **More Exit Effects** to open the Change Exit Effect dialog box

☐ Click an option from the Basic, Subtle, Moderate, or Exciting sections

☐ Click **OK**

Use More Motion Paths

Ribbon Method

☐ Select the text or object to be animated

☐ Click the **Animations tab**, click the **Animation Styles button** in the Animation group, then click **More Motion Paths** to open the Change Motion Path dialog box, shown in Figure PPT 5-4

☐ Click an option from the Basic, Lines & Curves, or Special sections

☐ Click **OK**

Figure PPT 5-4   Change Motion Path dialog box

APPLY EFFECT AND PATH OPTIONS

Apply Effect Options

Ribbon Method

☐ Select the text or object with an animation applied
☐ Click the **Effect Options button** in the Animation group, then click an option in the gallery
   OR
☐ Select the text or object with an animation applied
☐ Click the **Launcher** ⌾ in the Animation group to open a related dialog box
☐ Click the **Effect tab**
☐ Select appropriate options in the dialog box
☐ Click **OK**
   OR
☐ Select the animated text or object
☐ Click the **Animations tab**, then click the **Animation Pane button** in the Advanced Animation group
☐ In the Animation Pane, right-click the animation or click the animation list arrow, then click **Effect Options** to open the Effect Options dialog box
☐ Adjust options in the Enhancements and/or Settings sections of the dialog box

Modify Path Options

Ribbon Method

☐ Select the text or object with a motion path applied
☐ Click the **Animations tab**, click the **Effect Options button** in the Animation group
☐ Click an option in the Shapes section to change the shape of the path, click an option in the Sequence section to change the order of animation, click an option in the Origin section to lock or unlock the effect, or click an option in the Path section to edit the points of the path or reverse its direction
   OR
☐ Select the animated text or object

□ Click the **Animations tab**, then click the **Animation Pane button** in the Advanced Animation group

□ In the Animation Pane, right-click the animation or click the animation list arrow, then click **Effect Options** to open a related dialog box

□ Adjust options in the Settings section of the dialog box

Set Timing

Ribbon Method

□ Select the animated text or object

□ Click the **Animations tab**, then select options in the Timing group shown in Figure PPT 5-5

Figure PPT 5-5   Timing group on the Animations tab

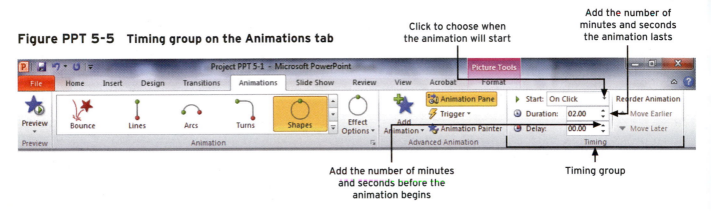

OR

□ Select the animated text or object

□ Click the **Animations tab**, then click the **Animation Pane button** in the Advanced Animation group

□ In the Animation Pane, right-click the animation or click the animation list arrow, then click **Timing** to open a related dialog box with the Timing tab displayed, as shown in Figure PPT 5-6

□ Select appropriate options, then click **OK**

Figure PPT 5-6   Timing tab

OR

□ Select the text or object with an animation applied

□ Click the **Launcher** ⬚ in the Animation group to open a related dialog box

□ Click the **Timing tab**

☐ Select appropriate options in the dialog box

☐ Click **OK**

Set Start Options

Ribbon Method

☐ Select the animated object or text

☐ Click the **Animations tab**, click the **Start list arrow** in the Timing group, then select an option

   OR

☐ Select the animated object or text

☐ Click the **Animations tab** on the Ribbon, then click the **Animation Pane button**

☐ If necessary, click the animation in the Animation Pane to select it

☐ Right-click the animation or click the animation list arrow, then click a Start option on the menu

   OR

☐ Select the text or object with an animation applied

☐ Click the **Launcher** 🔲 in the Animation group to open a related dialog box

☐ Click the **Timing tab**

☐ Click the **Start list arrow**, then click an option from the list

☐ Click **OK**

MANIPULATE ANIMATIONS

Change the Direction of an Animation

Ribbon Method

☐ Select the text or object with an animation applied

☐ Click the **Animations tab**, then click the **Effect Options button** in the Animation group

☐ Click an option in the menu, shown in Figure PPT 5-7 (Options in this menu vary depending on the type of animation applied.)

Figure PPT 5-7   **Effect Options button and menu**

   OR

☐ Select the text or object with an animation applied

□ Click the **Launcher** 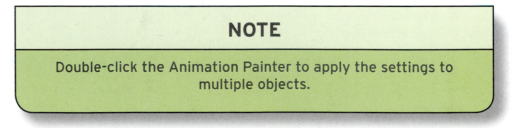 in the Animation group to a related dialog box with the Effect tab displayed

□ In the Settings section, click the **Direction list arrow**, then click an option from the list

□ Click **OK**

   OR

□ Select the text or object with an animation applied

□ Click the **Animations tab**, then click the **Animation Pane button** in the Advanced Animation group

□ In the Animation Pane, right-click the animation or click the animation list arrow, then click **Effect Options** to open a related dialog box with the Effects tab displayed

□ In the Settings section, click the **Direction list arrow**, then click an option from the list

□ Click **OK**

Attach a Sound to an Animation

Ribbon Method

□ Select the text or object with an animation

□ Click the **Animations tab**, then click the **Launcher** in the Animation group to open a related dialog box

□ Click the **Effect tab**, click the **Sound list arrow**, then click an option from the list

□ Click **OK**

   OR

□ Click the **Animations tab**, click the **Animation Pane button** in the Advanced Animation group

□ In the Animation Pane, right-click the animation or click the list arrow, then click **Effect Options** to open a related dialog box

□ Click the **Effect tab**, click the **Sound list arrow**, then click an option from the list

□ Click **OK**

Use the Animation Painter

Ribbon Method

□ Select the text or object with an animation applied

□ Click the **Animations tab**, click the **Animation Painter button** in the Advanced Animation group, then click an object or text box with the **Animation Painter pointer** to apply the animation

Shortcut Method

□ Select the text or object with an animation applied

□ Press **[Alt][Shift][C]**

□ Click an object with the **Animation Painter pointer** to apply the animation

---

NOTE

Double-click the Animation Painter to apply the settings to multiple objects.

Reorder Animation

Ribbon Method

□ Select the text or object with an animation effect applied

□ Click the **Animations tab**, click the **Move Earlier button** or **Move Later button** in the Reorder Animation section of the Timing group to move the animation earlier or later in the play order

OR
- □ Select the text or object with an animation effect applied
- □ Click the **Animations tab**, click the **Animation Pane button** in the Advanced Animation group
- □ Select the animation in the Animation Pane
- □ Click the **Re-Order Up arrow** ⬆ or the **Re-Order Down arrow** ⬇ to move the animation earlier or later in the play order

Select Text Options
Ribbon Method
- □ Select the text with an animation effect applied
- □ On the Animations tab, click the **Launcher** ▣ in the Animation group to open a related dialog box
- □ Click the **Text Animation tab**, shown in Figure PPT 5-8, click the **Group text list arrow** and click an option in the list
- □ Select other appropriate options in the dialog box, then click **OK**

Figure PPT 5-8   Text Animation tab

Remove Animations from Text or an Object
Ribbon Method
- □ Select the animated text or object
- □ Click the **Animations tab** on the Ribbon, click the **Animation Styles button** in the Animation group, then click **None**

  OR
- □ Select the animated text or object
- □ Click the **Animations tab** on the Ribbon, then click the **Animation Pane button** in the Advanced Animation group
- □ In the Animation Pane, right-click the animation or click the animation list arrow, then click **Remove**

  OR
- □ Select the numbered animation label beside the animated object on the slide
- □ Press **[Delete]**

Preview an Animation Effect
Ribbon Method
- □ Display the slide with the animated text or object
- □ Click the **Animations tab** on the Ribbon, then click the **Preview button** in the Preview group

APPLY AND MODIFY TRANSITIONS BETWEEN SLIDES

Add Transitions Between Slides

Ribbon Method

☐ Display a slide, then click the **Transitions tab** on the Ribbon

☐ Click the **More button** ⊟ in the Transition to This Slide group to open the Transitions gallery, shown in Figure PPT 5-9, then click an effect in the gallery

☐ To apply the transition to all the slides in the presentation, click the **Apply To All button** in the Timing group

Figure PPT 5-9   Transitions gallery

Modify a Transition Effect

Ribbon Method

☐ Select the slide or slides with a transition applied

☐ Click the **Transitions tab**, click the **Effect Options button** in the Transition to This Slide group and click an option in the list

Add Sound to a Transition

Ribbon Method

☐ Select the slide or slides with a transition effect applied

☐ Click the **Transitions tab**, click the **Sound list arrow** in the Timing group, then click an option from the list shown in Figure PPT 5-10

Figure PPT 5-10   Sound list arrow

Modify Transition Duration

Ribbon Method

□ Select the slide or slides with a transition effect applied

□ Click the **Transitions tab**, click the up and down arrows in the **Duration box** in the Timing group to set the length of the transition

Set up Manual or Automatically Timed Advance Options

Ribbon Method

□ Select the slide or slides with a transition applied

□ Click the **Transitions tab**, then click the **On Mouse Click check box** in the Timing group to set the next slide to advance when you click the mouse or click the **After check box** in the Timing group and adjust the number of minutes and seconds in the text box to set the amount of time before the slide advances

Remove Transitions Between Selected Slides

Ribbon Method

□ Select the slide or slides from which you want to remove the transitions

□ Click the **Transitions tab** on the Ribbon

□ Click the **More button** [▼] in the Transition to This Slide group, then click **None** in the gallery

PowerPoint

REVIEW QUESTIONS

TRUE/FALSE

Circle T if the statement is true or F if the statement is false.

T   F   1. The duration of an animation refers to when an animation starts to play.

T   F   2. To advance a slide automatically, click the On Mouse Click check box in the Timing group on the Transitions tab.

T   F   3. You can customize an animation in the Animation Pane.

T   F   4. Entrance, Emphasis, and Exit are types of transition effects.

T   F   5. You can change the order in which animation effects play on a slide.

MATCHING

Match the correct term in Column 2 to its description in Column 1.

Column 1

_____   1. Applies the same transition effect to all the slides in the presentation.

_____   2. Allows you to specify options for an applied animation.

_____   3. Used to copy animation settings from one object and apply them to other objects.

_____   4. An effect that controls how one slide is removed from the screen and the next one appears.

_____   5. A visual or sound effect added to text or objects that controls the flow of information and adds interest to a presentation.

Column 2

A. Animation Painter

B. Transition

C. Effect Options button

D. Animation

E. Apply to All button

PROJECTS

Project PPT 5-1

1. Open the data file **Project PPT 5-1.pptx**.

2. On slide 10, select the question mark clip art and apply an Entrance Fade animation.

3. Change the duration of the animation to 2 seconds.

4. Add the Grow/Shrink Emphasis effect starting after the previous animation.

5. Change the effect options for the Direction to Horizontal and the Amount to Smaller.

6. Preview the animation on the slide.

7. Remove the Grow/Shrink Emphasis effect.

8. Add the Shapes motion path.

9. Add the Dynamic Content, Rotate transition to all slides.

10. Set the timing on all slides so that each slide is displayed for three seconds before the next slide advances automatically.

11. View the slide show from the beginning.

12. Save the presentation as **Seminar.pptx** and close it.

PowerPoint

Project PPT 5-2

1. Open the data file **Project PPT 5-2.pptx**.

2. On slide 1, add a Fly in Entrance effect to the airplane clip art. Modify the effect options so the Fly In comes from the Bottom-Right.

3. On slide 12, add a Fly Out Exit effect to the airplane clip art. Modify the effect so the Fly Out goes to Top-Right.

4. Add the Wind sound to the Fly Out effect.

5. Add a delay of two seconds to the animation effect.

6. Add the Shape Entrance effect to the Summary title.

7. Reorder the animations on the slide to have the animation on the title play first.

8. Use the Animation Painter to apply the effect to the title of each slide in the presentation, including the first slide.

9. Apply the Cover transition to all slides in the presentation.

10. Change the transition effect direction for each of the following slides:
    - Slide 2: From Top
    - Slide 4: From Left
    - Slide 6: From Bottom
    - Slide 8: From Top-Right
    - Slide 10: From Bottom-Right
    - Slide 12: From Top-Left

11. View the slide show from the beginning.

12. Save the presentation as **Blue Yonder.pptx** and close it.

CRITICAL THINKING

Activity PPT 5-1

Open the PowerPoint Help window. Search for the videos *Animation basics for PowerPoint 2010* and *Add transitions to a PowerPoint presentation* and watch them. What is the purpose of adding animations and transitions to a presentation? How do you decide when it is appropriate to use animations and transitions? Create at least a five-slide presentation about what you think are the Do's and Don'ts of using animations and transitions. Be prepared to share your presentation with the class.

PowerPoint

POWERPOINT OBJECTIVE 6: COLLABORATING ON PRESENTATIONS

MANAGE COMMENTS IN PRESENTATIONS

Insert a Comment

Ribbon Method

☐ Select the appropriate slide or object to which the comment applies

☐ Click the **Review tab** on the Ribbon, click the **New Comment button** in the Comments group, then type the comment in the balloon that opens, as shown in Figure PPT 6-1

Figure PPT 6-1   Review tab and Comment balloon

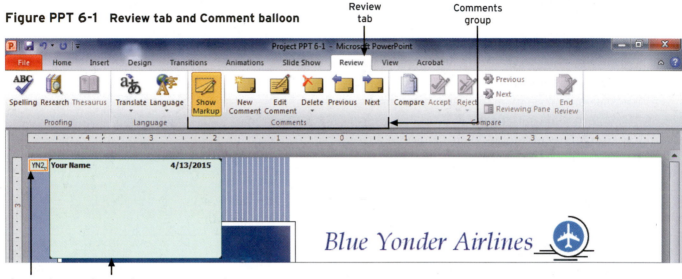

Comment thumbnail

Comment balloon

Shortcut Method

☐ Right-click an existing comment thumbnail, then click **New Comment** on the shortcut menu

☐ Type the comment in the balloon that opens

Edit a Comment

Ribbon Method

☐ Select a comment thumbnail

☐ Click the **Review tab** on the Ribbon, then click **Edit Comment** in the Comments group to open the comment for editing

☐ Use standard text editing techniques to modify the comment

Shortcut Method

☐ Right-click a comment thumbnail, as shown in Figure PPT 6-2, then click **Edit Comment** on the shortcut menu to open the comment for editing

☐ Use standard text editing techniques to modify the comment

Figure PPT 6-2   Comment thumbnail and shortcut menu

Right-click a comment thumbnail to display the shortcut menu

Show or Hide Markup

Ribbon Method

☐ Click the **Review tab** on the Ribbon, then click the **Show Markup button** in the Comments group to show comments, or to hide comments if they are showing

Move to the Previous or Next Comment

Ribbon Method

☐ If the comments are not visible, click the **Review tab** on the Ribbon, then click the **Show Markup button** in the Comments group

☐ Click the **Next** and **Previous buttons** in the Comments group as needed, then click each comment thumbnail on the slides to review the comments

Delete Comments

Ribbon Method

☐ Select a comment thumbnail

☐ Click the **Review tab** on the Ribbon, then click the **Delete Comment button** in the Comments group

OR

☐ Click the **Review tab** on the Ribbon, click the **Delete Comment list arrow** in the Comments group, then click **Delete All Markup on the Current Slide** or **Delete All Markup in this Presentation** to delete the desired comments

Shortcut Method

☐ Right-click the comment thumbnail, then click **Delete Comment** on the shortcut menu to delete the current comment

OR

☐ Select a comment thumbnail

☐ Press **[Delete]**

APPLY PROOFING TOOLS

Check Spelling

Ribbon Method

☐ Click the **Review tab**, then click the **Spelling button** in the Proofing group

☐ In the Spelling dialog box, shown in Figure PPT 6-3, make appropriate selections and use the buttons to ignore or change possible spelling errors

Shortcut Method

☐ Press **[F7]** to open the Spelling dialog box, then follow the steps in bullet 2 of the Check Spelling Ribbon Method

Figure PPT 6-3   **Spelling dialog box**

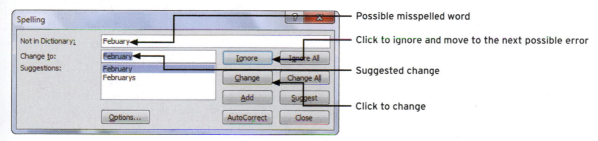

> **NOTE**
>
> Word automatically checks spelling as you type. PowerPoint flags words that might be misspelled with a wavy red underline. You can right-click a word that has a red wavy line and see a shortcut menu with suggestions for corrections.

Use the Thesaurus

Ribbon Method

☐ Position the insertion point in the word you would like to search for in the Thesaurus

☐ Click the **Review tab**, click the **Thesaurus button** in the Proofing group to open the Research task pane with a list of synonyms related to the search word

☐ To replace the search word with the new word, click the list arrow on the right side of the word, then click **Insert**, as shown in Figure PPT 6-4

☐ To find synonyms for a word in the list, double-click the word

☐ To select a different reference in which to search, click the **Reference Books list arrow**

Shortcut Method

☐ To look up a synonym for a word, right-click the word, point to **Synonyms** on the shortcut menu, then click an option from the submenu to replace it or click **Thesaurus** to open the Research Task pane where you can select additional search options

    OR

☐ To look up a synonym for a word, select the word, then press **[Shift][F7]**

☐ Follow the steps in bullets 3-5 in Use the Thesaurus Ribbon Method above

Figure PPT 6-4 **Inserting a synonym from the Thesaurus**

Research task pane

Search word

Reference Books list arrow

Word to search for in the Thesaurus

Click Insert to replace the selected word in the presentation with this synonym

Compare and Combine Presentations

Ribbon Method

☐ Open the presentation

☐ Click the **Review tab**, click the **Compare button** in the Compare group

☐ In the Choose File to Merge with Current Presentation dialog box, navigate to the file, click it, then click the **Merge button**

☐ Review the changes listed in the Reviewing pane, shown in Figure PPT 6-5

☐ Click a change listed in the Reviewing pane to display the item with a checkbox

☐ Click the checkbox to accept the change

☐ Save the merged file, then click the **End Review button** in the Compare group and click **Yes** or **No** to end the review

Figure PPT 6-5 **Merged presentation**

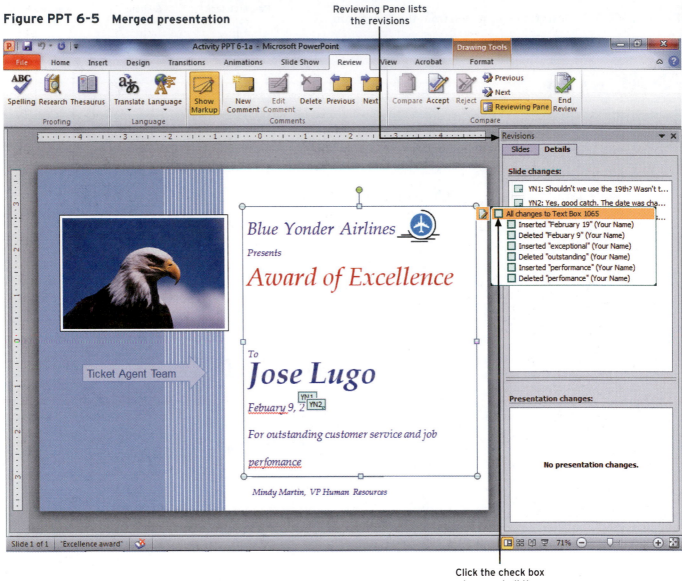

REVIEW QUESTIONS

FILL IN THE BLANK

Complete the following sentences by writing the correct word or words in the blanks provided.

1. When you click the New Comment button, a _____ opens in which you can type a comment.

2. To edit a comment, you must first select the comment _____.

3. The Previous and Next buttons are used to move between _____.

4. The results of a Thesaurus search are displayed in the _____ pane.

5. The New Comment button is located on the _____ tab.

MULTIPLE CHOICE

Select the best response for the following statements.

1. Use the _____ button to delete all the comments in a presentation.
   - A. Edit Comment
   - B. New Comment
   - C. Delete Comment
   - D. Show Markup

2. The Show Markup button displays _____.
   - A. slides
   - B. comments
   - C. handouts
   - D. outlines

3. Press _____ to start the spelling checker.
   - A. [Delete]
   - B. [F7]
   - C. [F9]
   - D. [Ctrl][S]

4. The _____ button lets you merge two presentations.
   - A. New Comment
   - B. Thesaurus
   - C. Compare
   - D. Show Markup

5. Use the _____ button to look up a synonym for a word.
   - A. Show Markup
   - B. Spelling
   - C. Compare
   - D. Thesaurus

PROJECTS

Project PPT 6-1

1. Open the data file **Project PPT 6-1.pptx**.

2. Check the spelling of the presentation and correct the two errors.

3. Show the Markup.

4. Read the comment.

5. Insert a new comment. Type **Yes, good catch. The date was changed to February 19. I'll make the change.**

6. Change the date to **February 19.**

7. Hide Markup.

8. Use the Thesaurus to find a synonym for the word *outstanding* near the bottom of the slide. Replace the word *outstanding* with the word *exceptional*.

9. Close the Research task pane if it is open.

10. Show Markup. Edit the comment you inserted. Change the last sentence to **I made the change.**

11. Delete the YN1 comment.

12. Save the presentation as **Lugo Award.pptx** and close it.

CRITICAL THINKING

Activity PPT 6-1

Open **Activity PPT 6-1a.pptx**. Compare and combine it with **Activity PPT 6-1b.pptx**. Review the changes. Accept all the changes in the text box, end the review, then save the file with the filename **Merged Presentation.pptx**.

Activity PPT 6-2

Open a presentation you have worked with in this unit. Critique the presentation by inserting comments explaining the strengths and weaknesses of the presentation in your opinion. Be sure to provide positive feedback where appropriate and carefully word your comments. Be prepared to share your critique with the class.

POWERPOINT OBJECTIVE 7: PREPARING PRESENTATIONS FOR DELIVERY

SAVE PRESENTATIONS

Save a Presentation as a Picture Presentation

Ribbon Method

☐ Click the **File tab**, click **Save & Send**, then click **Change File Type** in the File Types section of the center pane

☐ In the right pane, click **PowerPoint Picture Presentation** in the Presentation File Types section as shown in Figure PPT 7-1

☐ Click **Save As**

☐ In the Save As dialog box, type an appropriate filename in the File name text box, then click **Save**

☐ Click **OK**

OR

☐ Click the **File tab**, then click **Save As**

☐ In the Save As dialog box, type an appropriate filename in the File name text box, click the **Save as type list arrow** and click the **PowerPoint Picture Presentation** file type, then click **Save**

☐ Click **OK**

Figure PPT 7-1   Saving as a picture presentation

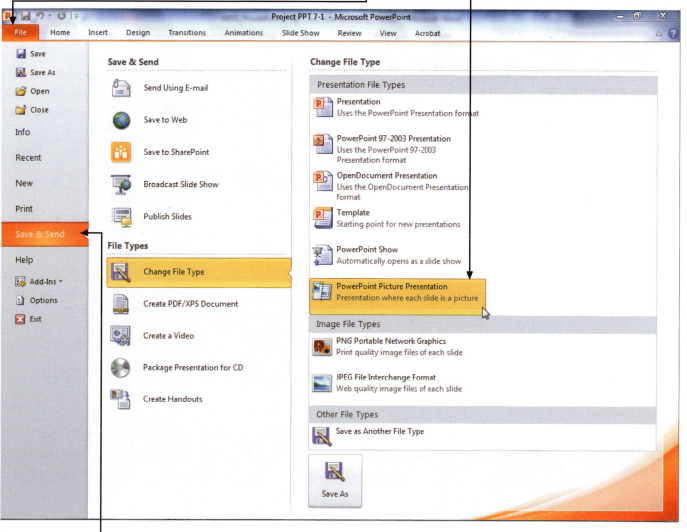

Shortcut Method

□ Press **F12**

□ In the Save As dialog box, type an appropriate filename in the File name text box, click the **Save as type list arrow** and click the **PowerPoint Picture Presentation** file type, then click **Save**

□ Click **OK**

Save a Presentation as a PDF

Ribbon Method

□ Click the **File tab**, click **Save & Send**, then click **Create PDF/XPS Document** in the File Types section of the center pane

□ In the right pane, click the **Create PDF/XPS button** in the Create a PDF/XPS Document pane

□ In the Publish As PDF or XPS dialog box, type an appropriate filename in the File name text box, click the appropriate **Optimize for option button**, change any other options as necessary, then click **Publish**

OR

□ Click the **File tab**, then click **Save As**

□ In the Save As dialog box, type an appropriate filename in the File name text box, click the **Save as type list arrow** and click the **PDF** file type, change any other options as necessary, then click **Save**

Shortcut Method

□ Press **F12**

□ In the Save As dialog box, type an appropriate filename in the File name text box, click the **Save as type list arrow** and click the **PDF** file type, change any other options as necessary, then click **Save**

Save a Presentation as an XPS

Ribbon Method

□ Click the **File tab**, click **Save & Send**, then click **Create PDF/XPS Document** in the File Types section of the center pane

□ In the right pane, click the **Create PDF/XPS button** in the Create a PDF/XPS Document pane

□ In the Publish as PDF or XPS dialog box, type an appropriate filename in the File name text box, click the **Save as type list arrow** and click the **XPS Document** file type, click the appropriate **Optimize for option button**, change any other options as necessary, then click **Publish**

OR

□ Click the **File tab**, then click **Save As**

□ In the Save As dialog box, type an appropriate filename in the File name text box, click the **Save as type list arrow** and click the **XPS Document** file type, change any other options as necessary, then click **Save**

Shortcut Method

□ Press **F12**

□ In the Save As dialog box, type an appropriate filename in the File name text box, click the **Save as type list arrow** and click the **XPS Document** file type, change any other options as necessary, then click **Save**

Save the Presentation as an Outline

Ribbon Method

□ Click the **File tab**, click **Save & Send**, then click **Change File Type** in the File Types section of the center pane

□ Click **Save as Another File Type** in the Other File Types section of the right pane

□ Click **Save As**

□ In the Save As dialog box, type an appropriate filename in the File name box, click the **Save as type list arrow**, then click **Outline/RTF**

□ Click **Save**

OR

□ Click the **File tab**, then click **Save As**

□ In the Save As dialog box, type an appropriate filename in the File name box, click the **Save as type list arrow**, then click **Outline/RTF**

□ Click **Save**

Shortcut Method

□ Press **F12**

□ In the Save As dialog box, type an appropriate filename in the File name box, click the **Save as type list arrow**, then click **Outline/RTF**

□ Click **Save**

Save the Presentation as an OpenDocument

Ribbon Method

□ Click the **File tab**, click **Save & Send**, then click **Change File Type** in the File Types section of the center pane

□ Click **OpenDocument Presentation** in the Presentation File Types section of the right pane

□ Click **Save As**

□ In the Save As dialog box, type an appropriate filename in the File name box, then click **Save**

OR

□ Click the **File tab**, then click **Save As**

□ In the Save As dialog box, type an appropriate filename in the File name box, click the **Save as type list arrow**, then click **OpenDocument Presentation**

□ Click **Save**

Shortcut Method

□ Press **F12**

□ In the Save As dialog box, type an appropriate filename in the File name box, click the **Save as type list arrow**, then click **OpenDocument Presentation**

□ Click **Save**

Save the Presentation as a Show (.PPSX)

Ribbon Method

□ Click the **File tab**, click **Save & Send**, then click **Change File Type** in the File Types section of the center pane

□ Click **PowerPoint Show** in the Presentation File Types section of the right pane

□ Click **Save As**

□ In the Save As dialog box, type an appropriate filename in the File name box, then click **Save**

OR

□ Click the **File tab**, then click **Save As**

□ In the Save As dialog box, type an appropriate filename in the File name box, click the **Save as type list arrow**, then click **PowerPoint Show**

□ Click **Save**

Shortcut Method

□ Press **F12**

□ In the Save As dialog box, type an appropriate filename in the File name box, click the **Save as type list arrow**, then click **PowerPoint Show**

□ Click **Save**

Save a Slide or Object as a Picture File

Ribbon Method

□ Click the **File tab**, click **Save & Send**, then click **Change File Type** in the File Types section of the center pane

□ Click **PNG Portable Network Graphics** or **JPEG File Interchange Format** in the Image File Types section of the right pane

□ Click **Save As**

PowerPoint

☐ In the Save As dialog box, type an appropriate filename in the File name box, then click **Save**

☐ In the Message box, click **Every Slide** to save each slide in the presentation as a graphic file, or click **Current Slide Only** to save only the selected slide as a graphic file

OR

☐ Click the **File tab**, then click **Save As**

☐ In the Save As dialog box, type an appropriate filename in the File name box, click the **Save as type list arrow**, then click the graphic file format you want

☐ Click **Save**

☐ In the Message box, click **Every Slide** to save each slide in the presentation as a graphic file, or click **Current Slide Only** to save only the selected slide as a graphic file

Shortcut Method

☐ Right-click the object you want to save as a picture file, click **Save as Picture** on the shortcut menu

☐ In the Save As dialog box, type an appropriate filename in the File name box, click the **Save as type list arrow**, then click the graphic file format you want

☐ Click **Save**

OR

☐ Press **F12**

☐ In the Save As dialog box, type an appropriate filename in the File name box, click the **Save as type list arrow**, then click the graphic file format you want

☐ Click **Save**

☐ In the Message box, click **Every Slide** to save each slide in the presentation as a graphic file, or click **Current Slide Only** to save only the selected slide as a graphic file

SHARE PRESENTATIONS

Package a Presentation for CD Delivery

Ribbon Method

☐ Insert a blank CD in the appropriate drive on your computer

☐ Click the **File tab**, click **Save & Send**, then click **Package Presentation for CD** in the File Types section of center pane

☐ In the right pane, click **Package for CD**

☐ In the Package for CD dialog box, shown in Figure PPT 7-2, type a name for the CD in the Name the CD text box

☐ Click the **Copy to CD button**

☐ In the message box, click **Yes** to copy all linked files to the CD

Figure PPT 7-2 **Package for CD dialog box**

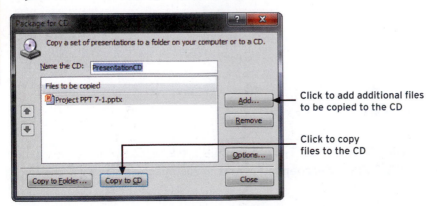

Create a Video

Ribbon Method

□ Click the **File tab**, click **Save & Send**, then click **Create a Video** in the File Types section of center pane

□ In the right pane, click the **Computer & HD Displays list arrow** and click an option from the list

□ Click the **Don't Use Recorded Timings and Narrations list arrow** and click an option from the list

□ Adjust the **Seconds to spend on each slide text box**, if desired

□ Click the **Create Video button**

□ In the Save As dialog box, type an appropriate filename in the File name box, then click **Save**

Create Handouts

Ribbon Method

□ Click the **File tab**, click **Save & Send**, then click **Create Handouts** in the File Types section of center pane

□ In the right pane, click the **Create Handouts button**

□ In the Send To Microsoft Word dialog box, shown in Figure PPT 7-3, select appropriate options, then click **OK** to launch Microsoft Word and display the handouts document

□ Click the **Save button** 🖫 on the Quick Access Toolbar to display the Save As dialog box

□ Type an appropriate name for the handouts in the File name text box, then click **Save**

Figure PPT 7-3   Send to Microsoft Word dialog box

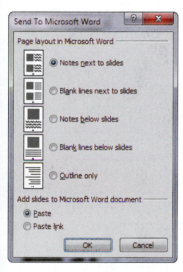

Compress Media

Ribbon Method

□ Click the **File tab**, click **Info**, then click the **Compress Media button** in the center pane, as shown in Figure PPT 7-4

□ Click an option from the menu to specify quality

□ In the Compress Media dialog box, view the compression progress bar until it is complete, then click **Close**

Figure PPT 7-4 Compress Media button and menu

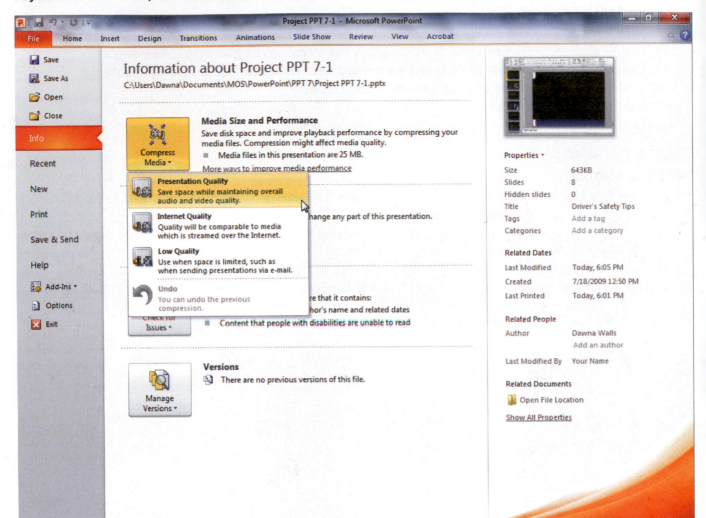

NOTE

The presentation must include an audio or video file for the
Compress Media button to appear in Backstage view.

PRINT PRESENTATIONS

Print Slides

Ribbon Method

☐ Click the **File tab**, then click **Print**

☐ In the Print area of Backstage view, shown in Figure PPT 7-5, click the **Print All Slides list arrow**

☐ Click an option from the list to print all slides, a selection, the current slide, or a custom range that you specify in the Slides text box

☐ Click **Print**

Figure PPT 7-5   Printing options in Backstage view

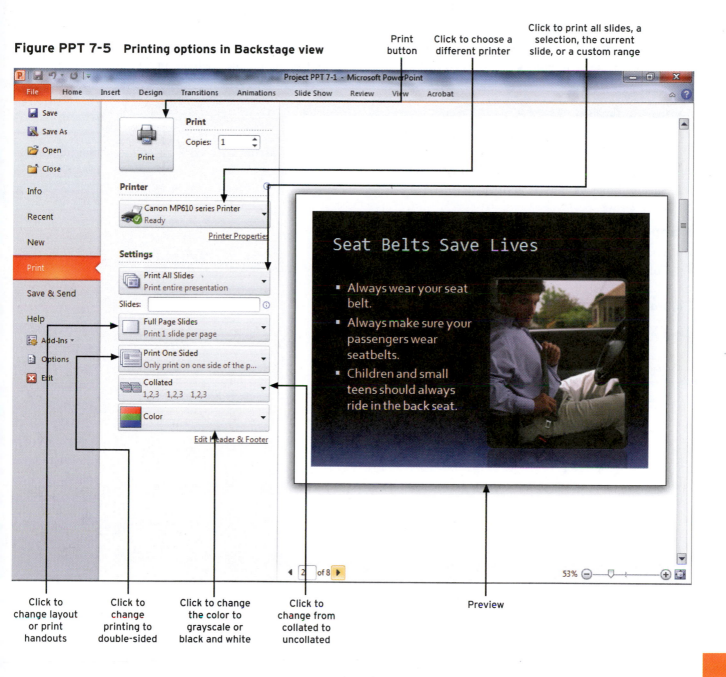

Print button

Click to choose a different printer

Click to print all slides, a selection, the current slide, or a custom range

Click to change layout or print handouts

Click to change printing to double-sided

Click to change the color to grayscale or black and white

Click to change from collated to uncollated

Preview

Shortcut Method
☐ Press **[Ctrl][P]**
☐ Follow the steps in bullets 2–4 in the Print Slides Ribbon Method on the previous page

Print Notes Pages or an Outline
Ribbon Method
☐ Click the **File tab**, and then click **Print**
☐ In the Print area of Backstage view, click the **Full Page Slides list arrow**, then click **Notes Pages** or **Outline** from the Print Layout section of the gallery
☐ Specify other options as desired
☐ Click **Print**

Shortcut Method

☐ Press **[Ctrl][P]**

☐ Follow the steps in bullets 2–4 in the Print Notes Pages or an Outline Ribbon Method on the previous page

Print Handouts

Ribbon Method

☐ Click the **File tab**, and then click **Print**

☐ In the Print area of Backstage view, click the **Full Page Slides list arrow**, then click an option in the Handouts section of the gallery, shown in Figure PPT 7-6

☐ Specify other options as desired

☐ Click **Print**

Shortcut Method

☐ Press **[Ctrl][P]**

☐ Follow the steps in bullets 2–4 in the Print Handouts Ribbon Method above

Figure PPT 7-6   **Options for printing handouts**

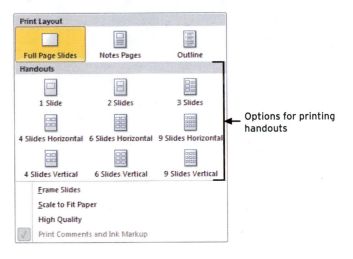

PROTECT PRESENTATIONS

Set a Password

Ribbon Method

☐ Click the **File tab**, click **Info**, click the **Protect Presentation button**, then click **Encrypt with Password**

☐ In the Encrypt Document dialog box shown in Figure PPT 7-7, type a case-sensitive password in the Password text box

☐ Click **OK**

☐ Reenter the case-sensitive password in the Reenter password text box in the Confirm Password dialog box

☐ Click **OK**

Figure PPT 7-7   **Encrypt Document dialog box**

> **NOTE**
>
> You must type your password exactly as it was set to be able to access the presentation again once it is password-protected.

Change a Password

☐ Click the **File tab**, click **Info**, click the **Protect Presentation button**, then click **Encrypt with Password**

☐ In the Encrypt Document dialog box, delete the characters in the text box, then type a new case-sensitive password in the Password text box

☐ Click **OK**

☐ Reenter the new case-sensitive password in the Reenter password text box in the Confirm Password dialog box

☐ Click **OK**

> **NOTE**
>
> If you decide to remove the password encryption from a presentation, just delete the characters in the Encrypt with Password dialog box, then click OK.

Mark a Presentation as Final

☐ Click the **File tab**, click **Info**, click the **Protect Presentation button**, then click **Mark as Final**

☐ Click **OK**, then click **OK**

PowerPoint

REVIEW QUESTIONS

TRUE/FALSE

Circle T if the statement is true or F if the statement is false.

T   F   1. Encrypting a file makes it read-only.

T   F   2. Passwords are case-sensitive.

T   F   3. The Create Handouts button lets you create handouts that can be edited and formatted in Microsoft Word.

T   F   4. Using the Custom Range option, you can print slides 2-4 of a 10-slide presentation.

T   F   5. [CTRL][P] is a keyboard shortcut for opening the Save As dialog box.

MATCHING

Match the correct term in Column 2 to its description in Column 1.

Column 1	Column 2
_____ 1. Helps improve performance and save disk space.	A. Mark as Final button
_____ 2. Allows you to create a video from your presentation.	B. PowerPoint Picture Presentation format
_____ 3. Saves a presentation with each slide as a picture.	C. PowerPoint Show format
_____ 4. Saves a presentation as read-only.	D. Compress Media button
_____ 5. Saves a presentation in a format that opens as a slide show.	E. Create a Video button

PROJECTS

Project PPT 7-1

1. Open the data file **Project PPT 7-1.pptx**.

2. Print handouts as follows: 9 slides per page, horizontally.

3. Save the file as **Driver Safety Presentation**.

4. Encrypt the presentation with a password. Type **DSpres*8** as the password.

5. Type **DSpres*8** to confirm the password. *Note:* the password is case sensitive.

6. Save and close the presentation.

7. Open **Project PPT 7-1.pptx**.

8. Save the presentation in the PowerPoint Show format named **Driver Safety Slide Show.ppsx**.

9. Close the file.

10. Open the **Driver Safety Presentation.pptx**. Type **DSpres*8** as the password.

11. Create a video of the presentation. Save it as **Driver Safety Video** using the default settings. (It may take a few minutes to convert the file to video. Check the status bar for progress.)

12. Close the **Driver Safety Presentation.pptx**.

13. Open the **Driver Safety Slide Show.ppsx** presentation.

14. Mark it as final.

15. Close the presentation.

PowerPoint

CRITICAL THINKING

Activity PPT 7-1

Use PowerPoint Help and the Internet to learn about creating strong passwords. Create a brief presentation about how to create strong passwords and how to store passwords. Password-protect your presentation, and be prepared to share your presentation with the class.

Activity PPT 7-2

What is a .pdf and an .xps? When should each be used? Search PowerPoint help to find out. Save one of your presentations as a pdf or xps.

POWERPOINT OBJECTIVE 8: DELIVERING PRESENTATIONS

APPLY PRESENTATION TOOLS

Add Pen and Highlighter Annotations

Shortcut Method

☐ View the presentation in Slide Show view, then right-click the slide you want to annotate

☐ Point to **Pointer Options** on the shortcut menu, then click **Pen** or **Highlighter** on the submenu as shown in Figure PPT 8-1

☐ Drag on the slide to create the annotation you want, then release the mouse button

Figure PPT 8-1   Shortcut menu

Menu Method

☐ View the presentation in Slide Show view, then move the pointer to the lower left corner of the screen

☐ Click the **Pen Options button** 🖊 on the Slide Show menu, then click **Pen** or **Highlighter** on the submenu

☐ Drag on the slide to create the annotation you want, then release the mouse button

Change the Ink Color

Shortcut Method

☐ View the presentation in Slide Show view, then right-click the slide you want to annotate

☐ Point to **Pointer Options** on the shortcut menu, point to **Ink Color** on the submenu, then click a new color in the palette

☐ Drag on the slide to create the annotation you want, then release the mouse button

Menu Method

☐ View the presentation in Slide Show view, then move the pointer to the lower left corner of the screen

☐ Click the **Pen Options button** 🖊 on the Slide Show menu, click **Ink Color** on the menu, then click a new color in the palette

☐ Drag on the slide to create the annotation you want, then release the mouse button

Erase an Annotation

Shortcut Method

☐ Display the slide that contains annotations you want to erase in Slide Show view

☐ Right-click the slide

PowerPoint

☐ Point to **Pointer Options** on the shortcut menu, click **Eraser** on the submenu, then click the **Eraser pointer** ✎ on an annotation to erase it or click **Erase All Ink on Slide** to erase all the annotations on the slide

Menu Method

☐ Display the slide that contains annotations you want to erase in Slide Show view

☐ Move the pointer to the lower left corner of the screen

☐ Click the **Pen Options button** 🖊 on the Slide Show menu, click **Eraser** on the menu, then click the **Eraser pointer** ✎ on an annotation to erase it or click **Erase All Ink on Slide** to erase all the annotations on the slide

Retain or Discard Annotations Upon Closing

☐ Make appropriate annotations as you advance through all the slides in the presentation

☐ At the end of the slide show, click to Exit or press **Esc**

☐ Click **Keep** or **Discard** in the message box that appears asking if you want to keep your ink annotations

---

SET UP SLIDE SHOWS

Set Up a Slide Show

Ribbon Method

☐ Click the **Slide Show tab** on the Ribbon, then click the **Set Up Slide Show button** in the Set Up group

☐ Specify the desired options in the Set Up Show dialog box, shown in Figure PPT 8-2, using Table PPT 8-1 as a guide

☐ Click **OK**

Figure PPT 8-2   Set Up Show dialog box

Table PPT 8-1   Set Up Show Dialog box

Section	Options
Show type	Choose whether show will be delivered by a speaker or browsed by an individual in a window or at a kiosk
Show options	Select whether to loop continuously, whether to show with or without narration or animation, and pen and laser pointer color
Show slides	Specify whether to show all or selected slides
Advance slides	Choose to proceed through slides manually or using timings
Multiple monitors	Set show to run on one or multiple monitors using Presenter view to use thumbnails to select slides, preview text, see Speaker notes in larger format, and run other programs that you don't want the audience to see during the presentation

Play Narrations

Ribbon Method

☐ Click the **Slide Show tab** on the Ribbon, shown in Figure PPT 8-3, then click the **Play Narrations check box** in the Set Up group to play any recorded Narrations during the slide show

Figure PPT 8-3   Slide Show tab

Set up Presenter View

Ribbon Method

☐ Click the **Slide Show tab** on the Ribbon, then click the **Use Presenter View check box** in the Monitors group

☐ Click **Check** or **Cancel** in the message box that may appear stating that this feature is for use with more than one monitor

☐ If necessary, make appropriate selections in the Screen Resolution dialog box to specify your main monitor and show monitor

Use Timings

Ribbon Method

☐ Click the **Slide Show tab** on the Ribbon, then click the **Use Timings check box** in the Set Up group to play any recorded timings during the slide show

Show Media Controls

Ribbon Method

☐ Click the **Slide Show tab** on the Ribbon, then click the **Show Media Controls check box** in the Set Up group to display media controls when you move the pointer over audio and video clips during a slide show

Broadcast Presentations

Ribbon Method

☐ Click the **Slide Show tab** on the Ribbon, then click the **Broadcast Slide Show button** in the Start Slide Show group

☐ In the Broadcast Slide Show dialog box, shown in Figure PPT 8-4, click the **Start Broadcast button**

☐ Log in with your Windows Live ID to connect to the broadcast service

☐ In the Broadcast Slide Show dialog box, click **Copy Link**, then click **Send in Email** to open an Outlook email you can use to invite others to view the broadcast with a web browser

☐ Click the **Start Slide Show button**

☐ After the slide show is over, click the **End Broadcast button** in the Broadcast group on the Broadcast tab

☐ Click the **End Broadcast button** to disconnect all remote viewers

Figure PPT 8-4   Broadcast Slide Show dialog box

NOTE

To broadcast a presentation, you need a Windows Live ID and an Internet connection.

Create a Custom Slide Show

Ribbon Method

☐ Click the **Slide Show tab** on the Ribbon, click the **Custom Slide Show button** in the Start Slide Show group, then click **Custom Shows**

☐ In the Custom Shows dialog box, click **New**

☐ In the Define Custom Show dialog box, click the **Slide show name text box**, then type the name of the slide show

☐ To add a slide to the show, click the slide you want to include in the slide show in the Slides in presentation section, then click **Add** as shown in Figure PPT 8-5

☐ To remove a slide from a show, click the slide in the Slides in custom show section, then click **Remove**

☐ To change the order of slides by selecting a slide or slides, click the **Move Up button** 🔼 or the **Move Down button** 🔽

☐ Click **OK**, then click **Close** in the Custom Shows dialog box

Figure PPT 8-5   **Define Custom Show dialog box**

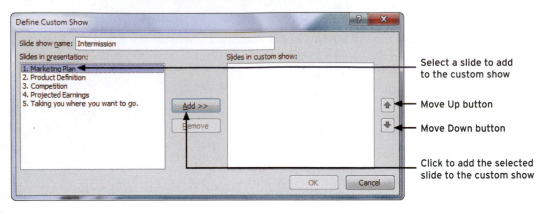

SET PRESENTATION TIMING

Rehearse Timings

Ribbon Method

☐ Click the **Slide Show tab** on the Ribbon, then click the **Rehearse Timings button** in the Set Up group

☐ The slide show begins to run, and the Recording toolbar, shown in Figure PPT 8-6, opens and times the slide

☐ Advance through the presentation, clicking the **Next button** 🡆 when sufficient time has passed for each slide

☐ Click the **Repeat button** 🔁 to restart recording the time for the current slide

☐ Click the **Pause button** ⏸ to pause the presentation and stop the clock

☐ Once all the slides have been rehearsed, click **Yes** in the message box that appears to keep the new slide timings, or click **No** to use other timings or try again

Figure PPT 8-6   **Recording toolbar**

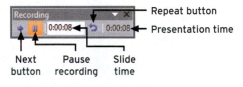

OR

☐ Click the **Slide Show tab** on the Ribbon, then click the **Record Slide Show button** in the Set Up group

☐ In the Record Slide Show dialog box, click the **Slide and animation timings check box**, if necessary, to insert a checkmark

☐ Click the **Narrations and laser pointer check box** to remove the checkmark

☐ Click **Start Recording**

☐ Follow the steps in bullets 2-6 of the Rehearse Timings Ribbon Method above

PowerPoint

NOTE

During a recording, you can right-click a slide to pause the recording and access the commands on the shortcut menu.

Keep Timings

Ribbon Method

☐ Follow the steps in bullets 1-5 of the Rehearse Timings Ribbon Method above to record timings

☐ Once all the slides have been rehearsed, click **Yes** in the message box that appears to keep the new slide timings and display Slide Sorter view with the time of each slide in the presentation

Clear a Slide's Timing

Ribbon Method

☐ Display the slide

☐ Click the **Slide Show tab** on the Ribbon, click the **Record Slide Show list arrow** in the Set Up group

☐ Click **Clear**, then click **Clear Timings on Current Slide**

Adjust a Slide's Timing

Ribbon Method

☐ Display the slide

☐ Click the **Slide Show tab** on the Ribbon, click the **Record Slide Show list arrow** in the Set Up group, then click **Start Recording from Current Slide**

☐ In the Record Slide Show dialog box, click the **Slide and animation timings check box**, if necessary, to insert a checkmark

☐ Click the **Narrations and laser pointer check box** to remove the checkmark

☐ Click **Start Recording**

☐ Follow the steps in bullets 2-6 of the Rehearse Timings Ribbon Method on the previous page

OR

☐ Display the slide

☐ Click the **Transitions tab**, then adjust the number of minutes and seconds you want to show the slide in the **After text box** in the Timing group

---

RECORD PRESENTATIONS

Start Recording from the Beginning of a Slide Show

Ribbon Method

☐ Click the **Slide Show tab** on the Ribbon, click the **Record Slide Show list arrow** in the Set Up group, then click **Start Recording from Beginning**

☐ In the Record Slide Show dialog box, shown in Figure PPT 8-7, select the appropriate recording options

☐ Click **Start Recording**

Figure PPT 8-7   **Record Slide Show dialog box**

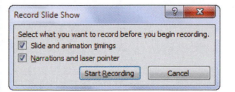

Start Recording from the Current Slide of a Slide Show

☐ Click the **Slide Show tab** on the Ribbon, click the **Record Slide Show list arrow** in the Set Up group, then click **Start Recording from Current Slide**

☐ In the Record Slide Show dialog box, select the appropriate recording options

☐ Click **Start Recording**

REVIEW QUESTIONS

FILL IN THE BLANK

Complete the following sentences by writing the correct word or words in the blanks provided.

1. Press the _____ key to end a presentation.

2. You can change the _____ color of a pen or highlighter used to make annotations.

3. _____ a presentation means to make it show continuously.

4. If you want to present only part of a slide show to an audience, you can create a _____ slide show.

5. The _____ menu is located in the lower left corner of the slide show.

MULTIPLE CHOICE

Select the best response for the following statements.

1. The Set Up Show button is located on the _____ tab.
   A. File
   B. Insert
   C. Animations
   D. Slide Show

2. When you _____ annotations in a presentation, the ink is removed from the slides.
   A. Keep
   B. Discard
   C. Copy
   D. Hide

3. _____ is a feature that lets you show the presentation on one monitor for the audience and display speaker notes and timings on another monitor for the presenter.
   A. Rehearse Timings
   B. Custom Slide Show
   C. Presenter View
   D. Play Narrations

4. The _____ command allows remote users to view your presentation in a web browser.
   A. Record Slide Show
   B. Broadcast Slide Show
   C. Custom Slide Show
   D. Set Up Slide Show

5. To record how long to display each slide, use the _____ button.
   A. Rehearse Timings
   B. Use Presenter View
   C. Broadcast Slide Show
   D. Set Up Slide Show

PowerPoint

PROJECTS

1. Open the data file **Project PPT 8-1.pptx**.

2. Rehearse the timings. Set each slide to appear for 5 seconds.

3. Set the presentation to be presented by a speaker, to loop continuously, to show without narration, and to advance slides using timings.

4. Start the slide show from the beginning.

5. Press Esc to end the presentation.

6. Change the slide show to advance manually.

7. Select slide 4 and start the slide show.

8. Use the pen to draw an arrow pointing to the gray East 3rd quarter projected earnings.

9. Use the highlighter to highlight the number 90.

10. Change the pointer back to the arrow and go to slide 1. Advance to slide 5.

11. On slide 5, end the presentation and keep the ink annotations.

12. Create a new custom slide show that includes the first and last slides. Name the slide show **Intermission**.

13. Save the presentation as **BY Marketing Plan.pptx**.

CRITICAL THINKING

Activity PPT 8-1

Create a 5-slide presentation about your favorite electronic gadget, such as a phone, video game system, watch, camera, or hand-held device. Explain what it does, what company makes it, how you use it, and what makes it great. Include appropriate graphics, animations, transitions, video, or audio. Rehearse the timings, add a narration, and set it to advance automatically. Use what you have learned to create a fantastic presentation to show to the class.

MICROSOFT OUTLOOK 2010 CERTIFICATION PREP

Getting Started with Outlook 2010

The Outlook Microsoft Office Specialist (MOS) exam assumes a basic level of proficiency in Outlook. This section is intended to help you reference these basic skills while you are preparing to take the Outlook MOS exam.

> ☐ Starting and exiting Outlook
> ☐ Setting up an Outlook profile
> ☐ Using the Ribbon
> ☐ Using keyboard KeyTips
> ☐ Opening Outlook tools
> ☐ Viewing Outlook tools
> ☐ Getting Help

START AND EXIT OUTLOOK

Start Outlook

Button Method

☐ Click the **Start button** on the Windows taskbar
☐ Point to **All Programs**
☐ Click **Microsoft Office**, then click **Microsoft Outlook 2010**
  OR
☐ Double-click the **Microsoft Outlook 2010 program icon** on the desktop
  OR
☐ Click the **Microsoft Outlook 2010 icon** on the Quick Launch Toolbar

Exit Outlook

Ribbon Method

☐ Click the **File tab** on the Ribbon, then click **Exit**

Button Method

☐ Click the **Close button** on the Outlook program window title bar

Shortcut Method

☐ Press **[Alt][F4]**

Refresh the Inbox

Ribbon Method

☐ Click the **Home tab** on the Ribbon, then click the **Send/Receive All Folders button** in the Send/Receive group
  OR
☐ Click the **Send/Receive tab** on the Ribbon, then click the **Send/Receive All Folders button** or the **Update Folder button** in the Send & Receive group

Shortcut Method

☐ Press **[F9]** to send and receive all messages in Outlook

SET UP AN OUTLOOK PROFILE

Button Method

☐ Click the **Start button** 🪟 on the Windows taskbar, then click **ControlPanel**

☐ In the Control Panel window, click **User Accounts and Family Safety**, then click **Mail**

☐ In the Mail Setup - Outlook dialog box, click the **Show Profiles button**

☐ In the Mail dialog box, click **Add**

☐ In the New Profile dialog box, type a name for the profile in the Profile Name text box, then click **OK**

☐ Navigate through the Add New Account wizard, beginning with the dialog box shown in Figure OL GS-1, making selections and specifying settings as appropriate to create the profile, then click **Finish**

☐ Click **OK** in the Mail dialog box

Figure OL GS-1   Add New Account dialog box

USE THE RIBBON

Display the Ribbon

Ribbon Method

☐ When the Ribbon is hidden, double-click any tab (other than the File tab), to display it as shown in Figure OL GS-2

Shortcut Method

☐ Right-click any tab, then click **Minimize the Ribbon** on the shortcut menu to deselect it

OR

☐ Right-click any Quick Access toolbar button, then click **Minimize the Ribbon** on the shortcut menu to deselect it

Outlook

Figure OL GS-2   The Outlook Ribbon

Hide the Ribbon

Ribbon Method

□ Double-click the active tab

Shortcut Method

□ Right-click any tab, then click **Minimize the Ribbon** on the shortcut menu to select it

   OR

□ Right-click any Quick Access Toolbar button, then click **Minimize the Ribbon** on the shortcut menu to select it

Work with the Ribbon

Ribbon Method

□ Click a tab on the Ribbon, click a button or a button list arrow in any group, then click a command or gallery option, if necessary

   OR

□ Click a **dialog box launcher** 🔲 to open a dialog box or a pane offering more options

Customize the Quick Access Toolbar

Ribbon Method

□ Right-click any Quick Access toolbar button

□ To hide that button, click **Remove from Quick Access Toolbar**

□ To add or remove a button, click **Customize Quick Access Toolbar**, click a command in the left or right column, then click **Add** or **Remove**

□ Click **OK**

   OR

□ Click the **Customize Quick Access Toolbar button** 🔽, click a command in the list or click **More Commands**, click a command in the left or right column, then click **Add** or **Remove**

□ Click **OK**

   OR

□ To remove a button, click the **Customize Quick Access Toolbar button** 🔽, then click the command in the list to deselect it

Reposition the Quick Access Toolbar

Ribbon Method

□ Right-click any Quick Access toolbar button

□ Click **Show Quick Access Toolbar Below the Ribbon**

   OR

□ Click the **Customize Quick Access Toolbar button** 🔽, then click **Show Below the Ribbon**

USE KEYBOARD KEYTIPS

Display Keyboard KeyTips

Shortcut Method

- [ ] Press **[Alt]** to display the KeyTips for each command on the active tab on the Ribbon and on the Quick Access toolbar, as shown in Figure OL GS-3
- [ ] Press the letter or number shown in the KeyTip for the specific active tab on the Ribbon
- [ ] Press additional letters or numbers as needed to complete the command sequence
- [ ] If two letters appear, press each one in order
- [ ] For some commands, you will find that you have to click an option from a gallery or menu to complete the command sequence
- [ ] The KeyTips turn off automatically at the end of the command sequence

Figure OL GS-3   Key Tips   KeyTip

Hide KeyTips

Shortcut Method

- [ ] Press **[Alt]** to hide the KeyTips for each Ribbon command

OPEN OUTLOOK TOOLS

Button Method

- [ ] Click the appropriate button in the Navigation Pane, using Table OL GS-1 as a reference

Shortcut Method

- [ ] Press the appropriate keyboard combination, using Table OL GS-1 as a reference

Table OL GS-1 Common Outlook Navigation Options

Command on	Navigation	Keyboard	Description
Mail		[Ctrl][1]	View new e-mail messages, create new e-mail messages, and move messages to folders
Calendar		[Ctrl][2]	View, create, and manage appointments
Contacts		[Ctrl][3]	Create, view, and edit contacts
Tasks		[Ctrl][4]	Schedule and assign tasks
Notes		[Ctrl][5]	Create and edit notes
Folder List		[Ctrl][6]	View the contents of a folder or create a new folder
Shortcuts		[Ctrl][7]	View and manage shortcuts to folders in Outlook
Journal		[Ctrl][8]	Create and edit Journal entries

VIEW OUTLOOK TOOLS

View the Inbox Folder

You can use the Inbox folder to send, receive, and read mail, as well as read and respond to any tasks or meeting requests. See Figure OL GS-4.

Figure OL GS-4   The Inbox

View the Calendar Window

You can use the Calendar to create appointments and events, organize meetings, view group schedules, and manage another user's Calendar. You can view the Calendar by day, week, or month. See Figure OL GS-5.

Figure OL GS-5   Calendar window arranged by week

View the Contacts Window

You can use the Contacts window to store e-mail addresses, addresses, phone numbers, and any other information that relates to your contacts, such as birthdays, children's names, or spouse's names. See Figure OL GS-6.

Figure OL GS-6   Contacts window

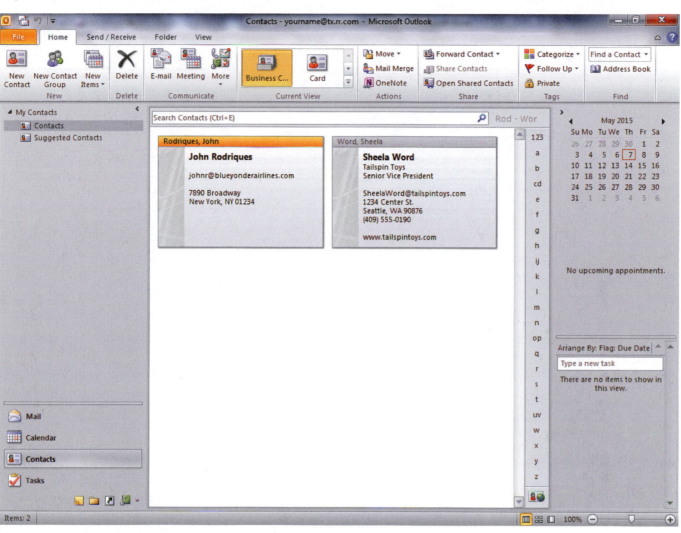

View the Tasks Window

The Tasks window contains a list of all tasks you have created for yourself or others, or that others have assigned you to do. You can use the tasks list to update the status of your projects, set a task as recurring, delegate tasks, and mark tasks as completed. See Figure OL GS-7.

Figure OL GS-7   Tasks window

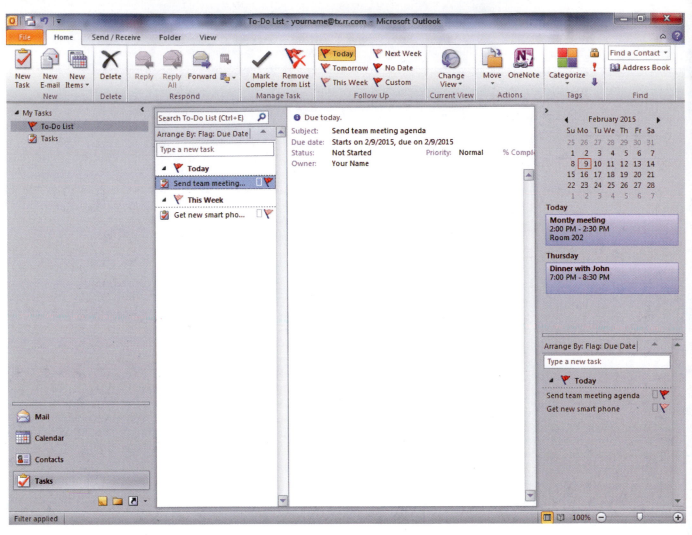

GET HELP

Ribbon Method

□ Click the **File tab**, then click **Help**

□ Click **Microsoft Office Help** to open the Outlook Help window

□ Use Table OL GS-2 as a reference to select the most appropriate way to search for help using the Outlook Help window, shown in Figure OL GS-8

Outlook

Table OL GS-2 Outlook Help Window options

Option	To use
Getting started with Outlook 2010	Click a link representing a topic you want to read about; click subtopics that appear until you see help text for the topic
Browse Outlook 2010 support	Click a link representing a topic you want to read about; click subtopics that appear until you see help text for the topic
Back button	Click to return to the previously displayed information
Forward button	Click to go forward in the sequence of previously displayed information
Stop button	Click to stop searching on a topic
Refresh button	Click to refresh the Help window content
Home button	Click to return to the Outlook Help window
Print button	Click to print the current page
Change Font Size button	Click to enlarge or shrink the help text
Show Table of Contents	Click to show the Table of Contents pane, showing topic links you can click
Keep On Top	Click to keep the Help window on top as you work; button becomes the Not On Top button, which you click to let the Help window go behind the current window as you work
Type words to search for box	Type a word, then click the Search button
Search button list arrow	Click the list arrow, then click the area, such as Content from Office.com, All Outlook, or Outlook Help
Search help using Bing	Type a word, then click the Search button or Type a word, then click the link downloads, images, or templates to search for those items on Office.com

Figure OL GS-8   Outlook Help window

Button Method
☐ Click the **Microsoft Outlook Help button** ❓ in the upper right corner of the Ribbon

☐ Use Table OL GS-2 as a reference to select the most appropriate way to search for help using the Outlook Help window

Shortcut Method
☐ Press **[F1]**

☐ Use Table OL GS-2 as a reference to select the most appropriate way to search for help using the Outlook Help window

REVIEW QUESTIONS

FILL IN THE BLANK

Complete the following sentences by writing the correct word or words in the blanks provided.

1. Double-click the active tab to _____ the Ribbon.

2. The _____ window displays appointments and events.

3. The _____ button has a picture of a question mark on it.

4. Press _____ to display the KeyTips for any active tab.

5. You can add and remove buttons from the _____.

MATCHING

Match the correct term in Column 2 to its description in Column 1.

Column 1	Column 2
_____ 1. Helps you create a profile	A. Contacts window
_____ 2. Refreshes the Inbox	B. Inbox
_____ 3. Contains a to do list	C. E-mail Account Wizard
_____ 4. Stores e-mail addresses	D. Send/Receive button
_____ 5. Displays mail received	E. Tasks window

PROJECTS

Project OL GS-1

1. If you do not already have one, set up a new Outlook profile.

2. Start Outlook.

3. View the Inbox.

4. Display the KeyTips.

5. Use the KeyTips to display the Send/Receive tab.

6. Display the Home tab.

7. Hide the Ribbon.

8. Display the Ribbon.

9. Reposition the Quick Access toolbar below the Ribbon.

10. Customize the Quick Access toolbar by adding the Print button.

11. Reposition the Quick Access toolbar above the Ribbon.

Outlook

12. Remove the Print button from the Quick Access toolbar.

13. Leave Outlook open for use in the next project.

Project OL GS-2

1. Display the Calendar window.

2. Display the Contacts window.

3. Display the Tasks window.

4. Display the Mail window.

5. Refresh the Inbox.

6. Display the Outlook Help window.

7. Type **help** in the textbox, then press **Enter**.

8. Close the Outlook Help window.

9. Exit Outlook.

CRITICAL THINKING

Activity OL GS-1

Open the Outlook Help window. Search for the video titled "Take a tour of Outlook 2010" and watch it. What other videos and articles are available? Browse through Help to see all the material available to help you learn more about using Outlook. Refer to Table OL GS-2 as a reference if you need help using the Outlook Help window.

Activity OL GS-2

Open Outlook and display the Mail window. Click on each of the tabs and start familiarizing yourself with the commands available in Outlook. Position the mouse pointer over commands to see an explanation. Next, explore the Calendar, Contacts, and Task windows. What similarities and differences do you see?

Outlook

OUTLOOK OBJECTIVE 1: MANAGING THE OUTLOOK ENVIRONMENT

APPLY AND MANIPULATE OUTLOOK PROGRAM OPTIONS

Set General Options

Ribbon Method

☐ Click the **File tab**, then click **Options** to open the Outlook Options dialog box with the General area displayed

☐ Select General options for working with Outlook, using the following categories: User Interface options, Personalize your copy of Microsoft Office, and Start up options

☐ Click **OK**

Set Mail Options

Ribbon Method

☐ Click the **File tab**, click **Options**, then click **Mail**

☐ In the Outlook Options dialog box, shown in Figure OL 1-1, adjust the settings for messages you create and receive using the following categories: Compose messages, Outlook panes, Message arrival, Conversation Clean Up, Replies and forwards, Save messages, Send messages, Tracking, Message format, and Other

☐ Click **OK**

Figure OL 1-1   Mail area of the Outlook Options dialog box

Set Calendar Options

Ribbon Method

☐ Click the **File tab**, click **Options**, then click **Calendar**

☐ In the Outlook Options dialog box, change the settings for calendars, meetings, and time zones using the following categories: Work time, Calendar options, Display options, Time zones, Scheduling assistant, and Resource scheduling

☐ Click **OK**

Set Tasks Options

Ribbon Method

☐ Click the **File tab**, click **Options**, then click **Tasks**

☐ In the Outlook Options dialog box, shown in Figure OL 1-2 select appropriate options for changing the settings that track your tasks and to-do items using the following categories: Task options and Work hours

☐ Click **OK**

Figure OL 1-2   **Tasks area of the Outlook Options dialog box**

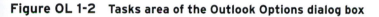

Set Notes and Journal Options

Ribbon Method

☐ Click the **File tab**, click **Options**, then click **Notes and Journal**

☐ In the Outlook Options dialog box, select the appropriate options to change the settings for Notes and the Journal using the following categories: Notes options and Journal options

☐ Click **OK**

Set Advanced Options

Ribbon Method

☐ Click the **File tab**, click **Options**, then click **Advanced**

Outlook

☐ In the Outlook Options dialog box, shown in Figure OL 1-3, select appropriate options for working with Outlook using the following categories: Outlook panes, Outlook start and exit, AutoArchive, Reminders, Export, RSS Feeds, Send and receive, Developers, Dial-Up connections, International options, and Other

☐ Click **OK**

Figure OL 1-3   Advanced area of the Outlook Options dialog box

Set Language Options

Ribbon Method

☐ Click the **File tab**, click **Options**, then click **Language**

☐ In the Outlook Options dialog box, select the appropriate options to Set the Office language preferences using the following categories: Choose Editing Languages, Choose Display and Help Languages, and Choose ScreenTip Language

☐ Click **OK**

MANIPULATE ITEM TAGS

Categorize Items

Ribbon Method

☐ In the appropriate folder, select the message(s), task(s), contact(s), or note(s) to categorize

☐ Click the **Home tab** on the Ribbon, click the **Categorize button** in the Tags group, then click an appropriate category in the menu shown in Figure OL 1-4, or click **All Categories** to open the Color Categories dialog box where you can create new categories, rename categories, delete categories, change the colors associated with the categories, or assign shortcut keys to a category

Figure OL 1-4   **Categorize button and menu**

OR

☐ To categorize an appointment, click the **Calendar folder** in the Navigation pane, click an appointment in the Calendar to select it and to display the Calendar Tools Appointment tab, click the **Categorize button** in the Tags group, then click an appropriate option in the menu

Shortcut Method

☐ Right-click a message, task, contact, calendar item, or note to categorize, click **Categorize** on the shortcut menu, then click an appropriate option in the submenu

Set Flags

Ribbon Method

☐ Select the message(s) you want to flag
☐ Click the **Home tab** on the Ribbon, click the **Follow Up button** in the Tags group, then click the appropriate flag in the menu, shown in Figure OL 1-5, or click **Custom** to open the Custom dialog box where you can set custom flag options

Figure OL 1-5   **Follow Up button and menu**

Shortcut Method

☐ Right-click a message, point to **Follow Up** on the shortcut menu, then click an appropriate option in the submenu
OR
☐ Click the **Flag icon** ⚑ to the right of an item in the message list to set a default flag
☐ If necessary, right-click the default flag and click a different flag option in the list

Set Sensitivity Level

Ribbon Method

☐ Open a new e-mail message

☐ Click the **launcher** 🔲 in the Tags group on the Message tab

☐ In the Properties dialog box, click the **Sensitivity list arrow** in the Settings section, click Normal, Personal, Private, or Confidential, then click **Close**

Mark Items as Read

Ribbon Method

☐ Select an unread message in the list

☐ Click the **Home tab** on the Ribbon, then click the **Unread/Read button** in the Tags group to mark the message as read

OR

☐ Open an unread message to automatically mark it as read

Shortcut Method

☐ Right-click an unread message, then click **Mark Read** on the shortcut menu

OR

☐ Select an unread message and press **[Ctrl][Q]**

Mark Items as Unread

Ribbon Method

☐ Select a read message in the list

☐ Click the **Home tab** on the Ribbon, then click the **Unread/Read button** in the Tags group

OR

☐ Open the read message, then click the **Mark Unread button** in the Tags group of the Message tab

Shortcut Method

☐ Right-click a read message, then click **Mark Unread** on the shortcut menu

OR

☐ Select a read message in the list and press **[Ctrl][U]**

View Message Properties

Ribbon Method

☐ Open a message

☐ On the Message tab, click the **launcher** 🔲 in the Tags group to open the Properties dialog box, shown in Figure OL 1-6

☐ Select appropriate options

☐ Click **Close**

Figure OL 1-6   Properties dialog box

ARRANGE THE CONTENT PANE

Show or Hide Fields in List View

Ribbon Method

☐ Click **View tab**, click the **View Settings button** in the Current View group to open the Advanced View Settings: Compact dialog box

☐ Click the **Columns button** to open the Show Columns dialog box, shown in Figure OL 1-7

☐ Click a field in the left column and click the **Add button** to show the new column

☐ Click a field in the right column and click the **Remove button** to remove a column from the view

☐ Select a field in the right column and use the **Move Up** and **Move Down** buttons to rearrange the order of the columns

☐ Click **OK**, then click **OK**

Figure OL 1-7   **Show Columns dialog box**

OR

☐ Click the **View tab**, click the **More button** in the Arrangement group to open the Arrangement gallery, then click **View Settings** to open the Advanced View Settings dialog box

☐ Follow the steps in bullets 2-6 in the Show or Hide Fields in List View Ribbon Method on the previous page

OR

☐ Click the **View tab**, then click the **Add Columns button** in the Arrangement group

☐ Follow the steps in bullets 3-6 in the Show or Hide Fields in List View Ribbon Method on the previous page

Shortcut Method

☐ Right click a field name, then click **View Settings** to open the Advanced View Settings dialog box

☐ Follow the steps in bullets 2-6 in the Show or Hide Fields in List View Ribbon Method on the previous page

OR

☐ To remove a column from the view, right click a field name and click **Remove this Column** on the shortcut menu

Show, Hide, or Move the Reading Pane

Ribbon Method

☐ To show or move the Reading Pane, click the **View tab**, click the **Reading Pane button** in the Layout group, then click **Right** or **Bottom** to display or move the Reading Pane as shown in Figure OL 1-8

OR

☐ To hide the Reading Pane, click the **View tab**, click the **Reading Pane button** in the Layout group, then click **Off**

Figure OL 1-8   Reading Pane

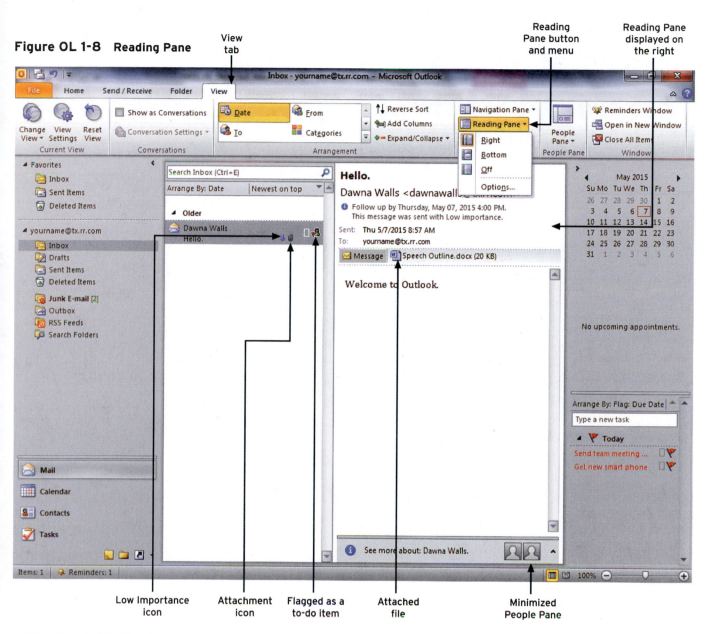

Shortcut Method

☐ To move the Reading Pane, position the pointer over the left or top border of the Reading Pane, then drag the **Resize Pane Vertical Pointer** ↔ or the **Vertical Resize Pointer** ↕ to change the view

Use the Reminders Window

Ribbon Method

☐ The Reminders window, shown in Figure OL 1-9, appears on your screen at the time set for a reminder or click the **View tab**, then click the **Reminders Window button** in the Window group to view the Reminders window

☐ Click **Dismiss All** to remove all reminders or select a reminder in the Reminders window then click **Open Item** to view the item, click **Dismiss** to remove the reminder, or click the list arrow to choose when you want another reminder and click **Snooze**

Figure OL 1-9   Reminders Window

Use the People Pane

Ribbon Method

☐ Click the **View tab**, click the **People Pane button** in the People Pane group, then click **Normal** to display the People Pane, shown in Figure OL 1-10

☐ Click one of the tabs to display different information about the person

☐ Click the **People Pane View Toggle arrow** to view information about other people

Figure OL 1-10   People Pane

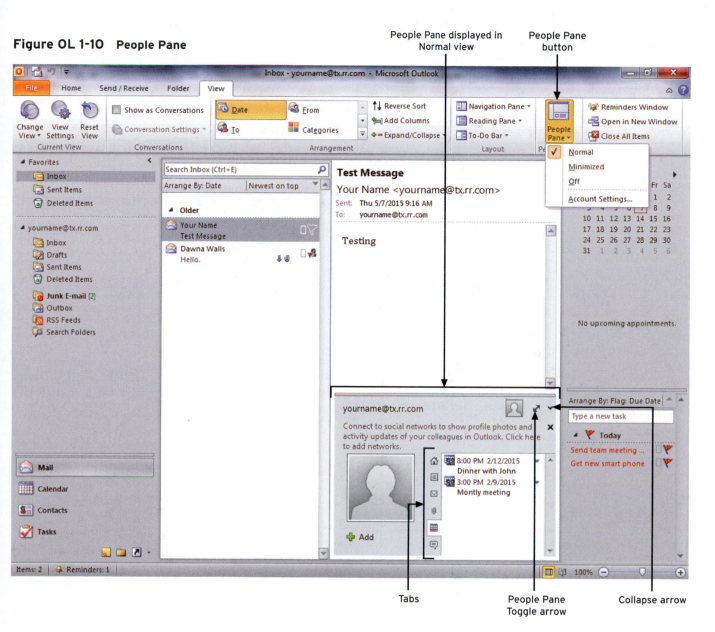

Shortcut Method

☐ Click the **Expand arrow** ▲ in the upper right corner of the minimized People Pane to display the People Pane

Minimize or Hide the People Pane

Ribbon Method

☐ Click the **View tab**, click the **People Pane button** in the People Pane group, then click **Minimize** to collapse it or click **Off** to hide it

Shortcut Method

☐ Click the **Collapse arrow** ▼ in the upper right corner of the People Pane to minimize it

Change the Size of the People Pane

Mouse Method

☐ Click the top border of the People Pane and drag the **Vertical Resize pointer** ↕ up or down to increase or decrease its height

APPLY SEARCH AND FILTER TOOLS

Use Instant Search

Ribbon Method

☐ In the Navigation pane, click a folder in which to search

☐ Type the word or words you want to search for in the **Instant Search box** as shown in Figure OL 1-11

Figure OL 1-11   Instant Search

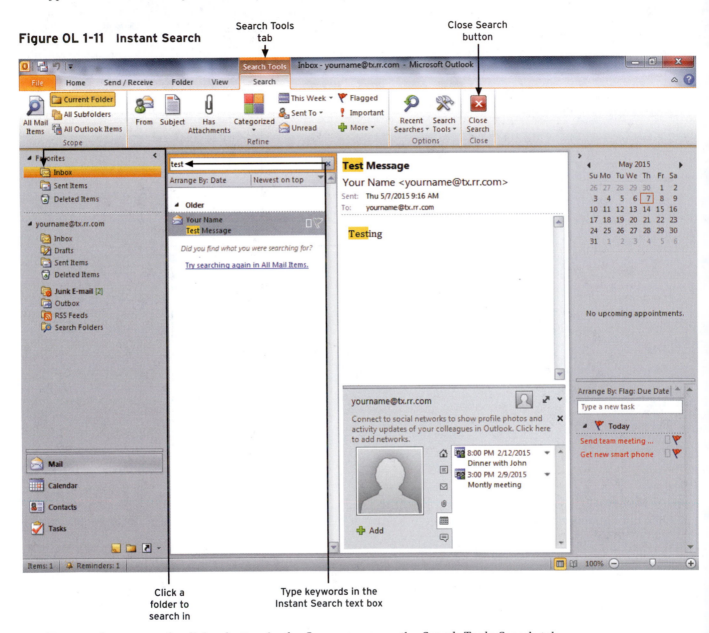

Click a folder to search in

Type keywords in the Instant Search text box

☐ To expand your search, click a button in the Scope group on the Search Tools Search tab

☐ To refine the search, click a button in the Refine group on the Search Tools Search tab

☐ To view a list of recent searches or to access additional search tools, click a button in the Options group on the Search Tools Search tab

☐ To remove the search, click the **Close Search button** in the Close group on the Search Tools Search tab

Shortcut Method

☐ In the Navigation pane, click a folder in which to search

□ Press **[Ctrl][E]**

□ Follow the steps in bullets 2-6 of the Use Instant Search Ribbon Method on the previous page

Filter E-mail Messages

Ribbon Method

□ Click the folder in the Navigation pane of the Inbox in which you want to filter e-mail messages

□ On the Home tab, click the **Filter E-mail button** in the Find group

□ Click an option from the menu, shown in Figure OL 1-12

□ To expand your filter, click a button in the Scope group on the Search Tools Search tab

□ To refine the filter, click a button in the Refine group on the Search Tools Search tab

□ To view a list of recent searches or to access additional search tools, click a button in the Options group on the Search Tools Search tab

□ To remove the filter, click the **Close Search button** in the Close group on the Search Tools Search tab

Figure OL 1-12   **Filter E-mail button and menu**

Use Built-in Search Folders

Ribbon Method

□ In the Inbox, click the **Folder tab** on the Ribbon, then click **New Search Folder** in the New group

□ In the New Search Folder dialog box, shown in Figure OL 1-13, click a built-in search folder, then click **OK**

Figure OL 1-13   **New Search Folder dialog box**

Shortcut Method

☐ In the Navigation pane, right-click the **Search Folders folder**, then click **New Search Folder**

☐ In the New Search Folder dialog box, click a built-in search folder, then click **OK**

OR

☐ Press **[Ctrl][Shift][P]**

☐ In the New Search Folder dialog box, click a built-in search folder, then click **OK**

PRINT AN OUTLOOK ITEM

Print Attachments

Ribbon Method

☐ Open a message with one or more attachments

☐ Select the attachment that you want to print

☐ On the Attachment Tools Attachments tab, click the **Quick Print button** on the Actions group to print the attachment with the default settings

OR

☐ In the message list, select a message with one or more attachments

☐ Click the **File tab**, click **Print**, then click the **Print Options button** in the Printer section of Backstage view

☐ In the Print dialog box, shown in Figure OL 1-14, click the **Print attached files check box** to print all the attachments to the default printer

☐ Click **Print**

Figure OL 1-14   Print dialog box

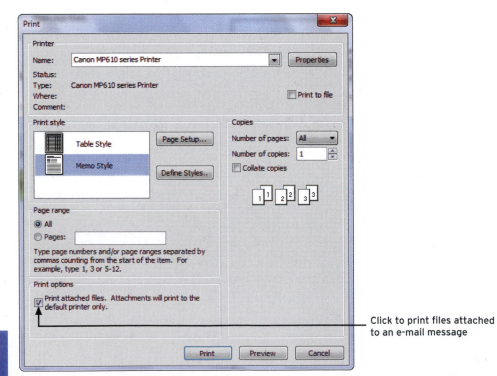

Click to print files attached
to an e-mail message

Print Calendars

Ribbon Method

☐ Click the **Calendar** folder

Outlook

☐ If necessary, use the Date Navigator to move to a different day, week, or month (Outlook prints the current day, week, or month by default)

☐ Click the **File tab**, click **Print**, then click appropriate options in the Printer and Settings sections of Backstage View, as shown in Figure OL 1-15

☐ Click **Print**

Figure OL 1-15   Print area of Backstage View

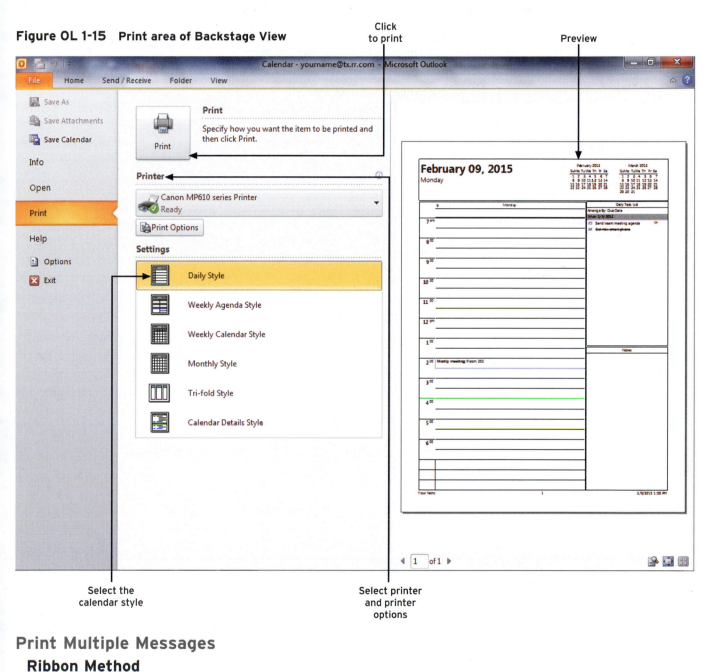

Print Multiple Messages

Ribbon Method

☐ Select the messages to be printed

☐ Click the **File tab** on the Ribbon, then click **Print**

☐ Select the Printer and Settings options

☐ Click **Print**

Shortcut Method

□ Select the messages to be printed

□ Right-click the selection, then click **Quick Print** on the shortcut menu to print the messages with the default settings

Print Multiple Contact Records

Ribbon Method

□ Click the Contacts folder that contains the contacts that you want to print

□ Click the **View tab**, then click **View Settings button** in the Current View group

□ In the Advanced View Settings dialog box, click the **Filter button**

□ In the Filter dialog box, shown in Figure OL 1-16, select options to display only the contacts you want to print

□ Click **OK**, then click **OK** again

□ Click **File tab**, then click **Print**

□ Choose Printer and Settings options

□ Click **Print**

Figure OL 1-16   Filter dialog box

Print Tasks

Ribbon Method

□ Click the task that you want to print

□ Click the **File tab**, click **Print**

□ Select Printer and Settings options

□ Click **Print**

    OR

□ Open the task that you want to print

□ Click the **File tab**, click **Print**

□ Select Printer and Settings options

□ Click **Print**

Shortcut Method

□ Right-click the task that you want to print

□ Click **Quick Print** on the shortcut menu to print the item with the default settings

Print Multiple Notes

Ribbon Method
□ In the Navigation Pane, click the Notes folder that contains the notes that you want to print
□ Select the notes that you want to print
□ Click the **File tab**, click **Print**
□ Select Printer and Settings options
□ Click **Print**

Shortcut Method
□ In the Navigation Pane, click the Notes folder that contains the notes that you want to print
□ Select the notes that you want to print
□ Right-click the selection, then click **Quick Print** on the shortcut menu to print the notes with the default settings

REVIEW QUESTIONS

TRUE/FALSE

Circle T if the statement is true or F if the statement is false.

T   F   1. The Quick Print command prints an item with the default settings.

T   F   2. In the Reminders Window, click Snooze to remove the reminder.

T   F   3. The Reading Pane can be turned on and off.

T   F   4. Normal, personal, private, or confidential are sensitivity levels.

T   F   5. Opening a read message automatically marks it as unread.

MATCHING

Match the button or keyboard shortcut in Column 2 to its description in Column 1.

Column 1	Column 2
_____ 1. Marks a message with a color.	A. Follow-up button
_____ 2. Is indicated by a picture of a bell.	B. Categorize button
_____ 3. Marks a message with a flag.	C. Reminder
_____ 4. Displays a preview of an e-mail message.	D. People Pane
_____ 5. Displays information about the sender of a message.	E. Reading Pane

PROJECTS

Project OL 1-1

1. Open Outlook.

2. Display the Reading pane at the bottom of the window.

3. Minimize the People pane.

4. Print the current month's calendar.

5. Turn off the Reading Pane.

6. Expand the People Pane.

Outlook

7. Remove the Importance field from the message list.

8. If you have a read message in your message list, flag it for follow up tomorrow and mark it as unread.

9. Add the Importance field back in to the message list. Move it to the beginning of the list.

10. Leave Outlook open for use in the activity.

CRITICAL THINKING

Activity OL 1-1

Use Outlook Options to customize Outlook. Refer to Outlook Help, if necessary, to complete the following steps.

1. In the Calendar, change the Work Week to Tuesday through Saturday.

2. Change the Time Zone to Central.

3. Display the Pacific and Central Time zones.

4. Add Holidays for the location of your choice.

5. Set the time zone to the time zone of your location.

6. Reset the Work Week to your specifications.

7. In Mail options, turn on the option to Always check spelling before sending.

8. In Tasks options, set the default reminder time to 10 am.

9. In Mail options, turn off the option to Always check spelling before sending.

10. Close Outlook.

OUTLOOK OBJECTIVE 2: CREATING AND FORMATTING ITEM CONTENT

CREATE AND SEND E-MAIL MESSAGES

Send and Address E-mail Messages

Ribbon Method

☐ In the Inbox, click the **Home tab** on the Ribbon, then click the **New E-mail button**

☐ In the Untitled Message window, shown in Figure OL 2-1, type the e-mail address(es) for the recipient(s) or the name of a contact group in the To and Cc boxes, separating each e-mail address with a semicolon (;), or to select recipient names from the Address Book, click the **To button** or the **Cc button** to open the Select Names dialog box, select the appropriate name(s), using Table OL 2-1 as a guide, click the To, CC, or Bcc button to add the name, then click **OK**

☐ In the Subject text box, type an appropriate subject for the message

☐ In the message body, type the message

☐ Click the **Send button**

Figure OL 2-1   Untitled Message window

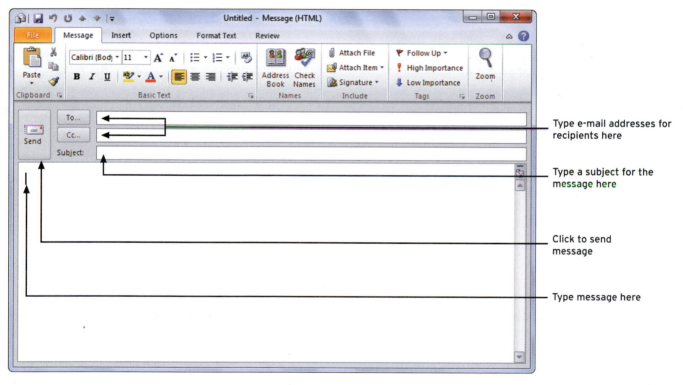

OR

☐ In the Inbox, click the **Home tab** on the Ribbon, click the **New Items button**, then click **E-mail Message**

☐ Follow the steps in bullets 2-5 in the Send and Address E-mail Messages Ribbon Method above

Shortcut Method

☐ Press **[Ctrl][Shift][M]** or **[Ctrl] [N]**

☐ Follow the steps in bullets 2–5 of the Send and Address E-mail Messages Ribbon Method above

Table OL 2-1   Message Addressing Options

Option	Sends
To	The primary recipient of the message
Carbon Copy (Cc)	A copy of the message, usually to people who do not need to respond
Blind Carbon Copy (Bcc)	A copy of the message to recipients whose names and addresses are not visible to the To and Cc recipients

Reply to or Forward an E-mail Message

Ribbon Method

☐ Open the e-mail message to which you want to respond

☐ In the Respond group on the Message tab, click one of the buttons described in Table OL 2-2

☐ Type the message in the message body, then add any additional recipients as appropriate

☐ Click the **Send button**

Shortcut Method

☐ Open the e-mail message to which you want to respond

☐ Press one of the keyboard combinations listed in Table OL 2-2, as appropriate

☐ Follow the steps in bullets 3–4 in the Reply to or Forward an E-mail Message Ribbon Method above

Table OL 2-2   E-mail Message Response Options

Command in the Respond group	Button	Keyboard combination	Action
Reply		[Ctrl][R]	To send a message that includes the original text and your comments directly to the original sender
Reply All		[Ctrl][Shift][R]	To send a message that includes the original message and your comments directly to the sender and all recipients of the original message
Forward		[Ctrl][F]	To send a message that includes the original message and your comments directly to the recipient(s) of your choosing, but not to the sender

Specify a Message Theme

Ribbon Method

☐ Select the text in an existing e-mail message or create a new e-mail message

☐ In the Untitled Message window, click the **Options tab**, click the **Themes button** in the Themes group, then click a theme in the gallery

☐ Complete the message, using the buttons in the Themes group to modify Colors, Fonts, Effects, or Page Color

☐ Click the **Send button**
   OR

☐ Click the **Home tab** on the Ribbon, click the **New Items button**, click **E-mail Message Using**, then click **More Stationery**

☐ In the Theme or Stationery dialog box, click a theme in the Choose a Theme column to see a preview in the right pane

☐ Select other appropriate options and click **OK**

Specify a Default Message Theme

Ribbon Method

☐ In the Inbox, click the **File tab**, then click **Options** to open the Outlook Options dialog box

☐ Click **Mail**, then click the **Stationery and Fonts button** in the Compose messages section of the dialog box

Outlook

□ In the Signatures and Stationery dialog box, click the **Personal Stationery tab** if necessary, then click the **Theme button** to open the Theme or Stationery dialog box shown in Figure OL 2-2

□ Click a theme in the Choose a Theme pane to see a preview in the right pane

□ Select other appropriate options, click **OK**, click **OK**, then click **OK** again

Figure OL 2-2   Theme or Stationery dialog box

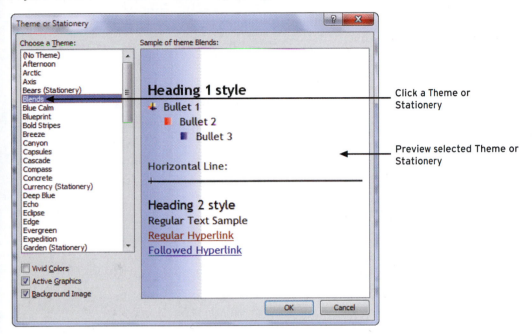

Specify Message Content Format

Ribbon Method

□ To change the default format for messages, click the **File tab**, click **Options** to open the Outlook Options dialog box, then click **Mail**

□ In the Compose messages section of the dialog box, click the **Compose messages in this format list arrow** and click **HTML**, **Rich Text**, or **Plain Text**

OR

□ To change the format for a single message, click the **Home tab**, click the **New Items button**, click **E-mail Message Using**, then click **HTML**, **Rich Text**, or **Plain Text** from the submenu

OR

□ To change the format for a single message, create a new e-mail message

□ Click the **Format Text tab**, then click **HTML**, **Plain Text**, or **Rich Text** in the Format group

Show or Hide the From and Bcc Fields

Ribbon Method

□ Create a new e-mail message, then click the **Options tab**

□ To show the Bcc field, click the **Bcc button** in the Show Fields group

□ To show the From field, click the **From button** in the Show Fields group

□ To hide the Bcc field, click the orange activated **Bcc button** in the Show Fields group

□ To hide the From field, click the orange activated **From button** in the Show Fields group

Set a Reminder for Message Recipients

Ribbon Method

☐ Open a new e-mail message

☐ On the Message tab, click the **Follow up button**, then click **Add Reminder** from the menu

☐ In the Custom dialog box, shown in Figure OL 2-3, click the **Flag for Recipients check box**, click the **Follow up list arrow** to choose the appropriate option

☐ Click the **Reminder check box**, click the date list arrow to choose the appropriate day from the calendar, then click the time list arrow to choose the appropriate time

☐ Click **OK**

Figure OL 2-3   Custom dialog box

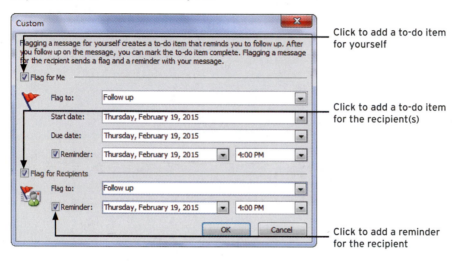

Specify the Sending Account

Ribbon Method

☐ Create a new e-mail message

☐ Click the **Options tab**, then click the **From button** in the Show Fields group to add the From field if it isn't displayed already

☐ Click the **From button**, then click the sending e-mail address in the list or click **Other E-mail Address** to open the Send From Other E-mail Address dialog box where you can click the From button to choose an address from your Contacts list or type in an address and click **OK**

Specify the Sent Item Folder

Ribbon Method

☐ Open a new or existing e-mail message, click the **Options tab** on the Ribbon, click the **Save Sent Item To button**, then click **Other Folder** to open the Select Folder dialog box

☐ Click a folder in the list or click the **New button** to open the Create New Folder dialog box, type the name of a new folder, then click **OK**

☐ Click **OK**

Configure Message Delivery Options

Ribbon Method

☐ Open a new or existing e-mail message

☐ Click the **Options tab**, then click the **launcher** ⌐ in the More Options group

☐ In the Properties dialog box, shown in Figure OL 2-4, select the appropriate options in the Delivery options section, then click **Close**

Figure OL 2-4   **Properties dialog box**

OR

☐ Open a new or existing e-mail message
☐ Click the **Options tab**, click the **Delay Delivery button** in the More Options group to open the Properties dialog box where you can specify a date and time for delivery or click the **Direct Replies To button** to open the Properties dialog to specify an e-mail address for replies to be sent to
☐ Click **Close**

Configure Voting Options
Ribbon Method

☐ Create a new e-mail message
☐ Insert the e-mail addresses of message recipients in the To:, Cc:, and/or Bc: text boxes
☐ Click the **Options tab** on the Ribbon, then click the **launcher** in the Tracking group
☐ In the Properties dialog box, click the **Use voting buttons check box**, click the list arrow and select an appropriate option or type the names of custom voting options separated by a semicolon
☐ Click the **Have replies sent to check box**, type or select an e-mail address, then click **Close**
☐ Type the message or poll question in the e-mail message, then click **Send** to send the message to recipients and allow them to vote by clicking **Vote** in the Respond group of the Message tab and clicking an option in the list
   OR
☐ Open a new e-mail message
☐ Click the **Options tab**, click the **Use Voting Buttons button** in the Tracking group, then click an option from the menu
☐ Click the **Direct Replies to button** in the More Options group
☐ Follow the steps in bullets 4-6 in the Configure Voting Options Ribbon Method above

Configure Tracking Options
Ribbon Method

☐ Open a new or existing e-mail message
☐ Click the **Options tab**, then click the **launcher** in the Tracking group
☐ In the Properties dialog box, click the **Request a delivery receipt for this message check box** and/or click the **Request a read receipt for this message check box**

☐ Click **Close**

OR

☐ Open a new or existing e-mail message

☐ Click the **Options tab**, shown in Figure OL 2-5, then click the **Request a Delivery Receipt check box** and/or the **Request a Read Receipt check box** in the Tracking group

Figure OL 2-5   Options tab

Send a Message to a Contact Group

Ribbon Method

☐ Create a new e-mail message

☐ Click the **To button** to open the Select Names dialog box

☐ Click a contact group in the list and click the **To button**

☐ Click **OK**

☐ Click **Send**

OR

☐ Create a new e-mail message

☐ Type the exact name of the contact group in the To text box, then press **Enter**

☐ Click **Send**

NOTE

A contact group is a set of e-mail addresses with a name. You can send the same e-mail message to the entire group by addressing the message to the contact group's name.

CREATE AND MANAGE QUICK STEPS

Perform Quick Steps

Ribbon Method

☐ In Mail, select a message in the list

☐ Click the **Home tab**, click an option in the Quick Steps gallery in the Quick Steps group to perform the action (The first time you use a Quick Step you will be prompted to complete the First Time Setup dialog box where you will configure options for the Quick Step)

Shortcut Method

☐ In Mail, right-click a message in the list

☐ Point to **Quick Steps** on the shortcut menu, then click a quick step in the submenu

Create Quick Steps

Ribbon Method

☐ In Mail, click the **Home tab**, click **Create New** in the Quick Steps gallery in the Quick Steps group

☐ In the Edit Quick Step dialog box, type a name for the Quick Step in the Name text box or leave the default name, My Quick Step (When you choose an action in the next step, the name may change automatically to the name of the action)

☐ Click the icon to the left of the Name box to open the **Choose an icon dialog box**, click an icon from the gallery, then click **OK**

☐ In the Actions section of the dialog box, click the **Choose an Action list arrow**, then click an option in the list

☐ To add another action to the quick step, click the **Add Action button**, click the list arrow, then choose another action and repeat as necessary

☐ In the Optional section of the dialog box, click the **Choose a shortcut list arrow** and click a shortcut key combination, if desired

☐ Type a description of the quick step in the Tooltip text box, if desired, as shown in Figure OL 2-6

☐ Click **Finish** to add the new quick step to the Quick Step gallery

Figure OL 2-6   Edit Quick Step dialog box

OR

☐ In Mail, on the Home tab, click the **More button** ⊡ in the Quick Steps group, point to **New Quick Step**, then click **Custom**

☐ Follow the steps in bullets 2-8 in the Create Quick Steps Ribbon Method above

OR

☐ In Mail, on the Home tab, click the **More button** ⊡ in the Quick Steps group, point to **New Quick Step**, then click an option in the list to create a new quick step based on a template

☐ In the First Time Setup dialog box, select options to configure the quick step

☐ Click **Finish**

Outlook

Shortcut Method
☐ Right-click a message
☐ Point to **Quick Steps** on the shortcut menu, then click **Create New** on the submenu
☐ Follow the steps in bullets 2-8 in the Create Quick Steps Ribbon Method on the previous page

Edit Quick Steps

Ribbon Method
☐ In Mail, on the Home tab, click the **More button** ⊟ in the Quick Steps group, then click **Manage Quick Steps**
☐ In the Manage Quick Steps dialog box, shown in Figure OL 2-7, click an option in the Quick step pane, then click the **Edit button**

Figure OL 2-7   Manage Quick Steps dialog box

Click to delete the selected quick step

☐ In the Edit Quick Step dialog box, select appropriate options, then click **Save**
☐ Click **OK**
   OR
☐ In Mail, on the Home tab, click the **launcher** ⊡ in the Quick Steps group
☐ In the Manage Quick Steps dialog box, click an option in the Quick step pane, then click the **Edit button**
☐ In the Edit Quick Step dialog box, select appropriate options, then click **Save**
☐ Click **OK**
   OR
☐ In Mail, on the Home tab, right-click a quick step in the Quick Steps gallery in the Quick Steps group
☐ Click **Edit (Quick Step)** on the shortcut menu
☐ In the Edit Quick Step dialog box, select appropriate options, then click **Save**

Shortcut Method
☐ In Mail, right-click a message in the list, point to **Quick Steps** on the shortcut menu, then click **Manage Quick Steps** in the submenu
☐ In the Manage Quick Steps dialog box, click a quick step in the Quick step pane, then click the **Edit button**
☐ In the Edit Quick Step dialog box, select appropriate options, then click **Save**
☐ Click **OK**

Delete Quick Steps

Ribbon Method

- In Mail, on the Home tab, click the **More button** ▾ in the Quick Steps gallery in the Quick Steps group, then click **Manage Quick Steps**
- In the Manage Quick Steps dialog box, click a quick step in the Quick step pane, then click the **Delete button**
- Click **OK**

OR

- In Mail, on the Home tab, click the **launcher** ⬎ in the Quick Steps group
- In the Manage Quick Steps dialog box, click a quick step option in the Quick step pane, then click the **Delete button**
- Click **OK**

Shortcut Method

- In Mail, on the Home tab, right-click a quick step in the Quick Steps gallery in the Quick Steps group
- Click **Delete** on the shortcut menu

OR

- Right-click a message, point to **Quick Steps** on the shortcut menu, then click **Manage Quick Steps** in the submenu
- In the Manage Quick Steps dialog box, click a quick step in the Quick step pane, then click the **Delete button**
- Click **OK**

Duplicate Quick Steps

Ribbon Method

- In Mail, on the Home tab, click the **More button** ▾ in the Quick Steps gallery in the Quick Steps group, then click **Manage Quick Steps**
- In the Manage Quick Steps dialog box, click a quick step in the Quick step pane, then click the **Duplicate button** to create a new quick step based on an existing one
- In the Edit Quick Step dialog box, change the name, if desired, then select appropriate options and click **Finish**
- Click **OK**

OR

- In Mail, on the Home tab, click the **launcher** ⬎ in the Quick Steps group
- In the Manage Quick Steps dialog box, click a quick step option in the Quick step pane, then click the **Duplicate button** to create a new quick step based on an existing one
- In the Edit Quick Step dialog box, change the name, if desired, then select appropriate options and click **Finish**
- Click **OK**

Shortcut Method

- In Mail, on the Home tab, right-click a quick step in the Quick Steps gallery in the Quick Steps group
- Click **Duplicate (Quick Step)** on the shortcut menu
- In the Edit Quick Step dialog box, change the name, if desired, then select appropriate options and click **Finish**

OR

- In Mail, right-click a message, point to **Quick Steps** on the shortcut menu, then click **Manage Quick Steps** in the submenu
- In the Manage Quick Steps dialog box, click a quick step in the Quick step pane, then click the **Duplicate button**
- In the Edit Quick Step dialog box, change the name, if desired, then select appropriate options and click **Finish**
- Click **OK**

Reset Quick Steps to Default Settings

Ribbon Method

- ☐ In Mail, on the Home tab, click the **More button** ▼ in the Quick Steps gallery in the Quick Steps group, then click **Manage Quick Steps**
- ☐ In the Manage Quick Steps dialog box, click a quick step in the Quick step pane, then click the **Reset to Defaults button**
- ☐ Click **Yes** in the Microsoft Outlook dialog box that appears asking if you want to reset Quick Steps to the default settings
- ☐ Click **OK**

    OR

- ☐ In Mail, on the Home tab, click the **launcher** 🔲 in the Quick Steps group
- ☐ In the Manage Quick Steps dialog box, click a quick step option in the Quick step pane, then click the **Reset to Defaults button**
- ☐ Click **Yes** in the Microsoft Outlook dialog box that appears asking if you want to reset Quick Steps to the default
- ☐ Click **OK**

Shortcut Method

- ☐ In Mail, on the Home tab, right-click a quick step in the Quick Steps gallery in the Quick Steps group
- ☐ Click **Manage Quick Steps** on the shortcut menu
- ☐ In the Manage Quick Steps dialog box, click a quick step option in the Quick step pane, then click the **Reset to Defaults button**
- ☐ Click **Yes** in the Microsoft Outlook dialog box that appears asking if you want to reset Quick Steps to the default
- ☐ Click **OK**

    OR

- ☐ In Mail, right-click a message in the list, point to **Quick Steps** on the shortcut menu, then click **Manage Quick Steps** in the submenu
- ☐ In the Manage Quick Steps dialog box, click a quick step in the Quick step pane, then click the **Reset to Defaults button**
- ☐ Click **Yes** in the Microsoft Outlook dialog box that appears asking if you want to reset Quick Steps to the default
- ☐ Click **OK**

CREATE ITEM CONTENT

Insert Graphical Elements

Ribbon Method

- ☐ Open a new or existing message
- ☐ Click the **Insert tab** on the Ribbon, shown in Figure OL 2-8
- ☐ Refer to Table OL 2-3 to insert graphical elements using buttons in the Illustrations, Text, and Tables groups

Figure OL 2-8   Insert tab

Table OL 2-3   Inserting Graphical Elements

To insert this Graphical Element	On the Insert tab	Then	Format the Graphical Element Using
Picture	Click the **Insert Picture from a File button** in the Illustrations group	In the Insert Picture dialog box, navigate to the appropriate drive and folder, then select an appropriate picture and click **Insert**	Picture Tools Format tab
Shape	Click the **Shapes button** in the Illustrations group	In the Shapes gallery, click an appropriate shape, then use the **Crosshair pointer** ╋ to draw the shape	Drawing Tools Format tab
WordArt	Click the **WordArt button** in the Text group	Select a **WordArt style** from the gallery, type the text in the text box that appears, and drag the WordArt into position in your message	Drawing Tools Format tab
SmartArt Graphic	Click the **SmartArt button** in the Illustrations group	In the Choose a SmartArt Graphic dialog box, click the category of diagram in the left pane, select a specific diagram layout and design in the middle pane, then preview your selection in the right pane and click **OK**	SmartArt Tools Design and Format tabs
Clip Art	Click the **Clip Art button** in the Illustrations group	In the Clip Art task pane, type the search criteria in the Search for text box, use the Results should be list arrow to identify the format to find, click the Include Office. com content check box if you want to search for clip art on Office.com, click **Go**, then click a clip art image to insert it	Picture Tools Format tab to modify the clip art
Screenshot	Click the **Screenshot button** in the Illustrations group	Click a thumbnail from the Available Windows gallery to insert it	Picture Tools Format tab to format or modify the screenshot
Chart	Click the **Chart button** in the Illustrations group	In the left pane of the Insert Chart dialog box, click the chart type, click the thumbnail for the desired chart in the center pane, then click **OK** Replace the sample data in the Excel worksheet with the labels and values for your chart, then click the **Close button** ☒ on the Microsoft Excel window	Chart Tools Design, Layout, and Format tabs
Table	Click the **Table button** in the Tables group, then click **Insert Table**	In the Insert Table dialog box, adjust the values in the Number of columns text box and the Number of rows text box to create the desired table, then click **OK**	Table Tools Design and Layout tabs

Insert a Hyperlink

Ribbon Method

☐ Select the text or picture you want to create as a hyperlink, click the **Insert tab**, then click the **Hyperlink button** in the Links group

☐ In the Insert Hyperlink dialog box, shown in Figure OL 2-9, click the option you want to link to in the Link to list, complete the rest of the Insert Hyperlink dialog box based on the Link to option you selected, then click **OK** (use Table OL 2-4 as a reference)

Figure OL 2-9 **Insert Hyperlink dialog box**

Shortcut Method

☐ Right-click the text or picture you want to create as a hyperlink, then click **Hyperlink** on the shortcut menu

☐ Follow the steps in bullet 2 of the Insert a Hyperlink Ribbon Method on the previous page

    OR

☐ Select the text or picture you want to create as a hyperlink, then press **[CTRL][K]**

☐ Follow the steps in bullet 2 of the Insert a Hyperlink Ribbon Method on the previous page

Table OL 2-4 **Inserting Hyperlinks Using the Insert Hyperlink dialog box**

To link to	Do this
An existing file	Click **Existing File or Web Page**, navigate to the appropriate drive and folder, click the file-name in the list, then click **OK**
A Web page	Click **Existing File or Web Page**, click the **Address text box**, type the **URL**, then click **OK** (*Note:* Make sure you are connected to the Internet to successfully follow this link)
Another place in the document	Click **Place in This Document**, select a location in the Select a place in this document list, then click **OK**
A new document	Click **Create New Document**, name the document, verify the drive and folder, choose to edit it now or later, then click **OK**
An e-mail address	Click **E-mail Address**, type the address and any other text to display, then click **OK**

FORMAT ITEM CONTENT

Use Formatting Tools

Ribbon Method

☐ Select the text to which you want to apply formatting, then use Table OL 2-5 and Table OL 2-6 as references to apply the format you want using the Basic Text group on the Message tab or the Font and Paragraph groups on the Format Text tab, shown in Figure OL 2-10

Figure OL 2-10   Format text tab

Format Text tab

Text formatting options

Paragraph formatting options

Table OL 2-5   Common Text Formatting Tools

Attribute to apply	Ribbon Method: Message tab/Basic Text group or Format Text/Font group	Shortcut Method: Mini toolbar	Shortcut Method: Keyboard	Launcher in the Message Tab/Basic Text group or the Format Text tab/ Font group: Font dialog box
Apply a new font	Click the **Font list arrow**, then click a font	Click the **Font list arrow**, then click a font	Press, [Ctrl] [Shift] [P] click the **Font scroll bar**, then click a font	Click the **Font list scroll bar**, then click a font
Apply a new font size	Click the **Font Size list arrow**, then click a font size, or type a value in the Font Size text box	Click the **Font Size list arrow**, then click a font size, or type a value in the Font Size text box	Press [Ctrl] [Shift] [P], then click the **Font Size scroll bar** and click a font size; or type the value in the Font Size text box	Click the **Font size scroll bar**, then click a font size; or type the value in the Font Size text box
Increase the font size one increment	Click the **Grow Font button** A˄	Click the **Grow Font button** A˄	Press [Ctrl] [>]	
Decrease the font size one increment	Click the **Shrink Font button** A˅	Click the **Shrink Font button** A˅	Press [Ctrl] [<]	
Clear formatting	Click the **Clear Formatting button**		Right-click, point to the **Styles command** on the Shortcut menu, then click **Clear Formatting**	
Apply bold	Click the **Bold button** B	Click the **Bold button** B	Press [Ctrl] [B]	Click **Bold** in the Font style list
Apply italics	Click the **Italic button** I	Click the **Italic button** I	Press [Ctrl] [I]	Click **Italic** in the Font style list
Apply underlining	Click the **Underline button** U, or click the **Underline list arrow** U ▾, select a preformatted underline or click **More Underlines** to open the Font dialog box, then refer to the directions in the last column	Click the **Underline button** U	Press [Ctrl] [U]	Click the **Underline style list arrow** and select a style, click the **Underline color list arrow**, select a color, then click **OK**

(continued)

Outlook

Table OL 2-5   Common Text Formatting Tools (continued)

Attribute to apply	Ribbon Method: Message tab/Basic Text group or Format Text/Font group	Shortcut Method: Mini toolbar	Shortcut Method: Keyboard	Launcher in the Message Tab/Basic Text group or the Format Text tab/Font group: Font dialog box
Apply highlighting to text	Click the **Text Highlight Color button** to apply the active highlight color or click the **Text Highlight Color list arrow**, then select a new color	Click the **Text Highlight Color button** to apply the active highlight color or click the **Text Highlight Color list arrow**, then select a new color		
Apply a new font color	Click the **Font Color button** to apply the active font color or click the **Font Color list arrow**, then select a color from a palette of available colors; or click **More Colors**, then create a custom color	Click the **Font Color button** to apply the active font color or click the **Font Color list arrow**, then select a color from a palette of available colors; or click **More Colors**, then create a custom color		Click the **Font Color list arrow** to select a color from a palette of available colors; or click **More Colors** to create a custom color
Change Case	Click the **Change Case list arrow**, then click an option in the list			Click an option in the Effects section, then click **OK**

Table OL 2-6   Common Paragraph Formatting Tools

Attribute to apply	Ribbon Method: Message tab/Basic Text group or Format Text tab/Paragraph group	Shortcut Method: Mini toolbar	Shortcut Method: Keyboard	Launcher in the Format Text tab/Paragraph group: Paragraph dialog box
Left	Click the **Align Text Left button**		Press **[Ctrl] [L]**	Click the **Alignment list arrow**, click **Left**, then click **OK**
Center	Click the **Center button**	Click the **Center button**	Press **[Ctrl] [E]**	Click the Alignment list arrow, click **Centered**, then click **OK**
Right	Click the **Align Text Right button**		Press **[Ctrl] [R]**	Click the **Alignment list arrow**, click **Right**, then click **OK**
Justified	Click the **Justify button**			Click the **Alignment list arrow**, click **Justified**, then click **OK**
Increase indent by preset .5"	Click the **Increase indent button**	Click the **Increase indent button**		
Decrease indent by preset .5"	Click the **Decrease indent button**	Click the **Decrease indent button**		
Line Spacing	Click the **Line Spacing list arrow**, then click a spacing option			Click the **Line spacing list arrow**, click a spacing option, then click **OK**

Apply Styles

Ribbon Method

☐ Select the text, click the **Format Text tab**, click the **Quick Styles button**, then click an appropriate Quick Style in the gallery

OR

☐ Click the **Format Text tab**, click the **Change Styles button** in the Styles group, click **Style Set**, then click an appropriate style set

OR

☐ Select the text, click the **Format Text tab**, then click the **launcher** ⬚ in the Styles group to open the Styles task pane

☐ Scroll the list of available styles, then click an appropriate style

Shortcut Method

☐ Select the text, right-click, then point to the **Styles command** on the shortcut menu

☐ Click a Quick Style in the gallery that opens or click **Apply Styles** at the bottom of the gallery to open the Apply Styles dialog box, click the **Style Name list arrow**, select a style, then close the dialog box

Create Styles

Ribbon Method

☐ Select the text, click the **launcher** ⬚ in the Styles group to open the Styles task pane

☐ Click the **New Style button** 🗚 to open the Create New Style from Formatting dialog box

☐ Select appropriate options

☐ Click **OK**

☐ Click the **Close box** ✖

Create Themes

Ribbon Method

☐ Open a new or existing message

☐ Click the **Options tab**, then click the **Themes button**

☐ Click a theme from the gallery

☐ Click the **Colors button arrow** to select a color scheme, click the **Fonts button arrow** to select a font scheme, click the **Effects button arrow** to choose an effect, or click the **Page Color button** to select a background color

☐ Click the **Themes button**, click **Save Current Theme**

☐ In the Save Current Theme dialog box, type a name for the theme in the File name box, then click **Save**

Use Paste Special

Ribbon Method

☐ Select the text or object

☐ Click the **Message tab**, then click the **Cut button** ✂ or **Copy button** 🗐 in the Clipboard group

☐ Click in the new location in the message where you want to paste the text or object

☐ Click the **Message tab**, click the **Paste button arrow** in the Clipboard group, then click **Paste Special**

☐ Select the appropriate options in the Paste Special dialog box, shown in Figure OL 2-11

☐ Click **OK**

Figure OL 2-11   Paste Special dialog box

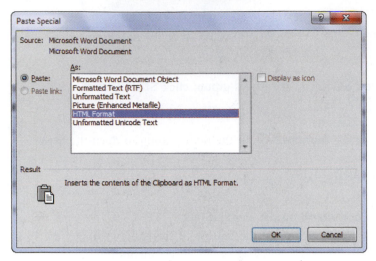

Shortcut Method

☐ Select the text or object

☐ Right-click the selected text or object, then click **Cut** or **Copy** on the shortcut menu

☐ Follow the steps in bullets 4–6 of the Use Paste Special Ribbon Method on the previous page
OR

☐ Select the text or object

☐ Press **[Ctrl][X]** to cut or **[Ctrl][C]** to cut or copy the selected text or object

☐ Press **[Ctrl][Alt][V]** to open the Paste Special dialog box

☐ Select the appropriate options in the Paste Special dialog box

☐ Click **OK**

Format Graphical Elements

Ribbon Method

☐ Select the graphical element

☐ Drag the selection handles to resize a graphic or drag the rotate handle to rotate the graphic

☐ Select options on the contextual tabs, such as the Picture Tools Format tab shown in Figure OL 2-12, to format graphical elements

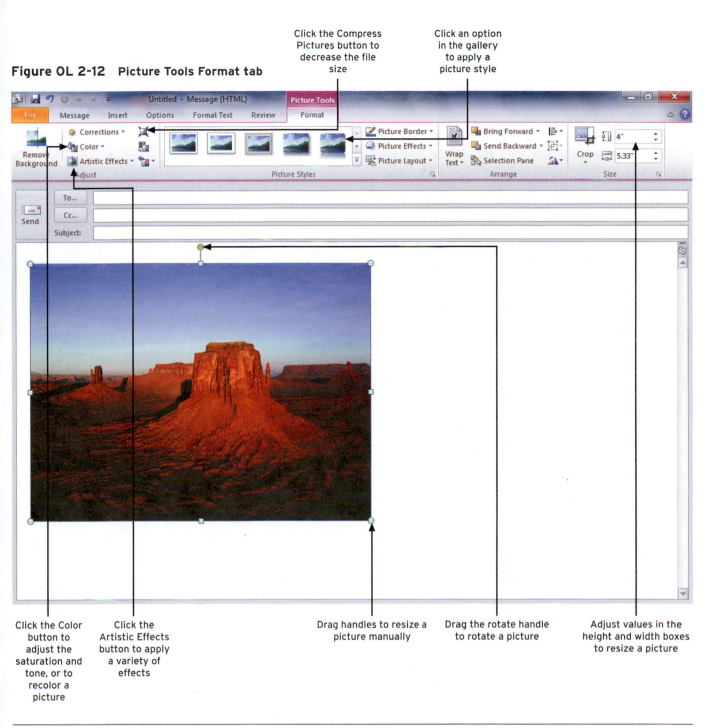

Figure OL 2-12   Picture Tools Format tab

Click the Compress Pictures button to decrease the file size

Click an option in the gallery to apply a picture style

Click the Color button to adjust the saturation and tone, or to recolor a picture

Click the Artistic Effects button to apply a variety of effects

Drag handles to resize a picture manually

Drag the rotate handle to rotate a picture

Adjust values in the height and width boxes to resize a picture

ATTACH CONTENT TO E-MAIL MESSAGES

Attach an Outlook Item

Ribbon Method

☐ Open a new e-mail message

☐ Click the Message tab, click the **Attach Item button** in the Include group, then click an option from the menu

☐ In the dialog box, click the item you want to attach, then click **OK**

OR

☐ Open a new e-mail message

☐ Click the **Insert tab**, then click Business Card, Calendar, Signature, or **Outlook Item button** in the Include group

☐ In the related dialog box, select appropriate options, click the file you want to attach, then click **OK**

Attach External Files
Ribbon Method
☐ Open a new or existing e-mail message

☐ Click the **Message tab**, click the **Attach File button** in the Include group

☐ In the Insert File dialog box, navigate to the appropriate drive and folder, click the file you want to attach, then click **Insert**

OR

☐ Open a new or existing e-mail message

☐ Click the **Insert tab**, then click the **Attach File button** in the Include group

☐ In the Insert File dialog box, navigate to the appropriate drive and folder, click the file you want to attach, then click **Insert**

REVIEW QUESTIONS

TRUE/FALSE

Circle T if the statement is true or F if the statement is false.

T   F   1. You can attach a calendar to an e-mail message.

T   F   2. Quick Steps allow you to automate repetitive tasks.

T   F   3. You cannot insert hyperlinks in the body of a message.

T   F   4. You can apply quick styles to the text in an e-mail message.

T   F   5. The Picture, Clip Art, and Shapes buttons are located in the Illustrations group on the Message tab.

MATCHING

Match the button or keyboard shortcut in Column 2 to its description in Column 1.

Column 1	Column 2
_____ 1. Inserts a text box for including a recipient that will receive a copy without others knowing.	A. Themes button
_____ 2. Lets you send a message at a later time.	B. Attach File button
_____ 3. Applies a new design to the message, including colors, fonts, and effects.	C. Show Bcc button
_____ 4. Allows you to create an e-mail poll.	D. Delay Delivery button
_____ 5. Has a picture of a paperclip on it.	E. Use Voting Buttons button

Outlook

PROJECTS

Note: To complete the Projects and Activities for this Objective, you must be connected to the Internet. In order to complete some tasks, you must have access to at least two e-mail addresses provided to you by classmates or your instructor.

Project OL 2-1

1. Open Outlook.

2. Create a new e-mail message.

3. Type your e-mail address in the To textbox.

4. Type **Reminder** in the Subject textbox.

5. Type **Don't forget to practice your speech!** as the body of the message.

6. Change the color of the text to Standard light blue, change the size to 18 point, and change the font to Impact.

7. Attach the data file **Speech Outline.docx**

8. Request a read receipt and add a reminder for the recipient to follow up today.

9. Send the message.

Project OL 2-2

1. You should have received the **Reminder** e-mail you sent in Project OL 2-1. If not, click the **Send/Receive** button.

2. Open the **Reminder** message. Click Yes to send the read receipt.

3. Create a Quick Step named Junk E-mail to move the message to the Junk E-mail folder. Type **Move to Junk E-mail folder** as the Tooltip text.

4. Use the Quick Step you created.

5. Click the Send/Receive button again, if necessary to receive the read receipt.

6. Open the **Read: Reminder** e-mail message, then close it.

7. Use the quick step you created to move it to the junk mail folder.

Project OL 2-3

1. Create a new e-mail message.

2. Insert the **Desert.jpg** picture from the Sample Pictures folder.

3. Change the size of the picture to 4" high and 5.33" wide.

4. Change the color to grayscale.

5. Add the light screen artistic effect.

6. Apply the Rotated, White picture style.

7. Remove the artistic effect and grayscale.

8. Compress the picture, using the Target output for e-mail.

9. Type a classmate's e-mail address or an e-mail address that the teacher has given you in the To: textbox.

10. Insert a Bcc field and type your e-mail address.

11. Create an e-mail poll using Yes;No;Maybe buttons and have the replies sent to your e-mail address.

12. In the subject of the message, type **Would you like to visit this place? Vote above.**

13. Send the message.

14. Wait a few moments. Click the Send/Receive button if the message hasn't yet arrived in your Inbox.

15. Open the message and vote in the poll, sending your voting response now.

16. Close the message.

17. Click the Send/Receive button.

Outlook

18. Open the voting results message.

19. Close all open messages and close Outlook.

CRITICAL THINKING

Activity OL 2-1

Create an e-mail poll using standard or custom voting buttons and set the delivery of the message to be delayed for one hour. Use a theme and at least one graphical element in your message. Send the message to at least five class-mates, friends, or relatives.

Activity OL 2-2

What is the difference between HTML, Rich Text, and Plain Text formats for e-mail messages? Use Outlook Help to find out. Experiment with formatting text using the three formats. What are the similarities and differences?

Activity OL 2-3

Apply a default theme or stationery to all your e-mail messages.

OUTLOOK OBJECTIVE 3: MANAGING E-MAIL MESSAGES

CLEAN UP THE MAILBOX

View Mailbox Size

Ribbon Method

☐ Click the **File tab**, click **Info**, click the **Cleanup Tools button**, then click **Mailbox Cleanup**

☐ In the Mailbox Cleanup dialog box, click the **View Mailbox Size button** to open the Folder Size dialog box, shown in Figure OL 3-1

☐ Click **Close**

Figure OL 3-1   Folder Size dialog box

Save Message Attachments

Ribbon Method

☐ Open the message that has the attachment

☐ Right-click the icon for the attachment, then click **Open** from the shortcut menu or double-click the attachment icon

☐ The file may open in protected view; click the link in the message box for more details or click the **Enable Editing button**

☐ Click the **File tab**, then click **Save As**

☐ In the Save As dialog box, navigate to the drive and folder where you want to save the file, then click **Save**

Shortcut Method

☐ Right-click the icon for the attachment, then click **Save As** from the shortcut menu

☐ In the Save As dialog box, navigate to the drive and folder where you want to save the file, then click **Save**

Save a Message in an External Format

Ribbon Method

☐ In the Inbox, click or open the message you want to save as a file

☐ Click the **File tab**, then click **Save As**

☐ In the Save As dialog box, navigate to the appropriate drive and folder, then type a name for the file in the File name text box

□ Click the **Save as type list arrow**, shown in Figure OL 3-2, click the appropriate file format using Table OL 3-1 as a reference, then click **Save**

Figure OL 3-2   Save As dialog box

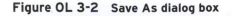

Table OL 3-1   Message File Formats

File format	Message can be opened in	Description	File extension
Text Only	Any text editor	Saves the text of a message to be opened and edited in a word processing program, but does not save all formatting	.txt
Outlook Template	Microsoft Outlook	Can be used to create other messages	.oft
Outlook Message Format	Microsoft Outlook	Saves the message intact	.msg
Outlook Message Format— Unicode	Microsoft Outlook	Saves the message in a format that supports multilingual data	.msg
HTML	Any browser	Can be displayed on the Web	.htm, .html
MHT	Any browser	Saves a message with multiple links or pages as one file with its additional resources intact	.mht

Ignore a Conversation

Ribbon Method

□ Select a message with a conversation that you want to ignore

□ Click the **Home tab**, then click the **Ignore button** in the Delete group

□ In the Ignore Conversation dialog box, shown in Figure OL 3-3, click **Ignore Conversation** to move the selected conversation and all future messages to the Deleted Items folder or click **Cancel**

Figure OL 3-3 Ignore Conversation dialog box

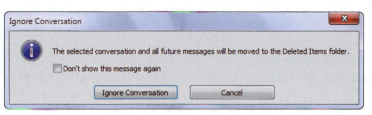

Shortcut Method

☐ Right-click a message with a conversation that you want to ignore, then click the **Ignore button** on the shortcut menu

☐ In the Ignore Conversation dialog box, click **Ignore Conversation** to move the selected conversation and all future messages to the Deleted Items folder or click **Cancel**

Use Clean-up Conversation Tool

Ribbon Method

☐ In the Inbox, select a message containing a conversation that you want to clean up

☐ Click the **Home tab**, click the **Clean Up button** in the Delete group, shown in Figure OL 3-4, then click **Clean Up Conversation**

Figure OL 3-4 Clean Up button and menu

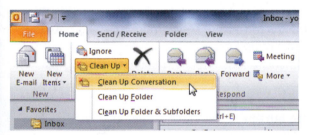

☐ In the Clean Up Conversation dialog box, shown in Figure OL 3-5, click the **Clean Up button** to move all redundant messages in this conversation to the Deleted Items folder or click the **Settings button** to adjust the Conversation Clean Up settings in the Outlook Options dialog box, click **OK** to close it, then click the **Clean Up button** to move redundant messages in the conversation

Figure OL 3-5 Clean Up Conversation dialog box

Use Clean-up Folder Tool

Ribbon Method

☐ In the Navigation pane, select a folder that you want to clean up

☐ Click the **Home tab**, click the **Clean Up button** in the Delete group, then click **Clean Up Folder** or **Clean Up Folder & Subfolders**

☐ In the Clean Up Folder dialog box, click the **Clean Up Folder button** to move all redundant messages to the Deleted Items folder or click the **Settings button** to adjust the Conversation Clean Up settings in the Outlook Options dialog box, click **OK** to close it, then click the **Clean Up button** to move redundant messages

OR

☐ In the Navigation pane, select a folder that you want to clean up

☐ Click the **Folder tab**, click the **Clean Up Folder button** in the Clean Up group, then click **Clean Up Folder or Clean Up Folder & Subfolders**

☐ In the Clean Up Folder dialog box, click the **Clean Up Folder button** to move all redundant messages to the Deleted Items folder or click the **Settings button** to adjust the Conversation Clean Up settings in the Outlook Options dialog box, click **OK** to close it, then click the **Clean Up button** to move redundant messages

Shortcut Method

☐ In the Navigation pane, right-click a folder that you want to clean up, then click **Clean Up Folder** on the shortcut menu

☐ In the Clean Up Folder dialog box, click the **Clean Up Folder button** to move all redundant messages to the Deleted Items folder or click the **Settings button** to adjust the Conversation Clean Up settings in the Outlook Options dialog box, click **OK** to close it, then click the **Clean Up button** to move redundant messages

CREATE AND MANAGE RULES

Create a Rule for Moving Messages

Ribbon Method

☐ To create a simple rule based on an e-mail message, select the message that you want to use to create the rule

☐ In the Inbox, click the **Home tab** on the Ribbon, click the **Rules button** in the Move group, then click **Always move messages from: (sender)** or **Always Move Messages To: (recipient)**

☐ In the Rules and Alerts dialog box, click a folder or click **New** to create a new folder, then click **OK** to run the rule

OR

☐ In the Inbox, click the **Home tab** on the Ribbon, click the **Rules button** in the Move group, then click **Create Rule**

☐ In the Create Rule dialog box, shown in Figure OL 3-6, select appropriate options in the When I get e-mail with all of the selected conditions section, click an option in the Do the following section, then click **OK**

☐ In the Success dialog box, click the **Run this rule now on messages already in the current folder check box**, if desired, then click **OK**

Figure OL 3-6 Create Rule dialog box

OR

☐ Open a message

☐ Click the **Message tab**, click the **Rules button** in the Move group, then click **Create Rule**

☐ In the Create Rule dialog box, select appropriate options in the When I get e-mail with all of the selected conditions section, click an option in the Do the following section, then click **OK**

☐ In the Success dialog box, click the **Run this rule now on messages already in the current folder check box**, if desired, then click **OK**

Shortcut Method

☐ Right-click a message that you want to use to create a rule, click **Rules** on the shortcut menu, then click **Create Rule**

☐ In the Create Rule dialog box, select appropriate options in the When I get e-mail with all of the selected conditions section, click an option in the Do the following section, then click **OK**

☐ In the Success dialog box, click the **Run this rule now on messages already in the current folder check box**, if desired, then click **OK**

Modify Rules

Ribbon Method

☐ Click the **File tab** on the Ribbon, click **Info**, then click the **Manage Rules & Alerts button**

☐ In the Rules and Alerts dialog box, select a rule from the list, click the **Change Rule button arrow**, select appropriate options, then click **OK**

OR

☐ Click the **Home tab** on the Ribbon, click **Rules** in the Move group, then click **Manage Rules & Alerts**

☐ In the Rules and Alerts dialog box, shown in Figure OL 3-7, select a rule from the list, click the **Change Rule button arrow**, select appropriate options, then click **OK**

Figure OL 3-7   Rules and Alerts dialog box

OR

☐ Open an email message

☐ Click the **Message tab**, click the **Rules button** in the Move group, then click **Manage Rules & Alerts**

☐ In the Rules and Alerts dialog box, select a rule from the list, click the **Change Rule button arrow**, select appropriate options, then click **OK**

Shortcut Method

□ Right-click a message, click **Rules** in the Move group, then click **Manage Rules & Alerts**

□ In the Rules and Alerts dialog box, select a rule from the list, click the **Change Rule button arrow**, select appropriate options, then click **OK**

Delete Rules

Ribbon Method

□ Click the **File tab** on the Ribbon, click **Info**, then click the **Manage Rules & Alerts button**

□ In the Rules and Alerts dialog box, select a rule from the list, then click the **Delete button**

□ In the Microsoft Outlook dialog box that appears, click **Yes** to delete the rule or click **No** to cancel the deletion

□ Click **OK**

OR

□ Click the **Home tab** on the Ribbon, click **Rules** in the Move group, then click **Manage Rules & Alerts**

□ In the Rules and Alerts dialog box, select a rule from the list, click the **Delete button**

□ In the Microsoft Outlook dialog box that appears, click **Yes** to delete the rule or click **No** to cancel the deletion

□ Click **OK**

OR

□ Open an e-mail message

□ Click the **Message tab**, click the **Rules button** in the Move group, then click **Manage Rules & Alerts**

□ In the Rules and Alerts dialog box, select a rule from the list, then click the **Delete button**

□ In the Microsoft Outlook dialog box that appears, click **Yes** to delete the rule or click **No** to cancel the deletion

□ Click **OK**

Shortcut Method

□ Right-click a message, point to **Rules** on the shortcut menu, then click **Manage Rules & Alerts** on the submenu

□ In the Rules and Alerts dialog box, select a rule from the list, then click the **Delete button**

□ In the Microsoft Outlook dialog box that appears, click **Yes** to delete the rule or click **No** to cancel the deletion

□ Click **OK**

MANAGE JUNK MAIL

Allow a Specific Message (Not junk)

Ribbon Method

□ Click the **Junk E-mail folder** in the Navigation pane

□ Select an e-mail message in the message list

□ Click the **Home tab** on the Ribbon, click the **Junk button** in the Delete group, then click **Not Junk**

□ In the **Mark as Not Junk dialog box**, shown in Figure OL 3-8, select appropriate options

□ Click **OK**

Figure OL 3-8   Mark as Not Junk

OR

□ Click the **Junk E-mail folder** in the Navigation pane

☐ Double-click an e-mail message in the message list to open it

☐ Click the **Message tab** on the Ribbon, click the **Junk button** in the Delete group, then click **Not Junk**

☐ In the **Mark as Not Junk dialog box**, select appropriate options

☐ Click **OK**

Shortcut Method

☐ Click the **Junk E-mail folder** in the Navigation pane

☐ Right-click an e-mail message in the message list, point to **Junk** on the shortcut menu, then click **Not Junk** on the submenu

☐ In the **Mark as Not Junk dialog box**, select appropriate options

☐ Click **OK**

NOTE

To permanently delete items in the Deleted Items folder or the Junk E-mail folder, right-click the folder, then click Empty Folder on the shortcut menu.

Filter Junk Mail

Ribbon Method

☐ In the Inbox, click the message that contains the user whose status you want to change

☐ Click the **Home tab**, click the **Junk button** in the Delete group, then click the option using Table OL 3-2 as a reference

☐ Click **OK**

OR

☐ In the Inbox, click the message that contains the user whose status you want to change

☐ Click the **Home tab**, click the **Junk button** in the Delete group, then click **Junk E-mail Options**

☐ In the Junk E-mail Options dialog box, make the appropriate selections, then click **OK**

OR

☐ Open the message from the sender whose status you want to change

☐ On the Message tab, click the **Junk button**, then click an option using Table OL 3-2 as a reference

☐ Click **OK**

Shortcut Method

☐ In the Inbox, right-click the message that contains the user whose status you want to change, point to **Junk**, then click an option using Table OL 3-2 as a reference

☐ Click **OK**

OR

☐ In the Inbox, right-click the message that contains the user whose status you want to change, point to **Junk**, then click Junk E-mail Options

☐ In the Junk E-mail Options dialog box, select appropriate options, then click **OK**

Outlook

Table OL 3-2 Junk E-mail Options

Use this option...	To do this...
Block Sender	Automatically move messages from this sender to the Junk E-mail folder
Never Block Sender	Automatically move messages from this sender to the Inbox
Never Block Sender's Domain (@example.com)	Automatically move messages from all senders who have the same domain to the Inbox
Never Block this Group or Mailing List	Used to ensure that messages from contact groups you belong to go to your Inbox instead of the Junk E-mail folder

MANAGE AUTOMATIC MESSAGE CONTENT

Include a Signature

Ribbon Method

☐ Click the **File tab** on the Ribbon, then click **Options**

☐ In the Outlook Options dialog box, click **Mail**

☐ Click the **Signatures button** in the Compose messages section

☐ In the Signatures and Stationery dialog box, click the **E-mail Signature tab**

☐ Click the **New button**

☐ In the New Signature dialog box, shown in Figure OL 3-9, type the signature name, then click **OK**

☐ In the Edit signature section of the Signatures and Stationery dialog box, type and format the signature text, select any other appropriate options under the Choose default signature section, then click **OK**

☐ Click **OK** in the Outlook Options dialog box

Figure OL 3-9 New Signature dialog box

Modify a Signature

Ribbon Method

☐ Click the **File tab** on the Ribbon, then click **Options**

☐ In the Outlook Options dialog box, click **Mail**

☐ Click the **Signatures button** in the Compose messages section

☐ In the Signatures and Stationery dialog box, select a signature from the Select signature to edit list

☐ In the Edit signature section, make the appropriate changes, then click **OK** in the Signatures and Stationery dialog box

☐ Click **OK** in the Options dialog box

Specify the Font for New HTML Messages

Ribbon Method

☐ Click the **File tab** on the Ribbon, then click **Options**

☐ In the Outlook Options dialog box, click **Mail**

☐ Click the **Stationery and Fonts button** in the Compose messages section

☐ In the Signatures and Stationery dialog box, click the **Font button** under New mail messages

☐ In the Font dialog box, select appropriate options, then click **OK**

☐ Click **OK** in the Signatures and Stationery dialog box, then click **OK** in the Outlook Options dialog box

OR

☐ Click the **File tab** on the Ribbon, then click **Options**

☐ In the Outlook Options dialog box, click **Mail**

☐ Click the **Stationery and Fonts button** in the Compose messages section

☐ In the Signatures and Stationery dialog box, click the **Theme button** under Theme or stationery for new HTML e-mail message

☐ Click a theme in the left pane of the Theme or Stationery dialog box to display a preview in the right pane

☐ Select an appropriate theme, then click **OK**

☐ Click the **Font list arrow** and choose an option

☐ Click **OK** in the Signatures and Stationery dialog box, then click **OK** in the Outlook Options dialog box

Specify the Font for Plain Text Messages

Ribbon Method

☐ Click the **File tab** on the Ribbon, then click **Options**

☐ In the Outlook Options dialog box, click **Mail**

☐ Click the **Stationery and Fonts button** in the Compose messages section

☐ In the Signatures and Stationery dialog box, click the **Font button** under Composing and reading plain text messages

☐ In the Font dialog box, select appropriate options, then click **OK**

☐ Click **OK** in the Signatures and Stationery dialog box, then click **OK** in the Outlook Options dialog box

Specify Options for Replies and Forwards

Ribbon Method

☐ Click the **File tab** on the Ribbon, then click **Options**

☐ In the Outlook Options dialog box, click **Mail**

☐ In the Replies and forwards section of the Outlook Options dialog box, shown in Figure OL 3-10, select appropriate options

☐ Click **OK**

Figure OL 3-10   Outlook Options dialog box

Set a Default Theme for all HTML Messages

Ribbon Method

☐ Click the **File tab** on the Ribbon, then click **Options**

☐ In the Outlook Options dialog box, click **Mail**

☐ Click the **Stationery and Fonts button** in the Compose messages section

☐ In the Signatures and Stationery dialog box, click the **Personal Stationery tab**, then click the **Theme button** under Theme or stationery for new HTML e-mail message

☐ Click a theme in the left pane of the Theme or Stationery dialog box to display a preview in the right pane

☐ Select an appropriate theme, then click **OK**

☐ Click the **Font list arrow** and choose an option for using fonts

☐ Click **OK** in the Signatures and Stationery dialog box, then click **OK** in the Outlook Options dialog box

Outlook

REVIEW QUESTIONS

FILL IN THE BLANK

Complete the following sentences by writing the correct word or words in the blanks provided.

1. A _____ is automatic text that appears at the bottom of each message.

2. The three formats for e-mail messages are _____, Rich Text, or Plain Text.

3. You can specify the font for new e-mail messages, add a signature, or apply a theme to messages by choosing _____ on the File tab.

4. The _____ button moves redundant messages to the Deleted Items folder.

5. The _____ button moves a selected conversation and all future messages to the Deleted Items folder.

MULTIPLE CHOICE

Select the best response for the following statements.

1. To view the size of the mailbox, click the _____ button in the Info section of Backstage view.
   - A. Account Settings
   - B. Cleanup Tools
   - C. Manage Rules & Alerts
   - D. Ignore

2. If you want to automatically move messages from a sender to the Junk E-mail folder, use the _____ option.
   - A. Block Sender
   - B. Never Block Sender
   - C. Never Block Sender's Domain
   - D. Never Block this Group or Mailing List

3. If you want e-mail messages to be moved to specific folders automatically when they arrive, you need to create a _____.
   - A. Font
   - B. Theme
   - C. Signature
   - D. Rule

4. The _____ button moves an item out of the Junk E-mail folder.
   - A. Never Block Sender
   - B. Junk
   - C. Not Junk
   - D. Block Sender

5. Junk E-mail commands are located on the _____ tab.
   - A. Home
   - B. Send/Receive
   - C. Folder
   - D. View

PROJECTS

Note: To complete the Projects and Activities for this Objective, you must be connected to the Internet. In order to complete some tasks, you must have access to at least two e-mail addresses provided to you by classmates or your instructor. If you use Outlook as your e-mail client, remove any rules, settings, categories, etc. after completing each Project and Activity.

Project OL 3-1

1. Open Outlook.

2. Set the default format for messages to HTML and apply the Industrial theme.

3. For the Font, choose the **Always use my fonts** option. Set the font for all new messages to **Cambria blue 12 pt.** Set the font for all reply or forwarded messages to **Calibri Red 11pt.**

4. Create a new mail message and send a test message to yourself.

5. View the test message, then send it to the junk mail folder.

6. Mark the message as Not Junk.

7. Change the theme and fonts for your e-mails to your specifications.

8. View the size of your mailbox.

9. Leave Outlook open for use in the next activity.

CRITICAL THINKING

Activity OL 3-1

Team up with two or more classmates to complete the following:

1. Create a rule to move all e-mail messages from one classmate to a new folder named Classmates.

2. Create a rule to delete all e-mail messages from one classmate.

3. Create a rule to forward e-mail from one classmate to another.

4. Send an e-mail message to each of the two classmates.

5. When you receive e-mail messages from your classmates, check to see if the rules you set up work. If they didn't, make adjustments now.

6. Create a rule that deletes e-mail with the word *won* in the subject. Send yourself an e-mail with the subject *You've won a million dollars* and watch the rule work.

7. Add one of your classmates to the Junk E-mail Blocked Senders List.

8. Add the other classmate to the Safe Senders List.

Activity OL 3-2

Create one or more signatures that you'd like to use in all your e-mails. Specify which one you'd like to use automatically for sent mail and for replies. Test them by sending a few e-mail messages to classmates.

OUTLOOK OBJECTIVE 4: MANAGING CONTACTS

CREATE AND MANIPULATE CONTACTS

Create a Contact

Ribbon Method

☐ Click the **Contacts folder** in the Navigation pane

☐ On the Home tab, click **New Contact** in the New group or click the **New Items list arrow**, then click **Contact**

☐ In the Untitled - Contact window, shown in Figure OL 4-1, enter the name, address, phone number, e-mail address, IM address, and other appropriate information for the person

☐ Click the **Save & Close button** in the Actions group on the Contact tab or click the **Save & New button** to save the contact and open a blank Untitled – Contact window so that you can add another new contact

Figure OL 4-1   Untitled - Contact window

Shortcut Method

☐ Press **[Ctrl][Shift][C]**

☐ Follow the steps in bullets 3–4 in the Create a Contact Ribbon Method above

Create a Contact from a Message

Shortcut Method

☐ Open the message that contains the contact you want to add

☐ Right-click the e-mail address or name of the contact you want to add, then click **Add to Outlook Contacts**

☐ Make any modifications in the Contact window, then click the **Save & Close button** in the Actions group on the Contact tab

Modify a Default Business Card

Ribbon Method

☐ Double-click the contact whose business card you want to edit

☐ On the Contact tab, click the **Business Card button** in the Options group

☐ In the Edit Business Card dialog box, shown in Figure OL 4-2, add and delete fields, format the card, make any other appropriate modifications, then click **OK**

☐ Click the **Save & Close button** in the Actions group

Figure OL 4-2   Edit Business Card dialog box

Forward a Contact

Ribbon Method

☐ Open a contact that you want to forward

☐ On the Contact tab, click the **Forward button** in the Actions group, then click **As an Outlook Contact** to open a new e-mail message with the person's contact information attached and the contact's name in the Subject text box

☐ Enter an e-mail address in the To text box

☐ Click **Send**

Update a Contact in the Address Book

Ribbon Method

☐ In the Contacts window, on the Home tab, click the **Address Book button** in the Find group

☐ In the Address Book: Contacts dialog box, shown in Figure OL 4-3, double-click a contact to open it

☐ Make the desired changes, then click the **Save & Close button** in the Actions group

☐ Click the **Close box** ![X] to close the address book

Figure OL 4-3 **Address Book: Contacts dialog box**

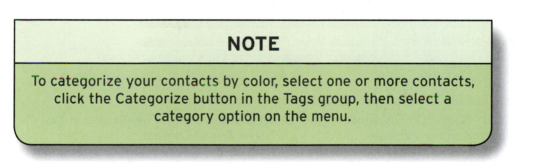

Shortcut Method

☐ Press **[Ctrl][Shift][B]** to open the Address Book

☐ Follow the steps in bullets 2–4 of the Update a Contact in the Address Book Ribbon Method on the previous page

> ## NOTE
>
> To categorize your contacts by color, select one or more contacts, click the Categorize button in the Tags group, then select a category option on the menu.

CREATE AND MANIPULATE CONTACT GROUPS

Create a Contact Group

Ribbon Method

☐ In Contacts, click the **New Contact Group button** in the New group

☐ In the Untitled – Contact Group window, shown in Figure OL 4-4, type the name of the group in the Name text box, then click the **Add Members button** in the Members group, then click **From Outlook Contacts** or **From Address Book**

☐ In the Select Members: Contacts dialog box, click a contact and click **Members** to add the contact to the group

☐ Repeat for each member, then click **OK**

☐ Click the **Save & Close button** in the Actions group on the Contact Group tab

Outlook

Figure OL 4-4   Untitled - Contact Group window

Click to add members to the group

Type a name for the group here

OR

☐ In Contacts, click the **New Contact Group button** in the New group

☐ In the Untitled – Contact Group window, type the name of the group in the Name text box, click the **Add Members button** in the Members group, then click **New E-mail Contact**

☐ In the Add New Member dialog box, shown in Figure OL 4-5, type the contact's name in the Display name text box, type the e-mail address in the E-mail address text box, select other appropriate options, then click **OK**

☐ Repeat for each member, then click **OK**

☐ Click the **Save & Close button** in the Actions group on the Contact Group tab

Figure OL 4-5   Add New Member dialog box

OR

☐ In Contacts, click the **New Items button** in the New group on the Home tab

□ Click **Contact Group**

□ Follow the steps in bullets 2–5 of the Create a Contact Group Ribbon Method

Add a Member to a Contact Group

Ribbon Method

□ In the Contacts window, double-click the contact group you want to modify

□ To add a new member, click the **Add Members button** in the Members group on the Contact Group tab

□ Click **From Outlook Contacts** or **From Address Book**

□ In the Select Members: Contacts dialog box, click a contact and click **Members** to add the contact to the group and then click **OK**

   OR

□ Click the **Add Members button** in the Members group, then click **New E-mail Contact**

□ In the Add New Member dialog box, type the contact's name in the Display name text box, type the e-mail address in the E-mail address text box, select other appropriate options, then click **OK**

Remove a Member from a Contact Group

Ribbon Method

□ In the Contacts window, double-click the contact group you want to modify

□ Click the name in the member list, then click the **Remove Member button** in the Members group on the Contact Group tab

Shortcut Method

□ In the Contacts window, double-click the contact group you want to modify

□ Click the name in the member list, then press **[Delete]**

Edit a Member's Information in a Contact Group

Ribbon Method

□ In the Contacts window, double-click the contact group you want to modify

□ Double-click the contact, make the modifications in the Contact window, then click the **Save & Close button** in the Actions group on the Contact tab

□ Make any other appropriate changes to the group, then click the **Save & Close button** in the Actions group on the Contact Group tab

Show Notes About a Contact Group

Ribbon Method

□ In the Contacts window, double-click the contact group

□ On the Contact Group tab, shown in Figure OL 4-6, click the **Notes button** in the Show group

□ Read or type notes in the window

□ Click the **Save & Close button** in the Actions group

Figure OL 4-6   **Contact Group tab**

Forward a Contact Group

Ribbon Method

□ In the Contacts window, double-click the contact group

☐ On the Contact Group tab, click the **Forward Group button** in the Actions group, then click **As an Outlook Contact** to open a new e-mail message that includes the name of the contact group in the Subject text box and the contact group attached as an Outlook Contact

☐ Click the **To button** to select contact recipient(s) or type the e-mail address(es) of the recipient(s) in the text box

☐ Add content to the body of the message, if necessary, then click **Send**

OR

☐ In the Contacts window, click the contact group

☐ On the Home tab, click the **Forward Contact button** in the Share group, then click **As an Outlook Contact** to open a new e-mail message that includes the name of the contact group in the Subject text box and the contact group attached as an Outlook Contact

☐ Click the **To button** to select recipient(s) or type the e-mail address(es) of the recipient(s) in the text box

☐ Add content to the body of the message, if necessary, then click **Send**

Shortcut Method

☐ In the Contacts window, right-click the contact group you want to forward, point to **Forward Contact**, then click **As an Outlook Contact** on the shortcut menu

☐ Click the **To button** to select contact recipient(s) or type the e-mail address(es) of the recipient(s) in the text box

☐ Add content to the body of the message, if necessary, then click **Send**

Delete a Contact Group

Ribbon Method

☐ In the Contacts window, click the contact group you want to delete

☐ On the Home tab, click the **Delete button** in the Delete group

OR

☐ In the Contacts window, double-click the contact group you want to delete

☐ On the Contact Group tab, click the **Delete Group button** in the Actions group

☐ Click **Yes** when a message box opens asking if you want to delete the contact group

Shortcut Method

☐ Right-click the contact group that you want to delete, then click **Delete** on the shortcut menu

Send a Meeting to a Contact Group

Ribbon Method

☐ In Mail, on the Home tab, click the **New Items button** in the New group, then click **Meeting**

☐ In the Untitled – Meeting window, shown in Figure OL 4-7, click the **To button**

☐ In the Select Attendees and Resources: Contacts dialog box, click the name of the contact group, then click the Required, Optional, or Resources button

☐ Click **OK**

☐ Type the subject of the meeting, type the location, adjust the start and end times of the meeting, then add content to the body of the message, if necessary, and click **Send**

Figure OL 4-7   Untitled – Meeting window

OR

☐ In Contacts, click the Contact Group to which you want to send a meeting

☐ On the Home tab, click the **Meeting button** in the Communicate group to open the Untitled – Meeting window with the contact group already inserted in the To text box

☐ In the Untitled – Meeting window, enter a subject and location, adjust the start and end times of the meeting, then add content to the body of the message, if necessary, and click **Send**

REVIEW QUESTIONS

FILL IN THE BLANK

Complete the following sentences by writing the correct word or words in the blanks provided.

1. The New Contact command is located on the _____ tab.

2. A group of e-mail addresses with a name is called a _____.

3. To remove a member from a contact group, click the _____ button.

4. [Ctrl][Shift][B] opens the _____.

5. [Ctrl][Shift][C] is the shortcut for opening a new _____ window.

MULTIPLE CHOICE

Select the best response for the following statements.

1. To accept changes made to a contact, click the _____ button.
   - A. Notes
   - B. Save & Close
   - C. Address Book
   - D. Forward

2. To share a contact with another person, use the _____ button.
   - A. Address Book
   - B. Forward
   - C. Notes
   - D. Delete

3. Use the _____ button on the Contact Group tab to add people to a Contact Group.
   - A. Forward Group
   - B. Remove Member
   - C. Save & Close
   - D. Add Members

4. One way to create a contact from a message is to right-click the _____, then click Add to Outlook Contacts.
   - A. message
   - B. subject
   - C. e-mail address
   - D. attachment

5. Electronic business cards may contain _____.
   - A. e-mail addresses
   - B. telephone numbers
   - C. business addresses
   - D. all of the above

PROJECTS

Note: To complete the Projects and Activities for this Objective, you must be connected to the Internet. In order to complete some tasks, you must have access to at least two e-mail addresses provided to you by classmates or your instructor.

Project OL 4-1

1. Open Outlook.

2. Create two new contacts using the following information.

Full name	Sheela Word	Jonathan Haas
Company	Tailspin Toys	Northwind Traders
Job title	Senior Vice President	Sales Manager
E-mail	SheelaWord@tailspintoys.com	JonathanHass@northwindtraders.com
Business Phone number	409-555-0190	816-555-0433
Address	1234 Center St.	2345 Main St.
	Seattle, WA 90876	Jackson Hole, WY 85432

3. Modify Sheela Word's contact information by adding her IM address (**sword123**) and her Web page address (www.tailspintoys.com). Use the Save & New command.

4. Create a new contact for Douglas Hite with the e-mail address: DouglasHite@tailspintoys.com.

5. Edit the Sheela Word business card. Add a blank line between the Business Address and the Business Home Page.

6. Change the color of her name to gray.

7. Remove the Work label from beside the telephone number.

8. Move the phone number down to below the Business Address.

9. Save the changes and close the contact.

Project OL 4-2

1. Create a contact group named **Networking group** using the Sheela Word, Jonathan Haas, and Douglas Hite contacts.

2. Remove Douglas Hite from the contact group.

3. Add a new member using her e-mail address: Pilar Ackerman, pilar@lucernepublishing.com to the contact group.

4. Save & close the contact group.

CRITICAL THINKING

Activity OL 4-1

Team up with one or more classmates to complete the following activity.

1. Create a contact group of friends, family, or classmates.

2. Forward the contact group to a contact on the list.

3. Send your contact group a meeting request.

4. Close Outlook.

OUTLOOK OBJECTIVE 5: MANAGING CALENDAR OBJECTS

Note: In order to complete many of the skills in this lesson, you will need to use a classmate or teacher's e-mail address, and for some skills, be on a network. If you use Outlook Calendar, make sure to undo any of the settings you change and delete any appointments that you set up.

CREATE AND MANIPULATE APPOINTMENTS AND EVENTS

Add Appointments to the Calendar

Ribbon Method

☐ In the Calendar, on the Home tab, click **New Appointment** in the New group or click **New Items** in the New group and click **Appointment**

☐ In the Untitled - Appointment window, shown in Figure OL 5-1, enter the subject, location, start and end time, and other appropriate information for the appointment

☐ Click the **Save & Close button** in the Actions group

Figure OL 5-1   Untitled - Appointment window

Shortcut Method

☐ Press **[Ctrl][Shift][A]**

☐ Follow the steps in bullets 2–3 in the Add Appointments to the Calendar Ribbon Method above
   OR

☐ In the Calendar, double-click a day (in Month view) or a time (in Day, Work Week, Week, or Schedule View) to open the Untitled - Appointment window with that information already included in the Appointment window

☐ Follow the steps in bullets 2–3 in the Add Appointments to the Calendar Ribbon Method on the previous page

Set Appointment Options

Ribbon Method

☐ Open a new or existing appointment

☐ On the Appointment tab, use the commands in the Options group to set appointment options

☐ To show how the time is marked on your calendar, click the **Show As list arrow** and click Free, Tentative, Busy, or Out of Office

☐ To add a reminder, click the **Reminder list arrow** and click an amount of time before the appointment

☐ To repeat the appointment on a regular schedule, click the **Recurrence button** in the Options group to open the Appointment Recurrence dialog box, where you can specify the Appointment time, Recurrence pattern, and Range of recurrence, as shown in Figure OL 5-2, then click **OK**

☐ To show or hide the time zones for the start time and end time of the appointment, click the **Time Zones button**

Figure OL 5-2   Appointment Recurrence dialog box

Print Appointment Details

Ribbon Method

☐ Open the appointment you want to print

☐ On the **File tab**, click **Print**

☐ Select appropriate options in the Print section of Backstage view, then click the **Print button**

Shortcut Method

☐ In the Calendar, right-click an appointment, then click **Quick Print** on the shortcut menu

Forward an Appointment

Ribbon Method

☐ Open the appointment you want to forward

☐ On the Appointment tab, click the **Forward button arrow**, then click **Forward** to attach the appointment as an Outlook attachment or click **Forward as iCalendar** to attach the appointment as an iCalendar file

Outlook

☐ In the new e-mail message that opens containing the attachment, enter an e-mail address in the To text box, type a message, if necessary, then click **Send**

Shortcut Method

☐ Right-click the appointment you want to forward, then click **Forward** on the shortcut menu

☐ In the new e-mail message that opens containing the attachment, enter an e-mail address in the To text box, type a message, if necessary, then click **Send**

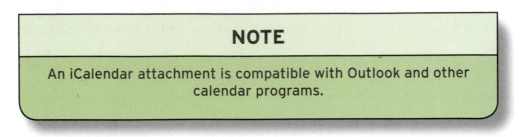

NOTE

An iCalendar attachment is compatible with Outlook and other calendar programs.

Schedule a Meeting with a Message Sender

Ribbon Method

☐ Open the e-mail message

☐ On the Message tab, click the **Reply with Meeting button** in the Respond group to open a new meeting request addressed to the sender of the message

☐ Click the **To text box**, then enter recipient names or type the e-mail addresses of the meeting attendees, separating each with a semicolon (;), or to select recipient names from the Address Book, click the **To button**, then in the Select Attendees and Resources dialog box select the attendees and resources from the Name list box, click the appropriate button for each name (Required, Optional, Resources), then click **OK**

☐ Enter the subject, location, start and end time, and other appropriate information, then click the **Send button**
OR

☐ Select the e-mail message in the list

☐ On the Home tab, click the **Reply with Meeting button** in the Respond group to open a new meeting request addressed to the sender of the message

☐ Follow the steps in bullets 3–4 in the Schedule a Meeting with a Message Sender Ribbon Method above

Shortcut Method

☐ Select the e-mail message in the list

☐ Press **[Ctrl][Alt][R]** to open a new meeting request addressed to the sender of the message

☐ Follow the steps in bullets 3–4 in the Schedule a Meeting with a Message Sender Ribbon Method above

CREATE AND MANIPULATE MEETING REQUESTS

Create a Meeting and Invite Attendees

Ribbon Method

☐ In the Calendar, on the Home tab, click the **New Meeting button** in the New group or click the **New Items button arrow** in the New group, then click **Meeting**

☐ In the Untitled - Meeting window, shown in Figure OL 5-3, click the **To text box**, then enter recipient names or type the e-mail addresses of the meeting attendees, separating each with a semicolon (;), or to select recipient names from the Address Book, click the **To button**, then in the Select Attendees and Resources dialog box, select the attendees and resources from the Name list box, click the appropriate button for each name (Required, Optional, Resources), then click **OK**

☐ Enter the subject, location, start and end time, and other appropriate information, then click the **Send button**

Figure OL 5-3   Untitled – Meeting dialog box

Shortcut Method
□ Press **[Ctrl][Shift][Q]**
□ Follow the steps in bullets 2–3 in the Create a Meeting and Invite Attendees Ribbon Method on the previous page
  OR
□ In the Calendar, right-click a day (in Month view) or a time (in Day, Work Week, Week, or Schedule View), then click **New Meeting Request** on the shortcut menu to open the Untitled – Meeting window with that information already included in the Meeting window
□ Follow the steps in bullets 2–3 in the Create a Meeting and Invite Attendees Ribbon Method on the previous page

Use Scheduling to Create a Meeting
□ In the Calendar, on the Home tab, click the **New Meeting button** in the New group or click the **New Items button arrow** in the New group, then click **Meeting**
□ Enter the subject, location, and other appropriate information
□ On the Meeting tab, click the **Scheduling button** in the Show group to display the free/busy grid to help you find the best time for the meeting based on the schedules of attendees
□ Click **Add Others**, then click **Add from Address Book**
□ In the Select Attendees and Resources dialog box, click the **Name only option button** to select it, if necessary
□ Enter the name of a person or resource that you want to invite to the meeting in the **Search text box**
□ Select the name from the Name box, click the Required, Optional, or Resources button, then click **OK**
□ Click a time for the meeting on the schedule or enter the start time and end time using the list arrows
□ Click the **Send button**

Set Response Options
□ Create a meeting request
□ Enter the e-mail addresses of attendees and type the subject, location, and other appropriate information
□ On the Meeting tab, click the **Response Options button arrow**, shown in Figure OL 5-4
□ Choose **Request Responses** to allow attendees to send you a response indicating if they will attend or not and/or choose **Allow New Time Proposals** if you want to allow attendees to propose a new time for the meeting
□ Click **Send**

Figure OL 5-4 **Response Options**

Response Options button and menu

Update a Meeting Request
Ribbon Method
☐ On the Calendar, open the meeting request which you want to update
☐ Make the changes to the meeting request, then click the **Send Update button**

Cancel a Meeting or Invitation
Ribbon Method
☐ In the Calendar, open the meeting request that you want to cancel
☐ On the Meeting tab, click **Cancel Meeting** in the Actions group
☐ Click **Send Cancellation** to send an e-mail to attendees notifying them of the cancellation
  OR
☐ In the Calendar, select the meeting request that you want to cancel
☐ On the Calendar Tools Meeting tab, click the **Cancel Meeting button**
☐ In the Meeting window, click the **Send Cancellation button**

Shortcut Method
☐ In the Calendar, right-click the meeting request that you want to cancel, then click **Cancel Meeting** on the shortcut menu
☐ In the Meeting window, click the **Send Cancellation button**

Propose a New Time for a Meeting
Ribbon Method
☐ In the Inbox, open the meeting request to which you want to respond
☐ Click the **Propose New Time button** in the Respond group
☐ In the Propose New Time dialog box, select a new time, then click **Propose Time**
☐ In the New Time Proposed message window, type a note if necessary, then click the **Send button**

MANIPULATE THE CALENDAR PANE

Arrange the Calendar View
Ribbon Method
☐ To change the Calendar view, refer to Table OL 5-1 to choose buttons in the Arrange group on the Home tab, shown in Figure OL 5-5

Figure OL 5-5   Arrange group on the Home tab

Arrange group

Table OL 5-1   Calendar Views

View	Description	Ribbon Method: Arrange group on the Home tab or the Arrangement group on the View tab	Shortcut Method: Keyboard shortcuts
Day	Displays one day's calendar	Click the **Day button**	[Ctrl][Alt][1]
Work Week	Displays all the days of the work week	Click the **Work Week button**	[Ctrl][Alt][2]
Week	Displays the entire week	Click the **Week button**	[Ctrl][Alt][3]
Month	Displays the entire month	Click the **Month button** or click the **Month button arrow**, then click **Show Low Detail**, **Show Medium Detail**, or **Show High Detail**	[Ctrl][Alt][4]
Schedule View	Displays the day in horizontal format useful for viewing multiple calendars	Click the **Schedule View button**	[Ctrl][Alt][5]

Change the Calendar Color

Ribbon Method

☐ On the View tab, click the **Color button** in the Color group, then click a color in the menu

Shortcut Method

☐ Right-click the calendar, point to **Color** on the shortcut menu, then click a color in the submenu

Display Calendars

Mouse Method

☐ In the Navigation pane, click the checkbox next to the calendar you want to display to insert a checkmark and display the calendar, as shown in Figure OL 5-6

Figure OL 5-6   **Show or Hide Calendars**

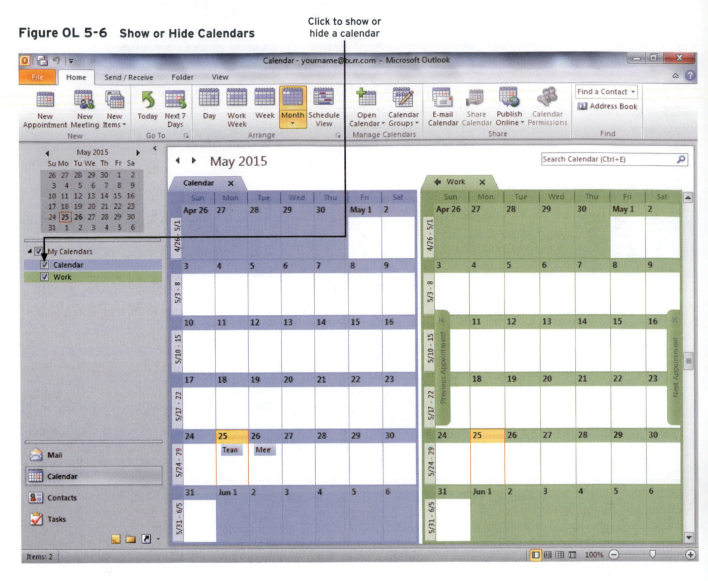

Shortcut Method

☐ In the Navigation pane, right-click the name of a calendar you want to display, then click **Show This Calendar** in the shortcut menu

Hide Calendars

Mouse Method

☐ In the Navigation pane, click the checkbox next to the calendar name to remove the checkmark and hide the calendar

Shortcut Method

☐ In the Navigation pane, right-click the name of a calendar you want to hide, then click **Hide This Calendar** in the shortcut menu

Create a Calendar Group

Ribbon Method

☐ In the Calendar, on the Home tab, click the **Calendar Groups button** in the Manage Calendars group, then click **Create New Calendar group**

☐ In the Create New Calendar Group dialog box, type a name for the group in the text box

☐ Click **OK**

☐ In the Select Name: Contacts dialog box, select members whose calendars you want to include in your group, then click the **Group Members button**

☐ Repeat for all the calendars you want to include in the group

☐ Click **OK**

OR

☐ Display the calendars that you want to include in a new group

☐ On the **Home tab**, click the **Calendar Groups button** in the Manage Calendars group, then click **Save as New Calendar Group**

☐ In the Create New Calendar Group dialog box, type a name for the group in the text box

☐ Click **OK**

REVIEW QUESTIONS

FILL IN THE BLANK

Complete the following sentences by writing the correct word or words in the blanks provided.

1. In the _____, you can hide a calendar by clicking the checkbox next to the calendar name to remove the checkmark.

2. If you make a change to a meeting request, you should use the _____ button to notify attendees.

3. If you often need to view multiple calendars at once, you should create a _____.

4. The _____ button lets you choose a new color for the calendar.

5. Press [Ctrl][Shift][A] to open a new _____ window.

MULTIPLE CHOICE

Select the best response for the following statements.

1. The _____ button displays the calendar in a horizontal format useful for viewing multiple calendars.
   - A. Schedule View
   - B. Month
   - C. Week
   - D. Day

2. A reminder is indicated by a picture of a _____.
   - A. Flag
   - B. Checkmark
   - C. Bell
   - D. Lock

3. The _____ button lets you view the free/busy grid to determine a time when all attendees are free.
   - A. Scheduling
   - B. Recurrence
   - C. Private
   - D. Appointment

Outlook

4. Which response option allows attendees to propose a new time for a meeting?
   - A. Request Responses
   - B. Tentative
   - C. Allow New Time Proposals
   - D. Accept

5. Which button allows you to repeat an appointment on a regular schedule?
   - A. Scheduling
   - B. Show As
   - C. Time Zones
   - D. Recurrence

PROJECTS

Project OL 5-1

1. Open Outlook.

2. View the calendar by work week.

3. View the calendar by day.

4. View the calendar by month.

5. Create a one-time appointment on the 15th of the current or next month with Dr. Chester from 1 pm to 2 pm at his office on 1234 Main St.

6. Set a reminder for the previous day.

7. Create a recurring Team Meeting appointment on the next Monday from 8 am to 9 am in the Conference Room. Set the recurrence to end after four occurrences.

8. Add your birthday to the calendar.

9. Open the birthday appointment, add a reminder for three days before the event, then forward it to a friend or classmate.

10. Leave Outlook open for use in the next activity.

CRITICAL THINKING

Activity OL 5-1

Note: Team up with three or more classmates to complete the following activity.

1. Create a meeting with your team.

2. Determine when attendees are available to meet using the Scheduling button.

3. Send a meeting request for tomorrow at noon to one classmate making his or her attendance mandatory. Invite another classmate as an optional attendee.

4. Propose a new meeting time.

5. Change the meeting time and send an update to all attendees.

6. Accept the new meeting time.

7. Add a new meeting attendee and send a meeting update to the new attendee.

8. Cancel the meeting.

OUTLOOK OBJECTIVE 6: WORKING WITH TASKS, NOTES, AND JOURNAL ENTRIES

CREATE AND MANIPULATE TASKS

Create a Task

Ribbon Method
- □ Click the **Tasks folder** in the Navigation pane
- □ On the Home tab, click the **New Task button** in the New group or click the **New Items button** in the New group and click **Task**
- □ In the Untitled – Task window, shown in Figure OL 6-1, enter or select the appropriate information for the subject, dates, priority level, reminder dates and times, and any other appropriate information
- □ Click the **Save & Close button** in the Actions group

Figure OL 6-1   Untitled – Task window

Shortcut Method
- □ In Tasks, press **[Ctrl][N]**
- □ Follow the steps in bullets 3–4 in the Create a Task Ribbon Method above
  OR
- □ In any area of Outlook, press **[Ctrl][Shift][K]**
- □ Follow the steps in bullets 3–4 in the Create a Task Ribbon Method above
  OR
- □ Right-click a blank area of the task pane, then click **New Task** on the shortcut menu
- □ Follow the steps in bullets 3–4 in the Create a Task Ribbon Method above

Manage Task Details

Ribbon Method

☐ Open a task

☐ On the Task tab, click the **Details button** in the Show group

☐ In the task window, enter or select appropriate information for the date completed, work hours, mileage, billing information, company, and any other information

☐ Click the **Save & Close button** in the Actions group

Send a Status Report

Ribbon Method

☐ Open the task

☐ Make the appropriate updates using the Status list arrow, Priority list arrow, and % Complete up and down arrows, shown in Figure OL 6-2

☐ To send an update to the contact who assigned the task, click the **Send Status Report button** in the Manage Task group, address the message, then click the **Send button**

☐ Click the **Save & Close button** in the Actions group on the Task tab

Figure OL 6-2   Updating the Status of a Task

Click to send a report to the contact who assigned the task

Click to adjust Priority

Click to adjust Status

Use arrows to adjust % Complete

Type a message, if necessary

Mark a Task as Complete

Ribbon Method

☐ Open the task whose status you want to update

☐ On the Task tab, click the **Mark Complete button** in the Manage Task group on the Task tab
   OR

☐ Select the task

☐ On the Home tab, click the **Mark Complete button** in the Manage Task group

   OR

☐ Open the task whose status you want to update

☐ Click the **Status list arrow**, then click **Completed** or click the **% Complete up arrow** until it reads 100%

Shortcut Method

☐ Right-click the task

☐ Click **Mark Complete** on the shortcut menu

Move or Copy a Task to Another Folder

Ribbon Method

☐ Select the task you want to move

☐ On the Home tab, click the **Move button** in the Actions group, then click a folder in the list or click **Other Folder** to select a different folder from the Move Items dialog box, then click **OK** or click **Copy to Folder** to move a copy of the task to the folder you select in the Copy Items dialog box, then click **OK**

Assign a Task to Another Outlook User

Ribbon Method

☐ Click the **Tasks folder** in the Navigation pane

☐ On the Home tab, click the **New Items button** in the New group, then click **Task Request**

☐ In the Untitled – Task window, type each recipient's name or e-mail address in the To text box separated by a semi-colon (;), or click the **To button**, select the appropriate recipient in the Select Task Recipient dialog box, then click **To**

☐ Enter or select the appropriate information for the subject, dates, priority level, and any other information

☐ Click the **Send button**

   OR

☐ Open an existing task

☐ On the Task tab, click the **Assign Task button** in the Manage Task group

☐ In the task window, type each recipient's name or e-mail address in the To text box separated by a semi-colon (;), or click the **To button**, select the appropriate recipient in the Select Task Recipient dialog box, then click **To**

☐ Enter or select other appropriate information or type a message, if necessary

☐ Click the **Send button**

Shortcut Method

☐ Press **[Ctrl][Alt][Shift][U]**

☐ Follow the steps in bullets 3–5 in the Assign a Task to Another Outlook User Ribbon Method above

   OR

☐ Right-click a blank area in the tasks pane, then click **New Task Request** on the shortcut menu

☐ Follow the steps in bullets 3–5 in the Assign a Task to Another Outlook User Ribbon Method above

Accept or Decline a Task Assignment

Ribbon Method

☐ In the Inbox, open the message containing the task request

☐ On the Task tab, click the **Accept button** or the **Decline button** as appropriate, in the Respond group shown in Figure OL 6-3

Figure OL 6-3   Task Request

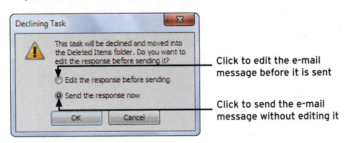

Click to Decline a task

Click to Accept a task

☐ In the Accepting Task or the Declining Task dialog box, shown in Figure OL 6-4, click the appropriate response option, then click **OK**

Figure OL 6-4   Declining Task dialog box

Click to edit the e-mail message before it is sent

Click to send the e-mail message without editing it

Update an Assigned Task

Ribbon Method

☐ Open the task that you want to update

☐ Make the appropriate updates using the Status list arrow, Priority list arrow, and % Complete up and down arrows

☐ On the Task tab, click the **Save & Close button** in the Actions group

Use Current View

Ribbon Method

☐ Click the **Tasks folder** in the Navigation pane

☐ On the Home tab, click the **Change View button**, then click an option in the gallery, shown in Figure OL 6-5

Figure OL 6-5   Change View button and gallery

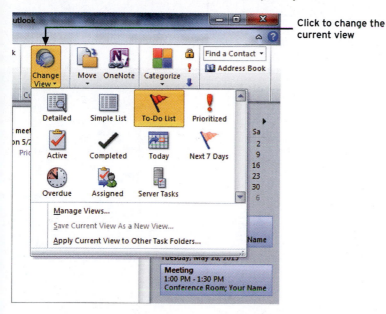

CREATE AND MANIPULATE NOTES

Create a Note

Ribbon Method

☐ Click the **Notes folder** ▢ in the Navigation pane

☐ On the Home tab, click the **New Note button** in the New group

☐ Type text in the note window that appears, as shown in Figure OL 6-6 (the note is saved automatically)

Figure OL 6-6   Creating a Note

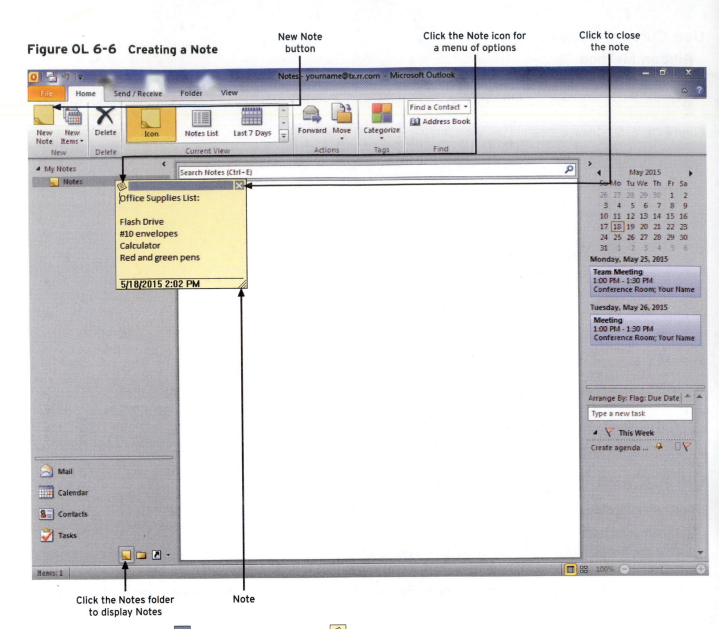

New Note
button

Click the Note icon for
a menu of options

Click to close
the note

Click the Notes folder
to display Notes

Note

☐ Click the **Close box** ☒ or click the **Note icon** 🗒 and click an option in the menu

Shortcut Method

☐ In Notes, press **[Ctrl][N]**

☐ Type text in the note window that appears

☐ Click the **Close box** ☒ or click the **Note icon** 🗒 and click an option in the menu

OR

☐ In any Outlook folder, press **[Ctrl][Shift][N]**

☐ Type text in the note window that appears, then click the **Close box** ☒ or click the **Note icon** 🗒 and click an option in the menu

OR

☐ Right-click a blank area of the notes pane, then click **New Note** on the shortcut menu

☐ Type text in the note window that appears, then click the **Close box** ☒ or click the **Note icon** 🗒 and click an option in the menu

Outlook

Change the Current View
Ribbon Method
- ☐ Click the **Notes folder**  in the Navigation pane
- ☐ On the Home tab, click an option in the **Current View group** or click the **More button** ⏷ and click an option in the Current View gallery

Categorize Notes
Ribbon Method
- ☐ In Notes, click a note to select it
- ☐ On the Home tab, click the **Categorize button** in the Tags group, then click a category on the menu
- ☐ If you haven't used the category before, you may be prompted to rename it in the Rename Category dialog box
- ☐ Type a name for the category, adjust the color or assign a shortcut key if desired, then click **Yes**

Shortcut Method
- ☐ In Notes, right-click a note, point to **Categorize** on the shortcut menu, then click an option in the submenu, shown in Figure OL 6-7

Figure OL 6-7 Categorize command on the shortcut menu

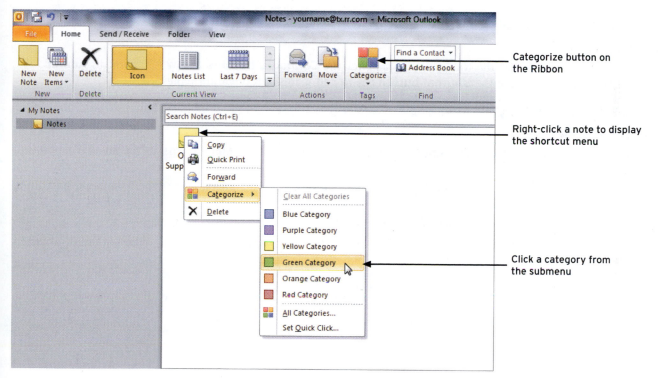

- ☐ If you haven't used the category before, you may be prompted to rename it in the Rename Category dialog box
- ☐ Type a name for the category, adjust the color or assign a shortcut key if desired, then click **Yes**

CREATE AND MANIPULATE JOURNAL ENTRIES

Automatically Record Outlook Items and Files
Ribbon Method
- ☐ Click the **File tab**, click **Options**, then click **Notes and Journal**
- ☐ In the Outlook Options dialog box, click the **Journal Options button**

□ In the Journal Options dialog box, shown in Figure OL 6-8, select appropriate options, then click **OK**

□ Click **OK**

Figure OL 6-8   Journal Options dialog box

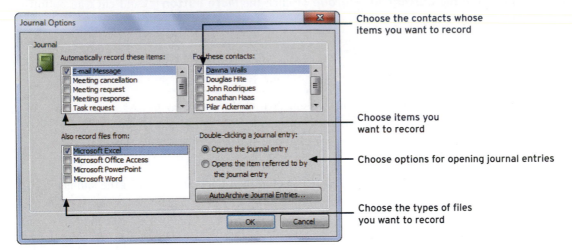

Choose the contacts whose items you want to record

Choose items you want to record

Choose options for opening journal entries

Choose the types of files you want to record

Add the Journal Button to the Navigation Pane

Ribbon Method

□ In the bottom right corner of the Navigation pane, click the **Configure buttons arrow** ▼, point to **Add or Remove Buttons**, then click the **Journal button** to add it to the Navigation pane

Create a Journal Entry

Ribbon Method

□ On the Home tab, click the **New Items button** in the New group, point to **More Items** in the menu, then click **Journal Entry** in the submenu

□ In the Untitled - Journal Entry window, shown in Figure OL 6-9, enter a subject, entry type, company, start time, duration and any other necessary information

□ On the Journal Entry tab, click the **Save & Close button**

Figure OL 6-9   Untitled Journal Entry dialog box

OR

☐ Click the **Journal button** 🗒 in the Navigation pane to display the Journal

☐ On the Home tab, click the **Journal Entry button** in the New group or click the **New Items button**, point to **More Items** in the menu, then click **Journal Entry** in the submenu

☐ Follow steps 2–3 in the Create a Journal Entry Ribbon Method on the previous page

Shortcut Method

☐ Right-click a blank area of the Journal pane, then click **Journal Entry** on the shortcut menu

☐ Follow the steps in bullets 2–3 in the Create a Journal Entry Ribbon Method on the previous page

   OR

☐ In Journal, press **[CTRL][N]**

☐ Follow the steps in bullets 2–3 in the Create a Journal Entry Ribbon Method on the previous page

   OR

☐ In any Outlook folder, press **[CTRL][SHIFT][J]**

☐ Follow the steps in bullets 2–3 in the Create a Journal Entry Ribbon Method on the previous page

Edit a Journal Entry

Ribbon Method

☐ In Journal, double-click a journal entry

☐ In the Journal Entry window, make any necessary changes

☐ Click the **Save & Close button** in the Actions group

   OR

☐ In Journal, right-click a journal entry

☐ In the Journal Entry window, make any necessary changes

☐ Click the **Save & Close button** in the Actions group

REVIEW QUESTIONS

TRUE/FALSE

Circle T if the statement is true or F if the statement is false.

T   F   1. After you create or modify a task, click the Save & Close button to save it.

T   F   2. Click the New Note button to create a journal entry.

T   F   3. When you type recipients' e-mail addresses in the To textbox, you should separate them with periods.

T   F   4. The priority list arrow lets you show how much of the task you have completed.

T   F   5. When you are done with a task, you can click the Mark Complete button to signify that the task is complete.

MATCHING

Match the button or keyboard shortcut in Column 2 to its description in Column 1.

Column 1	Column 2
_____ 1. Lets you delegate a task to someone else.	A. Categorize button
_____ 2. Sends an update to the contact who assigned the task.	B. Assign Task button
_____ 3. Allows you to turn down an assigned task.	C. Send Status Report button
_____ 4. Allows you to organize notes using colors.	D. Journal Options button
_____ 5. Allows you to automatically record Outlook items and files.	E. Decline button

PROJECTS

Note: To complete the Projects and Activities for this Objective, you must be connected to the Internet. In order to complete some tasks, you must have access to at least two e-mail addresses provided to you by classmates or your instructor.

Project OL 6-1

1. Open Outlook.

2. Create a new task. Type **Create agenda for project meeting** as the subject.

3. Set the start date as today and the due date in three days.

4. Set a reminder for two days.

5. Type **Include schedule** in the message textbox.

6. Save and close the task.

Project OL 6-2

1. Open the *Create agenda for project meeting* task.

2. Mark the status as *In progress* with a priority of *Normal* and *75% complete*.

3. Save and close the task.

Outlook

4. Create a note. Type the following text:

   Office Supplies List:

   Flash Drive
   #10 envelopes
   Calculator
   Red and green pens

5. Categorize this note using the green color, changing the name of the category to Office Administration.

6. Open the *Create agenda for project meeting* task and mark it as complete.

7. Create a journal entry with the subject *Promotion* to record a 30-minute conversation you had with your supervisor that started at 1 pm.

8. Save and close the journal entry.

CRITICAL THINKING

Activity OL 6-1

Team up with a classmate to complete the following:

1. Create and assign a task to each other.

2. When you receive the assigned task, decline it, and send the person a message explaining why you must decline.

Activity OL 6-2

Team up with a classmate to complete the following:

1. Create and assign a task to each other.

2. When you receive the assigned task, accept the task and send a status report on the assigned task back to the task owner.

Activity OL 6-3

Create at least three tasks that you need to complete in the next week. Use what you have learned to set due dates, reminders, and set the priority and status of the tasks. Create at least one journal entry and one note.

Outlook

APPENDIX: UNDERSTANDING WINDOWS 7 FUNDAMENTALS

EXPLORING THE WINDOWS 7 DESKTOP

Starting Windows 7

Ribbon Method

- □ Turn on your computer and the monitor, if necessary, to start Windows 7
- □ On the Welcome screen, click your **user name** and type your **password**, if prompted, to display the Windows 7 desktop, shown in Figure WIN-1
- □ Point to any icons on your desktop or taskbar, including shortcuts if there are any, to read the ScreenTip descriptions

Figure WIN-1   Windows 7 desktop

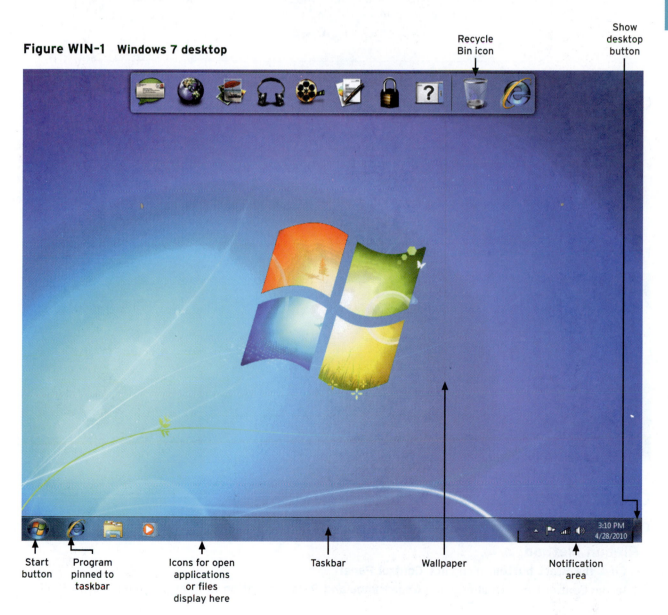

Recycle Bin icon

Show desktop button

Start button

Program pinned to taskbar

Icons for open applications or files display here

Taskbar

Wallpaper

Notification area

Identifying Parts of the Windows 7 Desktop

Ribbon Method

☐ Point to any icons on your desktop or taskbar, including shortcuts if there are any, to read the ScreenTip descriptions

☐ Click the **Start button** to open the Start menu

☐ Click the **date and time** in the notification area to see the calendar

---

NOTE

When you are working in a maximized program window and the desktop is not visible, you can always display it without closing the program window you are working in by clicking the Show desktop button on the right side of the taskbar.

Using Live Taskbar Preview

Ribbon Method

☐ With multiple programs, documents, or browser windows open, hover your mouse over an icon on the taskbar to see a thumbnail version of the window, shown in Figure WIN-2

☐ Point to a thumbnail image to see a full-screen preview

☐ Click the **full-screen image** to begin working with it or close the window by clicking the **Close button** on the thumbnail image

Figure WIN-2   Live Taskbar Preview thumbnail image

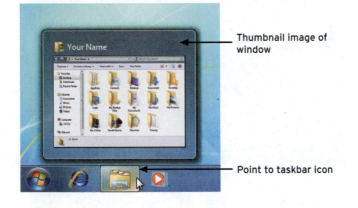

Thumbnail image of window

Point to taskbar icon

CUSTOMIZE WINDOWS 7

Changing Appearance and Personalization Settings

Ribbon Method

☐ Click the **Start button**, then click **Control Panel**

☐ In the Control Panel window, click **Appearance and Personalization** to display options, shown in Figure WIN-3

Figure WIN-3   **Control Panel Appearance and Personalization options**

Customize the Notification Area

Ribbon Method

☐ Click the **Show hidden icons button** on the taskbar, then click the **Customize link**, shown in Figure WIN-4

☐ In the Notification Area Icons window of the Control Panel, choose which icons and notifications to show or hide

Figure WIN-4   **Customize the notification area**

Link to customize the notification area

Show hidden icons button

Customize the Taskbar

Ribbon Method

☐ Right-click the taskbar and click **Properties**

☐ On the Taskbar tab of the Taskbar and Start Menu Properties dialog box, shown in Figure WIN-5, select the options you want, then click **OK**

Figure WIN-5   Taskbar and Start Menu Properties dialog box

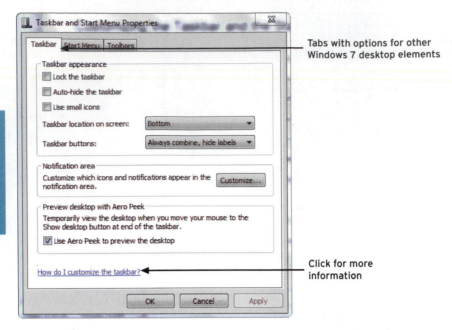

Tabs with options for other
Windows 7 desktop elements

Click for more
information

Customize the Start Menu

Ribbon Method

☐ Right-click the **Start button** and click **Properties**

☐ In the Start Menu tab of the Taskbar and Start Menu Properties dialog box, click the **Customize button**

☐ In the Customize Start Menu dialog box, shown in Figure WIN-6, select the options you want, then click **OK**

☐ Click **OK** to close the Taskbar and Start Menu Properties dialog box

Figure WIN-6   Customize Start Menu dialog box

Change User Account Picture

Ribbon Method

☐ Click the **Start button**, then click the picture at the top of the right pane of the Start menu

☐ In the User Accounts window of the Control Panel, click **Change your picture**

☐ In the Change Your Picture window, shown in Figure WIN-7, click a new picture, then click the **Change Picture button**

Figure WIN-7   **Change Your Picture window**

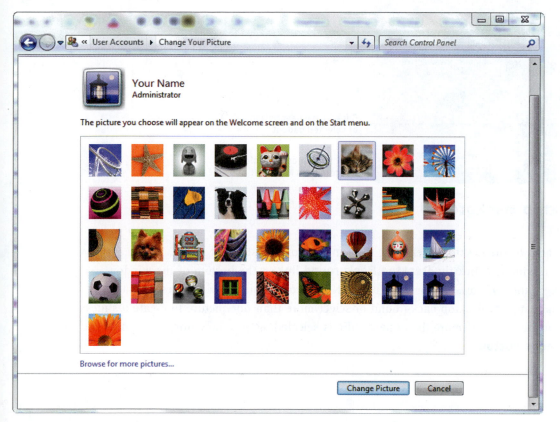

Customize Using Gadgets

Ribbon Method

☐ Right-click a blank area of the desktop, then click **Gadgets** to open the gadget gallery

☐ Double-click a gadget, shown in Figure WIN-8, to add it to the desktop

OR

☐ Download a gadget by clicking the **Get more gadgets online link**, shown in Figure WIN-8, in the gadget gallery

Figure WIN-8   Gadget gallery

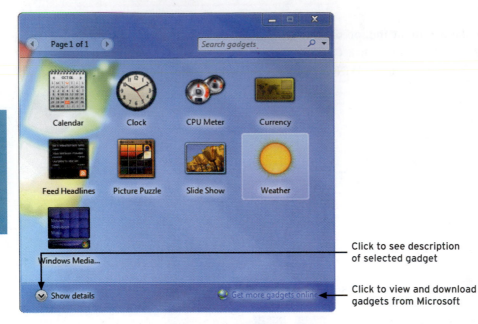

Click to see description
of selected gadget

Click to view and download
gadgets from Microsoft

Change the Desktop Background

Ribbon Method

☐ Right-click a blank area of the desktop, then click **Personalize** on the shortcut menu

☐ In the Personalization window, click the **Desktop Background link** at the bottom of the window

☐ In the Desktop Background window, shown in Figure WIN-9, scroll through the pictures available

☐ Click a picture to make it your desktop background or select more than one picture to create a slideshow

☐ Choose the picture position and, if more than one picture is selected, choose how often to change the picture

☐ Click the **Save changes button**

Figure WIN-9   Desktop Background window

Change the Screen Saver

Ribbon Method

☐ Right-click a blank area of the desktop, then click **Personalize** on the shortcut menu

☐ In the Personalization window, click the **Screen Saver link** at the bottom of the window

☐ In the Screen Saver Settings dialog box, shown in Figure WIN-10, choose the screen saver settings, then click **OK**

Figure WIN-10   Screen Saver Settings dialog box

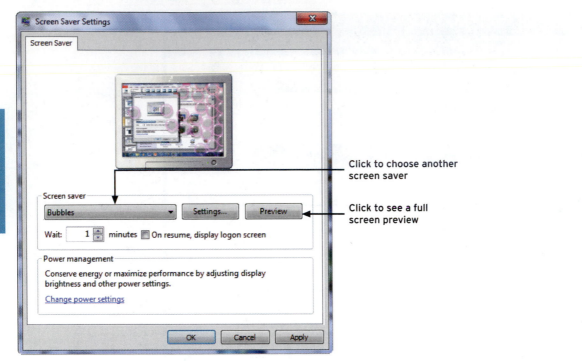

Click to choose another screen saver

Click to see a full screen preview

MANAGE FILES AND FOLDERS

Display Folders

Ribbon Method

□ Click the **Start button**, then click **your user name** at the top of the Start menu's right pane to display the folder window with contents of the personal folder for your user account, shown in Figure WIN-11

□ Use Figure WIN-11 and Table WIN-1 to become familiar with parts of a folder window

Figure WIN-11   Folder window

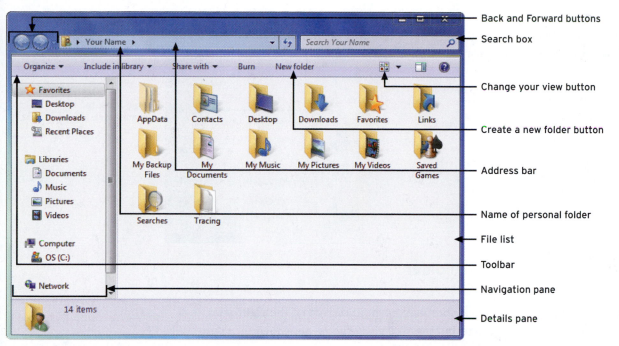

Win 7 Appendix

Table WIN-1   Folder window

Element	Used to
Navigation pane	Access common folders; quickly navigate to any folder on the computer
Back and Forward buttons	Return to the previously viewed folder in either direction
Address bar	Display your current location; navigate to another folder
Search box	Look for a file or folder in the current folder that contains the search word or phrase
Toolbar	Perform common tasks related to the folder that is displayed
Details pane	View information about the file such as the author, size, or date created
File list	Access the files and folders located in the current folder
Column headings	Change how the files are organized by sorting, grouping, or stacking; only visible in Details view
New folder button	Create a new folder
Change your view button	Change the types of information about a file or the icon size displayed in the folder window

Change Views

Ribbon Method

☐ Click the **Change your view button** repeatedly to toggle through the view options

OR

☐ Click the **Change your view button arrow** on the toolbar and then drag the slider or click another view, as shown in Figure WIN-12

Figure WIN-12   Change your view button and Views menu

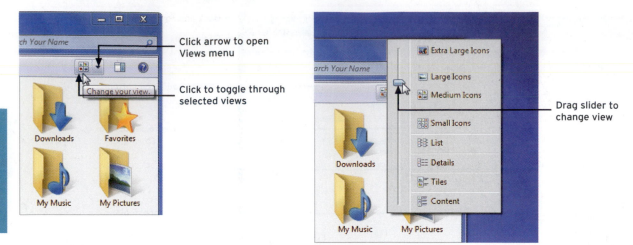

Delete or Rename a File or Folder

Ribbon Method

☐ Click the **Start button**, then click your user name in the top of the right pane

☐ On the toolbar, click the **Organize button** to display the menu, shown in Figure WIN-13

☐ Click **Rename**, type a new name, then press **Enter**

  OR

☐ Click **Delete**, then click **Yes** to confirm

Figure WIN-13   Organize menu

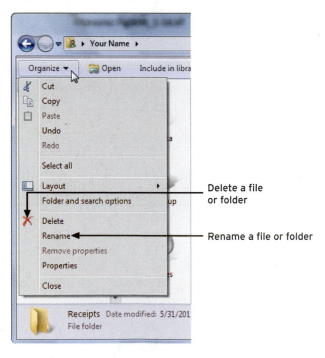

Move a Folder

Ribbon Method

☐ Click the **Start button**, then click your user name in the top of the right pane

☐ In the folder window, select the folder you want to move

☐ Drag the folder and drop it in its new location, as shown in Figure WIN-14

Figure WIN-14   Moving a folder

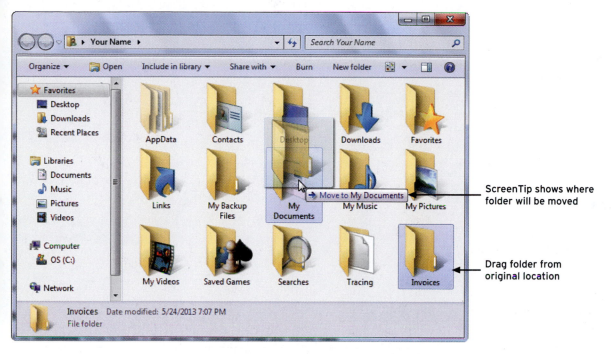

ScreenTip shows where folder will be moved

Drag folder from original location

GET HELP

Answer Questions, Troubleshoot Problems, and Get Instructions

Ribbon Method

☐ Click the **Start button**, then click **Help and Support** to display the Help window, shown in Figure WIN-15

☐ Type a word or phrase in the Search box

    OR

☐ Browse the topics by clicking the **Browse Help button**

    OR

☐ Get customer support options for your computer by clicking the **Ask button**

Figure WIN-15   Windows Help and Support

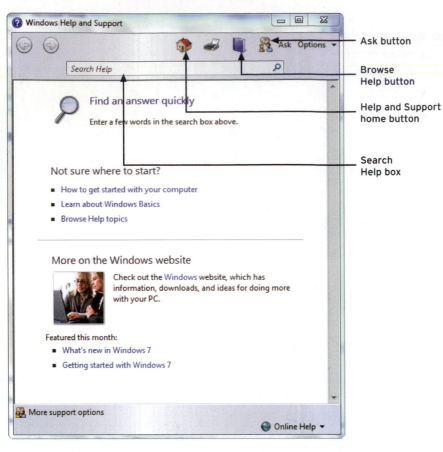

SHUT DOWN WINDOWS 7

Finish Working on the Computer

Ribbon Method

☐ Click the **Start button**, then point to the arrow next to the Shut down button, shown in Figure WIN-16

☐ On the menu, click an option, described in Table WIN-2

Figure WIN-16   Shut down button menu

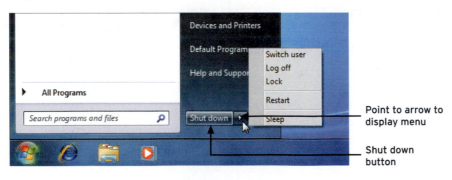

Table WIN-2   Shut down menu options

Option	Description
Switch User	Changes users on a computer without closing programs and files first
Log Off	Closes all the open programs, but does not turn the computer off
Lock	Displays the Welcome screen to prevent other people from accessing or viewing your work; useful when you will be away from the computer for short periods of time in a public place
Restart	Shuts the computer down and then starts it back up
Sleep	Power-saving mode that saves all files and programs to computer memory and allows you to quickly resume working

INDEX